REVOLUTION, SOCIALISM AND NATIONALISM IN VIET NAM

VOLUME ONE

By the same author:

The Nigerian Federal Election of 1959
The New States of West Africa
The Price of Liberty: Personality and Politics
   in Colonial Nigeria (with George D. Jenkins)
Structure and Conflict in Nigeria 1960–66
   (with Michael Vickers)
Arise Ye Starvelings: The Jamaican Labour Rebellion
   of 1938 and Its Aftermath
Strike the Iron: A Colony at War, Jamaica 1939–45 (2 vols)
Revolution, Socialism and Nationalism in Viet Nam
   Vol. Two *Viet Nam Divided*
   Vol. Three *Socialism in Half a Country*

REVOLUTION, SOCIALISM AND NATIONALISM IN VIET NAM

Volume One

AN INTERRUPTED REVOLUTION

KEN POST
Institute of Social Studies
The Hague

WADSWORTH PUBLISHING COMPANY
Belmont, California
A division of Wadsworth, Inc.

Printed in Great Britain.
First published in the United States in 1989.

ISBN 0–534–11941–7

For
Brother Seventy
and
The Tattooed Woman

Contents

List of tables and maps

Tables

Maps

List of abbreviations

ARVN	Army of the Republic of Viet Nam
BBC	British Broadcasting Service Summary of World Broadcasts, Part V (from April 1959 Part III) Far East, number alone for normal series, ES for Economic Supplements and W for Weekly series
CIP	Commercial Import Program
CPSU	Communist Party of the Soviet Union
DRVN	Democratic Republic of Vietnam
HT	*Hoc Tap* ('Study and Practice') (Hanoi)
ICL	International Communist League
ICP	Indochinese Communist Party
ICSC	International Commission for Supervision and Control
JPRS	Joint Publications Research Service, a US government agency
MAAG	(US) Military Assistance Advisory Group
NCKT	*Nghien Cuu Kinh Te* ('Economic Research') (Hanoi)
NCLS	*Nghien Cuu Lich Su* ('Historical Research') (Hanoi)
ND	*Nhan Dan* ('The People') (Hanoi)
NUF	National United Front
PP	*Pentagon Papers*
PRLP	Personalist Revolutionary Labour Party
QDND	*Quan Doi Nhan Dan* ('People's Army') (Hanoi)
RYCL	Viet Nam Revolutionary Young Comrades League
SEATO	South East Asia Treaty Organization
SFIO	French Socialist Party
SMM	Saigon Military Mission
USOM	United States Operation Mission
VNA	Viet Nam News Agency (Hanoi)
VNP	*Viet Nam Press* (Saigon)
VNQDD	Viet Nam National People's Party

Notes to readers

1. When using the notes to each chapter in conjunction with the Bibliography, it should be remembered that Vietnamese names are written with the family name first but individuals are addressed, even by strangers, by the last written, personal name (except, as a special distinction, for Ho Chih Minh). For example, Vo Nguyen Giap, will appear thus in a first note reference, but as Giap in further citations of the work..

2. Where Vietnamese periodicals are cited in the JPRS version, this means that the original was not available for this research.

3. Unless otherwise stated, 'tons' are always the metric quantity (tonnes). Ᵽ indicates currency in piastres, Đ in dongs.

Foreword and acknowledgements

This volume and those which follow it constitute an act of arrogance on two levels. First, it is arrogant of me to assume that anyone might wish to read so much of my prose, interlarded though it may be with frequent quotations. Second, and more important, the whole purpose of this study is arrogant, in the sense that I have consciously conceived it as a necessary intervention in the field of Vietnamese studies. That point requires further explanation if the reader who perseveres is fully to understand the thrust of my cumulative argument. I am making this massive intervention because, as someone who sees himself as a progressive, I am very worried about the way in which the Vietnamese Revolution, one of the most important phenomena in twentieth century history, is going to be presented to the interested public in the future. Vietnamese studies in the capitalist world have gone through a completely understandable cycle in the last twenty-five years, being built up by the concern with the increasing involvement of the USA, falling off dramatically with the end of the war in 1975 and, as a result of disillusionment on the left at the Sino-Vietnamese conflict, then beginning slowly to develop again (on the last phase see Butterfield 1983, Vlastos 1984 and Smith 1984). Available information indicates that the growth of publications which are above all motivated by a reassessment of US involvement in Viet Nam is likely to continue. For me, the problem is precisely that motivation.

The point is that the spirit of Rambo is abroad, and what is more not in his manifestation in *Rambo I: First Blood*, in which he killed his own compatriots, but in *Rambo II,* when his opponents and victims were Vietnamese and Russian. While the American public is led to anguish over those missing in action and to seek surrogate revenge for defeat, intellectuals are busily picking the scabs off past wounds and trying to decide, admittedly from different perspectives, what went wrong with the US intervention. (Sometimes the two levels come together, as in Stanley Karnow's ill-concealed glee at the problems which have faced post-1975 Viet Nam: see Karnow 1983, Chapter 1.) An inquest, however, can only establish cause of death, not the nature of the preceding life, and it is not the Vietnamese Revolution which died but US imperialism in a particular manifestation. The intervention by the US power bloc is not an adequate focal point for the future development of Vietnamese studies, or, indeed, for the wider issues, which the Vietnamese Revolution raises.

The exact nature of the problematic, as I would wish to raise it, is discussed below (pp. 6–9). Here I want to make explicit the more ideological nature of my intervention. It is intended to serve – and now my arrogance becomes clearer – as a point of reference to be set against the great bulk of what will appear in the coming years, for I see nothing written from an independent Marxist viewpoint on the horizon. Such an assessment seems to me essential both as part of the battle of ideas against the 'Rambo' intellectuals and liberal revisionists (on whom more below) and as a way of coming to terms with aspects of the specific Vietnamese experience and of the history of socialism in this century in general, which should justly give cause for doubt.

This does not explain, and certainly does not justify, the great length of my study. As one of the more perceptive (and anonymous) readers of a draft of this volume remarked, would it not be better to wait to produce a general work of synthesis until a body of monographs on various topics (which are at present notably absent) had been produced? Maybe, but for the combative reasons given above I cannot wait. Nor am I convinced that the necessary studies will be made, given the prevailing winds in Vietnamese studies, or that when they are they will be focused as I believe appropriately. Moreover, a fundamental question of method is involved. Ralph Smith, who will certainly dislike my approach, notes in introducing his own multi-volume work (on which more below) that 'Marxist–Leninist theory is in principle valid for all levels of social and political analysis, and even the most detailed aspects of grass-roots politics may have to be related to the global situation before conclusions can be reached' (Smith 1983, p. 12). Turning this round, I would say that such global factors as US intervention and the role of the Soviet Union and People's China can only be understood in conjunction with such matters as the fate of peasants, workers, ethnic minorities and women, the nature and role of the state and the Communist Party and much else upon which we have few or no studies up to now. Convinced as I am that the key issues of the second half of the twentieth century are national liberation and the attempt at socialist transformation of capitalist societies, I have allowed my vaunting ambition possibly to overleap itself and attempted a synthetic overview of the whole Vietnamese Revolution as a liberation struggle and an attempted social transformation. I leave it to others to show my lack of comprehension, to point out where I have put together the wrong pieces of the jigsaw, and to add more; I will have succeeded in my aim if I have provided a base upon which others can build and pointed out new directions they may take.

Despite its length, therefore, this work really is only a preliminary venture (and I will not take it amiss if, at the end, the reader may hope to be saved from my more developed writings). In addition to questions of innate intelligence, I have worked within two great limitations. First of all, at this stage we do not possess – nor will we in the foreseeable future ever possess – the necessary information for a full understanding of the nature and course of the Vietnamese Revolution. Even the liberation of some of the US documentation has only skimmed the surface of that murky well, and the archives in Moscow, Peking, Hanoi and the former Saigon are a mystery. Sometimes, like Salome, the various governments flick aside a veil to titillate us, but even the most prurient male chauvinist historians will never see below the seventh. There are of course newspapers and other published and unpublished materials in collections which are in principle accessible. A second limitation must be, therefore, whether or not one can in practice reach them. I have done what I could from a base in Western Europe, but history has determined that this is not the best possible. Ironically, someone based in Washington, DC or Ithaca, NY has the best chance of superseding my studies.

A certain defensiveness about this volume and its successors must not prevent me giving due thanks to those who have done all they could to help me. Above all, that means those who have held decision-making positions in the Institute of Social Studies over the last years. When I curse the Institute, as I too frequently do, for expecting me to add the role of bureaucrat to those of teacher and researcher, and thus intruding on my scholarly time, I forget what a truly remarkable institution employs me. It tolerates my deviant political views. With no apparent hesitation it has financed trips (sometimes more than once) to the USA, Britain, France, Viet Nam and Kampuchea when I have claimed them to be necessary for my work, has granted funds for the employment of assistants, and has provided unparalleled support in such matters as typing and copying. I hope to continue to enjoy these privileges, should the crisis of Dutch capitalism permit, and in any case remain grateful.

In identifying specific persons, my greatest single debt is to Nguyen Ngoc Luu. He taught me what I know of the Vietnamese language, introduced me to his culture, acted for a time as my diligent research assistant and now, as a colleague, continues to give me insights and help me with knotty pieces of translation. If nothing else, this study has gained me a valued friend. I also owe much to Christine White, who treated a newcomer to her field with enormous kindness and opened her personal collection of documents to him. While in the Socialist Republic of Viet Nam as a guest of the Committee for the Social Sciences my multitudinous questions were handled with unfailing courtesy by so many people that it seems best to give collective thanks; I have mentioned some individuals where appropriate in notes. Andy Vickerman, Huynh Kim Khanh, Peter Waterman, Anne Koch and a number of anonymous evaluators read part or all of the draft of this volume and made some important comments, to some of which I listened. Thanh Dam Truong helped with some basic translations. Once again, without that noble breed, librarians, I could have got nowhere, and my thanks are due in particular to those who helped me at Cornell University, the Library of Congress, the Cambridge University Library, the School of Oriental and African Studies of London University and, of course, the Library of my own Institute. Special mention should be made of Nguyen Ngoc Tri, who waits patiently for scholars to use the large collection of Vietnamese language material at the British Library in London over which he presides and which he was eager to put at my disposal. Lastly, other indispensable people gave the products of my typewriter a better physical shape; so many typists in fact were caught in full bloom by my drafts and withered away that I do not know them all; let Pien Moonen, my cheerful and efficient secretary, here stand for all. Koos van Wieringen has now added Viet Nam to his mastery of cartography.

Finally, a personal point, related to my linguistic competence. Like many Anglo-Saxons, I am an unfit inhabitant for the Tower of Babel, but soon after beginning to work on Viet Nam I realized that no serious study was possible without using material in the language of that country (though a remarkably large number of 'experts' seem to disagree). I therefore did what I could to acquire a reading knowledge, but this remains limited. I can find material for myself, translate with occasional help, and above all check other people's translations. The last I have done wherever the original was available so, unless noted, all translations must be taken as my responsibility and I will have to live with the consequences. In any case, I have treated references as basically intended for non-readers of Vietnamese, giving titles in English, for example; hopefully those wishing to trace them back to source will recognize the originals from my version. One evaluator pointed out, correctly, that it was inconsistent to do this and not give French or German titles only in translation. Repeating familiar arguments by Western capitalists, my chosen method is more economical (in space) and favours the most significant group of consumers (non-readers of Vietnamese). It should also be noted by specialists that I have followed the contemporary tendency to drop hyphens from Vietnamese proper names. Conversely, in cases where place names are very well known, such as Hanoi, I have not written them as two words as a Vietnamese would. Much to my regret, the typography to which I have access forced me to abandon the diacritical marks which are crucial to writing Vietnamese.

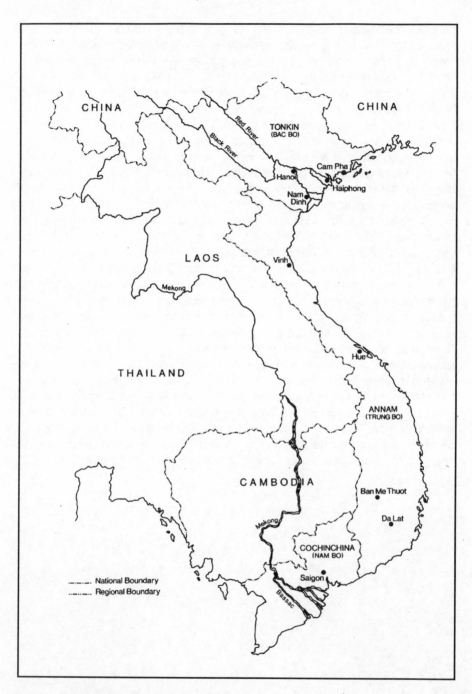

Map 1 Colonially divided Viet Nam

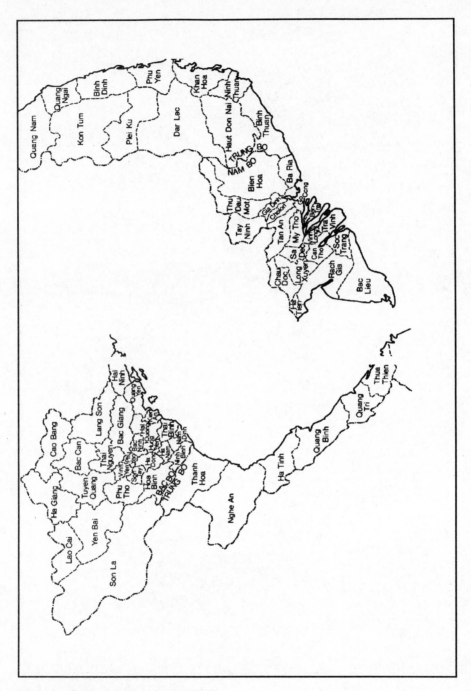

Map 2 Colonial Provinces 1945

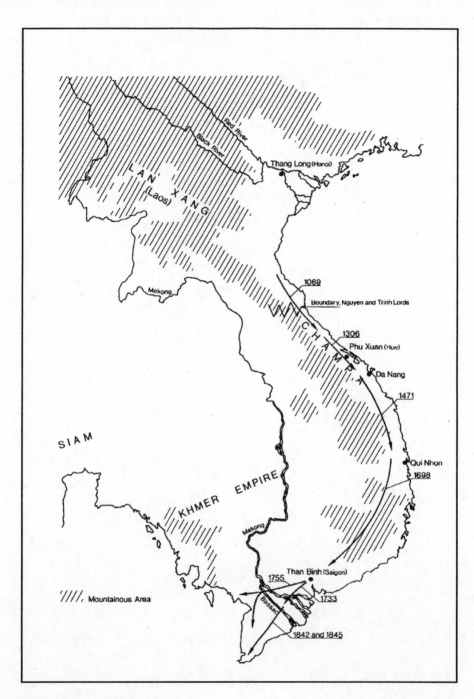

Map 3 Viet Nam (939–1860)

1 The trajectory of the Vietnamese Revolution

At the end of 1953 the Democratic Republic of Viet Nam (DRVN), led by President Ho Chi Minh, had been at war for more than eight years. Created by the August Revolution of 1945, it faced as formal adversary the French Union, which grouped the self-governing Associated States of Laos, Cambodia and the State of Viet Nam in Indochina with metropolitan France. In fact, the armed conflict, which now pitted Republic against State in contest for the same territory, was an extension of the liberation struggle which President Ho had been leading for nearly thirty years against French colonialism, now wearing a mask deemed appropriate for the post-Second World War international scene but no less concerned to reassert the control which that greater conflagration and the August Revolution had taken from it.

Turning point of a War

Late in 1953 the troops of the DRVN, led by General Vo Nguyen Giap, former teacher turned strategist, were poising themselves for a thrust into northern Laos, with the objectives of firmly establishing their allies, the Pathet Lao, there and, more importantly, of pulling the French Union forces off balance. In September the Politburo of the Viet Nam Workers' Party (as the Communists had termed themselves since February 1951) and its Central Committee Secretariat had finalized plans for the 'Winter–Spring' campaign, the opening

1

of the general counter-offensive which it was hoped would lead to victory. In December the operation began. The French high command pulled troops out of the Red River delta to counter it in Laos, but they did not catch up with General Giap's forces before the latter crossed back into Viet Nam. The objective of the first phase of the Winter–Spring campaign was achieved, with the delta, the stronghold of the French, opened to greatly extended activity by the liberation forces. Moreover, Giap was offered a probably unexpected bonus, with the stationing of a French Union force numbering eventually over 16,000 men at the remote highland district centre of Dien Bien Phu in an attempt to thwart another drive into Laos. Seizing the opportunity for a potentially decisive battle, in January Giap surrounded them with crack troops of the People's Army of the DRVN.

As 1954 began, the liberation war was not only moving towards a military climax. In November 1953 the political implications of the new campaign had been carefully explained to a conference of senior military cadres, addressed among other speakers by President Ho. At this time the Workers' Party Central Committee had in fact taken a momentous decision, namely to fight and negotiate at the same time. An approach would be made to the French government with a view towards combining the armed struggle with political manoeuvres out of which might come an eventual peace.[1]

The international linkages of the liberation struggle lay behind this new development. Western commentators have stressed that, as a recognized part of the world Communist bloc, the Democratic Republic was necessarily involved in the peace movement sponsored by the USSR, which Josef Stalin's successors had been emphasizing since his death in March, spurred on by the very practical prospect of the rearmament of the Federal German Republic within a new European Defence Community sponsored by the USA. Even more significant seems to have been the Vietnamese Communist leaders' direct perception of the USA as the growing menace to their ambitions in Indonesia, potentially a much more formidable enemy than France. Already, by early 1953, meeting more than half the French costs, the USA had to be forestalled by a political settlement before it could decide on even more massive intervention.[2] In these circumstances it was appropriate to combine military and political strategies in a proper Marxist–Leninist fashion. It is probable that the example of the recently concluded Korean War was also much in the minds of the Communist leaders, since 'fighting and talking' had been combined there for two whole years, from July 1951 until July 1953, when an armistice effectively divided the country in two. For their part, the Politburo members could well hope to get much more than their Korean comrades. The heady prospect of the success of the Revolution throughout the country was still before them, if they could wear away and then shatter the French Union forces while at the same time getting into place for a rapid handover of power by a French government demoralized by defeat. They knew that the last battle would be fought across a negotiating table, but now

2

saw that they must take position politically for this while manoeuvring for the final resolution of arms. Thus, still putting the main emphasis on arms, they saw the dual task at the end of 1953: 'We must strongly push forward the Resistance, destroy much more of the enemy's strength. Furthermore, it is only then that the enemy is prepared to negotiate concerning a peaceful solution for Viet Nam, respecting the right of our nation to freedom and independence.'[3]

President Ho and his lieutenants had reason to believe that the other side might be willing to talk. War-weariness was gripping both the successive French governments which arose from the effervescent politics of the Fourth Republic, and also the French people. The war had cost twice as much as the Marshall Aid given to rebuild the French economy after the Second World War. Although conscripts were not yet being used, death and mutilation of sons, fathers and husbands in far-off jungles and mountains appeared senseless to many, and sporadic campaigns against the 'dirty war' had been organized. These had naturally been a happy hunting ground for the French Communist Party once its final departure from the government in 1947 had left it free to replace the chauvinism which followed from accepting 'responsibility' with the themes of the world peace campaign. In February 1953, therefore, the French government had made informal contact with the Democratic Republic's delegation in Rangoon through a prince of the Vietnamese imperial house known for his nationalist sympathies.[4] This did not lead immediately to any major development, but it must have encouraged the Central Committee members to take the decision on their double strategy in November. At the end of that month President Ho made the new willingness to work towards a negotiated peace known to the world through an interview with a Swedish journal.[5]

In February 1954 the 'Big Four' (the USA, the USSR, Britain and France) announced after a meeting in Berlin that they intended to meet in Geneva in late April along with China and 'other states concerned' to discuss a final political settlement of the Korean conflict and a military and political settlement of the Indochinese question. The motivation of the French government is probably now clear; under pressure, it hoped to stabilize its position in the three Associated States with diplomatic support from its allies. The British power bloc, tottering on the crumbling foundations of its own imperial hegemony, faced by a difficult situation in the Suez Canal Zone and the still sputtering Communist insurrection in Malaya, would in the end have to follow any US lead. The Soviet Union's position must to a considerable extent be exposed by the methods of 'Kremlinology' rather than by access to documentation, but the dominant motives of its government at that conjuncture seem to have been determined by its broad policy of claiming to speak for the forces of peace and its more narrow concern with German rearmament. As for the other major Communist protagonist, the People's Republic of China, its

3

absence from the Berlin deliberations gives the clue to its main desires, namely to see itself recognized as a major power, particularly in Asia.

As for the USA, the liberation of the so-called 'Pentagon Papers' enables us to understand the position of its power bloc and government much more fully, and this is fitting given the increasing decisiveness of their policies for Vietnamese affairs over the next twenty years. The administration of President Eisenhower had yielded to French pressure at the Berlin conference with reluctance, feeling that negotiation without military victory would accomplish nothing, but increasing alarm was felt concerning the capacity of the French Union forces to win the shooting war, both in the Military Assistance Advisory Group (MAAG) on the spot, and hence in Washington. On 13 March the People's Army began its assault on Dien Bien Phu. The French government clearly indicated that it relied on greater US aid, immediately by the use of aircraft at Dien Bien Phu, and by April 1954 it was thought by the National Security Council in Washington that US ground troops might even have to replace those of France altogether. A report presented to the Council estimated the need at 275,000 US and allied troops, along with 330,000 from the Associated States, while the Pentagon planners, responding to this, raised the spectre of a full-scale Chinese intervention perhaps requiring some 190,000 more troops from the USA and its allies, and this even if atomic weapons were used.[6] In that sense, international negotiations seemed in Washington to be worth trying.

Hence, in a cautious frame of mind, a US delegation joined others from France, Britain, the Soviet Union, People's China, the Democratic Republic, the State of Viet Nam and the Kingdoms of Laos and Cambodia in Geneva in May 1954. On the 8th the mixture of plenary sessions and more limited meetings began, complicated by the fact that the US delegates were absolutely forbidden to meet the Chinese, the representatives of the State of Viet Nam refused all contacts with 'rebels', and they in their turn were treated with arrogance and condescension by the French. For the next two and a half months negotiations went on: their result, from the point of view of the Vietnamese Communists, fell very far short of what they might originally have expected.

When the DRVN delegation, led by Pham Van Dong – Deputy Prime Minister and Foreign Minister and one of Ho Chi Minh's earliest and most devoted followers – arrived amid the bourgeois comforts of Geneva they came as both patriots and Marxist–Leninist militants. In that sense they were the expressions both of many centuries of Vietnamese history and of the world revolutionary movement, centred on Moscow, which had emerged since 1917. It is the implications of these characteristics which will occupy us throughout this whole multi-volume study. Later in this chapter these general themes will be spelled out in detail. What needs to be made clear here is that this first volume turns around what was about to happen in the Swiss lakeside city in the middle of 1954. In brief, the DRVN delegation came believing that, with the help of their Soviet and Chinese allies, they were about to achieve a military ceasefire and political settlement which would guarantee them power throughout their country. They left in the bitter knowledge that, with the connivance of their allies, the first act of a counter-revolution had been carried out, depriving them of much that they had hoped to win. As we shall see in detail in Chapter 6, a series of concessions made by the Soviet and Chinese delegations, with little or no consultation with the DRVN representatives, had whittled the latters' original bargaining position down to immediate political control of less than half the territory and just over half the population, confined to the north of the seventeenth parallel. Below it, their enemies had partial control, with prospects of extending it, and that with the help of the US government. Thus, from the point of view of the Communist leaders and of many patriotic Vietnamese, the line which ran across the waist of Viet Nam cut through the web of its history. From the perspective at least of the former, it severed peasant from peasant, worker from worker, revolutionary intellectual from revolutionary intellectual, and so cut away one half of the Revolution from the other. Furthermore, the Vietnamese Revolution had been effectively isolated from those in Laos and Cambodia. In mid-1954 its future success was tied at Geneva to the holding of country-wide elections after two years. As we shall see in the successive volumes, the future of the Revolution in fact became one of continuing division of the country, a resumption of armed struggle in the South, and a savage war which ended in the reunification of a severely damaged country in 1975. In that sense, the Geneva Conference changed the whole trajectory of the Vietnamese Revolution.

The Nature of the Revolution

What happened at Geneva is an essential beginning for our analysis for two reasons. Firstly, the ultimate triumph of the Revolution was in effect delayed for more than twenty years. By transferring the decisive struggle from the battlefields to the formal, almost stylized, procedures of international negotiations the Vietnamese Communist leaders lost control of the political bargaining through which they had hoped to gain final victory. In effect they put themselves in the hands of their allies, who then acted more in their own interests than in those of the DRVN. In theory, the division of Viet Nam was temporary. In fact, as we shall see in a later chapter, the possibility of a Communist victory by political means could be blocked.

The Geneva events are also important for this study because concentrated in them were the general historical themes which characterize the Vietnamese Revolution and make it an important object of study. In travelling from far-off Asia to the Swiss centre of metropolitan capitalism the DRVN delegation symbolically underlined the centrality of their country's case to understanding the crucial shift in the location of the world socialist revolution from the capitalist centre to the colonial and semi-colonial periphery which had taken place since the Russian Revolution of 1917. The Vietnamese case is even more important than the Chinese case here, since it involved the most direct armed confrontation with the hegemonic capitalist power, the USA, and resulted in a defeat for the US power bloc of which the long-term effects are still to be seen. That constitutes one basic aspect of the Vietnamese Revolution, the issue of the relations between national liberation struggle and Marxist–Leninist socialism and their place in international politics in the twentieth century. The other is the whole question whether, given external pressures and a host of internal problems, socialist systems can in fact be built in former colonial countries or others, like Thailand – to take a Southeast Asian example – which became dependents of the capitalist powers though never actually annexed. In one way or another, everything which follows in this study is designed to come to terms with these issues.

It is in giving this shape to my problematic that I hope my study is to be distinguished from others and can serve, as I indicated in the Foreword, as a foil to them. The point is that, despite the attempts at reassessment and even to create a 'revisionist' historiography in recent years, the basic frame of reference remains the American experience, not the Vietnamese.[7] It is remarkable to me that when a distinguished group of intellectuals was brought together by the Woodrow Wilson International Center of the Smithsonian Institution on the tenth anniversary of the Paris Agreement of January 1973 which ended the direct US military intervention, with the mandate to discuss 'Vietnam as History', it was basically the history of the USA which they considered, not of Viet Nam.[8] My problematic is intended to look at Viet Nam and its people in their own right and above all to see the Vietnamese Revolution as a vitally important moment in world history, concentrating as it does the twin themes of liberation struggle and the building of socialism. This is not to say that the experience of Vietnamese has not been central to the work of others, as the use below of people like Duiker, Khanh, Long, Marr and Turley will show. Moreover, such scholars have been broadly or even highly sympathetic to the liberation struggle, though not necessarily to its Communist leadership. Nevertheless, their main impulse, as I see it, has remained reaction to US involvement and they have not tried to constitute a problematic wholly from the other side as it were.

There have been some indications of a 'revisionist' tendency, above all in the work of Ralph Smith, significantly a British rather than American scholar.[9] In his ongoing work he insists that US intervention has to be seen in a much broader international context than simply US–Vietnamese relations and that equal attention must be paid to the making of strategic decisions in Hanoi and Washington.[10] This breadth of approach creates an air of objectivity so that, as has been remarked of recent teaching about Viet Nam in the USA, Smith 'has unwittingly taken the role of the television news anchor man, the putatively disinterested analyst whose "objective" responses are set against the manifestly interested views of people with identifiable political affiliations.'[11] Yet now and again something else shows through; action taken by the representatives of the US power bloc is a response to Communist 'challenge' which threatens the established order of US hegemony, which in that sense becomes the norm.[12] By the time Smith comes to setting up his second volume, covering the period 1961–65, the defeat of 'any Communist attempt to change the global balance by force of arms' is seen as 'a precondition for the pursuit of detente in other spheres', while 'that ability was being put to the test' by the Vietnamese Revolution.[13] Viewed from the perspective of liberation struggle and the distinction between world revolution and great power interests (which Smith himself recognizes) 'détente' takes on a different meaning from the aspirations of liberals, not to mention successive US administrations. Even if a liberal revisionist school of Viet Nam scholars should emerge, it seems likely that they will feel more at home with détente than world revolution and Communist challenges.

What is in fact deep-rooted bias towards a 'western' perspective in even the best of the work on Viet Nam so far is made more profound by the failure to pay adequate attention, or even any at all, to the basic tenets of Marxism–Leninism. Yet it was these which impelled Ho Chi Minh and the other Vietnamese Communist leaders, and thus from an early stage the entire struggle for national liberation and socialism. It enormously weakens Smith's claim to be giving equal consideration to strategic decisions in Hanoi, for example, when he fails to establish something so basic as the influence of Lenin's doctrine of the two necessary stages of the Revolution. The present study will distinguish itself from others if for no other reason than because it will give due weight to the influence of Marxist–Leninist doctrine.

One other point needs to be added to this sequence of remarks. Even in the 'new' scholarship on Viet Nam it is remarkable how infrequently social forces are a real presence. In that situation, explanation is reduced to banalities such as 'Lyndon Johnson dreamed of a Great Society and not of Asian real estate' or 'One of the lessons of the whole thing is the need for an honest President'.[14] Hopefully a study inspired by Marxism can avoid such silliness. Whether it can avoid all kinds remains to be seen. In the meantime it is appropriate in this context to remember the approach advocated by Mao Tse-tung at a point when he was pushing for a more active advance of world revolution and against détente. He said:

The contradiction between the people of the world and imperialism is the primary one....There is the opposition of the people of all countries to the reactionary bourgeoisie and to reactionary nationalism. There are also the contradictions between the people of all countries and revisionism, the contradictions among imperialist countries, the contradictions among nationalist countries and imperialism, internal contradictions within imperialist countries, and the contradiction between socialism and imperialism.[15]

Although this study may not see them in exactly the same way, it is with these forces and contradictions that it will concern itself, in particular attempting to show how they came to shape the Vietnamese Revolution as an expression of a postulated world movement.

In looking at what happened in Geneva in mid-1954 we have already seen how closely intertwined were the Chinese and Vietnamese Revolutions. Both stemmed, of course, from the decisive breach in the front of world capitalism opened by the Bolshevik Revolution in Russia in 1917. It is now almost a platitude to point out that that seizure of power and what followed represented a profound deviation from what the intellectual masters of the Bolsheviks, Karl Marx and Friedrich Engels, had expected.[16] Since, for them, socialism was intrinsically associated with industrialization and the working class it could come only out of a full development of capitalism, the fosterer of the former and creator of the latter. In that sense no less a figure than V.I. Lenin remained until his death almost apologetic about what he and his Bolsheviks had accomplished, viewing their seizure of power as the product of special international circumstances and the chances of building socialism in the new Soviet Union as dependent upon revolutions in more developed countries.[17]

If such was the case, how much more extraordinary from a Marxist point of view (the one which hopefully informs this study) must be the facts that the second soviet system to be established was the Mongolian People's Republic in November 1924 and the third the Democratic Republic of Viet Nam in September 1945. The last of these is especially interesting viewed against the explicit opinion of Engels that colonial possessions like India and Algeria might at best achieve a nationalist revolution, but then as 'semi-civilized' countries would have to wait until Europe and North America were 'reorganized' after socialist revolutions there and then 'follow in their wake'.[18] When Lenin, at the Second Congress of the Communist International (Comintern) in July–August 1920 and the Baku Congress of Peoples of the East in the following September, had called on the revolution in Asia to redress the balance of its failure in Europe, he had taken account of this orthodoxy. Following a lead given by Marx (as was necessary even when innovating) he had already established the doctrine of the two stages of the revolution in countries like Russia. The first had to be a 'democratic' struggle against feudalism, historically led in western Europe by the bourgeoisie but now the prerogative of the working class supported by the peasantry because the 'classical' protagonists were too weak. In the second stage the greatly strengthened workers would eliminate what capitalist elements there were and move to the building of socialism. This doctrine was now extended further to the east, with a nationalist content added to the first stage to suit colonial conditions and stress laid on the peasantry as its mass base.[19]

These innovations made it possible to transfer Bolshevism to both China and Viet Nam. The leaders who emerged in the latter remained, in fact, among the most faithful adherents of the Leninist Comintern tradition, and we shall

8

have occasion to see this working itself out over a fifty-year time span. To a large extent, this implantation of Soviet Marxism–Leninism in Viet Nam revolved around one man, Ho Chi Minh, better known until 1945 as the revolutionary Nguyen Ai Quoc. Son of a scholar who had served as an official of the emperor, though by then within the French protectorate of Annam, and had become a specialist in traditional medicine after dismissal at the behest of the colonialists, Ho found his way to Paris in 1917, working as sailor, chef's assistant and in other such jobs on the way.[20] Already a nationalist who had lobbied for colonial independence among delegates at the Versailles peace conference in 1919, it was as a thirty-year old member of the French Socialist Party that he heard of Lenin's message of colonial liberation. The exiled photographer and painter of made-to-order Chinese 'antiques' later remembered this as a revelation and:

> ...step by step, during the course of struggle, by studying Marxism–Leninism while engaging in practical activities, I gradually understood that only socialism and communism can liberate the oppressed nations and the working people throughout the world from slavery.[21]

Thus, almost inevitably, he supported the majority at the Socialist Party Conference in December 1920 which decided to join the Comintern, and so became a founder member of the French Communist Party. His personal trajectory then took him through training as a Comintern agent to a meeting in Hong Kong in February 1930 to which we shall come in the next chapter.

We shall also come there to see why it was that by the mid-1920s a generation had emerged in Viet Nam some of whom were ready to listen to their countryman. What must be stressed is that what they heard and took unto themselves was the full body of Marxist–Leninist doctrine as it developed during the 1920s and 1930s. This was made certain by the fact that in April 1925 the Comintern Executive Committee had decided on a policy of 'Bolshevization' of all member parties, which Ho as its faithful servant was bound to implement.[22] Young Vietnamese men and women like Pham Van Dong (aged seventeen when he joined the predecessor of the Communist Party) were thus inculcated with what might be called the 'received ideas' of Soviet socialism, the body of theoretical propositions, strategic and tactical maxims and policy prescriptions which had been formulated since Marx's death and attained the status of dogma under Josef Stalin.[23] With the Comintern demanding 'iron proletarian discipline' as part of its Bolshevization line, and backed by the enormous prestige of the Communist Party of the Soviet Union (and later of the Chinese Communist Party), it is not surprising that the new generation of Vietnamese and their successors found it relatively easy to adhere unquestioningly to Marxism–Leninism (though some turned to its Trotskyist variant). As we shall see, its capacity to effect a symbiosis with the very old tradition of patriotism enormously reinforced this process, eventually bringing the

9

Communist-led nationalist movement to the strength which enabled it to force the French government to come to Geneva and later to defeat the US power bloc.

Finding a particular expression in the events in mid-1954 we may thus see a thirty-year history of development of the world revolutionary movement led by the Soviet Union, which found its greatest successes in Eastern Europe and Asia. In the former region, with the exception of Yugoslavia and Albania, it was less the indigenous movement than the victorious Red Army on the march from Moscow and Stalingrad in the last phase of the Second World War which secured the creation of new 'People's Democratic' states.[24] That was partially also the case in North Korea. In China and Viet Nam, however, the local comrades found their own way to power. The object of this study, therefore, is to analyse the specificity of the Revolution in the latter country in terms of four related themes.

First, we shall have to understand as clearly as possible what it meant in a former colony to have a revolution and to attempt the building of a soviet system in half the country while continuing the struggle for power in the other half. Had Engels spoken of Annam (the name he would probably have used then) in 1882, instead of another French possession, Algeria, he would directly have underlined the problem with which we must deal, how socialism might be built in a country in which neither of the founding fathers of Marxism (nor Lenin) would have envisaged it to be possible.

Second, how was the seizure of power accomplished, originally in August 1945 in the whole country, then in its northern half in July 1954, and finally twenty-one years later in the South? It is the basic proposition of this study that the forms this seizure took had a determining effect on the socialist construction in the North between 1958 (when it was launched) and the end of the war in May 1975, as of course they did upon what happened in the former South after reunification, which, however, lies outside this study's scope.

Third, how did the received ideas of Marxism–Leninism work themselves out in terms of both the seizure of power and the building of socialism in a former French Indochinese colonial possession? (Strictly speaking, of course, Viet Nam was three, the colony of Cochinchina and two protectorates, Annam and Tonkin.) Above all, how did the doctrine on the road to power stand up to nearly eight years of war with the mightiest state in the world, and what sort of socialism began to emerge in the North?

Fourth, how did the context of international relations within which the Vietnamese Revolution was situated affect its development? Obviously the original colonial status had a profound effect, indeed produced the revolutionary movement. Further, we have already seen from what happened in Geneva in mid-1954 how intimately the fate of the Vietnamese Revolution was linked with the policies of the USA, the Soviet Union and People's China. That linkage was to grow even stronger in the years ahead.

Two factors bind together these four themes. One is the specificity of Viet

Nam itself – the influence its history, culture and geography had upon the fifty years of struggle upon which these volumes will focus. It should already be apparent that the adherence of Ho, Dong, Giap and the other leaders of the Communist Party to the Soviet Union is the other. The concrete ways in which Vietnamese reality shaped ideas and actions can be left to emerge as we continue. The other question needs further preliminary elucidation, since a basic proposition of this study is that, although historical reality would have permitted no other pattern to emerge in the years with which we are concerned, the fact is that the Vietnamese leaders and people – above all the latter – paid an appallingly heavy price for their adherence to Marxist–Leninist received ideas and the 'socialist camp' led by the Soviet Union.

The Question of a Revolutionary Terrain

As we have already noted, the received ideas which were instilled into all its supporters by the Comintern covered a wide range of topics, some of them more applicable to the seizure of state power, others to what was supposed to happen after it. In this volume the former will be of most relevance; the latter will be examined later, at the beginning of the second volume. All that we need to do here is to note the crucial passage in which Lenin, in July 1920, laid down the doctrine which both bound together the seizure of power and what happened after it and also gave legitimacy to what Vietnamese, Chinese, Cuban and other leaderships have sought to do since:

> If the victorious revolutionary proletariat conducts systematic propaganda among them, and the Soviet governments come to their aid with all the means at their disposal – in that event it will be mistaken to assume that the backward peoples must inevitably go through the capitalist stage of development. Not only should we create independent contingents of fighters and party organizations in the colonies and the backward countries, not only at once launch propaganda for the organization of peasants' Soviets and strive to adapt them to the precapitalist conditions, but the Communist International should advance the proposition, with the appropriate theoretical grounding, that with the aid of the proletariat of the advanced countries, backward countries can go over to the Soviet system and, through certain stages of development, to communism, without having to pass through the capitalist stage.[25]

In terms of the seizure of power, with which this volume will be concerned, the point is that this requires a campaign fought across a particular terrain. In this study 'terrain' is not meant to be merely a metaphor, but to have actual meaning as a concept. Thus, in one sense it is what would conventionally be understood by the term, the land and water of Viet Nam itself which, as we shall see, was a not inconsiderable factor in shaping the Revolution. Much more important, however, was the terrain constituted from the class and other social struggles expressed both in contemporary action and in the cumulative weight of past experience. The point is that, although a terrain may not always be of a protagonist's choosing, a revolutionary movement in particular has to undertake its active *creation*. In other words, the history of past struggle has to be put into ideological forms which will give an advantage in the present one. More crucially, contemporary struggle has to be given a shape which makes it possible for the revolutionaries to find their way to victory.

In these two respects, the Vietnamese Communist leadership in effect discerned three contours which appeared to them to show what was the lie of the land. These were:

– socialism in its Marxist-Leninist version;
– a concept of internationalism, again derived from Marxism-Leninism;
– patriotism, something particular to Viet Nam itself.

The last may have been particular to the Vietnamese Revolution, but it was also fundamental, indeed in a very real sense primordial. The struggle of the Vietnamese people from the mid-1920s was to derive much of its strength from a sense of national identity which looked back in the popular conception to a 4,000-year history. The point is that patriotism, to use the term preferred by Party leaders and Communist scholars, did not take shape in twentieth-century Viet Nam as an ideological product of the past which weighed, in Marx's terms, like a nightmare on the brains of the living. Rather, it could be seen as having passed down through the generations, lovingly polished by the hands of all sorts and conditions of men and women, spanning all classes, even though rejected by some individuals, and finally coming into the custody of the revolutionary workers, peasants and intellectuals. In Chapter 4 we shall see in detail what was the reality behind this view. Here we must note that, like all other phenomena in the real world, Vietnamese patriotism was marked by a contradiction. Rooted as it was in social relations which had been superseded by the twentieth century, it could be freed in that epoch from immediate class associations and spread to all; but contemporary class and other interests prevented unanimity on what shape Vietnamese society and polity should ultimately take once they were free from foreign domination. The great majority of Vietnamese could be patriots, but not all could necessarily link this with an end to class and other oppression and exploitation.

Despite Lenin's best efforts, Bolshevik doctrine was never quite happy with nationalism/patriotism. Orthodoxy linked the ideology in class terms with the bourgeoisie, making it therefore something which would have to be superseded and could be a dominant motivation only in the first stage of the revolution. Moreover, particularly in colonial situations, it required the postulation of a 'national bourgeoisie' which could express it. It was the special triumph of the Vietnamese Communists that they were able to weld patriotism with Marxist–Leninist received ideas. From the foundation in 1930 of the Indochinese Communist Party (ICP) it kept constantly before its

12

adherents the goal not only of the end of foreign rule but also of a better society, with patriotic resistance always also implying a radical change in class and other social relations. There were times when the linkage became more obscure but it was never really broken. However, there can be no doubt that a series of prices were paid for this relative success. As we shall see, there were times during the struggle right up until 1975 when the contradiction between patriotism and socialism did emerge in the forms of uncertainty as to what was precisely the best base for the Revolution in a particular period, and of difficulties caused by previous judgements on this.

Socialism in its Marxist–Leninist variant contained another contradiction which was to have even deeper consequences. Since it really only came into play after mid-1954 in the North, I can leave its major exposition until Volume III. Here let it simply be said that a cumulative and enormous price was paid in Viet Nam for assimilating Bolshevik doctrine, namely the acquisition in some degree or other of all the economic and political distortions which characterize soviet systems. In the views of some, these are sufficient to make it impossible to regard such systems as 'socialist' at all.

Of more immediate relevance to this volume – although they will continue to figure until the last – are the contradictions arising from the Marxist–Leninist received ideas which dominated the Communist leaders' view of the seizure of power. This orthodoxy contained three essential elements:

– the concept of a revolution conducted in two stages – the first national and democratic in character, the second socialist;
– the idea that, in both stages, the revolution must be led by a vanguard party based upon the working class;
– the idea that the mass base of the revolution would have as its core a worker–peasant alliance, with the former class in the leading position.

Important contradictions would arise from these, in particular from the effect of the prerequisites for the first stage of the revolution upon the course of the second, and from the relationship between party and mass base.

In the Marxist–Leninist theory which was the inspiration of the Communists in Viet Nam, revolution and the working class were coupled always with internationalism; it was the workers of the world who were called on to unite, even in the Stalinist version which spoke also of building socialism in one country. This internationalism was to prove of enormous material and symbolic importance for the Party and its revolution, but it contained a contradiction which tended to reinforce the others. It was crucial that Vietnamese patriotism proved not to be of a cramped and chauvinistic kind, but one which could envisage an international struggle of which that in Viet Nam was a unique but integral moment.

Undoubtedly the linkages established by the ICP's relations with the Comintern from 1930 until that body's dissolution in 1943 sustained and developed the compatibility of patriotism, internationalism and the soviet version of

13

socialism. So did its contacts and those of its successor, the Workers' Party, with fraternal parties and governments from 1945. But the contradiction lay in the other movement established under Stalin, of commands issued from Moscow and subordination to Soviet interests. It can immediately be recorded that the material support of the USSR has, objectively speaking, always been a great contribution to the success of the Vietnamese Revolution. Nevertheless, a double price was paid. With internationalism ineradicably associated in the minds of the Vietnamese leaders with leadership from Moscow (apart from deviations toward Peking in the late 1950s and early 1960s, discussed later), the strength of the Marxist–Leninist model as derived from practice in the Soviet Union could only be increased. Beyond this, as we have already seen to be of overriding importance at Geneva, once the Communist leaders were in control of a state, the DRVN, their foreign policy and the whole Vietnamese Revolution became indissolubly linked with what the Soviet leadership was attempting to do upon the international scene. This, of course, had the most deleterious effects. Above all, it inevitably involved the Vietnamese liberation struggle in the international politics of the 'Cold War' which had emerged between the two giants of the post-Second World War era, the USA and the Soviet Union. Again, we have already seen some of the results of this involvement in looking at the events in Geneva in mid-1954, and it will loom increasingly large as this study proceeds.

The Road to Power

One further step needs to be taken in this presentation of necessary theory, namely to go beyond the concept of revolutionary terrain to the actual way it might be traversed on the way to the seizure of state power. For this purpose I shall employ a conceptualization also derived from the Marxist tradition and, like others used in this study, not necessarily incompatible with the Bolsheviks' position but capable of being distanced from it.

In the years during which the new Vietnamese vanguard was entrenching itself among French colonial subjects on the other side of the world, a sickly and misshapen but iron-willed Italian Communist was using his time in a fascist prison to consider the problem of seizing power. Upon some of the ideas of Antonio Gramsci, who died as a result of his incarceration, I can base my theorization of the problematic of the road to power and socialism in Viet Nam.

Gramsci was concerned above all with developed capitalist countries, what he called 'the West,' to which he counterposed 'the East' (for him pre-1917 Russia).[26] In the latter, to which by extension we may add China, Viet Nam and many others, Gramsci felt that 'civil society' was 'primordial', a label which we may read in terms of the complexities of social relations and consciousness in a country only partially penetrated by capitalism. Further, the state apparatus there was of particular significance as a bastion of the ruling class. In consequence, in such formations a protracted 'war of manoeuvre' would be required in order gradually to bring about the conditions for a revolutionary seizure of power. This kind of delayed frontal attack would not be necessary in conditions of developed capitalism, where power might be won through a relatively rapid 'war of position' involving political struggle in a situation of well-defined classes, and with a state apparatus which was only part of the defences of the ruling class. Like most of Gramsci's ideas, these are seedlings to be cultivated rather than fully-grown trees, which is one reason why in future chapters and volumes description, explanation and analysis will have to be punctuated with further theorization. To establish my problematic initially, however, one vital point must be made. In this study it is taken as axiomatic that in order to achieve a revolutionary overthrow of capitalism anywhere – whether in Italy or Viet Nam – both a war of position *and* a war of manoeuvre must be fought. Moreover, these two wars have to be fought together, overlapping in time, space and activity (and hence theoretically).

In this study, then, the war of position is the process whereby an organized leadership, such as that of the ICP and its successor the Workers' Party, which seeks to carry out a socialist revolution, puts itself at the head of a bloc of dissident class and other elements and, in so doing, roots itself so deeply that it cannot henceforth be eradicated by the power bloc which represents the dominant classes and its state apparatus. The war of manoeuvre is the politico-military process by which that leadership actually seizes power, propels itself, so to say, through the gates of the governor-general's or president's palace.

If the above discussion is taken along with the previous idea of the active creation of a revolutionary terrain, it will be seen that the wars of position and manoeuvre, as just defined, in fact constitute such a creation. My total argument thus runs: shift of the Marxist–Leninist-inspired revolution to the East (and the capitalist periphery in general) after 1920; attempts to create new terrains of struggle by vanguard parties; the launching of wars of position and manoeuvre in order to accomplish this and seize state power. The last part of this formulation requires further development before we can go on.

Obviously the taking of position amid existing social relations and struggle, the rooting of the vanguard, is a fundamental step. It can be seen in terms of five prerequisites. First, it needs a leadership, which we may see as coming from the social category which Gramsci termed the 'organic intellectuals'. This term will be explored in Chapter 2. Second, that group must be infused with a doctrine which serves them as a guide in both taking position and manoeuvring into power. In the Vietnamese case this was, of course, Marxism–Leninism. Third, and vitally important, a 'catchment area' of alienated class and other elements must exist to which the revolutionaries can find access and so create a base for themselves. Fourth, following from the third point, an organization must be created in order to hold that base together and move it in directions indicated by doctrine. Fifth, a similar necessity is an ideology, a combination of programme and inspirational message, through which increasing numbers of people can be moved.

That movement, of course, is the war of manoeuvre. Here the important point is Gramsci's view that in 'the East' such a war must necessarily be protracted. Struggling against colonial regimes or various forms of indigenous authoritarianism linked closely to foreign capital, socialist revolutionaries find it necessary to endure and have patience. Already, before Gramsci's death, the case of China had also shown that the protracted war must necessarily combine both political and military action. Indeed, in that country Mao Tse-tung was then emerging as the foremost Marxist–Leninist theorist of such a doctrine.[27] Moreover, in a remarkable case of serendipity, at this time Mao was also distinguishing between 'capitalist countries', where there would be 'a long period of legal struggle before the seizure of power', and 'semi-colonial and semi-feudal' China, where struggle would immediately have to take the form of 'insurrection and war'. In the former the rural areas would be seized from the cities; in the latter the reverse pattern would occur.

In a later chapter we shall see the significance of such ideas as the Vietnamese began to develop their own doctrines on manoeuvre and pro-tracted war.

The Shape of this Study

Whatever price they may have paid in the process (at whoever's expense), and whatever doctrinal changes they may have made on the way, it was the historical mission of the Vietnamese Communist leadership (and at the same time the personal genius of Ho Chi Minh) to direct the fusion in the period 1930–45 of the patriotism, internationalism and socialism which provided the contours of the Vietnamese Revolution as they saw it, and then to make the working class and its allied peasantry the major bearers of that combination. It was those leaders who also ensured that the process would be led by a Communist Party which counted among its members and supporters almost all the best of the country's intellectuals. After August 1945 the Revolution, at the same time patriotic, internationalist and socialist, drew upon itself the most bitter onslaughts over many painful years, but it could never be defeated. Ho Chi Minh could die in September 1969 knowing this, though unaware of the date of final victory.

In pursuing the themes opened up above and others better introduced later, we shall in fact trace the trajectory of the Vietnamese Revolution over fifty years. This series of volumes, therefore, will attempt to show how, taking shape clearly in 1930, though as a new expression of themes which in some cases were rooted very deeply in the past, the Revolution, by mid-1941, had found a firm terrain from which the ICP could make its way to power in August 1945. Attempted French reconquest was thwarted in a liberation war which prevented the full reincorporation of the country into world capitalism, but left it divided. The analysis of these developments forms this volume. From mid-1954 North and South Viet Nam experienced more than twenty years of the separate development in each of class and state, involving the laying of the foundations of a Soviet system in the former and the emergence of new forms of dependent capitalism in the latter. Both of these experiences were massively influenced by foreign intervention and war, but in the end the revolutionary forces triumphed over the power blocs of the USA and its local allies and the country was again united. This breach in the wall of international capitalism by the defeat of its hegemonic power provides one major justification for our taking the Vietnamese Revolution as a problematic for study. The other, of course intimately related to the first, is the importance of Viet Nam as a case of the attempted implementation of Marxist–Leninist doctrine in an ex-colonial country.

All historical studies must end somewhere, and the 'Great Spring Victory' won in 1975 by Party and people is a punctuation mark which my themes allow us to transform into a full stop. After that date the Vietnamese Revolution would continue, now with the task of capping unity and independence with a particular version of socialism, but thus opening new terrain which it is too early to chart. Other lesser marks punctuated the struggle. 1954 is a colon at which two separate regimes were imposed on a divided country, although fully to comprehend its effects will require us to push the analysis in this volume through 1956. The year 1960 is a semi-colon between the consolidation of the two regimes and the new struggle for reunification; 1965 is the colon at which massive and direct US intervention radically changed the ways in which this task had to be fulfilled. Early 1970 is another semi-colon, marking the broadening of the war to a fully Indochinese dimension. My subsequent volumes, though varying in scope and scale, are all bound by this periodization. This first volume will have the broadest historical sweep, concentrating on the period 1925 to 1956 but reaching back where necessary to try to extract the essence of 2,000 years of Vietnamese history.

Notes

1   My interpretation of the Vietnamese leaders' intentions in this and the preceding paragraph is based on *History of the Vietnamese People's Army* (in Vietnamese), 1977, pp. 530–6 and *Contribution to the Study of Dien Bien Phu* 1965, pp. 39–41 and 43–9.

2   This is the interpretation which I put on *History of the Vietnamese People's Army*, pp. 528–9 and 534. See also Porter 1980, pp. 232–3.

3   Circular of the Central Committee Secretariat, 27 December 1953, quoted in *Vietnamese People's Army*, pp. 536.

4   See Hammer 1966, p. 310.

5   The text may be found in Cole (ed.) 1956.

6   Annex to Document 30, 'NSC Action No. 1074–A,' 5 April 1954, *PP* I, p. 471, and Document 31, 'Army Position on NSC Action No. 1074–A,' p. 471 and calculation based

on p. 472. See also *PP* I, pp. 108–10. It should be remembered that the main text of this work is the draft of the history of the involvement of the USA in the second Indochinese conflict commissioned by the Secretary of Defense in 1967.

7   Two exceptions should be noted. Ever since 1954 the comparative advantage which French-speaking scholars have possessed has not been capitalized upon, and the amount of work on Viet Nam by them has been quite limited. Their point of reference and main object of study has tended to be French colonialism and the reaction to it, with some more contemporary acid-Gallic analyses of their US successors and lately some products of left disillusionment. Second, since 1975, a widely spread Vietnamese exile community has emerged and, while their publications have until now been mostly polemical, it is to be expected that the younger generation will employ its comparative linguistic advantage to take the graduate school-to-university professor path. This possibility scares me perhaps most of all, given the reactionary, if not fascist, tendencies which permeate the refugee communities, out of which have already come the murder of one progressive American academic and death threats to other people.

8   See Braestrup (ed.), 1984.

9   Duiker, Marr and Turley are Americans, Khanh and Long are Vietnamese with long US connections, including higher education.

10   See Smith 1983, Introduction, passim.

11   Vlastos 1984, p. 53.

12   See, for example, Smith 1983, pp. 16 and 261.

13   Smith 1985, p. 18.

14   Berman 1984a, p. 21 and 1984b, p. 36.

15   Mao 1962, p. 192.

16   For a summary discussion of the evolution of Bolshevik doctrine see Carr 1966, vol. 1, Chapter 1.

17   See Lenin, 'Better fewer but better', Lenin 1966, vol. 33, and Claudin 1975, pp. 63-71.

18   Engels, letter to Kautsky, 12 September 1882, in Avineri (ed.) 1969, p. 473.

19   On the Second Comintern Congress, see Carr 1966, vol. 3, pp. 253–61, and on the Baku Congress ibid., pp. 262–71.

20   The best English-language biography of Ho (though containing some errors and written before the availability of new materials published after his death) is Lacouture 1968. See also Rageau 1970. Duiker 1976, pp. 194–201, adds useful detail for the years up to 1925 by drawing on Vietnamese sources. There is no full biography in Vietnamese.

21   Ho Chi Minh, 'The Path Which Led Me to Leninism,' Ho 1977 (published April 1960), p. 252.

22   See 'Extracts from the Theses on the Bolshevization of Communist Parties Adopted at the Fifth ECCI Plenum,' Degras (ed.) 1960, vol. II, pp. 188–200.

23   The concept of the 'received ideas of socialism' is developed and applied in Post and Wright, 1989.

24   The specificities of Soviet (state socialist) states are the central theme of ibid.

25   'Report of the Commission on the National and the Colonial Questions', Lenin 1966, vol. 31, p. 244.

26   Gramsci's key text is 'State and Civil Society' in Hoare and Smith (eds.) 1971, but see also 'Notes on Italian History' and 'The Modern Prince.' An important discussion is Anderson 1976–77, and see also Sassoon 1980, pp. 134–50.

27   Mao 1938c, pp. 219–20. It is interesting that Mao saw the lengthy process as above all necessary in conditions of legality.

2 Colonialism and its enemies

In February 1930 Nguyen Ai Quoc, who would later become Ho Chi Minh, on Comintern instructions summoned to the British colony of Hong Kong representatives of the three Communist Parties which had come into being in Viet Nam. At a conference in a village near Kowloon he first listened to them denounce one another. Then, according to a later reminiscence, he made his decisive intervention: 'We won't discuss that story. I come here with the responsibility of unifying Communist forces. The line of the Communists is as follows: first make the bourgeois democratic revolution, later make the socialist revolution.'[1] Although at its foundation it counted only 211 members, the Communist Party of Viet Nam was created.[2] From then on, the Revolution had its vanguard party.

Ho and his comrades, as I suggested in the previous chapter, would have to construct a complex terrain of social struggle and find their way across it. In undertaking this, in fact, they carried with them a map, the ideas of Marxism–Leninism, which they believed to be infallible. As Pham Van Dong was to put it more than forty years later, speaking then as Prime Minister of the Democratic Republic vested in the North:

> Since its foundation, the Party has armed our people with knowledge and the most basic ideas of the epoch so that they may liberate themselves from all the chains of oppression and exploitation and build a new life for themselves. This knowledge and these ideas originate in Marxist–Leninist theory, the summation and highest peak of knowledge of all humankind.[3]

The first task which the Party set for itself was liberation from colonial rule, which the Comintern and its followers saw as involving a revolutionary seizure of power. We have already noted the essentials of Marxist–Leninist doctrine on this – that is, the vanguard party, mass base and a two-stage revolution. The purpose of this chapter and the next will be to trace the development of these in Viet Nam up until the decisive turning-point in May 1941. The necessary starting-point must be the impact of colonial capitalism upon an ancient Asian kingdom, and that will form the topic of this chapter.

Imperialism and History

During the second half of the nineteenth century the Vietnamese people and state experienced the trauma which was afflicting their Cambodian and Laotian neighbours, others in South East Asia like the Indonesians and Burmese, and peoples much further afield. In France, as in Britain, the Netherlands and other capitalist countries, growing industries created a new interest in raw materials and markets. In Asia, what drew men on above all was the great space and allure of China; the French hoped, in ignorance of geography, to penetrate up the Mekong River, like rats climbing up the hind leg of an elephant, and the Vietnamese imperial state stood in the way.[4] Its real travails began in 1859, when French forces seized Saigon. In 1862, hoping to blunt the appetites of the French with a moderate meal and prevent them holding a banquet, the Emperor ceded the three provinces around and to the east of Saigon, but with whetted appetites the French took the others to the west in 1867, creating the new Colony of Cochinchina. In the meantime a Protectorate had been declared over the Kingdom of Cambodia. A French attempt to seize Hanoi in 1873 resulted in the death of the French commander at the hands of local partisans, but in August 1883 the Emperor was forced to sign a treaty after the city was again captured and Hue, the capital, bombarded. In June 1884 another treaty confirmed the imposition of Protectorates over Tonkin and Annam, where in theory the Emperor was still to rule under French tutelage. (This was also the formal situation in Cambodia, and in Laos from 1893: for the five territories see Map 1.)

Armed resistance continued until as late as 1913 in Tonkin and Annam, but the Vietnamese people were henceforth under colonial rule, bringing to an end 900 years of independent history. This study does not pretend to provide an account of those centuries, although it will turn in the fourth chapter to those themes which are essential to an understanding of how the new Communist Party took its position between 1930 and 1941. In order to understand the experience of the Vietnamese people under French rule, however, and hence the emergence of the Communist Party (the main focus of this chapter) some basic points must be established here.

According to popular legend, the 4,000 years of Vietnamese history were those of a monarchical state founded by the eldest of one hundred sons of a

20

dragon king and a fairy princess, who were the ancestors of the Viet people. As a legitimizing myth this is better than that of the 'civilizing mission' of the French, and in any case provides us with one of the three structural continuities with which we are concerned here, the long-term existence of a centralized state apparatus.[5] At least after it emerged in the tenth (Christian) century from more than a thousand years of Chinese rule, the independent state based in the Red River valley can be seen as one of the factors which profoundly shaped the Kinh people – the Vietnamese proper – and the minority peoples, Muong, Thai, Tay and others, who were their immediate neighbours. It played a great part in class formation, since its apparatus served as an instrument for surplus extraction and hence exploitation. Much of this surplus went to sustain the imperial bureaucracy, recruited on the Chinese pattern by examination from among those schooled in a mainly Confucian body of ideas. The state also served to maintain a separate identity for the Kinh in face of threats from the Cham kingdom based in what became Annam, also from the Khmer rulers of Cambodia (which for long included later Cochinchina) and above all from the Chinese, whose invasion of Viet Nam in early 1979 was counted as the fourteenth such in the country's history.

Extraction of surplus implied taxes, and if it is indeed true that there is nothing certain in life except death and taxes, then in Viet Nam, as elsewhere in Asia, rice is the foundation for both. Its absence means starvation and its comparative plenitude provides enough to be squeezed out of the direct producers to support others. Rice cultivation requires land, water, seed, tools and human labour power (if possible supplemented with draught animals). It also means dependence on the weather. In Viet Nam two harvests are possible each year, but only if the rains come on time and in the right quantity, so that the Red River (in the south, the Mekong) and the others rise when they should and in the proper degree, and if the typhoons do not bring the sea sweeping on to the land. Another basic legend of the Viet puts the God of the Mountains and the God of the Waters in titanic combat; this expresses the slender dyke which the peasant, up to the present day, has walked between the new harvests, with their promise of continued life, and natural disaster and death for many. It is scarcely surprising that, with centuries of such anxiety behind them, rice became for the Vietnamese not merely a basic staple, a food (in special forms) for celebration and a source of alcohol, but also a less tangible force which permeated their culture. As a modern work puts it:

> At the very foundation of Vietnamese society the rice fields have throughout history supplied the society with a reason for being. The fields have provided the basis for a stable social structure, a discipline for work, and a rhythm of communal celebrations - in short, a contract between the society itself, the soil and the sky.[6]

When a group of workers at the Phu Rieng rubber plantation swore in September 1927 to kill their French manager and sealed the oath by drinking a mixture of their own blood and rice spirit, they were drawing from the deepest well of their people's culture for the symbolism of their resistance to colonialism.[7] The cultivation of rice, irrigated by a multitude of channels and protected by dykes at the cost of massive labour, is thus another basic structural continuity of Vietnamese history.

Wet rice cultivation involving elaborate water control and a centralized state apparatus were of course intimately, indeed causally linked, since one of the reasons for the development of central authority was doubtless the need to coordinate flood control and carry out projects too large for local resources.[8] Likewise, the third structural continuity of Kinh history was probably originated by the organizational needs of the growing of rice in paddy fields; I refer here to the village commune, the basic cell (though itself a grouping of families) of the Vietnamese social formation as it developed in the Red River valley and expanded beyond it. It seems likely that the more extended clan relationships of the Kinh lost their significance even before the Chinese conquest, as shifting cultivation requiring control of extensive territory, and thus relatively broad social units, was superseded by the intensive use of land for wet rice cultivation and the close cooperation of the fewer families this involved. As classes formed among the Kinh the original clan structure dissolved and lineages consolidated together as village communes: perhaps this reality lay behind the popular saying 'It is sometimes necessary to forsake distant cousins to live with near neighbours'.[9] In any case, however they originally formed, the communes (*xa*) emerged from the period of Chinese rule as the entities which carried out the work of irrigation and flood protection, grew the rice, and sustained the dominant class and state apparatus. Each rested among its ricefields and fishponds, marked off from the outside world by its bamboo hedge, whenever possible regulating its affairs internally, wary in its relations with the state representative who came to collect tax in kind, whether he journeyed from afar or lived nearby.

There remains plenty of room for debate among scholars concerning the real significance of the commune in Vietnamese history. What all can probably accept is its historical longevity and resilience, at any rate until exposed to the erosive acids of capitalism. Even then, so basic was it that, when the need to reconceptualize their reality hit Vietnamese intellectuals in the early decades of the twentieth century, nothing seemed better as a term for the Western idea of 'society' than '*xa hoi*' – 'association of communes'.[10] Throughout the preceding centuries, the commune and its peasant families had shown themselves better able to face foreign invasion and other convulsions than the power bloc and its state apparatus, which changed in composition and broke down while

...the Vietnamese village by its very rusticity had been an inviolable sanctuary of the nation. It was not that each village was capable of resisting individually. But these villages were found everywhere. They were not concentrated in any one place so that the adversary might have seized them as one lays hold of a capital, overthrows a dynasty, or subjugates a court.[11]

It will become clear that the communes were not without their own internal contradictions, but it is true that for hundreds of generations they were the basic organizational units of the Vietnamese social formation, able, whatever happened at levels above them, to 'shut like oysters, protecting their essential substance from the disorder of the outside world'.[12] It was in them that the ancestors of Nguyen Ai Quoc and his comrades lived and moved and had their being, and it was their problems, compounded by colonialism, which the Communist Party leaders had to face in the mid-twentieth century.

Colonialism and Transformation

Reference to how Vietnamese intellectuals came to conceptualize society is very much in order at this point, and an extra significance is given to Pham Van Dong's remarks in 1966, quoted above, by the fact that they were made at a conference of such people. When Dong joined the man who was to be his 'Uncle' for the next forty-four years, he did so – like most of his early comrades – as the expression of the crystallization of just such a new social category. French colonialism created the new Vietnamese intellectuals, and among them emerged the adherents of Marxism–Leninism.

It is indeed one of the satisfying ironies of history that this should be so. As Karl Marx noted, speaking then of British rule in India. 'There is something in human history like retribution; and it is a rule of historical retribution that its instrument be forged not by the offended, but by the offender himself.'[13] As we shall see, French rule in Viet Nam created, among other classes and groups, the three main ones which would serve as its undoing and that of the US power bloc later. These were two quite new social forces, the Western-educated intellectuals and the workers, and a peasantry which, already oppressed under the emperors, was further crushed under capitalism.

The basic task of the new rulers was to bring the five Indochinese territories into line with the needs of French capitalism.[14] The overall intention was what might have been expected at the time of the final burgeoning of European imperialism (and the beginning of that of the USA and Japan). Indochina was seen as a source of raw materials for French industries and a market for their products, but above all as a source of rice for the world market. During the fifty years' high tide of colonialism, Viet Nam and its population therefore experienced restructuring and a new economic differentiation designed to further the extraction of surplus by various French interests. It is important to avoid seeing this as the emergence of some sort of 'dualism', whether the feudalist–capitalist one of the unsophisticated Marxists or a rural–urban juxtaposition.[15] The colonial totality was certainly uneven, but it was

23

combined with a capitalism so dominant that it is difficult to speak of its articulation with any other form of production except on terms that were entirely its own.[16] The implications of this will become clearer as we proceed.

The necessary infrastructure for colonial exploitation, a massive programme of railway, road, canal, bridge and port development, was a first French priority. Ultimately even more significant was another very large state investment in drainage and land reclamation in western Cochinchina and the Mekong delta; between 1880 and 1930 the available agricultural land quadrupled, increasing between 1880 and 1900 alone from 522,000 hectares to 1,175,000. [17] This was not handed out or sold to the peasants but, along with land abandoned by fugitives from French reprisals and other areas seized by the conqueror, was sold at minimal prices to Frenchmen and to Vietnamese who had collaborated. Moreover, it was the peasant who ultimately paid for all this through a system of personal and land taxes and very lucrative state monopolies on the sale of salt, alcohol and opium, and what was in effect forced labour on construction work.

In order to administer tax collection and other state functions a new apparatus had to be developed. In Cochinchina, a colony, this could be created freely, without reference to the old bureaucracy which remained in place in the protectorates, Annam and Tonkin. In the South, therefore, collaborators of various kinds, often Catholic converts and of humble origins, were used at the lower clerical and interpreter levels.[18] French citizens naturally held all higher and most intermediate posts, although Vietnamese gradually gained some entry to the latter, particularly as a handful gained French citizenship (2,555 by 1937, 1,474 of them in the colony).[19] After 1880, Cochinchina was also able to boast a Colonial Council which could give an opinion on the colonial government's decisions, and a member of the National Assembly in France, both elected on very narrow franchises. In the protectorates, French control of what was formally still the Emperor's government was tight; the Council of Ministers for Annam was reorganized so that half of its members were French officials and one of them presided, and in Tonkin the imperial resident was replaced by a French 'High Governor'. The old system of recruitment of officials through examinations lasted until the administrative system was reorganized, which meant the end of the 'scholar-bureaucrats', the core of the old imperial system, as a social force, and also of the indigenous school system. However, the bulk of officials in the protectorates, even at high levels, continued to be Vietnamese, although now with a French education.[20]

The basic process of restructuring was over by the end of the First World War (1914–18), which witnessed a tightening grip on the economy as metropolitan demands for rice, soldiers and labourers had to be met. After the war, the French power bloc needed new wealth to replace that eaten up by the ravages of capitalism in global conflict, and the doctrine emerged of the 'valorization' ('*mise en valeur*') of the colonial possessions. Once again, that required capital investment, this time principally private.

The 1920s and 1930s thus witnessed two crucial developments which were of course intimately linked. First, investment and its effects on production, and hence exports and imports, strengthened the linkages of Indochina as a whole with French metropolitan capitalism and determined even more closely how the colonial economy would move. Second, in terms of the social revolution with which this study is concerned, the same period increased the pressure upon various class and other subordinated elements and opened them to radical political ideas.

In the period between the two world wars, therefore, Vietnamese underde-velopment was determined above all by the 4,170 million francs invested by private enterprise between 1924 and 1938, compared with only 490 million from 1888 to 1918.[21] Much of this went into mining and industry, continuing a trend begun during the war, but rubber was also a major concern. The tendency to invest in already established companies is shown by the fact that stock issues by existing concerns between 1924 and 1935 were more than twice those by new ones.[22] The period of increased investment thus did not mean a new direction for the colonial forces of production, and in any case came to an end when Indochina followed its masters into the world slump after 1929. Capitalism passes back its losses more readily than its gains to the exploited; ultimately to be absorbed by the peasants, workers and other poor, therefore, were such effects as a drop in stock issues from 729 million francs in 1929 to 40.8 million in 1935, and a fall on the Saigon market in the wholesale price of top quality paddy (unmilled) rice of 73.6 percent between 1929 and 1934.[23] Again as in France, from around 1936 there was something of an economic revival, and by 1939 wholesale rice in Saigon was back to 78.2 per cent of the 1929 price, but that was the year in which Indochina became engulfed in war, once more dragged in at the heels of France. As we shall see, it was the Second World War which gave the most deadly enemies of French colonialism their opportunity.

Having noted the main economic trends during the period when the French power bloc was in fullest control, it is time to examine certain developments in more detail, particularly in class terms; for those fifty years, marked as they were by the consolidation of colonial capitalism, wrought more changes than all the centuries that had gone before. We may begin with an observation by Jean Chesneaux, that an important series of discontinuities in the locations of major economic activity marks the transition from independence to French rule.[24] Discontinuities were also apparent in the type of activity. For instance, mining, which certainly had a long history, remained mostly in the highlands, but was now concentrated on non-ferrous metals such as zinc, chrome and tin. Chesneaux himself points out one very important new development in mining, the coal mines of Tonkin, with their own port at Cam Pha, the most important of these extractive activities.

Mining in general, as we have noted, was a major sphere of capital investment after the First World War. Capital also went into manufacturing, which basically meant agricultural processing, above all rice-milling in Saigon, and production of consumer goods such as textiles, sugar and matches; the biggest single such enterprise was the cotton mill at Nam Dinh in Tonkin, employing at peak periods as many as 5,000 workers. Haiphong, however, did boast a big cement works, and there was boatbuilding there and in Saigon and also some machine shops, for example at Vinh. It is important to note that not only were these new enterprises in terms of productive forces and relations of production, but they were also situated in centres which had not necessarily been economic poles before or, if so, they had been centres of trade, like Saigon's Chinese settlement, Cholon. In addition, to handle the changed flows of colonial commerce, new ports like Cam Pha and Haiphong replaced some old centres like Qui Nhon.

A similar pattern emerged in agriculture, the products of which remained the major exports. Thus, in the Tonkin midlands, north and west of the delta and between it and the highlands, French investors started coffee plantations in areas cleared in the late nineteenth century by French anti-guerrilla campaigns. Much more important, however, were two developments in Cochinchina – rubber and commercial rice production. The former was dominated by the big French companies like Michelin; by 1937 they controlled 68 per cent of the plantation area, and small owners (of less than forty hectares, often Vietnamese) only 6 per cent.[25] In all, rubber plantations took up some 130,000 hectares in the provinces north and east of Saigon.[26]

As for rice, we have already noted the prodigious opening of land for its cultivation west of Saigon, especially in the provinces known as the Trans-Bassac, up to the Cambodian border (which in fact remained only roughly demarcated). It has been estimated that about two-thirds of Cochinchinese riceland was brought into cultivation only after 1880, and between a quarter and a third from 1910 to 1930.[27] The whole process may be summed up in a quotation:

> Population rose consistently but spread unevenly. New lands were brought under rice cultivation in a process of static expansion rather than of balanced and diverse economic growth with new technology. The development of transportation and irrigation works aided this advance of the frontier, a movement first completed in the central region and still under way at the end of the colonial era in some parts of the eastern and western provinces. As part of the vast growth of rice export, a network of predominantly Chinese middlemen spread through the countryside to connect the Saigon exporters with the villagers.[28]

The Material Process of Class Formation

It was French capitalism in its imperialist form which had conquered Viet Nam, and extensions of the French capitalist class were the agents who

26

articulated all parts of the new economy. The capitalist class in the three possessions (in fact, in all five, if Laos and Cambodia are included) was a complex phenomenon, divided internally in various ways. Thus, it may be seen in terms of its fractions (mining, manufacturing, commercial, agricultural, financial) and as stratified by the different degree of control of its members over means of production – after all, the term 'capitalist' covers both the owner of a small rice mill and the head of the Bank of Indochina. Along with these two divisions came a third, the existence of ethnic segments within the capitalist class, distributed unevenly among its fractions and strata; thus, Frenchmen dominated the upper levels of all fractions, but Vietnamese (in effect, the Kinh) were well represented specifically in rice-growing and the Chinese (Hoa) in commerce, manufacturing and finance, while in the last there was a tiny but significant Indian element.

These three divisions were important because, as we shall see, the *internal* contradictions of various classes were part of the dynamic of class formation. This is well illustrated by the role of the Bank of Indochina. Formed in 1875, largely with capital from the giant Banque de Paris et du Pays Bas, it was given the power to issue the currency for the new Indochina and was thus tied closely to the colonial state apparatus, which was itself only an instance of the metropolitan one.   This became even clearer in 1931, when the Bank's monopoly over the issuing of currency was renewed for another twenty-five years while at the same time the French state took up 20 per cent of its shares.[29] By the late 1930s the Bank controlled a formidable range of enterprises in Indochina, particularly in manufacturing but also in transport, finance and mining, including the company which produced over 70 per cent of the coal.[30] Although it swallowed two rival groups in 1920 and 1924, it was not the only big financial power in Indochina; rubber in particular was linked to other financial houses and also had its own Société Financière des Caouchoucs. But if finance capital was the dominant fraction, binding all the others together, then the Bank of Indochina was its heart, able, through its control over currency and credit in collaboration with the state, to affect the performance and profits of every other enterprise, both large and small.

The Bank could impose unity from its position of vantage at the top of the capitalist class, where it merged the largely French financial and manufacturing interests. At the same time, another moment of a composite contradiction (fusing at one time divisions among fractions, strata and segments) was the struggle against the Bank's power by other capitalist interests. Here the most important element was the big landowners of Cochinchina. Since one man often controlled thousands of hectares of riceland and hundreds of tenants, this fraction represented the only sphere in which a substantial number of Vietnamese could expect to become really rich.[31] Although the large scale amounted in fact to something qualitatively new, emphasis must be laid on the backwardness of this element, content with the simple exploitation of tenant farmers and use of the profit thus made to enjoy the pleasures of Saigon, if not of Paris and the Riviera, rather than being interested in technical improvement or even direct management of production. Nevertheless, this was a very important group: rice from Cochinchina was the biggest part of Indochinese exports, reaching a peak of 2,390,000 metric tons in 1928, dropping to 1,320,000 in 1931, but topping 2 million again in five of the seven years 1934–40.[32] From this substantial material basis the Cochinchina landed interests could resist even the Bank of Indochina, as they did when its revaluation of the piastre in May 1931 in face of the world depression threatened to result in a decline of trade with other Asian countries.[33] Moreover, from it they also spread into the 'liberal' professions and to some extent into trade and industry.[34]

Nevertheless, we must remember that any contradictions within the capitalist class in Viet Nam were only secondary; the primary and crucial counterpositions were those between capitalists of different fractions on the one side and workers and peasants on the other. This three-cornered relationship, as we shall see, was fundamental to the development of the Vietnamese Revolution.

The expansion of capitalism after the First World War inevitably meant a growth of the working class which it had created, although to what exact size cannot be known. The figure always given is 221,000 for Indochina as a whole in 1929; of these 189,000 were in Viet Nam, although most of the others would have been Vietnamese migrants.[35] What must be clearly understood is that only those employed in European-owned establishments were counted, along with some government workers. Thus, 10,000 railway workers, 76,000 in manufacturing and commerce, 53,000 miners, and 81,000 plantation workers were covered. Excluded were the many thousands more who worked in Chinese and Vietnamese establishment and plantations, the dockworkers and masses of 'coolies' who carried goods in all market centres, construction workers and any other sort of daily paid labour. Le Thanh Khoi in consequence has suggested that a figure of 1 million might be more appropriate.[36] He, however, includes an unspecified proportion of the Cochinchina tenant farmers, who were proletarianized in the sense of minimal control over means of production, but were not wage-workers. There is also a problem concerning the inclusion of shop staff in the working class proper, as in the figure of 76,000 above. Nevertheless, whatever cavils might be made, the fact remains that the Vietnamese working class at the beginning of the 1930s probably numbered three or four times the 'traditional' figure.

More than that, as a number of scholars have pointed out, we are not dealing with some frozen figure. Capitalism in Viet Nam in the 1920s and 1930s was like a giant pump, drawing in people and expelling them again. Much labour, such as that on plantations or in construction, was in any case seasonal by nature. For that matter, labour on the rubber plantations was so terrible an experience that many workers broke contract and deserted and had to be replaced. It took the recruitment of over 75,000 plantation workers (a process often characterized by force and fraud) to hold together an actual labour force of 22,000 in the period 1925–1930.[37] Lastly, capitalists in Viet Nam behaved just as they did elsewhere in face of adverse conditions – they dismissed and rehired workers at will. The number of rubber plantation workers fell from 32,400 in 1930 to 11,250 in 1933 in face of the slump and then began to rise again.[38] Thus, taking seasonality, rapid turnovers, and dismissals and rehirings together, it is obvious that many more men (and some women) were exposed to the experience of wage labour – an estimated two-thirds in Tonkin for example – than a survey made at one point in time would indicate.[39]

As to the kind of life which a worker might normally expect, there is little to be said here; horror stories should be written by Edgar Allen Poe, not by historians, so long as it is understood that fact is involved, not fiction. One case can serve as a microcosm of the remainder. In the summer of 1941 the authorities at the Courtenay rubber plantation in Bien Hoa Province, east of Saigon, levelled the grave of one of their former employees because it had become an object of veneration by other workers. It was a nameless grave since, as was usual, the dead man had been known to his mates only by a shortened form of the number assigned to him by the estate management – Brother Seventy. Plantation workers under colonialism were not expected to have names, only to act as depersonalized agents for capitalist profit. They worked, and often they died. Brother Seventy, ill with malaria, was beaten by an overseer and forced to go on tapping trees for the sap which the workers called 'white blood'; soon he collapsed and died. Nevertheless, he earned a kind of immortality, for the anonymous ballad of 'Brother Seventy' was sung widely as part of the popular consciousness of resistance and struggle. [40]

Beatings, even murder, were ultimately less deadly than the slow grinding down of men and women by overwork and undernourishment, the undramatic sacrifice of lives and human potential. Brother Seventy was at least remembered in a song; thousands more went unsung to an early grave. Let the basic situation be put more 'scientifically.' It is evident that colonial capitalism in Viet Nam sought to make its profit by absolute rather than relative exploitation; that is, by long hours and hard work rather than mechanization and managerial efficiency. That meant relatively unskilled labour and low wages, which could always be reduced if profits were threatened. Thus, in June 1932 the rubber companies were authorized to cut men's wages by 25 per cent and women's by 30 per cent, while at the same time the government was paying the producers (who had enjoyed profits as high as 160 per cent in the years before the slump) a bonus to compensate for falling prices. Overall decline in wages in face of the world depression is shown in Table 2.1. [41]

In Viet Nam in the two decades before the Second World War, a working class did not merely exist in itself. It existed in relation to the peasantry, from which it was largely drawn, and the petty bourgeoisie of small manufacturers and traders. Indeed, at least around Saigon–Cholon, Haiphong, Hanoi and the larger provincial centres, they formed a continuum, with individuals combining forms of work from each or ceaselessly moving from one to another.[42] Unlike Marx's vision of communism, where one might be administrator, artist

Table 2.1 Fall in wages, 1931–36 (%)

	Hanoi	Haiphong	Tonkin	Annam	Saigon
Skilled	14.3	29.1	27.4	27.2	24.6
Male unskilled	27.8	29.7	12.9	35.1	27.0
Female unskilled	18.2	45.2	16.7	40.0	16.0

Source: Calculated from data in Thompson (unpublished), 1945, Table III, p.36

or fisherman by choice, colonial capitalism meant an enforced circulation from, say, vegetable grower to betel nut peddler to rice mill porter, or family combinations, perhaps wives, children and old people in the paddy field, father and grown sons in factories or on the docks. Moreover, when wage labour dwindled, any and every form of self-employment could be tried.

As for more permanently self-employed artisans, official figures in 1939 counted 95,670 in Tonkin (59.4 per cent in textiles), 12,652 in Annam (23.6 percent in textiles), and 19,034 in Cochinchina (22.8 per cent in textiles).[43] Although the accuracy of these figures may be doubtful, they do indicate that, in the centre and south, the productive core of the petty bourgeoisie had stood up less well to the inroads of capitalist imports of textiles and other goods.

In the early 1930s the peasants must have formed between 85 and 90 per cent of Viet Nam's 18,000,000 people. They were not, however, a homogeneous mass. Like other classes they were divided into fractions, strata and segments, although the last only in terms of the existence of a Khmer minority in western Cochinchina.[44] (This leaves aside the highland minority peoples, kept, by French policy, as separate as possible from the Kinh on a 'divide and rule' basis.) Three main fractions may be discerned, distinguished like all class fractions in two related ways. First, each combined means of production and labour power and had their surplus extracted in different ways within the margins of limited control over means and use of their own labour power which are common to all peasants. Second, patterns of social relations within each fraction varied, and thus the internal contradictions of the peasant class as a whole were complex. The existence of such variations meant that there was in fact no one 'peasant question' throughout Viet Nam, a characteristic which was to have profound effects on both the liberation movement and the building of socialism.

The three main fractions of the Kinh peasantry as it formed at the hands of French colonialism were as follows: the complex of basically subsistence cultivators (in the sense of having little rice for export) in the Red River delta of Tonkin, the midlands behind it and the coastal plains stretching down through Annam; the complex in eastern Cochinchina centred on the Mekong delta which produced rice for local use and export and some other food and cash crops – tobacco, peanuts; and the rice plantation tenants of western Cochinchina. (In the highlands of all three territories the ethnic minorities basically subsisted on rice, maize and other food crops.) At first sight these may appear to represent different degrees of penetration by capitalism. To some extent this is true, but what should be emphasized is that in fact each had its place in the capitalist totality.

Table 2.2 will permit comparisons to be made, but to complete the picture two more factors must be added.[45] First of all, tenants and sharecroppers, not shown in the table represented 24 per cent of the rural population in Tonkin, 13 per cent in Annam, and more than 57 per cent in Cochinchina.[46]

Table 2.2 Landowning, early 1930s

	Tonkin		Annam		Cochinchina	
	% of total	% of land	% of total	% of land	% of total	% of land
Owners of less than 5ha.	98.2	40.0	98.5	50.0	71.7	15.0
Owners of 5-50ha.	1.8	20.0	1.35	15.0	25.8	37.0
Owners of over 50ha.	0.02	20.0	0.008	10.0	2.5	45.0
Communal lands	–	20.0	–	25.0	–	3.0

Source: Adapted from Le Thanh Khoi 1955, p. 422.

The land they needed for survival had to be rented from actual owners. Secondly, there was a considerable variation in the density of rural population: 540 persons per square kilometre of cultivated land in Tonkin in 1936, 300 in Annam, 170 in eastern Cochinchina and 47 in the west of the colony.[47] Taken together, this meant that in Tonkin and Annam there was a particularly great hunger for land, generated by both social and demographic pressures.[48] That led to the division and subdivision of plots, with peasant families trying to subsist on fractions of a hectare, so that even a *sao* (360 square metres) was literally an object of combat. This in its turn meant that the renting of land was an absolute necessity for more than those officially described as tenants. In that sense, such figures as in Table 2.2 showing widespread landowning are extremely deceptive, and Table 2.3, although giving the situation at the end of the colonial period, is a useful corrective in that it brings out the relative dependence on renting.

Table 2.3 Relative dependence on rented land in Tonkin, 1945

	m²/per family member owned	m²/per family member farmed	% difference farmed/ owned
Landlords	10,093	11,256	11.1
Rich peasants	3,972	4,679	15.1
Middle peasants	1,372	1,688	18.7
Poor peasants	432	680	36.5
Casual labourers	124	252	50.8

Note: Figures are averages.
Source: Adapted and calculated from Nguyen Xuan Lai 1976, table p. 18.

In Tonkin and Annam, therefore, the general pattern was as follows. The communes still existed, taken over by the colonial state apparatus as administrative units, though nominally under the Emperor's authority.[49] As they had for centuries, the council of notables in each commune handled tax collection and state demands for labour, which by the 1930s were supplemented by visits from private contractors recruiting for mines and plantations. In that sense the commune was more than ever a prison for the majority of its members. Although from 1921 councils were formally elected in Tonkin (in Annam not until 1942), in both protectorates the members were almost invariably local landlords and rich peasants or their clients. Responsible, as in the pre-colonial era, for periodically allocating communal lands, now averaging a fifth to a quarter of the total, the village councils made sure that their members and friends benefited from the division.

With this intra-communal balance of power to facilitate it, a stratification already existing in pre-colonial times had consolidated. At its top level, a small group of mainly petty landlords rented out miniscule plots: there were officially only 180 holders of more than 50 hectares in Tonkin and 50 in Annam (although there were certainly other big landowners, since holdings could be spread to avoid taxes). The landlords extracted half or more of the crop each year from their tenants, in some areas up to 70 per cent, plus cash payments, unpaid labour and gifts on such occasions as the landlord's birthday or *Tet* (the lunar New Year). They and the rich peasants also acted as moneylenders, a frequently necessary recourse for tenants and other poor people in the face of taxes, poor crops and similar miseries. Interest rates ran from 6–10 per cent a month, in emergencies 2–5 per cent a day. The allies of the landlords, the rich peasants, either owned or rented more land than they and their family members could cultivate; they therefore necessarily employed labour at peak periods and could market a surplus. Middle peasants had enough land to sustain the family, with sometimes a surplus to sell, and enough family members to do the necessary work. However, if too large a proportion of their holdings was rented and if they got into debt, they might well lose their land and be pushed down into the ranks of the poor tenants – those who owned land but only an insufficient plot – or even of those who came lower still in the rural hierarchy, the totally landless who had only the hope of renting a patch or selling their labour power.

In pre-colonial times the communes had always included a layer of poor peasants who might, in bad conditions, be squeezed out and forced to wander abroad or rebel. The crucial changes under French rule were twofold and related. First, the pressure of rents was now greater and made much worse by heavier taxes: rates for the land and head levies had risen from 3 to 5.5 per cent of the crop under the old regime to 16 and 18 per cent in 1937, with very rare remissions for bad years.[50] Before the French conquest the pressure had become insupportable when crops failed; under the new regime, with a multitude of additional charges (on boats, buffalo and betel nuts, for example) the burden was unremitting and now all male commune dwellers were on the lists. (The notables who were responsible for collection could always try to pass on the greater burden of what were in any case fixed rates not scaled by income.) Secondly, those desperate to find the money to pay did not have to wander aimlessly from their village; they could hope to find work by travelling, in the plantations, mines, factories and docks.

It seems unnecessary to dwell on the conditions of life of the poor peasants, tenants, and landless labourers which followed from the above social relations.[51] Family incomes were just not enough. Above all, taxes had to be paid, and if there was no cash for this the poor peasant faced chaining and beating by the notables' bullies until he borrowed more or even sold a child as a servant. With this priority there was no cash to buy draught animals or better implements and thus improve productivity. There was no cash to educate the children who did not die in infancy, as around half did. There was very little to buy basic consumer goods like cloth, salt or kerosene for lamps; many peasants remained part-time artisans because they had to make things for themselves. Finally, there was probably nothing to buy food to supplement what was left after the rent in kind was paid. A life of grinding labour, debt, sickness and malnutrition faced the whole family, especially the female members.[52]

An extra word must be said concerning the experience of peasant women under colonialism, for they were to come to play a significant part in the Revolution. In general they remained what they had always been, labour power in the male-dominated households, often brought in as servants or secondary wives to the wealthier to swell the available workforce. Their social esteem stayed as it was in earlier epochs, and such new legal compilations as the Tonkin Civil Code of 1931 brought no real change. The earlier years of working class formation brought some into that new phenomenon, the rather large proportion (6,687 of 15,308 in capitalist enterprises in Tonkin in 1908) typical of the first stage largely based on textile production. After this the proportion fell (though women totalled 13.4 per cent in the agricultural plantations in 1929 and 13.6 per cent in the coal mines in 1939). Others found urban employment as prostitutes, an estimated 10,000 of them in Hanoi at the end of 1937. But, for most, their experience of exploitation remained that of peasant households.[53]

Taking refuge in more abstract analysis, how may the processes which lay behind these conditions be summarized? First, it is evident that the age-old communes of Tonkin and Annam could withstand the erosions of capitalism in the sense of not collapsing structurally, but at the price of forcing members to seek income outside and of increased contradictions within them. Secondly, these contradictions did not generate forces capable of changing the structure of the communes. Since even their wealthy members had rather scant resources, they could not react as feudal landlords often did in both Western and Eastern Europe (though in different ways) and turn the land and other resources over to production for a capitalist market. Similarly, they had no great sums to invest in non-agricultural enterprises in either the rural or the urban areas. On the other hand, the bigger landlords usually had additional urban occupations or in any case preferred to be absentees; it was estimated in 1943 that only 10 per cent of them directly supervised their lands.[54] Linked now with a capitalist mode of production, the peasants in the communes had insufficient resources of their own with which to ensure the reproduction both of themselves and their old mode of production. Since there was no way to transform the latter, it continued to be reproduced willy-nilly and village life consequently became a sort of imprisonment on half rations for the peasants. In Annam there seems to have been a marginally wider distribution of land ownership and markedly less tenants and sharecroppers than in Tonkin. On the other hand, climatic conditions were even less favourable than further north, an average of three out of six harvests were wholly or partially lost (1925 was particularly disastrous), and northern Annam at least was a permanent food-deficit area.

One last point should be made about the rural situation in the two protectorates. Despite the alarm which the more intelligent and sensitive observers occasionally expressed, these possessions were not some antiquated part of an economic dualism from the standpoint of French colonial capitalism. Rather, the pressures upon the peasants of Tonkin and Annam, exerted (it should be stressed) through taxes rather than the export market, ensured that capitalism would always have the supply of cheap labour which it needed for its absolute exploitation and often great profits. Although further research is needed to establish to what extent this was conscious policy, as was probably the case, it can at least be said that no major effort was ever made even to relieve the demographic pressure which the colonial authorities blamed for most ills. Shortly before the Second World War some attempt was made to move Kinh settlers into the highlands of Tonkin, but in eighteen months only 2,446 people were relocated.[55]

In Cochinchina capitalism was much more directly at work, but in two ways. In the eastern provinces (see Map 2) it had penetrated through the market, creating opportunities for sale of produce in Saigon–Cholon, items like fruits and vegetables for local consumption, tobacco for export and also local use, and rice for export. The point was that these specializations represented the work of a peasantry which had already been in place for some time, since these were the first provinces settled in what had become Cochinchina, starting as the move into Khmer territory began in the seventeenth century. They, therefore, contrasted strongly in class structure with provinces settled since 1880, some much more recently than that. Thus, to set against the figures for land ownership shown globally for the colony in Table 2.2, we should note that, in My Tho province, peasants with less than five hectares represented 80.2 per cent of total owners and had 26.9 per cent of the cultivated land, while in Cholon province they represented 73.3 per cent and had 27.9 per cent of the land. In Bac Lieu, by way of contrast, poor peasants represented only 38.3 per cent, but with much less land, 3.3 per cent. Middle peasants with 5–10 hectares were also much better represented in the delta provinces, with 15–20 per cent of the total land in My Tho, Cholon and Tan An.[56] If we compare eastern Cochinchina with Tonkin and Annam, we can suggest the existence of proportionately less but even more marginal poor peasant owners and a considerably better placed middle stratum (having as much land as middle and rich together in the protectorates), which was probably the basis of the move to cash crops. Historically this situation no doubt resulted from the later settlement of eastern Cochinchina and the much greater availability of land to the early settlers. Even the passing of two centuries had not sufficed, by the 1930s, to produce the degree of pressure on land and the kind of differentiation within the peasantry which had occurred over a much longer period further north.

Not that the situation of the peasantry in eastern Cochinchina was a happy one. Many were still tenants and sharecroppers. Although their communes were less tight-knit than the far older ones in Tonkin and Annam, they were still cramping enough, similar instruments for extraction of taxes and labour, similar scenes of the notables' oppression and corruption.[57] Disease, hunger and hopelessness were often the fate of the poor, who had to seek work where they could to try to make some cash; French estimates in 1916 were of around 200,000 men wandering abroad in the colony as a whole, and those of a modern scholar are 2–300,000 in the 1920s and 5–700,000 in the mid-1930s, in a population of around 4.5 million.[58]

In 1916 many of the wanderers would have headed west. There they would have found a quite different rural world of the big rice plantations and the great French and Vietnamese landowners. Many of them would have become tenants of the wealthy, whose method of making a profit was simple. Plantations were not developed like those for rubber, with large capital investments and use of wage labour, but parcelled out to tenants as separate farms, with 40–60 per cent of the crop going to the owner. Since he did little more than loan money in advance of crop to the tenants at the customary exorbitant interest rates, doing nothing to raise technological levels, the landlord had a particularly painless existence, provided he could employ sufficiently ruthless overseers to supervise while he was away (which was most of the time) and keep on good terms with the local commune officials. It was on this basis that Cochinchina rose to be one of the three biggest rice exporters in the world, with Burma and Siam, but with a low level of productivity per hectare.[59]

The landowner, so far as his agricultural activities were concerned, was a very primitive capitalist, investing money in land and cash advances but leaving hiring of labour to his tenants and thus realizing his surplus in the form of rent in kind (sometimes money).[60] Outside agriculture he might be more developed, owning rice mills, transport concerns or manufacturing enterprises. Certainly he did not regard himself as a capitalist, or as any kind of exploiter of his tenants. As Bui Quang Chieu, one of the biggest landowners and unusually qualified as an agronomist, father of the first Vietnamese woman doctor and member of the Colonial Council, said in that august body in November 1936:

> We are one of the rare countries where there is not a hereditary nobility. Nor are we in a country where there are closed castes. All of us have emerged from the Third Estate.... All our parents were poor; in consequence we have deep links with the working class.[61]

Certainly a better picture of the approach of Chieu's class as a whole to their tenants and the peasants in general is to be gained from an official report concerning the owner of 4,000 hectares in Ca Mau:

> Thefts of fish from the ditches, expulsions by force of smallholders, the burning of harvests belonging to his neighbors, and physical attacks by hired assailants at his command have served in the preceding years to intimidate the population of the region who dread this man. Brought to the tribunal at Bac Lieu rather often, he has always succeeded in squashing the affair by buying witnesses and intimidating his adversaries.[62]

If in 1916 there was still a chance for the poor peasant of eastern Cochinchina to move west, at risk of finding himself in the power of such a one as our Ca Mau landowner, by the mid-1930s that chance had virtually gone. The western provinces were in fact themselves very diverse, not necessarily everywhere being suitable for growing rice as an export crop.[63] Along much of the Cambodian border, for example, there remained wild and only sparsely settled territory. As the usable land filled up, the need for settlers and seasonal labourers diminished. With no large local urban centres, there were no concentrations of non-agricultural wage labour or market-oriented handicrafts to provide alternative employment. Opportunities in public works, quarrying or silk-weaving did exist, but did not add up to many jobs.[64] By the eve of the Second World War the process of western settlement had worked itself out and the contradiction was apparent. In the earlier period, shortage of labour had meant that land had to be given by the owners on a tenancy basis in order to get it worked; however, the institutional arrangements for this proved so exploitative that, in the absence of alternatives, and with the impact of the world depression, the tenants found themselves in a situation of declining rice consumption, falling wages and a reversion to more labour-intensive techniques because they could not afford animals or more elaborate implements.[65] Although the pressure was certainly not so bad as in the protectorates, it was beginning to be felt.

The Process of Class Formation: Consciousness and Political Practice

People and classes produce and reproduce themselves in a material world and, in that way, lay out the foundations for a complex terrain of social struggle. Part of this enterprise involves the creation of a perhaps even more complex world of perceptions, of speculation, of explanation, which attempts to come to terms with that reality. The constructs of the human mind which result, however close to, or remote from, material reality, are important determinants of action, and some of that action may be a protest against the prevailing distribution of class and other social power, even an attempt to change it. In colonial, as in pre-colonial Viet Nam that element was never absent.

Thus, it is possible to postulate the existence of a popular culture of resistance, rooted in the peasantry in its pre-colonial origins but extending from them into the petty bourgeoisie and new working class. Carried over from the Confucian ideology, which had been a form of social control by the imperial bureaucracy, was both a doctrine of obedience to divinely ordained authority and a concept of the moral responsibility of those who wielded authority. If their evil deeds were too manifest, if natural disasters seemed to indicate that heaven had withdrawn its mandate, their rule could be called into question. Also of great importance, above all in Cochinchina, was the tradition of 'folk Buddhism' as a source of resistance.[66]

Again, in what Antonio Gramsci called the 'common sense' of the poor – their everyday perceptions – this questioning generated the aphorisms, poems, proverbs and jokes which are the biting critique of the semi-literate or letterless worldwide. Thus, it was said 'In rank the peasants after, scholars first,/But hunting for scarce rice the rank's reversed', or 'The rich are deaf, the nobles blind'. Sometimes the divine order itself might be questioned – 'Why this unequal tilt of Heaven's scales,/That one enjoys in full, the other fails?'.[67] Behind such sentiments lay other popular beliefs which had less direct political significance but were concerned with explaining the universe and assessing human character – geomancy, divination, the reading of faces. In appropriate circumstances these could provide material for political consciousness; the faces of later political leaders were sedulously read for clues to their real nature.

Nor were there lacking the agents who might interpret, develop and fuse popular beliefs and turn them into a consciousness. It must be recognized that extreme discontent most often took organized form as banditry, with little or no explicit social content.[68] Nevertheless, Buddhist monks, close to the people, might sometimes carry over criticism of the way in which the rich blocked the path of virtue into stirring others to act. As in China, there were secret societies whose leaders might decide that the best way to help their members was to make over the world in a preferred image. Thus, in March 1913 and February 1916 there were attempts to seize Saigon itself by the followers of a young mystic, fortune teller and healer who had proclaimed himself the son of the deposed Ham Nghi emperor.[69] It is important to note that it was always in Cochinchina, with its loose control through the communes, its more intense penetration by the capitalist market, its 'frontier' traditions and its admixture of Khmer cultural elements that the more exotic cult flowers bloomed. The final fruits, Cao Dai and Hoa Hao, will be discussed later, but some idea of the complex syntheses which colonialism produced can be seen in the case of a woman arrested at the end of 1940 in Ca Mau. Claiming to be a priestess, she had twice been tattooed, once in 1926 by a village schoolteacher suspected of 'Communism and Theosophy', the second time in 1933 by a Khmer, this time with Khmer characters, masonic insignia, and the dread words 'Liberté-Egalité-Fraternité'.[70]

The tattooed woman was arrested at a time when a Communist-led rising was being suppressed, and with this point another social factor should be brought into the discussion. As we shall see later, the tradition of rebellion in the centre and north passed a watershed in 1930–31. Out of the common sense of the rural and urban poor – even fused, as it was in the south, with popular religion – faced with the might of the colonial state only the sort of limited and ultimately hopeless action which took place in Saigon in 1913 and 1916 could emerge. What was needed were intellectuals – more closely attuned to the ideas generated by modern capitalism, originally in the West – who could give a wider vision of a feasible future to those of the poor who were ready to try to make a better one. By the mid-1920s such an element had come into existence, representing a third creation of colonial capitalism, along with the workers and a more deeply brutalized peasantry.

Intellectuals are not a class, but a social category characterized by its role in developing and disseminating ideas. Members of the category may in fact be drawn from any class but, given that to perform the role at least some formal education is an advantage, they are more likely to be drawn from such occupations as teachers, journalists and lawyers. In class terms this aligns them with the element to which reference has not yet been made, the middle strata, who, like the petty bourgeoisie, occupy an intermediate position between capitalists and workers. Members of the middle strata are not a class, for they have no distinctive relation to labour power or means of production; like the workers they sell their labour power, but unlike them on the other hand they neither produce nor maintain use value, and they are paid from the surplus value the workers (and peasants) produce. Members of the middle strata (there are more than one, as in classes) extend the role of the capitalist: like managers, they perform necessary services to production (engineers, corporate lawyers); provide consumption services (hotel managers, shop assistants); operate the world of ideas (teachers, journalists). They therefore have a characteristically contradictory set of social relations, on the one side serving the personal and class needs of capitalism, on the other employed by it and hence with potentially conflicting interests.

Intellectuals in particular find their class positions by service relations with others. Following Gramsci again, we may distinguish between 'organic' intellectuals within capitalism, who serve either the capitalists or the workers, and 'traditional' intellectuals related to pre-capitalist ruling classes.[71] In serving a class, the intellectuals 'give it homogeneity and an awareness of its own function not only in the economic but also in the social and political fields'.[72] Obviously Gramsci's ideas imply that intellectuals have to be created, either consciously or unconsciously, by the classes which need them. Thus in Viet Nam the old imperial state created the scholar-bureaucrats it needed through the elaborate system of examinations in Confucian learning which it borrowed from China. French colonial capitalism, of course, used many of its own nationals, but after some three decades realized that it could not function by simply combining these with the 'traditional' intellectuals it took over from the pre-colonial state (as Gramsci envisaged under capitalism). Moved probably by a mixture of contempt for the traditions they represented and straight racism, as we have already noted, it abolished the basis of their existence in the protectorates.[73]

In practice, on the other hand, it had become apparent to the French that they could not rule without help from Western-educated Vietnamese. Locals had necessarily to be used in various clerical and service occupations, and could not be prevented from qualifying in France for the higher professions of lawyer, doctor, engineer or agronomist. With the foundation of the University of Hanoi in 1917 it was in fact officially recognized that some highly trained people were useful, if kept few and tightly controlled. Between 1918 and 1944 only an estimated 3,000 students were enrolled, however, for the whole of Indochina.[74]

A tiny number of revolutionary intellectuals (Vo Nguyen Giap, for example) was to be drawn from the more highly educated. However, on the whole colonialism was successful in forming the necessary organic intellectuals for its capitalist class. This began with those born between the French occupation and 1900, among whom were to be found conservatives like Tran Trong Kim or Pham Quynh, who felt that Viet Nam could benefit from its association with France, although they were not traditionalists who opposed all change. In practice, they could not preach the old Confucianism, which had well served the emperors of the past and which the French administrators had hoped would do as much for them. Vietnamese Confucianism was a paper flower imported from China rather than a transplant, sturdy enough but not really capable of growth. Tran Trong Kim, an educationalist, who laboured to infuse the new school syllabuses with the old values, was able to find enough to say about Vietnamese Confucianism to fill only 15 of the 805 pages in his book, *The Confucian Teaching*.[75]

As for resistance to French rule, by the mid-1920s two generations of intellectuals had failed to give an adequate lead to the peasants, workers and other oppressed. Thus, the first years of Vietnamese resistance, termed the Can Vuong ('Loyalty to the Emperor') period, after the edict issued in July 1885 when the Ham Nghi emperor left his capital for the mountains and called on his subjects to rise against the invader, were not really sustained by the traditional elements.[76] The senior officials in particular had no staying power. The real struggle was therefore soon left to the peasants, with whom the Confucian intellectuals were linked through the village scholars. These were another important part of the élite of notables who ran communal affairs – examination graduates who had retired from, or never actually joined, the bureaucracy and who usually earned their living as local teachers preparing the sons of other notables (and bright offspring of poorer peasants) to compete. The village scholars thus came to occupy an important but contradictory position, at once the chief disseminators of official Confucian ideology and spokesmen for, and counsellors to, the peasantry. Both moments in fact projected them into a leadership position in the first resistance struggle after 1885.

The idea that early resistance was not only based on, but truly expressed, the sentiments of the peasantry is borne out by its distribution. Thus, the main weight lay in northern Annam and southern Tonkin; earlier in Cochinchina, although the peasantry did fiercely resist the invader, the leadership tended to stay in the hands of high officials and the movement quickly died away after defeats in 1867. Further to the north, it may be suggested that the tightly structured communes provided a more solid basis. More specifically, it has been estimated that over 40 per cent of the risings took place in only three provinces, Thanh Hoa, Ha Tinh and Nghe An, the last the family home of Nguyen Ai Quoc.[77] These were areas with particularly strong traditions of producing successful examination candidates and hence a well developed presence of village teachers. Quoc's father revived a family tradition of success and married his teacher's daughter. The point is that the peasants fought, and thus established a tradition of anti-French resistance which could await a more formidable leadership. Even more important, by in effect moving beyond the old intellectuals and finding new leaders like the peasant De Tham, they had begun the process of building a new revolutionary terrain.[78]

Some of the distance that still had to be travelled after another generation of intellectual resisters can be seen in the careers of Phan Boi Chau (1867–1940) and Phan Chu Trinh (1872–1926). As can be seen from their dates, these two spanned the last period of the old scholar-bureaucrats (both passed high-level examinations) and that of the emergence of the generation of intellectuals which will be our key concern. What is important about them from our immediate point of view is that neither solved the problems of the creation of an appropriate terrain for a Vietnamese Revolution. Trinh, the critic, avoided direct political activity; Chau, the conspirator, saw the winning of power as a quick blow by a small dedicated group. Both had grave weaknesses.[79]

The weakness of being a critic under colonialism, as under any authoritarian regime, was that success in your vocation attracted invidious attention. In January 1908 Trinh's Eastern Capital Free School in Hanoi was closed by the authorities, after functioning for less than a year. During that time it had brought Western science and mathematics and other ideas to the budding new generation of intellectuals, including women; campaigned to spread the use of quoc ngu, the modified latin script developed by the missionaries which made literacy much more widely accessible, and bitterly criticized the old scholar bureaucrats and, by easy association, the French rulers. Perhaps the most important idea it disseminated was the identity of 'people' and 'country', the basis of modern nationalist ideology.[80] Poetry and aphorisms, central to Vietnamese popular culture, spread these ideas far beyond the school's walls. When, in March–April 1908, serious peasant demonstrations against taxation broke out in Quang Nam province in Annam and spread to Quang Ngai and Phu Yen, the School was blamed and closed.[81] Trinh was arrested and sentenced to life imprisonment, but allowed to go into exile in France, where he stayed until 1925, a sort of legendary man of principle. His welcome on his return was tumultuous, his funeral not long after, the occasion for a massive demonstration. In the years of his physical absence, his concept of the salvation of the Vietnamese nation through the adoption of new ideas had firmly taken root.

If Trinh was the legendary critic, Chau became the legendary activist. At first in favour of modernizing Viet Nam as a monarchy, on the lines of Japan, to which he organized a migration of some 200 students, he later turned to China and republicanism.[82] It is important to remember that, in the early decades of the twentieth century, there were alternatives to European models for Asian intellectuals smarting under colonialism – imperial Japan which had carried out its own bourgeois revolution and the post-1911 China of Sun Yat-sen which, this time sweeping aside the emperor, was attempting one. With Japan fast becoming a colonial power itself in Korea and Taiwan, and anxious to please its Western forerunners by dropping support for Asian dissidents, emphasis swung for Chau and his followers to the new China. Sun and his Kuomintang party had gained control of southern China, but Chau's Restoration Society, founded in 1912, had to find a way to follow suit. With their leader living abroad, first in Japan, then China, Chau's followers attempted to seize Hanoi in July 1908. They were involved in the conspiracy round the Duy Tan emperor (whose secretary was Pham Van Dong's father) in May 1916 and the rising in Thai Nguyen province (in Tonkin) in August 1917.[83] After this Chau became increasingly isolated from Vietnamese reality. Sentenced to death in his absence, in June 1925 he was betrayed, probably by his secretary, into the hands of French agents in Shanghai. His sentence was commuted to life imprisonment after a massive popular campaign, and he spent his last fifteen years under house arrest in Hue.[84]

Whatever the influence of their careers and views both Trinh and Chau failed in their anti-colonial mission, in the sense that French rule continued. The former in any case eschewed direct political action. The weakness of Chau and his followers was that, like Auguste Blanqui in nineteenth century France itself, they believed that a conspiracy of the élite was enough organization and a quick coup was the road to power, with no broader base than subversion of some units of the French colonial forces. This revealed a fundamental incapacity to understand the true nature of class relations and exploitation and the potential basis for the social and national revolution in the workers, peasants and other poor. Chau's circle thus displayed a rather typical tendency of intellectuals to overestimate themselves. It was only the Communists after 1925 who really understood that, by turning to the exploited and oppressed classes, Vietnamese revolutionary intellectuals could take the true path to political power and that this meant a very different kind of organization.[85]

People like Nguyen Ai Quoc, Pham Van Dong and Vo Nguyen Giap derived these ideas from Marxism–Leninism. They came to that 'summation and highest peak of the knowledge of all humankind' as part of a general ferment among Western-educated Vietnamese which swelled after the First World War. By that time it was evident that Confucianism could not serve as a source of new ideas, and that the educational and conspiratoral efforts inspired by Phan Chu Trinh and Phan Boi Chau could be questioned as paths to liberation. For some of those born in the first decade of the twentieth century which spanned Phan Chu Trinh's Eastern Capital Free School, the situation demanded more.

Neither those intellectuals who were already mature when the French took over (whether in the south in the 1860s or the centre and north in the 1880s), nor those who were educated just before or after and therefore represented a transitional generation, were able, even if so disposed, to fight wars of position and manoeuvre and so build a revolutionary terrain. For that, organic intellectuals of a quite different kind, oriented to workers, peasants and other oppressed groups, were needed. The crux of the matter is whether such elements in fact created their intellectuals, as Gramsci supposed they would, or received them from outside. First of all, we must note that the Italian Communist denied that the peasants could give birth to organic intellectuals.[86] This is not strictly true; the two mentors of the tattooed woman arrested in 1940 are almost certainly cases in point. Peasants do produce their own ideologues and organizers (or recruit them from closely allied groups like craftspersons and traders), although usually these are prophets or people on the make who ultimately do little or nothing to satisfy peasant interests. From our point of view, however, the important organic intellectuals are those who can span peasants, workers and a range of the dispossessed. Secondly, according to Marxist–Leninist orthodoxy, workers should produce these for the rest. Lenin had tried to establish this in his 1902 pamphlet, *What Is To Be Done?*, but with ambiguities which left another view possible.[87] The ambiguity was very important in the case of Vietnamese Communists, for whom Lenin's views were of course sacrosanct. When Lenin had said that political struggle must initially be brought to the working class from outside, to what extent did he mean by non-workers, or was it merely that political struggle as such was not innate to workers? The importance of this issue for the Vietnamese case is that, under colonial conditions, the chances for intellectuals to rise from the ranks of workers were in any case slim. A small and above all fluid class, subject to intense repression, was also not marked by members with much chance to acquire education. Nevertheless, the necessary revolutionary intellectuals did appear and, as already noted, they were the splendidly ironic products – for the most part – of the colonial education system itself.

It is important at this point to appreciate the size of the 'catchment area' which was about to supply leaders to the revolutionary terrain. Taking the crucial period 1920–25, in those six years a maximum of around 16,000 young people (overwhelmingly boys) would have passed through or entered upper primary schools.[88] To these may be added some among those who had graduated before and the handful of people educated in France, along with those determined enough to teach themselves. Most, of course, 'simply left school, accepted arranged marriages, and fitted quietly into the existing system – the men accepting desk jobs, the women obeying their in-laws and bearing children'.[89] A catchment area of perhaps 5,000 in the vital period of ferment seems a generous estimate.

These potential leaders of a new resistance to French rule, the third expression of Marx's principle of 'historical retribution', were driven by a common impulse, what David Marr has described as an attempt 'to seize hold of several millenia of knowledge in a few years', to find 'a set of beliefs that both explained reality and provided the means to alter it'.[90] This obviously marked them off from the village scholars who had led the first resistance struggle and, by its intensity of feeling, from the generation of Phan Chu Trinh and Phan Boi Chau. Why then were the years 1920–25 such an important transitional period? First, it may be suggested, because they saw the education according to Western methods and ideas of the first full generation which had never known anything but French rule. (In Cochinchina, it was the second generation; there colonial ideological influences were stronger and took longer to combat.) Second, those years came immediately after the demands made on Indochina to contribute wealth and men to the French war effort.

A new sense of history, nation and patriotism was in fact crystallizing. All too painfully linked by the circuits of capital to one another and to the outside world, Tonkin, Annam and Cochinchina, those recent scabs, were forming beneath them a new Vietnamese tissue. The first resistance to the French had been in the name of the emperor, but the collaboration which followed destroyed the dynasty's moral authority in the eyes of the new intellectuals. As we shall see in Chapter 4, the imperial system had been a necessary part of the older Kinh nation; the new Vietnamese nation, which the most advanced saw as going beyond the Kinh to the minorities, would have an 'essence' (tinh hoa) as independent of emperors as of Confucianism. Rather, the sifting of the past for themes, which is always part of the emergence of nationalism as an ideology, produced in this case an idea which offered great possibilities – of Viet Nam as a nation of patriotic heroes and heroines. As one of the most prominent of the new generation, Nguyen An Ninh, put it in a speech in March 1926, 'Our country has given birth to innumerable heroes... men [sic] who know how to die for their land.'[91] Moreover, intellectuals like Duong Ba Trac arrogated to their own category the tasks both of expressing the essence, as the emperors had once done for the Kinh, and of 'saving the age' (cuu the) in a new display of heroism.[92]

To patriotism in its new guise, however, a small minority of the intellectuals was to add something else – the Marxism–Leninism which seemed to them, at the end of the first quarter of the twentieth century, to be the supreme explanation of reality and the obviously most effective guide to changing it. A third reason why the years after 1920 were a crucial period in the transition is that gradually, through the presence of people like the future Ho in France itself, through the somewhat easier publishing and circulation conditions in Cochinchina, and through contact with Vietnamese exiles and their socialist and Communist friends in south China, the necessary literature reached Viet Nam.[93] Gradually Marxist–Leninist ideas entered the general discourse. The formation of a group of potential leaders of new wars of position and manoeuvre, however, occurred with greater speed, and initially outside the homeland.

Recruits were ensured by the translation of the debate of 1920-25 into organization and action. In 1923 Nguyen An Ninh launched a newspaper, *La*

Cloche Felée, in which he both addressed himself to radical nationalist youth and published Communist documents. Three years later he received his first prison sentence, but educated youth was by then on the march. Excited by the capture of Phan Boi Chau and the return and death of Phan Chu Trinh, students and teachers took part in a wave of demonstrations and school strikes in March–May 1926. Subsequent expulsions and dismissals only served to radicalize some, providing recruits to two new parties, the Great Viet Revolutionary Party and the Viet Nam National People's Party, known from its Vietnamese initials as the VNQDD. Much more important for the future, youthful intellectuals (but also workers and peasants) were to be attracted to a third organization, the Viet Nam Revolutionary Young Comrades League (Viet Nam Thanh Nien Cach Mang Dong Chi Hoi) (RYCL).[94] From this was to grow the Indochinese Communist Party.

Notes

1   'Some ideas concerning the first branches of the Party and the Indochinese Communist Party,' *ND*, 16 January 1965, p. 3.
2   *Fifty years of activity of the Communist Party of Viet Nam* 1979 (in Vietnamese), p. 29.
3   'The intellectual stratum of the Vietnamese people, of the Democratic Republic of Viet Nam, is contributing much and giving repeatedly to the anti-American cause, to national salvation,'*ND,* 8 January 1966, p. 2.
4   For detailed discussions of the motives and methods of French imperialism in Southeast Asia see Le Thanh Khoi 1955, pp. 365–72 and 1981, pp. 287–91; Buttinger 1958, Chapter VI; Brötel 1971; Cady 1954; Osborn 1969; and Taboulet 1955 and 1956.
5   In singling out these three elements of continuity I follow Nguyen Luong Bich 1963b (in Vietnamese).
6   Mus and McAlister 1970, p. 46. This is a partial adaption and translation of Mus 1952; see therefore also that work, p. 14.
7   For this incident see Brocheux 1975, p. 80. The significance of the symbolism of this incident may be underlined by another quotation from Mus and McAlister:
     Offerings of the first fruits of the peasant world – the rice that is burned sacrificially on the altar or the drinking of distilled rice – express the quintessence of the earth that produced it. This rice is permeated – as the earth is – with the souls of the ancestors who lie buried near the fields where it was produced. (1970, p. 79).
8   On this point see Van Tan 1968 (in Vietnamese), especially p. 24.
9   Quoted in Vu Quoc Thuc 1951, p. 16.
10 See Woodside 1976, p. 54. The term was itself borrowed from the Chinese *shi hui* which was in turn taken from the Japanese *shakai;* such were the cultural ripples caused by Western capitalism throughout East and Southeast Asia.
11 Mus and McAlister 1970, p. 50, and Mus 1952, p. 20. It should be noted that Paul Mus and his disciples, McAlister (see McAlister 1969) and Fitzgerald (Fitzgerald 1972), have been the main Western proponents of the interpretation of Vietnamese history and culture through the continuity of the commune. In my view, their line of thought has two related weaknesses. First, by focusing on communes as repositories of values they avoid the issues of class relations and exploitation and the contradictions they engender. Second, and in consequence, they tend to overemphasize the unity of these village communities.
12 Fitzgerald 1972, p. 43.
13 Marx and Engels 1960, p. 91.

14   The following discussion will, of course, focus on the three in Viet Nam. Work on the others is long overdue, though it cannot be said that scholars have in any way exhausted what needs to be done on the history of Cochinchina, Annam and Tonkin, names naturally offensive to Vietnamese patriots but in my view meaningful at least until 1945. Basic general treatments may be found in Khoi 1955 and 1981, and Chesneaux 1955, Isoart 1961 and in Buttinger 1967, vol. I. Ngo Vinh Long 1973 is also important, as is Thuc 1951. Essential if older works with varying focuses which everyone uses, including Communist historians, are Bernard 1934, Gourou 1936 and 1945, Henry 1932, Robequain 1944. Recently, work on colonial Viet Nam has been raised to a new height by Murray 1980. To these should be added Dumarest 1935 and Thompson 1937. From the Vietnamese Communist point of view see the official *History of Viet Nam* 1971, vol. I, and Nguyen Khac Vien 1974 and 1975. A short but interesting Trotskyist analysis is Anh Van and Roussel 1947. Other works will be referred to in specific places in the following pages.

15   The latter is a major theme of the work of Vu Quoc Thuc, while the disadvantages of the 'Communalist mentality' were also stressed by his contemporary on the staff of the University of Hanoi, Vu Quoc Thong, in his work published in 1952.

16   I have attempted to theorize the questions of totality and articulation in two previous works, both of them located historically in a colonial situation: see Post 1978 and 1981. For broad discussion in a compatible theoretical frame see Murray 1980, Chapters 1–4 and 7.

17   Buttinger 1967, p. 521, n. 5.

18   On this new social phenomenon see Woodside 1976, pp. 8-12.

19   Figures from McAlister 1969, p. 71.

20   For this transformation see Jumper and Hue 1962, pp. 96–101. The whole of their Part Two is a useful discussion of French colonial administration.

21   Thuc 1951, pp. 186–7.

22   For figures see ibid., p. 188.

23   Ibid., pp. 188–9, and paddy prices calculated from data in Sansom 1970, pp. 260 and 262.

24   See Chesneaux 1971.

25   Robequain 1944, p. 207.

26   Figure from Woodside 1976, p. 210.

27   Gran, (unpublished), 1975, p. 61 and see also Tables 2.1 and 2.2, pp. 62–3.

28   Ibid., pp. 88–9.

29   See Lancaster 1961, pp. 62–3.

30   For a list see Buttinger 1967, Vol. I, p. 50, n. 79. A discussion of the Bank from a Marxist perspective is to be found in Anh and Roussel 1947, pp. 23–6. See also Murray 1980, pp. 132–54.

31   In 1930–31 Frenchmen were probably cultivating around 11 per cent of the concession land under rice; Sansom (1970, p. 51) estimates that, even allowing for new grants in 1931, the total is unlikely to have exceeded 15 per cent. As closely as can be estimated, it would seem that in 1938 the European (overwhelmingly French) ownership of all concession land, for rice, rubber, tea and minor crops, totalled about 11.8 per cent (calculated from figures in Buttinger 1967, p. 167).

32   Figures from Sansom 1970, pp. 260 and 262.

33   On this Hémery 1975, pp. 28–33.

34   See Brocheux, (unpublished), 1969, English translation, Cornell University Library, pp. 173–4, for a discussion of the investment outside agriculture. Further on the Cochinchinese bourgeoisie see Smith 1971.

35   There appears to be only one source, used by everyone, *Le Travail en Indochine*, a pamphlet published by the colonial Labour Inspection office in 1929, which I have not seen myself. A somewhat more accessible reproduction of this data is in Goudal 1937, Appendix I, Table 12.

36   Khoi 1955, p. 429.

37 Robequain 1944, p. 82. These figures seem to cover only some of the plantations.
38 Figures cited in Hémery 1975, p. 214.
39 Thompson, (unpublished), 1945, p. 4.
40 The story of Brother Seventy may be found in Woodside 1976, pp. 210–11
41 See Huynh Van Phuong 1935, pp. 134.
42 There is a detailed and admirable analysis of the constellation in Saigon-Cholon, their suburbs and the surrounding villages in Hémery's book, pp. 197–231. It can only be hoped that other scholars will do the same for other centres.
43 Thompson, (unpublished), 1945, Table IV, p. 37, with calculations.
44 Similarly, ethnic segmentation was not crucial among the working class, although there was such an element of Chinese in Haiphong and the coal mines.
45 It should be noted that virtually all discussions of land tenure in colonial Viet Nam are based on Henry 1932, which was heavily criticised by Gourou 1936 on methodological and other grounds: see especially pp. 356–8. The main points to remember about Henry are, first, that his presentation disguises the existence of landowners combining several plots of land by treating each as a separate holding, and second that the picture of widespread land ownership in Tonkin and Annam gives a false impression of peasant stability and security. See also Murray 1980, Chapter 8.
46 Khoi 1955, pp. 422 and 423.
47 Thuc 1951, pp. 193–4.
48 French geographers and agricultural specialists in the colonial era, like Gourou, tended to put great emphasis on demographic questions. This was a conscious or unconscious way of avoiding facing social contradictions.
49 A salutory discussion of relations within the communes and their integration into the total system may be found in Popkin 1976, pp. 436–53. His comments are particularly important as a critique of the Paul Mus school (see note 11 above), though his own attempt to broaden his discussion by use of a rather simple games theory is not very impressive (see in particular pp. 447–52). See also Popkin 1977, Chapter 4.
50 Scott 1976, p. 106, citing an early manuscript version of Long's *Before the Revolution.*
51 A graphic picture is drawn in Ngo Vinh Long 1973, especially in the translated pieces in the second half. For an analysis by a Communist scholar see Nguyen Xuan Lai 1976, pp. 15–55, and the discussion in Truong Chinh and Vo Nguyen Giap, 1974. If these are felt to be biased sources, Buttinger 1967, pp. 162–81, might be more acceptable.
52 Data to illustrate this paragraph are in Gourou 1936, table p. 359; Goudal 1937, Appendix I, Table 12; and Nguyen Xuan Lai 1976, pp. 40–50.
53 Mai Thi Tu and Le Thi Nham Tuyet 1978, pp. 94–107 *passim.* A sketch of the position of peasant and working class women under colonialism can also be found in *Women of Viet Nam in The Struggle for National Liberation* 1948, pp. 4–7, and in Bergman 1975, pp. 40–8.
54 Woodside 1976, p. 126.
55 Thuc 1951, pp. 195–6.
56 Figures drawn from Hémery 1975, pp. 200–1, to whom I owe the idea of the distinct character of the eastern provinces. For a detailed discussion of this fraction of the Vietnamese peasantry see ibid., pp. 198–209.
57 On the Cochinchina communes see Popkin 1976, pp. 453–60. His analysis suffers, in my view, from the failure to recognize the two variants of peasant incorporation into production in the colony.
58 Gran (unpublished), 1975, pp. 513 and 544.
59 1.45 tons per hectare in central Cochinchina in 1938 and 1 ton in the west, 3.4 in Japan, 1.8 in Siam and 1.61 in Burma (1939): see Gourou 1945, p. 370; Long 1973, p. 51; and Lai 1976, p. 43 note.
60 Analysing a similar situation in the Philippines, Brian Fegan, drawing on the work of Hans Bobek, has called this 'rent capitalism'. See Fegan 1982.

61 Quoted in Brocheux, (unpublished), 1969, pp. 169–70.
62 Quoted in Gran, (unpublished), 1975, pp. 315–16.
63 For discussion of this diversity see ibid., pp. 66–89.
64 See Brocheux (unpublished), 1969, pp. 187–99, who tends to attach more importance to these activities.
65 This deterioration is spelled out in Sansom 1970, pp. 34–45.
66 On this see especially Hue-Tam Ho Tai 1983, Chapters 2 and 3.
67 Freely translated, in an attempt to convey something of the flavour of the original, from Vietnamese texts in Duong Dinh Khue 1976, pp. 31, 37-8 and 138.
68 For a discussion of this phenomenon in the south see Gran, unpublished, 1975, pp. 51–2 and 545-50.
69 For details see Marr 1971, pp. 221–3 and 230–1, and Tai 1983, pp. 69–75.
70 Brocheux, (unpublished), 1969, p. 186.
71 See in particular Gramsci's 'The Intellectuals' and 'Notes on Italian History' in Hoare and Nowell Smith (ed.) 1971, and discussion in Sassoon 1980, pp. 134–50. For further discussion along lines being developed here see Post and Wright 1988, Chapter 2.
72 Gramsci, 'The Intellectuals,' Hoare and Nowell Smith, p. 5.
73 On the racist content of Western education offered to young Vietnamese see Kelly 1984.
74 Figures from McAlister 1969, pp. 78–80; see generally pp. 77–82.
75 Woodside 1976, p. 105. Kim's book is discussed on pp. 103–5. On Kim and Quynh see also Marr 1981, pp. 109–15.
76 Strictly speaking, *Vuong* should be translated as 'King', the title by which the ruler was usually known within the country, 'Emperor' (*Hoang De*) being reserved for external purposes as part of the assertion of equality with the Chinese ruler. For the sake of simplicity I have used only one title, and pay the price here with an inaccuracy. The most detailed account of this early resistance to appear so far is Marr 1971, Chapter 3. See also Truong Buu Lam 1967 and, for a Communist interpretation, Nguyen Khac Vien 1975, Chapter I.
77 Marr 1971, p. 47, n. 9.
78 For a discussion of the reasons for the failure of the early resistance see Duiker 1976, pp. 27–30. On De Tham see Vien 1975, pp. 23–5.
79 Space forbids a broad discussion of the two men here, but reference may be made to Marr 1971, the bulk of which deals with them, and 1981, passim, and Duiker 1976, Chapters 3, 4 and 5. Work by Vietnamese scholars, Communist and otherwise, can be found referred to there.
80 On the Free School's activities see Vu Duc Bang (unpublished) 1971, Chapter V.
81 For the suppression of the School see ibid., pp. 168–75.
82 The Japanese migration is well described in ibid., Chapter II.
83 I follow Duiker 1976, p. 75, rather than Marr 1971, p. 233, in linking Chau to the 1916 affair: the former had new evidence at his disposal.
84 Anti-Communist writers have repeated with enthusiasm the story that it was Nguyen Ai Quoc who sold Chau to the French, to get rid of a rival; see, for example, Turner 1975, pp. 8–10. In the absence of definitive evidence, choice of culprit will be governed by ideology; suffice it to say that there is no objective evidence against Quoc and Chau himself blamed his secretary (see Duiker 1971, p. 85). Reference to Turner occasions a necessary general comment. As is to be expected, there is a group of experts on Vietnamese affairs who are overtly anti-Communist, just as another group is explicitly sympathetic. Most prominent in the first group are Hoang Van Chi, Dennis Duncanson, Bernard Fall, Patrick Honey and Robert Turner. Not only do I find their political views unacceptable, but they can give no insight into the action of the Vietnamese Communists because they have no real understanding of the theory which lies behind it, their use of Vietnamese sources is often very inadequate, and they sometimes misinterpret data (on this see Porter 1972). I have used the work of these scholars, therefore, only when data

could be obtained from no other source and then with care. Another anti-Communist expert is Douglas Pike, whose 1978 work is specially relevant to this volume. He is less susceptible to the above criticisms than the others, but is of course reluctant to recognize that Marxism–Leninism contributed to the success of the Vietnamese Communists, stressing rather the influence of the 'heritage of traditionalism' and 'spirit of *doc lap* ("independence")' on the leaders. It is particularly significant that Pike adheres (perhaps unconsciously) to the 'Communism as a pathological condition' school. This is revealed by his language, the above factors being said to involve a 'warped economic condition and deep psychological scars', a 'peculiar style of politics', and a 'distorted sense of Vietnam's relations with the external world' (Pike 1978, pp. xi-xii).

85   Emphasis on the organizational capacity of the Vietnamese Communists throughout does not imply an endorsement of the common position among Western scholars that their ultimate victory can be ascribed to their ability to secure a monopoly on nationalist sentiment by their powers of organization. This view derives from Chalmers Johnson's attempt to explain the USA's 'loss of China' (my phrase) in 1949: see Johnson 1962. As we shall see, this provided the ideological base for much of the US action in Viet Nam and fortunately proved a false guide. Even the work of an opponent of US intervention, Alexander Woodside, is marked by it; although infinitely more learned and sophisticated than most of us, his basic theme reduces to the drive by modern Vietnamese intellectuals to find ways of creating 'organized groups' *(doan the)* and the superior ability of the Communists to do so. As I hope to show in this study, underlying both organization and nationalism as employed by them was the theme of radical structural change to put an end to exploitation. This may have been less explicit or more so, but it was always there and marked off the Communists from all others.

    Another more liberal scholar, William Duiker, in his 1981 book also takes the organizational capacities of the Party as a major reason for its success and adds a similar argument, the potency of the new doctrine of 'people's war', in which the Vietnamese 'carried on the Maoist tradition'. Duiker does recognize the importance of the ability to combine the themes of patriotism and social revolution, but I would regard the two other major factors he cites as much more suppositious. First, he sees the Vietnamese Revolution in a strangely Hegelian way, as an 'act of human will', 'the product of individual human action'. The action involved, second, was that of the 'young generation of patriotic scholar-elites', who were 'the traditional ruling class'. Although recognizing that Marxism was 'a persuasive alternative' to this generation, he thus in effect, by imposing a spurious class continuity, treats the Vietnamese Revolution as basically a continuation of an age-old patriotism. Moreover, the stress on individual will (especially that of Ho Chi Minh), which he prefers as an explanation to 'a collapse of the old order' (itself a highly simplified dichotomy), in effect squeezes out the element of social revolution and the vital contribution of masses of exploited people (see Duiker 1981, pp. 321–29, *passim).*

86   Gramsci, 'The Intellectuals', in Hoare and Smith (eds.) (1971), p. 6.

87   For an able analysis and defence of Lenin see Landau 1977.

88   Calculated from Marr 1981, pp. 37-8.

89   Ibid., p. 38.

90   Ibid., pp. 331 and 329. Since Marr's book is an important and exhaustive study of the emergence of the new intellectuals between 1920 and 1945, it is necessary to distinguish my approach from his (while noting that I can never match his erudition). My focus is on what he calls 'the winners', whereas his broader concern includes the proposition that 'Losing, like winning, has its own creative process, its own historical momentum' (p. x). However, precisely one of my problems with his book is that he effectively makes it impossible to see a *process* at work, for two reasons. First, he gives no clear class or general sociological grounding to the concept of 'intellectuals' (which he also calls interchangeably 'intelligentsia'). Second, he imposes upon himself methodologically a

frame of treatment by themes which blocks the reader from seeing evolution and change in terms of the intellectuals as a social category. A further problem is that by leaving the question of peasant ideas and attitudes to another volume (no mention is made of workers), as he deliberately chooses (p. ix), he omits the only real basis for understanding who won and who lost, namely the relative ability to appeal to the oppressed.

91   Quoted in Duiker 1976, p. 148.

92   Woodside 1976, p. 70. Chapter 3 of this work is indispensable reading alongside Marr 1981.

93   The first translation of a basic Marxist textbook into Vietnamese seems to have been one of Bukharin and Preobrazhenski's *ABC of Communism*, in September 1929: see Marr 1981, p. 347. In 1928-30 Hue was in fact a centre for publishing works incorporating Marxist concepts: see ibid., pp. 252–3.

94   English-language authors usually speak of the Youth League, ignoring the word 'Comrades'. This was indeed omitted from the title used in China (Viet Nam Revolutionary Youth League), but I follow the version used in Viet Nam itself: see *History of the Struggle of the Vietnamese Workers and Trade Unions (1860–1945)* (in Vietnamese) 1977, p. 57, note. With the League begins the history of the Communist movement in Viet Nam. There is as yet no definitive account in a Western language, but the closest so far is Huynh Kim Khanh 1982, pp. 63–89. (Khanh holds different views on the League's name: see his n. 48, pp. 63–4). His book is the best so far on the whole early history of the Party, but for the period up to 1941 see also Duiker 1976 and 1981, and Hodgkin 1981, Chapters 9 and 10. Reference should also be made to Sampson, unpublished, 1975. Still worth reading, though outdated in parts, is Sacks 1959. A longer time perspective is covered in Rousset 1975 and 1984, which are written from a Trotskyist perspective. All Western accounts rely heavily for material on the Communist movement's early years on Volume IV of the official *Contribution à l'histoire des mouvements politiques de l'Indochine française* 1930–34. Reference may also be made to the discussions in Chesneaux 1955, Isoart 1961 and McAlister 1967, 1969, and to the work of Chi, Duncanson, Fall, Pike and Turner. An interesting attempt to deal with Viet Nam, Laos, Cambodia and China together in this early period is Marchese 1971. Vietnamese Communist scholars have naturally done much work on Party history and pre-history: see the nine volumes edited by Tran Huy Lieu and others, *Reference Materials On the History of the Contemporary Vietnamese Revolution* (in Vietnamese) 1956–58; *Events in Party History,* vol. I, 1920–45, and vol. II, 1945–54 (in Vietnamese) 1976 and 1979: and *Fifty years of activity of the Communist Party of Viet Nam* (in Vietnamese) 1979. Summary presentation of work in Vietnamese can be found in Vien 1975 and in *Brève histoire du Parti des Travailleurs de Viet Nam (1930-1975)* 1976.

3 Communism and the war of position

In the previous chapter we looked first at the impact of colonialism on the people of Viet Nam and then at the way in which it created its own enemies. By the mid-1920s they were being given organizational expression.

Toward a Communist Party

The RYCL was formed in June 1925 by Nguyen Ai Quoc, not in Viet Nam but Canton; Quoc had been sent to China with a Soviet delegation, his mandate from the Comintern to develop a Communist movement in his native land. Canton was already a place of refuge for supporters of Phan Boi Chau and younger revolutionaries, and Quoc was able to enlist members from among them. In so doing, he established the geopolitical linkage between north Viet Nam and south China which was to become of crucial significance at various times in the future.[1] Quoc was gradually able to bring people in for training from Viet Nam itself – probably several hundred over the next three and a half years: thanks to the alliance which existed between the Kuomintang and the Chinese Communist Party it was possible to use the facilities of the former to familiarize his new cadres with principles of both political and military organization. These militants, when sent back, were used with great patience to build up the kernel of a movement which could in time become a party, while Marxist–Leninist ideas were spread, along with those of nationalism, by the

RYCL's periodical *Thanh Nien* ('Youth'). Doctrinal priority was given, however, to the 'national' over the 'world' revolution, a formulation not in line with orthodox Marxism–Leninism.[2]

In this clandestine work two major problems faced Quoc and his lieutenants. First and foremost came the question of positioning the new movement and eventual party within the class relations of the two protectorates and colony. Second, this task had to be accomplished within the framework of policy laid down by the Comintern which, as Stalin asserted his control in the late 1920s, became ever more rigid.

In April 1927 Chiang Kai-shek, Sun Yat-sen's successor as head of the Kuomintang, broke with the Chinese Communists and tried to wipe them out. Quoc was forced to return for a while to the Soviet Union, but the RYCL was allowed to use Kuomintang facilities until the end of 1928.[3] After this the base was shifted to Hong Kong, not so satisfactory a location with the threats of interference by British intelligence and their possible collaboration with the French; Quoc was eventually arrested, but released on a legal technicality after a year and a half (1931–33).[4] Nevertheless, organizational work went on – the building of a vanguard in accordance with Leninist theory. From it emerges a pattern, the linking of support among students and staff in key secondary schools with working class elements. The illicit copies of *Thanh Nien* were studied outside the classroom at the Protectorate College in Hanoi, the Middle School in Nam Dinh, the Bonnan High School in Haiphong, the colleges at Vinh and Qui Nhon, the Chasseloup-Laubat College in Saigon and others while the textbooks carefully compiled by Tran Trong Kim were studied within. The more politically advanced students no doubt sought to make contact with workers. In any case, when selected individuals from among those who had graduated (or been expelled) were spirited away for further training, their orders on return from late1928 at least were to join the ranks of the working class.[5] Not only this, but they were active in establishing 'Red' trade unions, consolidated in Tonkin in particular by a special congress in July 1929.[6]

The process of 'proletarianization' of its cadres was undoubtably the most important move in the war of position made by the RYCL in its five and a half years' life. During the 1920s the working class at least doubled in size, and from our point of view it had three important characteristics. Despite the recent recruitment of its majority, there were scattered throughout it older workers who had become experienced in the daily battle of the shopfloor; moreover, some of them had served in French industry or the armed forces during the First World War and had come into contact with socialist ideas as a result. Thus the working class formed some organic intellectuals for itself. On the other hand, with not only strikes but unions remaining illegal, French colonial policy gave no opportunity for relatively skilled workers, such as those at the Saigon Arsenal, to crystallize as a 'labour aristocracy' in craft unions, or, indeed, for union bureaucracies to develop in general, so that there was no element within the working class especially disposed to collaboration.

These two characteristics go far towards explaining the third important feature of the Vietnamese working class from the mid-1920s, its increasing militancy. Sporadic action began as early as 1920 in the form of work stoppages and other protests such as mutilating rubber trees.[7] A turning point was marked by the strike in August 1925 at the Saigon Arsenal, which was highly political since it was occasioned not only by basic demands for higher wages but by protest at the order to work on a French warship bound for China in a show of imperialist might. The most prominent strike leader was Ton Duc Thang, later to succeed Ho as President of the DRVN, thirty-seven that month and already brought to Communism by his service in the French navy and participation in the mutiny in the Black Sea in 1918 against French intervention in the infant Soviet Union.[8] In the last years of the decade, the number of workers who went on strike rose from 6,000 (1928) to 10,000 (1929) to 27,000 (1930).[9] What was happening to the most advanced of them is graphically conveyed in the reminiscences of Hoang Quoc Viet, later to become head of the whole trade union movement in North Viet Nam. A mechanic in a colliery since he had to leave the Haiphong technical school after participation in the protest against the arrest of of Phan Boi Chau, he had already been active in organizing strikes when he met the RYCL leader in the port city. 'He talked to me about labour,' Viet later recalled, 'about workers and capitalists, about surplus value. Every word of his penetrated my mind like water in a piece of dry chalk.'[10]

The extent to which this was happening in the working class, new and raw as it was, must not be exaggerated. At the end of the 1920s it would appear that only some centres in Tonkin and northern Annam had effectively been touched, along with Saigon in the south. The big concentration of workers on the rubber plantations, for example, had not yet really been penetrated by the RYCL, except for the Phu Rieng holding from early 1928.[11] Nevertheless, a class now existed which could provide a potential basis for a revolutionary transformation, and, however unevenly, the Marxist–Leninist water was being drawn to the chalk.

It would also appear that by 1930 only limited contact had been made with the peasantry, though the movement of those in need of work between urban and rural areas ensured some. At least in Nghe An and Ha Tinh provinces of northern Annam peasant associations had come into existence; official party history claims a membership of 70,000 for the whole country.[12] Other rural contacts, very recent in 1930 but to prove of great importance a decade later, were with the Nung and Tay people in Cao Bang province; migrants from the latter minority in particular were accustomed to seek work in the coal and tin mines, and thus could come into contact with the RYCL, and in 1920 the Tay in Lang Son province has risen against colonial taxes and forced labour on the railway.[13]

Although the RYCL was not involved directly, the formation in early 1926 of the Women's Labour Study Association in Hue showed that a tiny minority of sisters were also moving. Although some of them had contacts with Marxist-oriented intellectuals, the Association members themselves, however, still had far to go, with 'labour' for them remaining above all cooking and sewing.[14]

By mid-1929 the RYCL had in fact made enough class and other contacts and recruited enough potential leaders to have accomplished its historical task. The measure of this is that there was now dispute among its 1,700 members as to whether or not to move to the creation of a fully-fledged party. In June 1929 dissident members in Tonkin created the Indochinese Communist Party, then the remainder launched 'Annamese Communism' (actually based in Cochinchina) in August. To muddy the waters further, the Revolutionary Party, already permeated by Marxist–Leninist ideas, turned itself into the League of Indochinese Communists, based in Annam.[15] By that time the Comintern had already ordered unification in October 1929, the results of which we noted at the beginning of Chapter 2.

With the founding of the unified Communist Party in February 1930 the future Ho Chi Minh created the necessary instrument for laying out a revolutionary terrain over which he and his comrades could travel to power and the building of socialism. In early 1930 there was still very far to go. It is important to recognize here that when Nguyen Ai Quoc, as a faithful servant of the Comintern, ratified the end of the RYCL, with its priority of national revolution, he placed much more emphasis on internationalism, which could only mean the world movement centred on Moscow. Indeed, this claimed priority over any national struggle. As the Comintern Executive Committee's 'Theses on Bolshevization' had put it in April 1925:

It must be brought home to the broadest masses that in the present epoch serious economic and political battles of the working class can be won only if they are led from one centre and on an international scale.[16]

Similarly, Quoc could no longer use the sort of 'petty bourgeois' language (by Moscow standards) of a world revolution leading to all uniting as 'brothers in one house' and of 'universal harmony' among all peoples which featured in the text he had written for training his young followers, *The Revolutionary Road*.[17] Organizationally, contacts would now have to be deepened with the Comintern's Eastern Department through its Far Eastern Bureau in Shanghai, the Pan-Pacific Trade Union Secretariat in the same city (which acted for the Profintern, the international trade union body), and potentially with the Krestintern, Moscow's peasant organization, and its Youth International and International of Women.[18] Above all, of course, the Comintern would now have to be the fount of doctrine for the new colonial Communist Party.

The Comintern and Doctrine

The last point makes it necessary to clarify a central theme of this study, above all in face of the already published work of Huynh Kim Khanh. Although there is as yet no definitive history of the first decades of the Vietnamese Communist Party and may never be one without access to certain archives likely to remain closed, Dr Khanh's is in many ways the closest yet. It is obvious to anyone reading my work and his that he is infinitely more erudite than myself. On the other hand, the present treatment does not seek to present a history of the Party in the way that he does, and in light of what *is* my concern – namely to show what has happened when Marxist–Leninist doctrine was displaced to a colonial and then post-colonial setting, with an apparently high degree of ultimate success in achieving revolutionary objectives – it is necessary to clarify my position in face of his.

The point is that Dr Khanh is insistent on the importance of Marxism–Leninism, but treats it as an 'imported' product requiring 'grafting' into 'indigenous' nationalism.[19] He presents the period 1930–45, therefore, as essentially a conflict between factions in the ICP, one of which truly represented Vietnamese national interests and the other extraneous, even alien ones.[20] Although he states that a later 'indigenization' might be possible, I feel that his view of these first fifteen years of Vietnamese Communism is dangerously oversimplified. I do not think that the tension between socialism and internationalism (albeit in their Marxist–Leninist versions) on the one hand and Vietnamese patriotism on the other took this polar form, with the external elements – as he hints rather than states – an obstacle to the liberation struggle. Indeed, as we shall see, the central patriotic concept of 'saving the nation' was to come directly from the Comintern. Rather, in my opinion, national and social liberation would not have been possible at all without the fusion of Marxism–Leninism with Vietnamese history and present reality. The pattern was thus dialectic rather than polar. Consistently seeking to take a Marxist–Leninist standpoint, the Vietnamese leaders were directed by this towards real problems with had to be solved and factors of decisive importance in their revolutionary trajectory. No other doctrine, certainly not a limited nationalism, could have served in this way. On the other hand, in working received ideas out in the context of Vietnamese reality, Ho and the others found it necessary to make either unconscious or conscious but unacknowledged shifts in the doctrine, involving either changes of emphasis or more extensive reformulations. It was this process, rather than a triumph in fact of 'indigenous' patriotism over 'imported' Marxism–Leninism, which ensured success, although, as I emphasized in the first chapter, this meant great contradictions and a very heavy price.

It may of course be that our differences are an expression of the fact that Dr Khanh is a Vietnamese and not a Marxist, while I am a Marxist and not a Vietnamese. I do feel, however, that what he presents is a metaphor rather than a theory, and therefore an inadequate analytical tool; that his grasp of Marxism–Leninism is limited; and that he fails to distinguish clearly enough among the three levels – the very real struggle against capitalism on an international scale, the role of the Comintern in this, and Soviet foreign policy. My own arguments and analysis will continue, therefore, to try to bring out these lines. More specifically, I shall go on to argue that:

- the Marxist–Leninist doctrine of a two-stage revolution made it possible to lay relative emphasis at different times upon class or national struggle, thus providing an effective instrument for analysing Vietnamese reality and guide to action;
- the doctrine was always flexible (or ambiguous) enough to permit effective positioning and manoeuvring;
- the shifts of emphasis upon forms of struggle in Viet Nam occurred above all in response to changes in the line of the Comintern and Soviet foreign policy, not because there were clearcut divisions among comrades.

The doctrine of the two stages of the revolution was affirmed once again at the Sixth Comintern Congress in September 1928, where it was declared that in China, India 'and similar colonial countries' the 'bourgeois–democratic revolution' was in progress and was 'organically linked with the national liberation struggle against imperialist domination.[21] This Congress was particularly important for the development of Communism in Viet Nam, since it was the immediate inspiration of the pressures from the rank and file to create a Party to replace the RYCL and also the major influence upon the positions the new unified one took in 1930. In this respect, we should note that it was at the sessions in September 1928 that Stalin, now rapidly coming to dominate the Soviet leadership, pushed the world movement into a militant stand in expectation of growing capitalist crisis. Special emphasis was given to places like China and Viet Nam: 'At the world level, the most important strategic tasks of the Communist International in the proletarian struggle are concerned with the revolutionary battle in the colonies, semi-colonies, and dependent countries.'[22] Moreover, Communists there were expected to take a combative line and to give a lead to the bourgeois democratic revolution, during the course of which they were to lead the workers and peasants in breaking the power of the exploiting classes 'at whose back imperialism stands', organize 'soviets' of workers and peasants and set up a Red Army, 'establish the dictatorship of the proletariat and peasantry' and consolidate 'the hegemony of the proletariat'.[23]

Although these strategic instructions for the wars of position and manoeuvre (to use my terminology) were meant to apply to colonies as well as to China, there is evidently an ambiguity here concerning the timing of the seizure of power and gaining of independence in the former, especially since this was only to be 'completely guaranteed by the victory of the proletariat in the leading capitalist countries'.[24] Also, the Vietnamese comrades would have read quite clearly in the 1928 Comintern Programme: any alliances with the 'national reformist' or 'bourgeois' opposition to imperialism were to be temporary, must not 'in any way restrict communist freedom of agitation among the masses' and must involve simultaneously 'the most relentless ideological and political struggle against bourgeois nationalism'.[25] In fact there were problems here in relating this to the 'united front' tactics which had been a consistent part of Comintern policy since 1920.

As soon as Lenin and other Bolshevik leaders had taken a serious look at revolutionary prospects in the 'colonies and semi-colonies', they had perceived a sociological reality of peripheral capitalism, which we have noted in the case of Viet Nam – namely the very complex class structures created by capitalist penetration and dominance of previously existing class systems. This made some sort of united front tactics of class alliance more or less axiomatic.[26] In the absence of a large and developed working class, a revolutionary movement would have to construct a terrain of social conflict composed of a diversity of elements. Above all, this involved finding some relationship first with the peasantry and second with a putative 'national bourgeoisie,' one part of which, at least, might have cause to oppose imperialism.

Already at the Second Congress of the Comintern in 1920 Lenin himself had laid it down that:

> It would be utopian to believe that proletarian parties in these backward countries, if indeed they can emerge in them, can pursue communist tactics and a communist policy, without establishing definite relations with the peasant movement and without giving it effective support.[27]

From this point on it was axiomatic for Communists in countries like China or Viet Nam to seek 'the consistent pursuit of the peasant agrarian revolution', as the Comintern Programme adopted in September 1928 put it.[28] From the very first year of existence of the new unified Vietnamese party, as we shall see shortly, the issue of taking position among the peasants and making their interests part of the revolutionary terrain was an absolutely central one.

As for the 'national bourgeoisie', the basic question in Viet Nam was whether such a thing really existed at all, in the sense in which such a class force in India gave strength to the Congress Party and in China to the Kuomintang.[29] Next to French capital, Chinese-owned capital, oriented basically to south China, was the most important. The approximately 6,000 Cochinchina landlords were 'national' in a literal sense, but inextricably linked to rice exports and hence to the French, and more generally international, market. The nature of colonial capitalism in fact scarcely permitted any form of local control of local means of production, labour power and markets, because there were no effective boundaries which could be drawn around these, to mark them off from what was controlled by foreign, basically French, capital.

Beyond very simple levels more typical of petty bourgeois production than capitalist, technology, as made concrete in equipment and tools, had to be imported, along with technical knowledge. Generalized poverty made local markets small and uncertain. Government policy on such matters as licensing, taxation and tariffs, obviously more open to French than to local pressures, and the control of credit by the Bank of Indochina and other financial institutions (there was one small Vietnamese bank, founded in 1927) governed all possibilities of extracting and realising surplus value.

What this meant *politically* is that, without a clearly separate structural base for them, there could be no permanent parties or other organizations taking a 'national bourgeois' line, though it could well be put forward by some group at times. Thus the Constitutionalist Party in Cochinchina, formed in 1917 and counting among its leaders Bui Quang Chieu (the big landlord), was not without nationalist impulses, at least in its earlier years. In 1920 and 1923 it was involved in resistance to attempts by French companies to obtain monopolies over sale of *nuoc mam* (the indispensable fish sauce) and rice in Saigon. (The Party had also tried a boycott of Chinese merchants in 1919.) Politically, it sought increased Vietnamese participation through elections; probably its greatest success was the granting in 1922 of 10 seats out of 24 on the Colonial Council to locals and the enlargement of the electorate to a scarcely generous 20,000. The Party won all 10 seats in October 1926 and remained dominant electorally, but it remained the mouthpiece of the rich and after 1930 tended to become even more conservative. [30]

Nevertheless, Comintern policy in whatever phase dictated that the new ICP should seek at least a temporary alliance with the national bourgeoisie, which required the existence of an organized political force. In its absence, as we shall see, the Party was forced to rely on, or even create, substitutes.

The ICP Takes Position and Loses Ground

A token of the new Vietnamese Party's adherence to the Comintern and internationalism was its change of name in October 1930 to the Indochinese Communist Party, on instructions from Moscow. Its international and regional orientation, however, left it with the problem of taking a position relative to the various local class forces in a way which would be compatible with Comintern doctrine. The programme adopted at the founding Congress of the Party in February 1930 had already been generally in accord with the decisions taken by the International in 1928, since it spoke of the direct formation of a workers' and peasants' government in Viet Nam which must undertake both national democratic tasks and those which would lead to socialism. Thus French imperialism, feudalism and also the 'counter-revolutionary bourgeoisie' were to be overthrown, land owned by these elements was to be distributed to peasants, banks and other foreign-owned enterprises were to be nationalized, existing taxes were to be abolished and replaced by a progressive system. This first statement of policy also included equality of the sexes.[31]

The more extended 'Political Theses' adopted at the meeting of the Central Committee in October 1930, drafted by the ICP's first Secretary General, Tran Phu (who had been trained in Moscow) clearly distinguished two revolutions in Indochina, the 'bourgeois democratic' and the socialist.[32] Although one of the tasks of the former would be to set up a workers' and peasants' government, this would preside only over the preparations for the latter, since 'the...Indochinese revolution...cannot yet tackle directly the problems of socialist organization, the country's economic capacity is still very feeble, feudal vestiges are still numerous, the balance of class strength does not yet favour the proletariat, moreover imperialist oppression is still suffered.'[33] In these circumstances the first revolutionary stage would be 'agrarian and anti-imperialist' in nature, with its main economic measures being the handing over of the land of local and foreign owners to middle and poor peasants and the nationalization of large enterprises owned by foreigners. Upon this basis, local industry could develop, 'proletarian organization' and 'proletarian leadership' would gain strength, the balance of class forces would shift to that class, and it would be possible to advance to the socialist revolution. A further precondition of the second stage in Indochina was seen to be the building of socialism in the Soviet Union and the existence of a current period of 'proletarian revolution throughout the world'; in these circumstances (as Lenin had suggested in 1920) socialism could be built in Indochina without a preceding period of capitalist development. One further statement of great importance should be noted. In October 1930 the ICP Central Committee endorsed the view that 'the struggle of the worker and peasant masses has a very clearly independent character [and] is not necessarily influenced by nationalism as it formerly was'.[34] Immediately at its beginning, therefore, the Party was not identifying itself directly with the new phase of nationalism which found political expression rather in the VNQDD and preferred to give class struggle firm priority over that based on national identity.

By late 1930, in fact, the ICP faced no real competition from what the Comintern would have termed its 'petty bourgeois' rivals. The Revolutionary Party and the VNQDD each drew their supporters from middle strata intellectuals, lower-level officials and the petty bourgeoisie. Both were nationalist in ideology, but the Revolutionary Party's socialist leanings made it relatively easy for the ICP to attract its members, even, it seems, where the former was strongest, in northern Annam. The VNQDD had its base in Tonkin. Founded in December 1927, and consciously modelled on the anti-Communist Kuomintang, it was a tougher nut for the ICP to crack. In the event, the French authorities spared them the trouble. Heir to Phan Boi Chau's conspiratorial methods, in early 1930, relying on subverted units of the colonial forces, the VNQDD intended to raise the banner of revolt in various places in Tonkin. The

Yen Bai mutiny, key to the whole plan, miscarried in February 1930, the French put down the Party with their usual ruthlessness, and only a rump of the leadership was left in exile in south China.[35]

In late 1930, therefore, the Comintern lines for colonial parties which Tran Phu obviously followed – priority to class struggle, avoidance of close links with 'bourgeois' and 'petty bourgeois' elements on a nationalist basis, a militant attempt to take position among workers and peasants – seem a reasonable guide for a new Communist organization in Viet Nam. Significantly, however, the workers and peasants had not waited for the Party to develop its own ideas before attempting to make their own history. Another of the tasks of the Central Committee in October 1930 was to attempt to come to terms with the massive upsurge which was shaking the foundations of all three colonial divisions of Viet Nam. This was the rising usually known as the Nghe-Tinh Soviets movement, which certainly began and was most extensive in Nghe An and Ha Tinh provinces in north Annam but was far more besides.[36]

It would appear that the leaders of the new Communist Party decided to mark its appearance by fomenting a wave of strikes and demonstrations on 1 May 1930, International Labour Day.[37] Even in this they were running hard to keep ahead of the workers, since the first four months of 1930 had already been marked by important strikes in Haiphong (the cement works), Saigon, on the Phu Rieng rubber plantation, where the workers had seized control for a few days, and at the Nam Dinh textile mill.[38] The 1 May appeal met a response at various places in Tonkin and Annam, but the most significant was to prove to be in Vinh and Ben Thuy in Nghe An province of northern Annam. With perhaps 7–8,000 workers concentrated in the port, saw-mill, match factory, locomotive repair yards, textile mills and smaller enterprises they had been an obvious target for the 'proletarianization' of RYCL cadres – with considerable success, if it is indeed true that in March 1931 Nghe An and Ha Tinh provinces contained 2,011 of the Party's 2,400 full members.[39]

What gave the Nghe Tinh Soviets movement proper its impetus was the close connections which the workers of Vinh and Ben Thuy maintained with the surrounding villages. Thus, the events of 1 May in the towns were paralleled by a peasant demonstration against a notorious landlord, and then in June–July a further strike released workers to go into the rural areas and agitate. They met a ready response. As we have already noted, the misery which was the daily lot of peasants throughout Viet Nam was always especially immanent in northern Annam, and in the middle months of 1930 it was becoming hideously apparent that the ironic sequence of flood and drought had ruined the May rice crop. In August there were more strikes and the rural movement really took off; peasants marched and rioted, drove out local officials, released prisoners, burned records and government buildings. By mid-September, following an earlier example, local peasant councils – 'soviets' – were being set up to replace the collapsed communal administration of the notables in Nghe An, and soon after in Ha Tinh.

By that time also, southern Annam and rural Cochinchina (but to a much lesser extent Tonkin) were gripped by the same peasant demonstrations, with 'soviets' reported in a few places in the colony. From early 1931 to a peak on 1 May, urban strikes and rural risings convulsed the colony; 13 provinces out of 21 were in some degree affected.[40] Conversely, urban activity in the protectorates was largely spent by early 1931. In Nghe-Tinh the struggle continued under increasingly difficult circumstances – namely growing famine and brutal repression. Thousands were arrested, shootings were indiscriminate, villages were bombed, the Foreign Legion was used as only mercenaries inspired by a racist ideology can be. In April and May almost the whole of the Party's Central Committee including its Permanent Commission, which directed day-to-day affairs, was arrested, among them Tran Phu. At the beginning of August Nghe-Tinh followed the rest of the country into sullen silence.

The movement in 1930–31 had been in part a dialectic between workers and peasants, with each inspiring the other to rise in their own way. But it was the latter in Nghe-Tinh who were more radical, who tried to wipe out existing institutions and create new ones. In northern Annam there was a steady escalation of objectives, beginning with a protest against taxes, literally murderous when famine was impending and all cash was needed to buy food; this explains the attacks on notables and burning of tax registers. Then communal land was seized and redistributed in 63 per cent of the 173 villages where the soviet movement took hold.[41] When the October 1930 harvest also failed, stores of rice began to be seized from landlords and rich peasants, then land: in Nghe-Tinh as a whole this was the equivalent of only 2.8 per cent of the communal land taken, but in Ha Tinh alone it was equal to 31.3 per cent.[42]

What must be emphasized is that none of this really represented an 'anti-feudal' movement of the sort envisaged by the ICP's Political Theses. The movement against tax-paying was a direct confrontation between commune and state apparatus, very like those of the pre-colonial centuries, rather than a fight between peasants and landlords. The emphasis in the next phase of struggle on communal land is also quite distinct. It must be understood that these two provinces, especially Ha Tinh, were areas of more extensive petty land ownership than Annam as a whole, but with less communal land and petty landlords (see Table 3.1). This situation, it may be suggested, placed particular weight on access to the limited amount of communal land, both for small owners who had insufficient amounts and petty landlords who would like to lease out more. Given that village notables represented the latter and manipulated allocations in their favour, it is not surprising that seizure of this land should have been a feature of the uprising, though scarcely an attack on a 'feudal class.' Even when landlords' holdings began to be seized in the third phase, the conflict was of limited extent – mostly in Ha Tinh where there was markedly less communal land. It is nonetheless interesting that the movement should have deepened through its phases into an assault on privately owned means of production, with this radicalization even matched in the last phase by the collective cultivation of confiscated land in some Ha Tinh villages.[43]

Table 3.1 Landholding in Nghe-Tinh

	Annam	Nghe An	Ha Tinh
Landowners as % of population	12.4	28.1	22.4
Landlord as % of owners	10.1	8.1	5.9
Communal Land as % of total cultivated	25.58	22.04	15.91

Source: Vu Huy Phuc 1968 (in Vietnamese), pp. 6–7 and 8.

The failure of the rural movement to conform to expected class patterns was shown in the ICP's inability to keep analytically abreast of events. In a tactical document which the founding Congress adopted in February 1930 it had been specified that the Party must 'rally the majority of the peasant masses, carry out agrarian revolution and overthrow the gang of landowners and feudalists'.[44] In face of what was actually happening in October 1930, however, these lines were inadequate. Thus, the directive sent out to district committees in Nghe An, passing down instructions from the Regional Committee for Annam, restricted itself on the question of land to 'Confiscate communal ricefields, communal lands in the hands of notables and landlords, distribute to the poor peasant. Suppress land rents, wipe out debts.'[45] The interests of poor peasants in Nghe-Tinh could not adequately be seen as an 'anti-feudal' struggle, because they involved a different sort of target. According to a later historian, the Central Committee at its meeting in October decided that it was a strategical error to try to distinguish between big and small landlords.[46] It thus admitted that it was difficult to find a real feudal class to attack.

In later years Party leaders were to come to see the Nghe-Tinh movement as marked by 'leftist and sectarian' ideas, typified by this endorsement of a broad rural struggle which led, especially in Ha Tinh, to attacks on rich and even middle peasants, petty notables and the educated, including the use of violence against them.[47] Indeed, this emphasis on broad unity rather than division was later to be taken further, and the view was to be that the national bourgeoisie and petty bourgeoisie should have been brought in on a nationalist basis.[48] That, it may be suggested, was the product more of subsequent Party experience than of a reading of the reality of 1930–31, of what the workers and peasants were actually doing, or indeed of the position taken on class versus national struggle in October 1930. In any case, the ICP did not have the organizational capacity to build a broad front in its first year of existence, or for that matter even to keep control of events. It had only a handful of cadres for the whole country and was just beginning to get its apparatus into place; the committee for Nghe An itself was only set up in late February 1930, and the May Day demonstrations were no doubt its first major exercise. Although there was a dialectic upsurge between workers and peasants, and between parts of the country, it was the interpenetrations of classes which determined this, not skilful orchestration by the Party, the top leadership of which was never in control of events. Indeed, it is of particular interest that the Central Committee seems to have anticipated failure from the beginning. Thus, in September 1930 it wrote to the Regional Executive Committee for Annam that 'we have to act in such a way as to firmly maintain the influence of the Party on the Soviets, on the masses, so that when we fail the meaning of the Soviets will have taken root deeply in the minds of the masses and the strength of the Party and the peasant associations is maintained.'[49]

The establishment of village 'soviets' in Nghe-Tinh, so much emphasized by Communist historians, seems in fact to have been a purely local initiative and was perhaps a spontaneous action by the peasant associations rather than something coming from the Party leaders (who themselves imposed that name). Later judgement was to see late 1930 as not an 'optimum moment' for such a move, and to distinguish it from the leadership of the whole uprising by the ICP.[50] At the same time the Central Committee seems to have been concerned to keep the Party somewhat in the background. In the same letter to the Regional Executive it was laid down that 'All village affairs should be handled in the name of the Soviet and never in the name of the Party or the peasant association'.[51] Lower level cadres were no doubt frenetically active, and paid the price in arrests and summary executions, but their activities could be curiously far apart. Thus, while in Nghe-Tinh in January 1931 starving peasants were seizing rice from the better-off, in Cochinchina the clandestine unions were organizing the workers in a commemorative week for Lenin and Rosa Luxemburg, necessarily remote figures it might be thought. It does not seem surprising that, in the two Annamese provinces, participation in these activities was described by a later historian as small and of short duration.[52]

Nevertheless, what happened in 1930–31 must in no way be underestimated; in a sense it was the Vietnamese equivalent of Russia's 1905, sketching the outlines of bigger things to come. First, though finally crushed, the peasants and workers had shown that they could shake the foundations of colonial capitalism, even by largely spontaneous and uncoordinated action. They had directly demonstrated that the Comintern was correct to emphasize class action as the central form of struggle. Second, the ICP had learned vital lessons, even at the cost of losing many of its cadres, including most of its top leadership. Third, and of very great importance, the Party had firmly identified itself with struggle against colonialism and capitalism and, in so doing, had laid the foundations for linking radical economic and social change with the national struggle, whatever its current reservations about the latter. 'Saving the age' and 'national salvation' as themes for intellectuals could from now on, in practice if not in theory, begin to be linked to land reform, improved pay and conditions for workers and generalized democratic freedoms, the bridge being the Party's concern with destroying French rule and the confiscation of plantations, mines and factories owned by foreigners and their local allies.

Fourth, and deserving the utmost emphasis, in 1930–31 there appeared in outline what was to take full shape over the next decade, the actual sociological rooting of the ICP in the class structure as Marxism–Leninism enjoined. If the first task in the contest for power was to fight a war of position to build, as it were, a place to stand on a concrete terrain of class forces, then this is when the ICP decisively took the high ground. The crucial location was classes, following up the efforts of the RYCL. It did not matter that the working class was small, because it was concentrated in sufficient numbers at important locations – Hanoi, Haiphong, the coal mines, Nam Dinh, Vinh-Ben Thuy, Saigon-Cholon. Thus there existed relatively dense masses of workers which the Party could penetrate and in which it could root itself. Neither did it matter that the working class was mostly new and thus closely linked to the urban petty bourgeoisie and peasantry. In fact, this was the Party's great advantage, for it meant that the movement from working class to other basic organizations was made much easier. It may indeed be suggested that the firmest roots of all were precisely in the suburbs and the villages closest to the urban concentrations of workers. In the case of Saigon, for example, this meant places like Go Vap just to the north, or Hoc Mon a little further out at the end of the tramline, where wage workers in big and small enterprises, artisans, petty traders, porters, rickshaw pullers and cashcrop-growing peasants actually lived together. There Party cadres could live with less chance of detection, action committees could be formed, district and provincial committees could come together for sessions knowing that police spies were likely to be known and that warning of raids could be given.[53]

For the vital initial taking of position by the new ICP leadership, at least up until mid-1941, the creation of a new Vietnamese working class by French colonialism was thus the most important act of the oppressor. That is not to say that workers and revolutionary intellectuals alone were sufficient to give hope of liberation to the oppressed. As the events of 1930–31 proved, even if through failure, Party and working class needed the weight of peasants, youth, women, ethnic minorities and others behind them to become really effective. The Vietnamese Revolution as a social and political phenomenon could not be understood if that were not made clear. But it may be said that, together, the Party and the working class resembled the human brain and central nervous system, not very large in mass compared to the whole body, without a great musculature of their own, but able to direct the efforts of the rest, to impel it to achieve determined goals. The Party leadership decided and sent impulses through its ranks and into the working class, from which (as well as more directly) they could be transmitted into the masses of peasants, artisans and traders. The organization of that transmission and the symbols in which its impulses were encoded varied from period to period, but the 'brain' and 'central nervous system' were always there. It will be an important part of this whole study to see how their linkages changed.

Finally, one other thing was derived by the leadership from the experience of 1930–31. They learned that, to expel the French, a war of manoeuvre would have to be fought. The ICP eventually would have to be politically, and in a certain form militarily, strong enough to seize the state apparatus as a whole, not just to support localized insurrection. In 1928 the Comintern had laid down the pattern of combining the 'general strike' and 'armed insurrection' as authoritative.[54] In time the ICP was to find its own form of this in the doctrine of the General Uprising.

Ten Years of Uneven and Combined Development

In the period 1925–30 decisive events had taken place in Viet Nam, if we view it from the perspective of the shift of the world revolution to 'the East'. The Comintern had in April 1925 ordered 'bolshevization' and in September 1928 a more militant class struggle. The tiny group of Vietnamese Marxist–Leninists had responded to these calls. They had taken the crucial steps in building a revolutionary terrain by implanting Comintern doctrine and making the first links among peasants, workers and organic intellectuals. They had created a revolutionary nucleus of 'proletarianized' leaders and had formulated their first programme. Then the catastrophe of 1930–31 had hit them – describable as such because, in necessarily playing a very active part in the upsurge both leadership and militants were decimated by French repression. Thus, from 1931 first of all the nucleus had to be kept in being, then lost terrain recaptured and after that expanded. It is a tribute to the ICP leaders and the rank and file that all this was done and that, surviving a new repression in 1939–40, the Party moved to a decisive shift in ideology and organization in May 1941.

The period 1931–35 was one of necessary rebuilding of the movement, complicated by further arrests of top leaders in October 1932 in Cochinchina. Nevertheless, it was in that colony that the rebuilding progressed most successfully, since political life there was somewhat more open than in Annam or Tonkin; the colonial state had to provide for expression of the interests of smaller French settlers, in addition to the great landlords and firms, and this conversely also gave openings for the ICP to organize and propagandize. To a large extent, therefore, the Party's revival was built around publishing a legal newspaper, *La Lutte*, which first appeared in Saigon in April 1933, and competing (with success) in elections for the Saigon municipal council. An unusual feature of this activity was the collaboration between the ICP and the talented group of Trotskyists, in particular Ta Thu Thau, who had gained an urban following which rivalled that of the Party.[55]

In the two protectorates, the colonial administration made mild gestures towards reform without really grasping it. All that we need now note is the entry onto the stage of the young Emperor Bao Dai, brought back from his education in France to give the impression of a new era, and the similar appointment of his two new ministers – the intellectual Pham Quynh whom we have already met, and the young provincial governor Ngo Dinh Diem, whom we shall meet again. This time, the latter – a Catholic, strong anti-Communist and conservative nationalist – lasted only a few months before withdrawing into the wings to await a better moment. Despite the great difficulties in Tonkin, which made it necessary to locate the regional leadership among the Tay in Cao Bang (and to have a Tay as its head), the ICP there and in Annam did slowly make progress in putting its basic organization into place. Nor should one other sphere of its operations be forgotten, the prisons and detention camps scattered throughout Indochina, with around 10,000 political prisoners after 1930, who often suffered and died there but who also studied and learned and became even tougher cadres.[56]

During the 1930s leadership outside the prisons (and often inside – for about half were, in time, arrested) was in the hands of comrades like Le Hong Phong who had been trained in the Soviet Union, and had often been brought there from residence in France. Given that others like Pham Van Dong, Truong Chinh, Vo Nguyen Giap and Le Duan were in prison following the 1930–31 uprising, it is thus to people like Phong and Tran Van Giau that the credit must go for preserving and rebuilding the Party.[57]

Nor was the future Ho Chi Minh involved in the rebuilding, except that in distant Moscow he helped train some of the returnees.[58] It is indeed a remarkable fact that for 10 years the future President of the DRVN played no real part in the Party's activities. It seems very likely that, from the Comintern's point of view, he was in fact in some disgrace.[59] His arrest in Hong Kong in June 1931 had been only part of a series of disasters which hit the Comintern's Far Eastern Bureau after the smashing of the Chinese Communist Party's Southern Bureau in Shanghai had given the Kuomintang and foreign security forces much information on the Comintern network; two other key agents as well as Nguyen Ai Quoc were arrested.[60] This, combined with events in Viet Nam, would obviously cause heart-searching in Moscow, and when Quoc reached the Soviet capital a couple of months after being released from gaol in Hong Kong in January 1933 (having been reported dead in the meantime), he would be a likely candidate for self-criticism and retraining. (In this context it is interesting to note that in May 1931 Li Li-san, one of the most prominent leaders of the CCP, had been summoned to 'stay here to study for a few months and to work with the Comintern in order to correct his mistakes'.)[61] In December 1934 Quoc was openly criticised in an ICP journal for 'nationalist vestiges', failing to understand Comintern directives, and advocating 'reformist and collaborationist' tactics between January and October 1930 – significantly the period before the Comintern had ordered the more internationalist reorientation, and renaming, of the unified party.[62]

Nguyen Ai Quoc was to re-emerge in 1941 to help the ICP develop a new patriotic message, but in the meantime the Party maintained its firm class line. The ICP's 'Programme of Action' published in June 1932 stressed the leading role of the working class and strongly attacked the local bourgeoisie which sought to represent itself as a national leadership.[63] Similarly, a meeting of the Central Committee in March 1931 had noted the need for a rapid correction of the tendency of the Party's Association of Anti-Colonialist Women to cut itself off from women workers, defining the urgent task as 'to organize women workers in the Trade Unions, the women peasants in the Peasant's Association, and women small traders in the Union of Traders; that is, to organize the masses of women workers and poor women'.[64] No doubt buoyed up by the fact that even French repression did not prevent strikes and demonstrations by workers in 1932–33, the ICP leadership would thus have had no problems with the Comintern position on Indochina taken in mid-1933: 'The most urgent task of the forthcoming revolution is to form a workers' and peasants' government in order to effect the tasks of the bourgeois democratic revolution and liberate the country from foreign domination.'[65] At the Party's First Congress held in Macao in March 1935, which Nguyen Ai Quoc did not attend, the idea of a relatively narrow class front, based on the workers, was again affirmed.

On the other hand, before the First Congress there were already signs that, on the international level, Communists were re-examining the militant class line of the Comintern's 'Third Period' policy inaugurated in 1928. The decisive turning-point was the coming to power of Adolf Hitler and the National Socialists in Germany in January 1933. Both the Soviet and the French Communist Party leaders began to contemplate a new Germany expanding through military means. In May 1934 it was announced that the Seventh Comintern Congress would be held in the autumn to consider the new situation, and in June, anticipating a new turn, the French made an alliance with the Socialist Party (SFIO). [66] The important point here, of course, is that these two foreign leaderships were the most important influences upon the ICP. In July 1935, when the Comintern Congress met after a delay, the decision was taken in effect to abandon the class struggle in favour of the broadest possible front against fascism and the threat of war.[67] This was a turning-point for the Comintern as a whole. It had now become principally an instrument of Soviet foreign policy and its attempt to face the fascist menace. The supreme directive body of the world Communist movement now resolved that in normal circumstances it would not interfere in the internal affairs of individual parties.[68] In fact, they were effectively set upon a course which would increasingly involve them in accommodations, real or attempted, with bourgeois parties on a national basis. Even beyond this, in the main report presented to the Comintern Congress Georgi Dimitrov, the veteran Bulgarian leader, made a strong attempt to capture nationalism for his international movement. 'The interests of the class struggle of the proletariat against its native exploiters and oppressors', he declared, 'are in no contradiction whatever to the interests of a free and happy future of the nation. On the contrary, the Socialist Revolution will signify the *saving of the nation* and will open up to it the road to loftier heights.'[69] Although this was evidently not intended to apply to colonial peoples, whose main exploiters were not 'native', it was to give a major opening to the ICP.

In July 1936 the Second Plenum (full meeting) of the ICP Central Committee, held in Shanghai (again without Nguyen Ai Quoc), decided that the 'direct and immediate' aim was not to overthrow imperialism and carry out the 'agrarian revolution', but to struggle against 'colonialist reactionaries' who sided with fascism and for 'democratic liberties, food and clothing and peace'.[70] The abandonment of class struggle, if so doing would accommodate any element prepared to take an anti-fascist position, was expressed in the Vietnamese context in building the broadest possible Indochinese Anti-Imperialist People's Front. The ICP Central Committee instructed branches to 'relegate class struggle to the background' in order to obtain support from at least 'some elements of the national bourgeoisie'. After some resistance this line was adopted.[71] One important difference from the general result of the application of the new Comintern line must be stressed; whereas Communist Parties were now expected to surrender leadership of the front if necessary, in Viet Nam there was no rival to the ICP, certainly not the Constitutionalists. Unlike the Chinese Party in the 1920s, the ICP would not have to collaborate with any other organized class force.

The application of the new line on the united front in Viet Nam was marked by an even more significant development. In September 1936 a letter addressed to comrades in Cochinchina, which seems to have been intended finally to lay down the new policy, defined the principal task in Indochina as the 'emancipation of nations'.[72] At the same time, an article in a new Party journal was defending the use of such language as 'Fatherland' and 'compatriot' when appealing to the masses.[73] The new line as applied in Viet Nam was thus taking shape not merely as a United Front of all possible elements against fascism but more positively as an affirmation of the distinct qualities of the nation as it had evolved in history, which might be shared by individuals of other than worker or peasant background.

Just as the ICP Central Committee was pushing home the new line, a change of government in France opened further opportunities. In mid-1936 the menace of fascism brought electoral victory to the Popular Front and a government including Socialists and supported by Communists. In Indochina that meant a considerable relaxation of control over political activity, to the ICP's benefit. Many prisoners were released, including Vo Nguyen Giap, Hoang Quoc Viet, Pham Van Dong, Le Duan and Truong Chinh. With these and other prison-hardened cadres to help it, the ICP went into a flurry of organization and publishing, creating new unions, peasant associations and all kinds of other bodies, with appropriate newspapers and journals. In Cochinchina the Party worked more or less in the open – in Annam and Tonkin through the renamed Indochinese Democratic Front, headed by Dong and Giap. None of this meant, however, an end to direct working class struggle in the period 1936–39; 1937 was in fact a peak year for strikes.[74] Rather, such action could be said to have given the weight to all the rest.

A further significant feature of the new activity was the appearance of the first real attempt to analyse the situation of the peasantry. In 1938 Truong Chinh and Vo Nguyen Giap published pseudonymously *The Peasant Question*..[75] Both authors were young intellectuals, among the best-educated Vietnamese of their day, who had been caught up in the ferment of 1925–26, which brought Chinh to the ICP through the RYCL and Giap to the Party in the early 1930s. Although they did not put forward any specific programme of rural reform, their new attention to the plight of the peasants was a notable development in the ICP, made the more necessary by their continuing class action, as in the waves of struggle in Cochinchina and Tonkin in April–June 1937.[76]

This continuing class militancy of workers and peasants under Communist leadership provided an important link with the previous period of upsurge. It distinguished the ICP from what other parties were doing; in this same period the French CP was discouraging worker action and supporting French colonialism.[77] In the years after the 1930–31 defeat, a class struggle line had encouraged the ICP to fight back and to dig itself in, continuing the war of position. From mid–1936 it began to widen its contacts by open activity without in fact having to abandon its more clandestine work and organizing for social struggle.

During the years 1936–39 one price which the ICP paid for the chance to contact many thousands more Vietnamese was a break with the Trotskyists, who could not stomach the new line of cooperation with bourgeois elements and the dropping of revolutionary aims and class struggle which this entailed, at least formally. In May 1937 the break became final; Ta Thu Thau and his comrades retained control of *La Lutte* and much of their popularity in Saigon-Cholon, even defeating ICP lists in elections for the municipal council and Colonial Council.

Forty years later, the Party's official history was to paint these years as ones of complete success in combining open and clandestine action.[78] Khanh, on the other hand, portrays them as a period when the ICP 'foundered in ideological confusion and interfactional disputes'.[79] The truth, in my view, lies somewhere between the two but with a bias towards the Party's version. Disputes over relations with the Trotskyists and other issues certainly roiled the ranks in Cochinchina and made it difficult for the leaders to keep members there in check.[80] From this time the leadership in the colony tended to develop its own line, to which we must return. Again, the broad united front policy meant adopting demands like universal suffrage or the eight-hour working day from which one would not automatically find one's way to land reform, say, or nationalization. Certainly this was far from independence, and on one level the ICP followed the French Party closely and abandoned that demand. No less a person than Nguyen Ai Quoc, now on a mission for the Comintern in China, reported back to Moscow in July 1939 that both 'close relations' with the metropolitan party and avoiding the 'excessively high' demand for independence were necessities.[81]

On the other hand, as already noted, the ICP had been given the opportunity by the change in Comintern policy and Popular Front government in France to extend its contacts and propaganda very considerably. If French police estimates are to be believed, it grew from 800 active members in 1935 to 2,000 in early 1939, with 40,000 supporters.[82] Faced early in 1938 with a new government in Paris which marked a swing to the Right, the Central Committee plenum in March was able to assess 'front' work critically and, among other measures, set in train clandestine organization in expectation of repression of the open activity.[83] This capacity to maintain both levels of positioning and manoeuvring during 1936–39 was to serve it in good stead. Also of enormous importance, as we shall shortly see, was the opportunity to follow up and develop the new nationalist line taken by the Seventh Comintern Congress. In this respect, in the context of world revolution, there was a crucial distinction between the developed countries of 'the West' and the colonies and 'semi-colonies' of 'the East'. Communist parties in the former were committed, after mid-1935, by the line laid down in Dimitrov's report to a war of manoeuvre determined by the wheeling and dealing of national politics, which sometimes, as in the French case, involved abandoning the call for colonial independence. Away from the capitalist centre, however, their comrades, committed only to the first stage of the revolution, could take up the theme of 'the saving of the nation'.

There is another way in which we may put the Popular Front period – indeed the 1930s as a whole – into perspective. During those years there emerged the figures (some of them, like Dong, Duan or Chinh already top leaders) who will constantly recur as key decision-makers in this study. There was, of course, a high mortality rate; Tran Phu, for example, did not survive imprisonment. More time would be needed for some to rise from local leadership roles to the centre of the Party. But a very important feature of the Vietnamese Revolution remains the extraordinary continuity (as well as the very small size) of the crucial leadership group. If we take the thirteen members of the Party's Politburo (eleven full and two alternates, all men) in the mid-1960s – a pivotal point both in the balance between building socialism and fighting foreign aggression and in this study – we find that at least seven had joined the RYCL sometime between 1925 and 1930, while the last to join the Party enrolled in 1937.[84] All except Ho were born between 1900 and 1917. At least eight, and possibly eleven, were educated to upper primary level or above and can be regarded as intellectuals by occupation. (Nguyen Chi Thanh, a poor peasant, and Van Tien Dung, a textile worker, became self-educated intellectuals through their political work as local leaders in the 1930s.) A notable total of eight were born in Annam, all in the narrow 'waist' provinces later split between North and South, four in Tonkin and one in Cochinchina.

With these basic characteristics already to hold them together, three other factors contributed to making this the most long-lasting and cohesive leadership in Marxist–Leninist revolutionary history, which never lost a member except to death until Hoang Van Hoan fled to Peking in 1979. First, all were total Vietnamese patriots, steeped in the essence of their country's history. Second, all were convinced Marxist–Leninists who learned their theory while engaged in practice. Third, all had their characters shaped in the revolutionary movement; above all, it may be suggested, by their common quality of what might be called controlled passion. This passion came from shared hardship (all but two certainly served time in prison), but above all from their desire to see their people free; the control derived from the rigour of Marxist–Leninist theory and the discipline of Party organization.

Taking Position in Wartime

In September 1939 the future Ho Chi Minh and all his comrades had to face an entirely new international situation, with the outbreak of the Second World War. This was complicated by the fact that in the previous month the increasing divergence between Soviet foreign policy and the demands of world revolution had been dramatically expressed by the signing of a pact between Stalin's USSR and Hitler's Germany.

Particularly in Europe there was a great grinding of gears as Communist Parties sought to reverse directions and reconcile Stalin's move with the anti-fascist crusade. The ICP leaders were spared such open embarrassment. On 3 September France went to war with Germany and, on the pretext of the ICP's Soviet affiliations, declared it to be illegal on 24 September. ICP publications were suppressed and 2,000 people arrested – 800 in Cochinchina alone.[85] The only option now was to concentrate on direct and basically illegal struggle.

In November 1939 the Central Committee of the ICP held its Sixth Plenum to assess the new situation. While maintaining that the workers and peasants were the 'two main forces of the revolution' and that the bourgeois democratic stage must involve an agrarian revolution, the meeting decided that, in conditions of world war, national liberation must have the main emphasis. In order to secure maximum support for this, the idea of a radical redistribution of land was dropped; expropriations would be restricted to French landowners and Vietnamese collaborators. The concept of worker–peasant soviets was also abandoned in favour of the much more bourgeois form of a federation of Indochinese democratic republics. As for tactics, moreover, although the meeting spoke of preparing for 'violent action' the chosen vehicle was a reconstitution of the previous Indochinese Democratic Front as an Anti-Imperialist National United Front.[86]

When the Central Committee met a year later for its Seventh Plenum it again took the position that 'we are not yet in a revolutionary situation'.. For the first time maintaining that the movement among the workers was weaker than that of the peasants, it still regarded the latter as unevenly developed; moreover, 'As yet there exists no anti-imperialist movement among intellectuals and students'– a somewhat surprising observation, the reasons for which are probably related to the smashing of the Party's open activity in urban areas. Two rather more favourable factors were specified. Firstly, a 'number of minority groups have enthusiastically joined the anti-imperialist revolution', and secondly, the 'masses have begun to use highly effective forms of struggle, such as political and armed struggles, although these forms have not been popularized and carried out in a decisive manner'.[87] Both these comments must have been derived from the Party's recent experience in the Bac Son rising.

The background to that event was the arrival on Vietnamese soil of troops of yet another imperialist power, Japan. In May–June 1940 France had been smashed by Hitler's forces and dismembered, half directly occupied, the other part under the puppet Vichy regime. That in itself, and the arrival of a Vichy-appointed Governor General for Indochina, were enough to produce a new political conjunction, but in September the Japanese, able to treat any Vichy administration as a dependant because of their alliance with Germany, landed 6,000 troops at Haiphong and moved others over the border from China. The object was to block the flow of supplies to Chiang Kai-shek's Chungking government, still holding out against Japan after three years of war. The Japanese forces coming from the north clashed with French troops in the highlands near Bac Son and dispersed them. The Tay then seized the chance to rise. ICP cadres had been active in the area since 1933 and, although the rising fell back into a guerrilla movement after its defeat, were able to form two fighting units in the Bac Son area and send another into Cao Bang.[88] It was in these circumstances that the Seventh Plenum decided to develop revolutionary bases and launch local uprisings where it seemed appropriate, with a general uprising as the final target.[89]

As the Seventh Plenum recognized, Bac Son was a most important development in the war of manoeuvre. It pushed the Party away from civil politics and towards that of arms and what followed was to develop into the policy of establishing base areas under its control. The need for such secure zones was amply demonstrated immediately after the Plenum by a second much greater failure, that of the rising in Cochinchina in late November–December. In fact, the Central Committee had instructed an emissary from the south to return with orders not to rise, but he was picked up by the French security police before he could pass on the order. The Cochinchina regional committee was apparently planning something like the VNQDD rising of February 1930 on a larger scale, relying on subverted troops of the colonial forces who were being readied to fight off an attempt by Thailand (formerly Siam) to fish in the muddied waters of French defeat by annexing Cambodian territory. Mutiny by the Vietnamese units was supposed to mesh with general uprisings and a march on Saigon. Warned by the capture of the Central Committee's messenger, the colonial government repressed the badly coordinated, if widespread, outbreaks with its usual thoroughness and perhaps more than its usual ferocity. Besides their dead, the ICP leaders could count thousands more members and supporters arrested (among them Le Duan and Le Hong Phong, the latter dying in gaol).[90]

The Bac Son rising had apparently served another important purpose, namely to bring to the centre of Communist Party discourse the concept of 'national salvation'– at least in the sense of appealing to the masses in the name of the 'Viet Nam Anti-Imperialist League for National Salvation'.[91] Duong Ba Trac's 'saving the age' as a task of intellectuals had been transformed into the mission of the Party, concentrated, no doubt, by Dimitrov's invocation of 'saving the nation' at the Comintern's Seventh Congress. This was confirmed when, in May 1941, the Central Committee of the ICP met for its Eighth Plenum at Pac Bo, just across the border from China whence Nguyen Ai Quoc returned to his native land after thirty years to preside. The meeting surveyed the situation and took a wide range of crucial decisions.[92] First, assessing the international conjunction, it accurately predicted that the Axis powers would invade the Soviet Union, and took this to mean that they would be defeated, that world revolution would spread, and that socialist systems would be established in more countries after the war. With this scent in its nostrils, the Central Committee obviously saw Viet Nam as a candidate for revolution and the subsequent building of socialism, but the question that followed was how to achieve a sufficient mass base for this? Taking up the line explored at its Sixth and Seventh Plenums, the Central Committee confirmed the shift of emphasis: the struggle was now to be seen not as one of class, but as one of bringing together vast majority of Vietnamese of all classes in a fight for national liberation. As the Eighth Plenum's final resolution put it:

At this moment, sectional and class interests should be subordinated to the vital interests of the country, the nation. Should we not at this moment solve the problem of national liberation, succeed in demanding independence and freedom for the whole nation, not only would the country and people remain beasts of burden forever, but also the sectional and class interests could not be restored for an eternity.[93]

In other words, the class interests of workers and peasants in particular were to be subordinated to the cause of a national independence which would be common to Vietnamese capitalists and landlords as well. In fact, the only elements to be excluded from the class bloc which the Party now hoped to lead would be those who had actively collaborated with the French.

Social classes were certainly not forgotten. An elaborate analysis was made of the internal and external balance of forces, for example, in which the 'vanguard' was still the 'proletariat' and the 'direct reserve army' was formed by the peasants but now also by 'anti-imperialist popular strata in the whole country'.[94] In tribute to Moscow and the Comintern, this seems to have been directly modelled on Stalin's analysis of the 'strategic leadership' in the Russian Revolution in his 'The Foundations of Leninism', a work no doubt known to any Vietnamese who had studied in Moscow. Nevertheless, as we have already seen, the Eighth Plenum did not push any class issue which might contradict what it now sought to do, the achievement of the broadest possible front against French and Japanese imperialism.[95]

From this decision immediately followed two others. It was felt that henceforward, although the Party still continued to call itself 'Indochinese', the revolutions in Viet Nam, Cambodia and Laos should be treated separately. Given that the movement in the first of these was much further developed than in the others this was logical, but that position, of course, tended to reinforce the conceptualization of the ICP's task on the national level. Even more important for future developments in Viet Nam, the shift in balance of the struggle from class to nation was now projected into policy towards agrarian change, obviously central in a country with a population which was almost 90 per cent peasant. Again following the line taken at the Seventh Plenum, the Central Committee in May 1941 abandoned the idea of an agrarian revolution leading to a massive restructuring of landholding in favour of the poorer peasants. Land redistribution, in fact, disappeared entirely from Party policy, except for village communal land. The class content of agrarian policy was now reduced to lowering of rents and interest on debts (certainly very necessary) and 'progress toward giving land to the tillers'.

A fourth important decision at the Pac Bo meeting related to the actual taking of power by the Party. Again in line with the Seventh Plenum, the Eighth resolved that the 'central task' in this respect was to prepare for general armed insurrection, the prelude to which could be 'partial insurrection in every region'. (Under the direction of Nguyen Ai Quoc, the establishment of bases in mountainous areas had already been started.)[96] Probably because of the tight coordinating control which this sort of strategy would need, direction of affairs was now placed in the hands of a three-man Standing Bureau of the Central Committee, led by Truong Chinh, the newly elected General Secretary of the Party. It was also recognized that more cadres – organizers and propagandists – were going to be needed.

The most important organizational decision in May 1941, however, was to set up the Viet Nam Independence League (Viet Nam Doc Lap Dong Minh), universally known as the Viet Minh, which was to lead the struggle for the next ten years. This was to be a general umbrella under which could be grouped all 'patriotic' elements – of course, under the leadership of the ICP. Further, and in order to mobilize mass membership, previous organizational attempts by the Party were to be extended into a series of 'National' Associations, for workers, peasants, youth, women and, as they developed further, intellectuals, old people, soldiers and others. The building-up of these over the next few years would give the necessary social basis to the new emphasis on national liberation.

In the period 1925–41 the new Communist leaders had thus followed a trajectory which, through an indispensable emphasis on class struggle, had first allowed them to find a firm footing on the social terrain of colonial Viet Nam. Their Marxist–Leninist concepts of socialism and internationalism encouraged them to do so, but from about 1936 also permitted the quest for a broader feeling on a patriotic basis. That in turn involved the invocation of pre-colonial history. In May 1941 the Party in seeking to position itself took hold of the history of Viet Nam in a special version – one of a nation which could produce heroes and heroines when necessary, which was in need of salvation, worthy of it, and capable of being saved – under the leadership of the ICP. The patriotic game was now afoot, and what was to be gained and what lost would work themselves out over the years to come.

Notes

1   On this see Brocheux 1981 and Huyhn Kim Khanh 1982, pp. 64–6.
2   On RYCL doctrine see Khanh 1982, pp. 79–88.
3   Sacks 1959, p. 118.
4   Given my necessarily very abbreviated statement of the reason for Quoc's release, which differs from all other sources, reference must be made to Governor of Hong Kong to S.H. Cunliffe Lister, 31 January 1933, in Colonial Office Box 129/539, file 92610 'Nguyen Ai Quoc arrest of,' Public Record Office, London. Another perspective on these events can be found in Duncanson 1974.
5   As an example of ambiguity in student–worker relations the case of Haiphong may be quoted. There the League set up its first two groups in June 1929, in the Bonnan High School and the cement plant, but each produced its own magazine (see Le Quan, 'The process of establishing the Communist Youth League', *ND*, 25 March 1961, p. 3).
6   On this see 'The History of the Vietnamese Workers' and Trade Union Movement (1860–1945)' 2, 1976, pp. 30–1. This whole series of articles is a valuable source.
7   See Phan Thanh Son 1971, pp. 164–5. This essay is derived from Son's *thèse de 3e cycle* for the Sorbonne (1968). That in its turn is an important work because Vietnamese studies of the formation of the working class as a political force remain generally inaccessible because of language: thus, Tran Van Giau has written four volumes on the period up to 1945, all under the title *The Vietnamese Working Class* (1957, 1962 and 1963). More recent important works in Vietnamese are Ngo Van Hoa and Duong Kinh Quoc 1978, and Cao Van Bien 1979. I benefited greatly from discussion with Professor Cao Van Luong of the Institute of Historical Research in Hanoi in March 1980. For those who can read Russian there is also Mkhitarian 1967.
8   For this strike see Son 1971, pp. 167–8.
9   Giau 1962, p. 83.

10   *A Heroic People* 1965, p. 156.

11   See Brocheux 1975, pp. 78–82.

12   See Nguyen Khac Vien 1975, p. 74.

13   See Elliott 1974, p. 13, especially notes 44 and 45, and pp. 15–18. The first branch of the new Communist Party was established among the Tay in April 1930: see Institute of Minority Studies, Committee for Vietnamese Social Science (in Vietnamese) 1978, p. 178.

14   On the League see Marr 1981, pp. 214–20. The whole of Chapter 5 is a very valuable source on the early women's movement. See also Bergman 1975, pp. 48–56, and *Women of Viet-Nam* 1948, pp. 9–12, for organization and resistance in general.

15   For further details see Khanh 1982, pp. 116–23. Figures for RYCL membership from *Fifty years of activity of the Communist Party of Viet Nam,* p. 24.

16   Degras (ed.) 1960, vol. II, p. 199.

17   For a partial text see *History of the Communist Party of Viet Nam: Excerpts from Party Documents* 1979 (in Vietnamese), vol. I, p.14.

18   An acquaintance of Quoc in Moscow during 1927–28 later stated that he had been one of the founders of the Krestintern: see Wollenberg 1970, p. 22.

19   Khanh 1982, pp. 20–1.

20   For a summary of his views see ibid., pp. 332–33.

21   'Programme of the Communist International Adopted at the Sixth Congress,' Degras (ed.) 1960, pp. 536 and 537.

22   Ibid., p. 521.

23   Ibid., p. 536.

24   Ibid., p. 537.

25   Ibid., p. 541.

26   For more on this at the general, theoretical level see Post and Wright 1989, Chapter II.

27   'Report of the Commission on the National and the Colonial Questions', Lenin 1966, pp. 241–2.

28   'Programme of the Communist International Adopted at its Sixth Congress', Degnas (ed.) 1960, p. 506.

29   For discussion by a DRVN scholar see Nguyen Cong Binh 1961 (in Vietnamese).

30   For further discussion of the Constitutionalists see Duiker 1976, passim; Hémery 1975, pp. 113–20; and Smith 1968, Chapter VI, and 1969.

31   Two (slightly different) versions of the programme can be found in translation in Tran Huy Lieu 1960, pp. 13–14, and Ho Chi Minh 1977, pp. 39–41. I have followed the Vietnamese texts given in *History of the Communist Party of Viet Nam: Excerpts from Party Documents,* vol. I, 1979.

32   A partial text of the 'Political Theses' is to be found in Nguyen Khac Vien 1974, pp. 277–82, and in English in Vien 1975, pp. 233–40. Vietnamese text in *History of the Communist Party...Documents*, op. cit., 1979 (some, as here, are in fact full texts).

33   *Documents* 1979, pp. 38–9.

34   Ibid., p. 38.

35   On the Revolutionary Party see Duiker 1976, pp. 153–7; Sacks 1959, pp. 119-22; and Smith 1968, pp. 103–4. On the VNQDD and Yen Bai see Duiker 1976, pp. 155–65; Sacks 1959, p. 119; Smith 1968, pp. 104–6; and Khanh 1982, pp. 91–7.

36   For discussions of the Nghe-Tinh movement see Lieu 1960, which summarises the work of North Vietnamese historians; Duiker 1973 and 1976, Chapter 12; Osborne 1974; Scott 1976, pp. 120–49; Ngo Vinh Long 1978; Bernal 1981 and Khanh 1982, pp. 151–71. A study (in Vietnamese) which I have found of particular value is Vu Huy Phuc 1968. For the role of the working class see 'The History of the Vietnamese Workers' and Trade Union Movement (1860–1945)', 3, 1976, pp. 26–30. My interpretation differs, sometimes radically, from these. In that regard, detailed comment upon Ngo Vinh Long seems in order. His unpublished thesis, 'Peasant Revolutionary Struggles in Vietnam in the

1930's' (Harvard University, 1978) has not been available to me, but the 1978 article is drawn from it. Long requires comment because of his view that there is 'overwhelming evidence of an effort at national coordination' in the events of 1930–31 (p. 15). This is very much opposed to my own interpretation. The problem is that Long never produces any real evidence to support his view. Indeed, much of what he mentions (the condemnation by the ICP Central Committee in September 1930 of what was being done in Annam as 'not appropriate to the situation' (p. 23); the warning against 'unnecessary demonstrations' in Nghe Tinh in October (p. 26); the condemnation of 'leftist tendencies' by the Central Committee in March 1932 (p. 28)) suggests rather hesitation and inadequate control on the part of the ICP leadership. Again, he seems to assume that declarations by the Central Committee are equivalent to effective action: thus, the formal unification of the Party in February 1930 did not immediately ensure 'centralized coordination', as he assumes (p. 15), and calling on branches to 'share the flames' (my preferred translation of *chia lua*) does not in itself ensure or coordinate action (pp. 25–6). The bulk of his discussion is of Nghe An and Ha Tinh, where the ICP was certainly strongest, being able to build on work by the RYCL and Revolutionary Party; elsewhere Party members would have had to be superhuman to have coordinated on such a wide scale; there were just not enough of them. Lastly, my own study of the uprising in Jamaica in May–June 1938 has shown that it is quite possible to have very widespread action by peasants and workers which is self-mobilized and spreads very rapidly; in that case, an estimated tenth of the whole population became involved without any central direction or even formal organization existing (see Post 1978). For me, then, the essential point about the events of 1930–31 is that the new unified Party sought to begin its war of position and in so doing aroused forces which it was far beyond its capacity to organize. It did the best it could to give a lead, especially in Nghe-Tinh, but the leadership realized from early on that the uprising would be smashed. It was, and the whole affair was a big set-back for the Party.

37   A leaflet to this purpose can be seen in Room 4 of the Museum of the Revolution in Hanoi.
38   Details of these strikes may be found in *Events in Party History*, vol. I, pp. 164–8. For the events at Nam Dinh, where is should be remembered that the workforce was largely female, see Vu Can 1967, pp. 202–6, and for conditions leading up to the strike, pp. 196–202.
39   *Fifty years of activity…*, p. 37. The preceding months of struggle must have helped boost the Nghe Tinh total, but the ICP undoubtedly built on earlier work by the left faction of the Revolutionary Party.
40   For a map see Hémery 1975, pp. 15–17.
41   Phuc 1968, p. 6.
42   Ibid., p. 12.
43   Ibid., For the importance of communal land as an issue in Nghe Tinh see Ngo Vinh Long 1978, p. 18.
44   'Summary of Party Programme,'*Excerpts from Party Documents* 1979, p. 28.
45   Phuc 1968, p. 10.
46   Ibid.
47   Lieu 1960, p. 52.
48   Ibid., pp. 51–2.
49   Quoted in Trung Chinh 1961 (in Vietnamese), p. 3: original document in the National Archives, Hanoi.
50   See Hong Quang 1962 (in Vietnamese), p. 7.
51   Ibid.
52   Lieu 1960, p. 42.
53   The clearest picture of this class interpretation can be derived from a careful reading of Hémery's admirable study of Cochinchina, especially Chapter 5. It is hoped that one day we may have equivalent studies of the class situation in the 1930s in the Hanoi and

Haiphong areas, and also for smaller centres like Vinh-Ben Thuy and Nam Dinh, where the urban-rural linkages were probably more direct, without the complex suburban structure which at least characterized Saigon–Cholon–Gia Dinh.

54   See 'Programme of the Comintern Adopted at its Sixth Congress', Degras (ed.) 1960, especially pp. 522–3.

55   The most detailed study of this group, and of the whole 1931–39 period, is Hémery 1975. For the Trotskyists, Sacks 1959 is still important. A major recent discussion forms part of Rousset 1978.

56   Hémery 1975, Chapter 4, deals with the prison system and political prisoners. For interesting reminiscences of first-hand experiences see the contribution of Hoang Quoc Viet in *A Heroic People*, 1965. See also Khanh 1982, pp. 162–3.

57   I do not think that Huynh Kim Khanh really establishes his argument for the existence in these years of two factions, the returnees, whom he calls the Stalinists, and those originating from the RYCL, termed by him the Communists. In his subsequent analysis the latter are a shadowy group, while the former, obviously for him the exogenous factor importing foreign doctrine, are the ones who in fact are prone to disobey the Comintern, including collaborating with the Trotskyists (pp. 195-6 and 198-9).

58   For his activities during these years see Nguyen Khanh Toan, 'En URSS avec l'Oncle Ho' in *Avec l'Oncle Ho* 1972.

59   See Duiker 1975, pp. 32–3; Hémery 1975, pp. 53–4; Rousset 1978, p. 128; and especially Khanh 1982, pp. 181–6.

60   See McLane 1966, p. 147.

61   See Chen 1969, n. 75, pp. 30–1.

62   See Huynh Kim Khanh 1982, p. 185.

63   See the quotations in Sacks 1959, p. 130, and Rousset 1978, p. 126: There is a French text of the 1932 Programme in *Partisans* 48, July–August 1969, and part of the Vietnamese in *Excerpts from Party Documents* 1979.

64   Quoted in Mai Thi Tu and Le Thi Nham Tuyet 1978, p. 118.

65   Quoted in Sacks 1959, p. 131. I do not agree with him that this contrasts with the 1930 ICP Programme and represents a 'return to the formula of the two-stage revolution'. This had not been abandoned, though the Comintern's 1928 line was to put the leadership in the first stage into working class hands, even though its objectives were 'bourgeois democratic' and 'anti-feudal' in nature. It should be noted that the quotation is from 'Tactical and Organizational Questions of the Communist Parties of Indochina and India: Questions and Answers,' published in *Pan Pacific Worker*, a Comintern organ, in July 1933. The author was given as 'Orgwald', and McLane 1966, p. 43, n. 64, suggests that this was Nguyen Ai Quoc; I am more inclined to accept Duiker's identification as Dimitri Manuilsky (1975, p. 30). I also disagree with McLane that the views in this document represent an anticipation of the 1935 United Front concept: the 1928 Comintern line involved an alliance of classes, but specified the leading role of the working class and its party.

66   For a discussion of these developments on Marxist lines see Dornhorst 1977, pp. 9–12.

67   On the Congress see Claudin 1975, pp. 183–99, and Dornhorst 1977, pp. 11–18.

68   Degras (ed.) 1960, vol. III. p. 354.

69   Dimitrov 1935, p. 80, original emphasis. I basically follow here the line of analysis taken in Dornhorst 1977.

70   *Fifty years of activity...* 1979, p. 49.

71   Duiker 1975, pp. 32-3.

72   Quotations from and discussions of this document can be found in Hémery 1975, pp. 288–9, and Rousset 1978, pp. 153–4. No Vietnamese text is available, so we must depend on the French text in the colonial archives, but I accept its genuineness. I follow Hémery in using the word 'nations', though the original French text says 'races' (Rousset

1978, p. 154 note). I am advised by Nguyen Ngoc Luu that the original was probably *giong noi* which is susceptible to both translations.

73   See the quotation in Hémery 1975, p. 291.
74   See 'The History of the Vietnamese Workers' and Trade Union Movement' 5, 1976, pp. 25–8.
75   Translated by Christine White as *The Peasant Question (1937–1938)* 1974.
76   For details see *Events In Party History*, vol. I., pp. 421–5.
77   See Mortimer 1984, pp. 261–2.
78   *Fifty years of activity...*1979, pp. 54–5.
79   Khanh 1982, p. 231.
80   For this see ibid., pp. 223–25.
81   'Concerning the line [and] standpoint of the Party during the period of the national democratic front', *Selected Party Documents* 1979, pp. 196 and 197. An English version is in Ho Chi Minh 1977.
82   Duiker 1975, pp. 31 and 37–8. Probably the last category are those in ancillary organizations.
83   *Fifty years of activity...* 1979, p. 53.
84   The full members were Ho Chi Minh, Pham Van Dong, Le Duan, Truong Chinh, Vo Nguyen Giap, Le Thanh Nghi, Pham Hung, Nguyen Duy Trinh, Le Duc Tho, Nguyen Chi Thanh and Hoang Van Hoan; the alternates were Van Tien Dung and Tran Quoc Hoan. Ho, Dong, Chinh, Nghi, Hung, Tho and Hoang Van Hoan began in the League. Duan may also have done so, but in any case was a very early member of the ICP, as were Trinh and Thanh and probably also Tran Quoc Hoan. Giap, later the Party's military expert, came over in 1933 from the Revolutionary Party and Dung, who was to be the commander of the final victory in 1975, joined the ICP in 1937.
85   Figures from Duiker 1976, p. 259.
86   For the Plenum Resolution see *History of the August Revolution* 1972, pp. 14–16. There is a complete Vietnamese text in *Excerpts from Party Documents,* op. cit., vol. I.
87   These quotations from the Seventh Plenum Resolution are drawn from Hong Chuong 1965 (in Vietnamese), p. 45. An incomplete Vietnamese text is in *Excerpts*, vol. I.
88   See Duiker 1976, pp. 262–6, and Chu Van Tan 1974, pp. 33–5.
89   *August Revolution* 1972, pp. 20–1.
90   On this see Hong Chuong 1965. For an account in English which does not use this source see Duiker 1976, pp. 266–70.
91   There is a leaflet of the League in Room 6 of the Hanoi Museum of the Revolution.
92   The basic Party account is *Fifty years of activity...* 1979, pp.59–62. See also *History of the August Revolution,* pp. 24–30; Duiker 1976, pp. 275–7, and 1981, Chapter 4: and Khanh 1982, pp. 256–63. A complete Vietnamese text of the Plenum Resolution is in *Excerpts*, vol. I.
93   *Excerpts*, p. 321. The last phrase is literally 'for ten thousand years.'
94   See *Excerpts*, pp. 23–4. For an interesting retrospective discussion see Thanh Dam 1975 (in Vietnamese).
95   A detailed historical survey of the evolution of Vietnamese Communist 'united front' tactics, written from an orthodox Leninist perspective but well-based on sources, including Russian and Vietnamese language materials, may be found in Lulei 1979.
96   *August Revolution* 1972, pp. 23–4.

4   A usable past

Before moving the history of struggle on from May 1941, it is necessary first to look briefly forward and then backwards at greater length. Thus, on 15 May 1975 Le Duan, First Secretary of the Workers' Party of Viet Nam spoke at a meeting in Hanoi called to celebrate the 'Great Spring Victory' which, two weeks before, had put Saigon in the hands of the liberation forces, overthrown the Thieu regime and at last united Viet Nam. Himself a dedicated Communist, speaking at a moment of enormous triumph for a party which had struggled for forty-five years to achieve it, Duan's emphasis was naturally upon the future, but also on the past; the present triumph was portrayed by him not merely as that of his party and recent generations of the Vietnamese people but as the culmination of 'our nation's 4,000-year history', and the heroes and heroines of liberation struggle whom he mentioned stretched back to the first century of the Christian era.[1] As a young railway clerk at the end of the 1920s the First Secretary had himself experienced the upsurge of intellectual excitement which had as one of its main focuses the nature of pre-colonial history. That interest, arising in face of French colonial rule, had a particular end. As one historian has put it, 'In re-evaluating history, intellectuals wanted to develop a usable past which could connect them with and help to propel them into a worthy future.'[2] It was to prove a major asset of the Vietnamese Communist intellectuals that they were able to use history as one of their strongest weapons in the war of position. This they were able to do because they forged it into a very specific shape, structured around the theme which we

80

noted at the end of the last chapter – that of Viet Nam as a nation of patriotic heroes and heroines who over many centuries had fought against foreign invaders.

This idea, which was not 'received' from outside in the sense discerned in Chapter 1 but generated within, could be used by the Communist leadership upon two levels. First, they looked to it to provide concrete content for the message which they were endeavouring to spread as they tried to find access to a variety of sources of support in their war of position. In that sense, history was a resource which provided content to ideology. Second, following from this and even more deeply important, they drew from it the message that the weight of history was behind them, that the contemporary struggle could be seen as the culmination of past efforts. In that sense there was an almost millennial quality about the message of history as patriotism. It tapped very deep roots among many Vietnamese of all classes, and was a major source of that quality of controlled passion noted already among Party leaders but which was shared by others.

In thus attempting to incorporate the past into the present revolutionary terrain, the leaders naturally used Marxism–Leninism as their guide. Above all, the terrain involved was that of the first stage of the struggle, the national democratic revolution, since socialism would mean a radical break with history – in classical language the entrance upon *true* history. In approaching the first stage, received ideas directed them towards the mobilization of the peasantry to overthrow the feudal order and the waging of struggle for national independence in which that class would also be the mass base; both tasks involved the bourgeoisie, which had interests alike in overthrowing the feudal nobility and building a nation state. The point is that, once again, Comintern orthodoxy directed the Vietnamese towards appropriate targets in their war of position, even though, as we shall see, taken literally the interpretation of history which it enjoined was not sustainable. When doctrine pointed to nationalism as a force which could move broad masses of people, and to the peasantry as the most important part of this, it was correct. It was not correct in leading Communist activists (and historians) to characterize pre-colonial Viet Nam as 'feudal', dominated by a landlord class of the kind predicatd by Marx, and to associate nationalism with a rising bourgeoisie. As for the historical reality, it might better be said that:

– the crucial relationship for the peasantry in pre-colonial Viet Nam was with the state at one level and the commune at the other, not the 'classical' lord-serf relationship;
– Vietnamese 'feudalism' could not give birth to a bourgeoisie, an essential feature of its Western form;
– nationalism was centred on the state, not on a non-existent bourgeoisie, and had a second level of existence as peasant patriotism.

The implications of this are that, by the time of the French conquest, no class forces had emerged, except in a certain sense the peasants, who were the

81

'custodians' of patriotism. This, as we shall see, was of enormous importance, since it left the Communists free to portray the class content of patriotism in the way which suited them best as part of the work of ideology-building necessary to the war of position.

The Foundation of a Nation

The earliest history of the Viet people has produced myths of more than one kind – notably the ancient legends of the people themselves, which obviously reflect important themes in that history, and the more recent constructs of colonial, neo-colonial and, let it be said, socialist scholars.[3]

According to legend, the oldest son of the Dragon and the Fairy who were the ancestors of the Viet peoples founded the Hung Kingdom of Van Lang. Modern scholarship reveals that its material base was rice production using bronze as well as polished stone tools on inundated fields which had to be protected from floods if not directly irrigated.[4] Such also was the basis of the Kingdom of Au Lac, formed in 258 BC when another monarchical union of tribes which had evolved to the north of the Red River delta extended its power to the sea. Although historians and archaeologists disagree on its exact nature, it would seem that this new Kingdom represented a higher degree of class and state formation than its predecessor, able to mobilize enough labour power to build the great earthworks of Co Loa, near modern Hanoi, maintain a standing army and mass-produce bronze weapons.[5] These abilities, however, did not prevent conquest from the north by a Chinese warlord in 208 BC, while in 111 BC the extension of the Han emperor's rule to southern China brought the Viet people also under his sway. The next thousand years of their history were to be ones of foreign rule.

Two extremely important shifts had thus apparently occurred among the Kinh even before Chinese rule – from tribes to a centralized state and from clans to village communes. In both cases, that is, there was a shift from a basis of kinship relations to those defined by economic, political and spatial criteria. Under Chinese rule, though not necessarily only as a result of it, agriculture developed much further. Irrigation and flood control techniques, iron tools (especially ploughshares) and extended use of water buffaloes made it possible to enlarge cultivated areas and increase productivity.[6] As for the centralized state, from around the middle of the first century AD Chinese control through a professional bureaucracy was greatly extended. Vietnamese were recruited to it, and Chinese cultural influences made themselves more generally felt; Confucianism, Buddhism and Taoism, the three great sources of ideology at all class levels, began their long permeation of Vietnamese society.

Not that the Viet of the Red River Valley ever forgot during the millennium of Chinese rule that they were descendants of the Dragon and the Fairy, a distinct people, marked off immediately from their rulers by such customs as tattooing, teeth-blackening and betel nut chewing, which the Chinese sought sporadically to suppress. It is not easy to see any transcendent feeling of identity in the earlier uprisings against Chinese rule, of which there were at least eleven major ones in that period, some of them even briefly securing renewed independence.[7] The first seem rather to have been expressions of the Viet aristocrats' discontent when pushed into second place by northern pro-consuls. (Nevertheless the leaders of two of them, the Trung sisters (39–43 AD) and the Lady Trieu (246 AD), were among the national heroes and heroines mentioned in May 1975 by Le Duan.) However, the Red River Viet were in effect bound to develop a stronger sense of common identity when to a shared language and culture and history of unity under one state were added centuries of foreign rule and relegation to an inferior status as barbarians subject to the Middle Kingdom of the Heavenly Emperor.

In the same way that we may take it that by the mid-tenth century the Viet of the south were clearly marked off from the Chinese and hence from their own northern cousins who remained under Chinese rule, it can also be assumed that those of the Red River Valley had evolved far enough economically and politically to be fully distinguished from the Thai-speaking peoples and other highland groups.[8] This is symbolized in their own name for themselves, Kinh, which, significantly, also means 'capital city'. Although they continued over the next centuries to call their kingdom Dai Viet – Great Viet – it will be convenient to use the specific name for the majority people and speak of the Vietnamese in situations where both they and the others were involved as historical subjects.[9]

Around the time of the Geneva Conference, a Communist historian, writing for a general audience, summed up the results of a thousand years of Chinese rule thus:

> Compelled to adopt the conqueror's way of living and culture, the Vietnamese people during the long period of slavery, refused to be assimilated and managed to absorb from this contact what was necessary to build up a national culture, to elaborate their own personality, and thereby to create forces to liberate Viet-Nam from the foreign yoke, to maintain its independence for about ten centuries and to contribute its share to the civilization of the old Asiatic world.[10]

Was this enough to make them a nation? By the strict orthodoxy expressed in Marxist–Leninist received ideas the answer must be negative. By the facts of Vietnamese history, however – and fortunately for the twentieth century Communist leaders – the Kinh proper were able to consolidate as a nation, if not by the tenth century and their liberation from Chinese rule, then at least by the thirteenth.

Even before his rise to power, orthodoxy on what constituted a nation had been established by Josef Stalin, himself a member of one of the minorities within the Tsarist empire. Writing in 1913 he had declared that:

A nation is a historically constituted, stable community of people, formed on the basis of a common language, territory, economic life, and psychological make-up manifested in a common culture.[11]

Further, he had insisted that if 'a single one of these characteristics' were absent 'the nation ceases to be a nation'.[12] No doubt Ho Chi Minh and any other Vietnamese comrades trained in France or the USSR were familar with these views. It may be speculated that the matters of language, territory, psychology and culture – despite the slippery nature of the last two concepts – would have created relatively few problems in the Kinh context. However, the question of a 'common economic life' might have given pause for thought, especially since Stalin also gave it a definite class content. A nation, he wrote, 'is not merely a historical category but a historical category belonging to a definite epoch, the epoch of rising capitalism'.[13] In class terms, therefore, nationalism as an ideology was associated with a bourgeoisie seeking to consolidate itself as a capitalist ruling class. This made the Vietnamese case more difficult.

In part, this is because Stalin did not define in detail that which he also referred to as 'community of economic life' and 'economic cohesion'.[14] It is evident that this was bound up with the operation of a capitalist market on a wide scale, but the Bolsheviks, in adopting this position as orthodoxy, did not take it further than this. However, as part of an exchange of views in 1929, Stalin did clarify his position a little – though his piece was not published till twenty years later, and so could not be known to Ho and the others. Speaking now from the centre of power, the CPSU General Secretary thus denied the possibility of a pre-capitalist nation emerging in Western or Eastern Europe, 'because there were as yet no national markets and no economic or cultural centre, and, consequently, there were none of the factors which put an end to the economic disunity of a given people and draw its hitherto disunited parts together into one national whole'.[15] A basic objective of this chapter, therefore, is to show that, as the revolution moved in the twentieth century from West to East and thus sought to come to terms with the struggle for national liberation, this orthodoxy of Marxism–Leninism was both incorrect and caused unnecessary complications. To put it in another way, in cases like Viet Nam (and China) nations could arise without an aspiring capitalist class as their bearers, and bringing a socialist and a national struggle together did not necessarily have to involve taking a position relative to leadership by such a class. Provided basic patterns of production and exchange were compatible with one another, a 'national market', and hence a mercantile bourgeoisie, were not essential. A centralized state erected upon such basic commonalities of production and exchange and drawing surplus from them was sufficient to provide the necessary economic as well as political cohesion. (Significantly, Stalin did not even mention the political factor.) Such a state had come into existence in northern Viet Nam by the thirteenth century.

The Consolidation of the Centralized State

Three short-lived dynasties after the liberation of 939 failed to stabilize the new state structure, as various Kinh warlords competed for mastery.[16] In 1009, however, a fourth, the Ly, established itself: in the following year its founder transferred the capital to Thang Long, on the site of the modern Hanoi, and the rule of his descendants lasted until 1225. Following this, the Tran dynasty ruled until 1400. In those four centuries the Vietnamese social formation, from village commune to state apparatus, first fully consolidated itself. Thus, its cultural, linguistic, political and territorial integrity were established. The Kinh people were brought into relationship with the Thai, Nung and other ethnic groups of the mountainous areas by campaigns and dynastic marriage alliances which established a system of tributaries on the northern and western edges of the Red River delta.[17] Many battles were fought against the Cham kingdom, which occupied the narrow waist of what is now central Viet Nam and comprised an Austro-Indonesian population ruled by an aristocracy which had taken over Hindu religious practices and political forms, and also the Hindu-influenced Khmer kingdom centred in modern Kampuchea.[18] Although in 1069 it extended its territory at the expense of the Cham to just south of what much later became the famous seventeenth parallel, things did not always go well for the Kinh dominant class. There were seven major Khmer invasions in the years between 1128 and 1216, and in the last half of the fourteenth century almost continual fighting against the Cham was one of the factors that exhausted the Tran rulers. The biggest threat, on the other hand, continued to come from the north. When the Chinese emperor attempted to reassert suzerainty in 1075–77 he was met by an incursion of Vietnamese troops and then defeat when his own armies counter-invaded. Although the Heavenly Emperor's face was saved by a temporary cession of territory, the Vietnamese–Chinese boundary was henceforth fixed as one between sovereign states. Then, in 1257, 1284–85 and 1287–88 came the biggest test of the pre-colonial Vietnamese state – invasion by the Mongol rulers of China which gave the southern state its most epic victories and another national hero hailed by Le Duan in 1975, General Tran Hung Dao.[19]

There can be little doubt that all these struggles to assert a Kinh identity and to preserve an independence from Chinese and Mongols, not only for the Kinh but also for the highland peoples (a Nung general was one of the commanders against the Chinese in 1075), increased the power of the state. This was clearly expressed at the ideological level by the ascription of an imperial dignity to the Kinh ruler in face of the invasion by the Chinese emperor's armies in the eleventh century. In a poem written as a call to battle by the Kinh commander, Ly Thuong Kiet (another hero cited by Le Duan), it was claimed that:

> The southern country is ruled by a Son of Heaven,/This is laid down definitely in the Heavenly Book,/Those who came to violate it against the divine order/Will certainly be defeated.[20]

More than just an equal place in the divine order was adopted by the Kinh ruler in the south in imitation of his admittedly more powerful northern neighbour. In 1075 the Chinese system of examinations for entrance to the bureaucracy was taken over as the basis for a regularization and institutionalization of the state apparatus. A code of laws had already been ordered to be prepared in 1042. The duty of military service was imposed under the Ly and a military academy established by the next dynasty. Both Ly and Tran emperors were also ready to intervene in the economy, directing the building of canals and dykes, regulating the sale and mortgage of land and limiting enslavement to such categories as prisoners-of-war and debtors. These developments found expression in ideology. Adoption of the Chinese system of training for the bureaucracy and the special education directed towards success in the entrance examinations meant the adoption of the Confucian classics. Under the Ly their doctrines faced strong competition as official ideology from Buddhist teachings, since Buddhist monks stood high in the favour of a dynasty whose founder had been brought up in one of their temples. Under the Tran, however, it was seen that the three central obediences of Confucianism – of child to parent, wife to husband and subject to ruler – represented an excellent glue for the social fabric for those who wished to reproduce the existing balance of class power. Buddhism and Buddhist monks as imperial advisors were pushed away from the centre, although they retained a strong grip on the common people.[21] The role of the state apparatus, as personified by the emperor, also was mediated into ideology. In 1048 a temple was built to the gods of earth and the harvest, where the emperor sacrificed four times a year to ensure the crop; each year he also went into the fields and with full ceremony initiated the ploughing of the ricefields.[22] In general, the symbolic position of the emperor was well expressed by the Chinese character used for the word 'ruler,' which showed the three levels of heaven, man and earth vertically linked.[23]

By the end of four centuries of independence, however, we may safely say that the Kinh had become something more than subjects of an emperor who claimed to be the representative of heaven. They had become a unified people conscious of themselves as such and with a pantheon of heroes and heroines.[24] They had their own territory centred on the Red River Valley but with 'a narrowing coastal strip running south like a spear into Champa', most of which they had held for much longer than four hundred years.[25] They had a history of consolidating and holding this territory in face of Cham, Khmer and, above all, the Chinese and Mongols. They had a common basic economy, which gave them a common culture of the family as a working unit, a rice-based diet, and a religion which in the main was intended to celebrate and perpetuate the agricultural process. They had their own language, which by the fourteenth century was beginning to distinguish its written form more clearly from Chinese by the use of *nom*, a simplified form of the characters derived from the north: already by then the classic *Book of Poems* had been rendered into the new form.[26] Such a development would not have been possible without the permission, if not sponsorship, of the state, and a further crucial factor in the development of a Kinh nationality was the common experience of unity under a centralized state. More than that, the state apparatus was active in fostering the sense of identity, more especially by the writing of official history; around 1272 the first major work, *History of Great Viet*, now unfortunately lost, was compiled.[27] Thus, there was certainly a generalized consciousness of common identity, exemplified in the famous conference in the Dien Hong palace at the end of 1284, when it was the overwhelming support of elders representing all the villages of the empire, not just the counsels of nobles and officials, which pushed the emperor into resisting the Mongol armies.[28]

By the 1960s historians in the DRVN were themselves giving prominence to the centralized state as an element of continuity in Vietnamese history which had played an important part in fostering a sense of national identity.[29] In the 1930s and 1940s, however, the situation was one of greater ambiguity. Marxist–Leninist doctrine saw the 'feudal' state as incapable of giving structure to a nation. As Stalin put it in his 1929 piece, 'how could nations have arisen and existed before capitalism, in the period of feudalism, when countries were split up into separate independent principalities which, far from being bound together by national ties, emphatically denied the necessity for such ties?'[30] Even if we postulate the feudal European state as composed of separate fiefs with a common overlord, rather than of completely autonomous units, as Stalin said, the point is basically correct. The feudal state was in effect a corporation of landholders with the same liege, held together ideologically by the concepts of fealty and oath. Such a state structure would be most unlikely to give shape to a national identity and provided no ideological basis for the concept of a 'nation state', in which the latter entity derived its legitimacy from the expression of the first. On the other hand, precisely because he discerned profound differences when he turned his attention outside Europe, Karl Marx had postulated an alternative mode of production to the feudal one – the Asiatic mode. I do not intend to enter into any debate concerning the appropriate label to place on pre-colonial Viet Nam;[31] the important thing to note here is that in October 1930, when Tran Phu's 'Theses' laid down the orthodoxy that feudalism characterized, in fact, the whole of Indochina, the Comintern still left open the possibility of the alternative analysis.[32] It was not until 1939 that Stalin in his 'Dialectical and Historical Materialism' expunged the Asiatic mode from the armoury of Marxist theoretical concepts. It seems almost certain that the ICP's first Central Committee in 1930 followed Stalin's May 1927 specification of China as dominated by 'survivals of feudalism', the exact phrase (*di kich phong kiem*) used of his own country by Tran Phu.[33]

We should now turn to consider class formation during Vietnamese pre-colonial history, partly to see in what its 'feudalism' consisted and above all to see the nature of the peasant condition during those centuries.

State and Class: Some Historical Realities

The basic class of the Vietnamese social formation was the peasantry, those who, in the dominant Kinh nationality, produced the rice within the village communes. In theory the emperor owned all the land, putting part of it at the disposal of members of a commune, which existed with the sanction of a charter from him, kept in its combined temple and assembly hall. There was also a village head appointed from the centre, although it seems likely that it was often a local man. But it was the commune members, or at least the older males among them, who controlled the use of the land through the village council which periodically re-allocated the communal land. Although private ownership developed, communal land must frequently have been the greater part of the total area.[34] It followed from this that it was the commune as a whole from which surplus was levied, with the assessment of individual contributions left to its members, through their council. The basic class relationship was thus not the European feudal one of the supposedly mutual obligations of an individual peasant and his lord; rather, it was that of the corporate village with the state apparatus, personified as the emperor. Concealed non-cooperation and even open rebellion were the peasants' final resort when external pressure appeared too great for solution by the normal means by which the commune regulated its affairs.

From whence came that pressure? In the first instance from the state apparatus, through its hierarchy of provincial and district officials, who transmitted to the village heads the demands for labour services to build dykes and canals, temples and similar public works, for rice and other agricultural products, and for contingents when needed for the army. However, the state apparatus was also securing the necessary means for the ruling class to reproduce its power. Who, then, were the ruling class? At its core was the emperor's extended family with its several generations of siblings, wives, concubines and children and more distant relatives, numbering perhaps several thousand people.[35] Grouped around these would be the similar extended families of those who had become wives or concubines, imperial favourites, top military commanders or those who had done some service to the imperial family and thus earned incorporation into the ruling class. Another incorporated element, given that by the end of the eleventh century the Vietnamese social formation included non-Kinh peoples, were the chieftains of the latter who had been subordinated to the Kinh state.[36]

The most ambitious, energetic and favoured nobles and the senior bureaucrats in fact formed a power bloc, which we may define as the constellation of elements which directly manipulate the state apparatus in order to influence the formation and execution of policies. This bloc, necessarily linked with the ruling class or classes and centred of course round the emperor, did not necessarily express immediately all their economic and political interests.

Within it the bureaucrats would be in a subordinate position, since they were subject to periodic review and discipline.

What made the Kinh nobility a class was possession of the right, bestowed by the emperor for a lifetime or longer, to extract the surplus in a given area from the communes standing upon it, surrendering part to the state or keeping the whole. Thus the ruling class controlled the means of production and labour power, but again through the medium of the commune and its own organization. The right to appropriate the surplus, or part of it, from designated communes was also the economic basis for the provincial governors and other senior bureaucrats; lesser ranks received payment in kind from the taxes syphoned back to the emperor at the capital. It would be incorrect, however, to group the nobility and senior bureaucrats as one class.[37] The latter were rather a sort of middle stratum, between peasants and nobles, enjoying an income directly in proportion to rank, not to the extent of the land and people they controlled only so long as they held office. As a historian in the DRVN noted:

> The truth is that with their functional status, the mandarin stratum – like all other bureaucracies of other eras – were salaried executives of the existing ruling class. They did not create socio-economic relationships and the particular relations of production of an era. Therefore, it is not possible to consider mandarins, officials, who were paid for fulfilling social functions, as a class. Salaries of mandarins, officials, actually were the forms of distribution of the means of consumption which they could enjoy because of the performance of their functions.[38]

Nevertheless, the designation of bureaucrats as a subordinate part of the pre-colonial Vietnamese power bloc and the suggestion of limits upon their ability and that of the nobility to control the basic means of production are not meant to imply that they were too weak to extend their power. As we have just noted, from the early years of the Ly dynasty, the nobility in particular were sometimes given control for services rendered, not only of land and part of the revenues to be derived from the labour of the people upon it, but also the whole of the surplus produced. Thus Marshall Ly Thuong Kiet, who defeated the Chinese in 1077, is said to have had 10,000 households of dependants on lands granted for his partial exploitation and another 4,000 whose surplus was entirely for his benefit.[39] It is evident that the existence of the second category of grants could create an impulse towards the establishment of private estates by the nobility, if they could exploit some situation of weakness on the part of the emperor so that he allowed estates to be passed on to the next generation. Such seems to have become increasingly common under the Tran; already in 1266 the nobles were sufficiently powerful to secure a decree permitting them to enslave vagabonds and those without work and use them to open up new lands which the nobles might then exploit.[40]

Thus, one of the main contradictions of the pre-colonial social formation was that between the nobility and the centralized state personified in the emperor, each defining the other's existence but the one interested in usurping control of more and more of the surplus produced by the peasants and the other in ensuring its flow to the centre. In this situation the bureaucracy also found itself in a structural contradiction – on the one hand the direct agent of the emperor, on the other (at least at its senior levels) impelled to maximize its own private wealth. These contradictions, of course, can only be understood in relation to the most primary contradiction of all, that between the state apparatus and its bureaucracy along with the nobility and the peasants from whom the surplus was squeezed.

These were not the only contradictions in the class structure of pre-colonial Viet Nam. The village communes – the basic units which give the history of that country much of its special character – were also gripped by contradictions of their own. Firstly, we must note the one inherent in the position of the commune within the process of surplus extraction just described. On the one hand, its capacity to unite internally and face outwards provided some mitigation of the power of nobles and bureaucrats to extract from its members at will. But on the other hand, the structure of the commune imprisoned the peasants and put them at the disposal of the wealthy and their state apparatus.

In discerning a second contradiction – again of the communes' place within the structure as a whole – we may agree, reviewing centuries of Vietnamese history, that as units of production, of administration, and of mobilization of the population when necessary (in face of foreign invasion) they were certainly remarkably stable and long-lived. But the other aspect of this was their incapacity to change, however challenged. They could reproduce themselves simply by the geographical diffusion of replicas of existing communes where new territory could be opened up, but could create no new social forces within themselves to meet a new conjunction involving elements outside.[41] The stability was determined by their internal cohesion, stemming from centuries of intense cooperation among their members necessitated by irrigated rice cultivation. At the same time, as Vu Quoc Thuc pointed out, this intimate parochialism bred characteristics which virtually ruled out new social relationships.[42] The passion for landed property, which could only be quite small, reinforced the endless perpetuation of petty agricultural production. Few opportunities for increasing wealth outside agriculture existed, since the similarity of one commune to another limited trade, and each produced most of its own consumer goods internally; the same held true, in fact, among families. No peasant wished to appear too much richer than his fellow, because that would mean being assessed for a larger share of the commune's tax.

At the same time, it must not be supposed that each commune was some rustic republic of equal citizens, unmarked by internal contradictions. Within each, there was a definite stratification characterized by at least three layers. As we have already noted of the colonial period, landlords and rich peasants, allied politically and sometimes by family to the bureaucrats and with one of their number nominated by the state as village head and grouped together by

90

their control of the village council, could always manipulate such matters as tax levies and distribution of communal lands to suit themselves. This would be at the expense of middle and poor peasants, who might be inscribed on the tax rolls but had little control over affairs. Still lower on the communal scale were those who did not possess enough to pay taxes, who had to pick up work wherever they could, who might in times of stress have to cut loose from the village and wander off to find sustenance elsewhere, often as brigands or slaves. In times of particular dearth, if floods, drought or typhoons struck or the state became more exacting than usual, members of the middle and poor strata might well be relegated into this one.

Moreover, it must be remembered that women in general had no voice outside the family circle, and were limited there by patriarchy backed by Confucian ideology. They played an important economic role, in agriculture (where men maintained the hydraulic system but women did much else), handicrafts and trading, and it was a popular saying that 'husband's property comes from wife's labour'. Women were indeed valued as sources of labour power, so much so that daughters-in-law, who added to the resources of a household, were more esteemed than daughters, who would go to another. In 1103 an imperial grant was made to redeem girls sold by their families and marry them to widowers and young men who could not afford bride price; all males had to be given access to unpaid female labour in the imperial system.[43]

Finally, there was a part of the population which was even outside the communes, lacking therefore the limited protection which they could give – slaves, both domestic and agricultural (the last often non-Kinh prisoners of war), and actors.

In the final decades of the fourteenth century, various of these class contradictions were calling the whole system into question. The immediate cause of their exacerbation was constant fighting with the Cham kingdom, involving both invasion from the south with accompanying devastation (Thang Long the capital was twice captured and sacked) and the levying of increased taxes and contingents of troops. This, however, only brought to a head the longer-term effects of the growth of private land ownership and landlordism, marked by such measures as the decree of 1335 permitting the private annexation of public lands and that of 1365 permitting hiring of labour.[44] With non-noble landlords also emerging, it was necessary, as early as the last Mongol invasion, to grant titles to those who supplied rice to the army, and this tendency for surplus to be concentrated in landlord hands rather than in state granaries continued.

By the end of the fourteenth century, landlord, noble and state pressures on the peasantry were severe and the Tran dynasty seemed to have lost the mandate of heaven. In 1400 its last child emperor was deposed by the general, Ho Quy Ly, who had halted the Cham invasions. Ly, already regent, now made himself emperor. The Ming emperors of China used this usurpation as an excuse to invade Great Viet once more in 1407, and the Vietnamese peoples again experienced foreign rule until 1428.

An Expanding Social Formation

The period of Chinese rule in the fifteenth century lasted only a fraction of the time taken up by their earlier hegemony, but it had considerable impact. Control of the population was strict, with family registers and identity papers, and such customs as teeth-blackening were forbidden. Naturally, taxes were extracted for the benefit of the northern emperor, and Kinh nobles who had collaborated with the invaders against the usurper Ly now found further chances to extend their private holdings. In this situation, popular support gradually rallied around Le Loi, a landowner from south of the Red River delta, who launched a resistance war in 1418 and finally drove out the Chinese in 1428. The dynasty which he founded was to last 350 years, and he himself, yet another of the national heroes mentioned by Le Duan in May 1975, was to become famed by the Vietnamese Communists as a liberator and early master of guerrilla warfare.

Le Loi, as the emperor Le Thai To, and some of his successors up to the early sixteenth century, especially Le Thanh Tong (1459–97), laboured mightily to restore state and society and to some extent succeeded.[45] The founder of the new dynasty distributed land to needy peasants, taken from nobles who had collaborated with the Chinese, the estates of those who had died without issue, and areas which had been newly cleared but not registered. Both he and his successor forbade the private expropriation of communal lands and re-established their periodic redistribution. Hydraulic works were attended to and supervised by special officials. The central state apparatus and army were reorganized, and reforms carried out in the examination system for entry to the bureaucracy. The Thanh Tong emperor ordered a new codification of the law. The sponsorship of a more 'national' history and literature continued. Great Viet became a power throughout South-east Asia, receiving embassies from Java and sending its troops as far as the Lao state on the middle Mekong.

But these measures expressed only one set of moments of the contradictions which placed nobles against the centralized state, nobles and officials against the peasant, and divided communes internally. No permanent shift in the balance occurred, the other moments were at most weakened for some generations. As a class, the nobility survived, still able to take land for itself. The state apparatus assumed more aspects of control, extending into prohibition of gambling and suppression of 'parasites.' Frequent wars meant a greater burden on those who paid the taxes and provided the soldiers. Minority peoples, who had supported the Kinh against the Chinese, were driven into rebellion by the state exactions. Ideologically, recourse was made to an even stricter Confucianism. Old customs, such as that which allowed a wife to remain in her parent's household for up to four years after marriage, were suppressed and treatises written on the proper conduct of all classes and strata. Thus, nine of the '24 points of education' related to women, who were enjoined to the 'Four Virtues' and 'Three Obediences' (of daughter to father, wife to husband, and widow to son).[46] In the end the new dynasty did not bring with it structural change; nor could it, because in the last resolve it represented only another permutation among noble factions, not a new social force.[47]

Thus, while it may be possible to agree with Nguyen Khac Vien that what he calls the 'feudal monarchy' reached its peak under the Le emperors of the fifteenth century, and even that the monarchy and bureaucracy for a time played a positive role, it must be stressed that they represented only the highest peak in a pre-colonial history of troughs and peaks, cycles of rise and decline of the centralized monarchy governed by the slow, tidal shifts of the class contradictions outlined earlier.[48] It could be argued that, for something under a century, the class basis of the regime shifted to the wealthier peasants in the communes, whose private plots were no longer taxed and who benefited the most from the now more closely regulated distribution of communal land. The Le regime of the fifteenth century, however, was marked by an important contradiction: the class which was its basis was not the ruling class. The reforms of Le Thai Tho and his early successors, as we have noted, brought the nobility under control but certainly did not destroy them; thus, partisans of Le Loi and their descendants were given grants of silver and land, even though these remained revocable at imperial will.[49] By the third decade of the sixteenth century, as we shall see, the nobility were again fatally exerting themselves as the dominant class. Nevertheless, before looking at this, attention must be drawn to one new development of the fifteenth century which was to have the most profound implications for the whole future history of Viet Nam, shaping the lives of Nguyen Ai Quoc, Brother Seventy and all their contemporaries, and determining the course of the liberation struggle and building of socialism. That development was the launching of the '*Nam Tien*,' the 'advance to the South' (see Map 3).[50]

The Changing Shape of Viet Nam

This movement had effectively begun as early as 1069, when the first areas were conquered from the Cham, and this gradual encroachment had continued: thus, the usurper Ho Quy Ly had pushed the frontier forward into the modern Quang Nam and Quang Ngai provinces of what later became South Viet Nam. Nevertheless, it may be argued that it was in the late fifteenth century that the balance decisively shifted, when in 1471 the Cham kingdom was finally broken and reduced to a rump doomed to disappear. For the next four hundred years and more, Vietnamese peasant families, who found themselves trapped in poverty within the old communes, uprooted and moved south to find empty space suitable for rice-growing where new communes could be founded. There was also state-sponsored migration, often in the form of settlements of soldiers, who could both hold the frontier of the moment against Cham and Khmer attack and grow rice and other crops. The more adventurous or ambitious nobles, too, took an imperial commission to clear new areas, often with slave labour, and found their own estates. But the main social force behind the move must surely have been the anonymous enterprise of the ordinary peasants, who eventually filled up an area of land much greater than that of the Kinh heartland by the same patient process by which they had colonized that region and the first provinces, like Thanh Hoa, opened to the south of the Red River delta. Amoeba-like, the old communes threw off new ones, sending parties or individual families south to start again.

The results of this process of migration will provide constant themes for the remainder of this study, and its importance cannot be over-emphasized. To a large extent, the history of Viet Nam in its last centuries before colonial rule was to be the history of a moving frontier, as a social formation which numbered perhaps 5 or 6 million inhabitants in the early fifteenth century pushed slowly south.[51] This implied a change in the physical terrain of social action, in social relations and in culture.

In a real sense, therefore, the time of troubles into which the northern-based kingdom was about to enter in the early sixteenth century marked a shift in its nature. Taking Stalin's characteristics of a nation as our guideline, it may be suggested that, poised now for the final move into the deep south, over five centuries of independence had constituted the Kinh people as a stable community with a common language, culture and basic economic life in terms of uniform patterns of production and exchange. A centralized state bound everything together and deliberately fostered a consciousness of national identity. However, this was not a feudal state, but a much more elaborate apparatus staffed by a professional bureaucracy and centred on a semi-divine emperor. Although a hereditary nobility represented a major element in its power bloc, the state above all undertook surplus extraction directly in a very 'non-feudal' way. At the base the state rested on the village communes, which had some capacity to regulate their own affairs and for which a direct contact with the bureaucracy had more meaning than that with local nobles.

Moreover, the operation of local cults of national heroes and heroines in particular allows us to hypothesize the existence of two levels of national feeling.[52] As noted, this was projected as part of the ideology supporting the state, as in the claim that the Kinh emperor was of equal rank to the Chinese. On the other hand, patriotism (to use the term preferred by later Communist activists and scholars) was very real for the peasants. A telling example from the viewpoint of this study was the way in which later migrants to Siam actually carried the cult of the deified hero Tran Hung Dao, conqueror of the Mongols, out of the national territory altogether and unsupported by the state. There, in 1928, a visiting Nguyen Ai Quoc made great efforts to come to grips

94

with cult temples, mediums and seances, writing a secular 'hymn' to be used in revering the hero. Such were the attractions of a usable past for a revolutionary trying to mobilize the masses.[53]

Peasant patriotism was to make them a major force in the twentieth century revolution against capitalism, colonialism and imperialism. In fact, the rebelliousness which they were to show above all in 1930–31 surfaced as a strong characteristic by the mid-eighteenth century. This adds to our theme of patriotism the essential dimension of class struggle. As we shall now go on to see, the prolonged crisis of the old system which began in the early 1500s eventually created insupportable conditions of oppression for the peasants.

Decline and Restoration

The renewal of the power of the centralized monarchy by the Le dynasty lasted only three generations before being called into serious question once again. From 1504 the emperors were marked by debauchery rather than good works, and the nobles by renewed ambition rather than loyalty.[54] In 1527 one of them took the throne, but some nobles and officials remained loyal to the Le, and eventually in 1596 the usurping faction was pushed north to a small area on the Chinese border, where it held out until 1677. This did not mean that the Le emperor was to wield unquestioned power; indeed, he retained little if any, since the two families which had been most instrumental in defeating the usurpers, the Nguyen and Trinh, held the real power while allowing a puppet emperor to mask their rule. Not that they ruled in concert: by 1605 the country was divided into two separate spheres, the Trinh effectively the rulers north of a line roughly on the modern eighteenth parallel, the Nguyen south of it. After constant fighting from 1627–73 the two families called a truce and each controlled its own area in the name of the emperor.[55]

While at war with one another and after, the Trinh and Nguyen lords pursued policies which made them pale copies – one could even say caricatures – of the most powerful emperors of the Ly, Tran and later Le dynasties.[56] That is to say that the Trinh in the north retained the familiar state structure, although with two significant exceptions. After 1729 shortage of funds caused them to put bureaucratic promotions up for sale and to open the previously restricted examinations, at least at the regional level, to anyone able to pay a fee.[57] At the administrative base, after 1732 the position of village head was left to the choice of the leading men of the commune, without any control over the appointment from the centre.[58] While this would obviously reinforce contradictions within the communes, the peasants' external relations were not really eased by Trinh attempts at rural reform, as in 1708 and 1711, when regularization of distribution of communal land was attempted and private estates forbidden. Such measures remained dead letters, but much more effective was the gathering of taxes, on the communes, on persons, on salt and increasingly customs dues. The result of this taxation was massive rebellions in the 1740s, three of them simultaneously during some years.

The Nguyen in the south, who finally established their capital at Phu Xuan (the modern Hue), had to build a state apparatus more or less from scratch, but took the familiar as their model. A significant variation was their introduction of an examination system open to all, and less attention seems to have been paid to it. As a result, the son of an actor, who had not been allowed to compete in the north, even rose to be a minister, and it is not too far-fetched to see this as a symbol of the relative openness of the class system in the south. The point was that the Nguyen lords badly needed people, while conversely the Trinh areas were probably feeling the effects of overpopulation.

The Nguyen wanted settlers to move south, and they assumed the political lead in opening the new lands, especially in waging frequent war upon the Khmer empire, which was also under pressure from the powerful state of Siam to its west, based on the Chao Phraya valley. As the Khmer state collapsed, its eastern provinces passed into Kinh hands; a milestone event was the occupation of what became Saigon in 1690. Naturally, the ruling class grouped round the Nguyen lords wished to keep this process of settlement under control by carving out estates for themselves, and the state also set up military settlements. But that class was not as strong as in the Kinh heartland; part of it was even recruited from Chinese and other foreign soldiers of fortune. On the other side of the class contradiction, the villages which were being established were also not exactly like those in the north. Certainly they were based on rice cultivation, but the plentiful streams and rivers of the Mekong delta made cooperation for irrigation purposes less essential and plenitude of land meant larger holdings and a more spread population. In this situation village rites to express solidarity and even the cohesiveness of families became a less marked feature of communal life. It may be also that the condition of the peasantry was less hard in the newer lands of the south than in the older provinces around the Nguyen capital; there, as we shall shortly see, it was bad enough to induce revolt.

Before passing on to the mightiest of all the uprisings of pre-colonial Vietnamese history, however, three other developments of this early period of the effective division of the country must be noted. First, there was a Buddhist revival, which took place during the eighteenth century under both the Trinh and the Nguyen. Confucianism was becoming exhausted as an instrument of the state, and its usefulness as an ideology of the power bloc had come into doubt. So temples were built by the state once more, as under the Ly, and Buddhist priests could move in higher circles once again. Second, the latter half of the eighteenth century in particular saw a growth of literature much more rooted in the life of the people and written in the vernacular and in *nom*, although the most famous work of all, *Lament of a Soldier's Wife*, by Dang Tran Con was in fact initially in Chinese characters.[59] Third, a new alien element had appeared as a participant in Vietnamese affairs – European traders and missionaries, the advance guard of mercantile capitalism. By the second decade of the seventeenth century the Dutch were backing the Trinh lords and the Portuguese the Nguyen; by 1660 French bearers of Christianity and seekers for more secular profit were firmly in alliance and had representatives in the Trinh's main trading port.

The full implications of this new presence were to take two centuries to reveal themselves and, by the time they did, the Trinh and the Le dynasty had been swept away and the Nguyen had risen to new heights. Nevertheless, the ascension of the southern lords was anything but direct; in between they endured defeat and long travail.

By the third quarter of the eighteenth century it was evident that both the Trinh and the Nguyen lords had exhausted their capacities, and in so doing had brought the peasantry to perhaps the lowest point of misery they had yet plumbed. In the north especially, there was little left for very many but helpless, hopeless wandering. It was in an area settled something over a century earlier, however, and not in the Kinh heartland, that the greatest of the peasant rebellions of pre-colonial Vietnamese history began in 1771.[60] At the village of Tay Son, which stood between the highlands and the coastal plain opened up to settlement by the Nguyen lords south of Hue, three brothers, Nhac, Lu and Hue, raised the banner of revolt in 1771. Bearing the ubiquitous family name Nguyen, they had little else in common with the Nguyen rulers, though the brothers were descended from a prisoner of war settled in the area by them, and the eldest, Nhac, had at one time been a minor local official. The brothers' original following was composed of the usual uprooted elements, and naturally expanded on a peasant base, but the new movement had at least two unusual features. Firstly, the leaders themselves were drawn from the middle levels of small landowners, better-off peasants and minor bureaucrats rather than from discontented nobles.[61] Secondly, Nhac had also been a trader and the brothers were supported, and probably financed, by Kinh merchants, perhaps discontented with the inroads into their profits made by the Nguyen lords' heavy reliance on revenue from import duties, and resentful of Chinese competition.[62]

Although the brothers claimed at first to be restoring the power of the Le emperor, in 1778 Nhac raised himself to the imperial dignity, after a series of campaigns which had wiped out all but one of the Nguyen princes, Nguyen Anh, who managed to hold the lower south with backing from the Siamese kingdom, now recovering from a disaster at the hands of the Burmese in 1767. In 1782, however, Nhac and Hue (the middle brother, Lu, was never so prominent) captured Saigon, paying off their debt to the merchants by massacring thousands of their Chinese counterparts in its twin city of Cholon. Sorely pressed, Nguyen Anh turned for help to the French, using as intermediary a missionary bishop; fateful signs of future developments were being written on the wall. In 1786 Nguyen Hue turned north and finished off the rule of the Trinh lords, who had dared to meddle in events in the territory of their old rivals; Thang Long was captured and Hue became the Quang Trung emperor. Then the Chinese invaded again in 1788, ostensibly on behalf of the deposed Le dynasty, and Hue, a brilliant general, smashed them, thus earning himself a place as another of Viet Nam's national heroes, duly mentioned by Le Duan in May 1975.

This was the peak of the Tay Son movement. With the conquered territory divided between Hue in the north and Nhac in the centre, and strong rivalry between them, Nguyen Anh was able to advance from the extreme southwest, where he was sheltered under the Siamese umbrella, and build a new base around Saigon, using military settlements and encouraging both nobles and peasants to open new lands. Slowly he advanced northward, nibbling away at his rivals' territory and aided militarily by French mercenaries and weapons. In 1792 the Quang Trung emperor died, aged only forty, and the next year his eldest brother and later rival died. In 1801 Anh retook the city of Phu Xuan; in 1802 he took Thang Long, and emerged as the Gia Long emperor, the first Vietnamese ruler to hold sway on the entire modern terrain, from the gate of China to the Ca Mau peninsula.

The long political division of the country had been accompanied by its enormous extension in area, and the Tay Son movement had brought the two developments into line by uniting the country again, or, more accurately, by giving Nguyen Anh the chance to do so. Ultimately the rebel brothers found their greatest historical significance in wiping out the Trinh, giving the *coup-de-grâce* to the Le and opening the way for a new dynasty which was to achieve more. Despite attempts to restabilize the disintegrating northern communes, increased use of *nom* and a literary florescence – marked by at least one extraordinary figure, the poetess Ho Xuan Huong – for which they were not directly responsible, the Tay Son brothers could do little more than fall back on a rebuilding of the age-old state apparatus.[63] Behind that, of course, lay the perennial problem for pre-colonial Vietnamese reformers and rebels alike, the absence of a newly emerging social class upon which their efforts could be based. All Nhac and Hue were able to do in the end was to sponsor the attempted reformation of the old nobility to incorporate their own adherents, and retain its power bloc with the bureaucracy, albeit with rather more emphasis on its military component. That in itself reflected another weakness endemic to pre-colonial political change, the need to fight constant campaigns which prevented stabilization of the regime and meant more extortion from the peasantry. Lastly and more specifically, the Tay Son leaders made a fatal mistake in allowing Nguyen Anh to consolidate a base in the south after 1788 from which he was able to launch his successful offensive and gain the imperial throne.[64]

The Last Period of the Pre-colonial Formation

The kingdom which was restored by Gia Long, now for the first time officially entitled Viet Nam, began in three circumstances which no other new dynasty had faced. First, the country was now much larger in size than the one ruled by Ly, Tran or Le emperors and Trinh and Nguyen lords, with a great new rice-producing delta added to it and more land west of that to be fully settled and developed. Second, long years of wars and exactions by the state and nobility had worn the whole social fabric perilously thin, even inducing, as we shall shortly see, a shift of some importance in the balance of class forces. Finally, although the new Viet Nam was probably more significant as a Southeast Asian power than ever before, with yet another Chinese invasion defeated and the Khmer kingdom reduced to a tributary, the new Nguyen emperors faced a potential foreign challenge like none other in their country's history – a newly expansive European capitalism. It is in the light of these three elements in the historical conjunction of the first half of the nineteenth century that we must view the peasant experience and the nation in the last period of Viet Nam's pre-colonial independence.

The new dynasty had necessarily to do what others had done - namely restore the central power and the economic life which must produce the surplus on which it was based.[65] Particularly under Gia Long and his successor, the Minh Mang emperor (1820–41), the main bureaucratic institutions were reorganized and extended along with the hierarchy of officials and their emoluments.[66] For the first time the entrance examinations for the bureaucracy were opened to all, indicating a shift in the basis of the regime. Another very important change, in 1839, was to restrict the incomes of officials to direct payments of rice and silver; henceforth they had no more control over revenue derived from specified land or villages. Not only was the power of the emperor and his immediate associates over the bureaucracy thus increased; the general powers of control by the state apparatus were extended. The means varied. Thus, a series of new citadels were built, modelled on seventeenth-century French designs, though with added Vietnamese architectural flourishes. The population could be controlled not only militarily but through registers of population and land, ancient devices now revived and involving the first systematic survey of landholding in the south. We should also note the code of laws drawn up under Gia Long in 1812, the first concerted attempt to do this since the late fifteenth century.

The most important means of controlling the population, however, remained the commune. Here the vast bulk of the population found their daily existence, and through its corporate life channelled their relations with the state. A number of important economic measures were directed towards preserving communal lands from sale and ensuring their regular distribution, though with the innovation that this should be done equally, not according to rank or title. From the rents of these communal lands, or by their direct cultivation, provision was made for such needs as the maintenance of widows and orphans, helping the poor to pay taxes, meeting part of the cost of maintaining local recruits, and paying for teachers and educational materials. The other land in the commune was 'personal share land', divided according to rank, title and age on principles reintroduced from the Le period by Gia Long. Under this system every adult male would have at least a minimum holding (non-titleholders ranged from 0.18 to 1.53 hectares) as long as he remained on the registers, and another to sustain him in old age when he left the register; widows and orphans and the chronically sick also received shares.[67]

There can be little doubt that the contradictions within the commune, expressed by the differences in personal shares, interfered with the operation of what, on paper, seems like a sort of local welfare system. Moreover, as under all previous dynasties, taxes were levied on riceland and persons, with the main burden falling as ever on the ordinary peasants, as did that of compulsory labour on public works, although some attempt seems to have been made to collect taxes in kind at seasons best suited to the payers. State-sponsored drainage of new land in the north and continued settlement in the south (often by military colonies in the more recently Khmer-claimed areas) gave some chance to migrate and relieve population pressure. Lastly, the Nguyen state paid considerable attention to hydraulic works; in 1829 a 'Comprehensive Record of Public and Private Dikes in the North' was prepared.[68]

The role of the commune under the Nguyen and its relations with the state should also be seen in the context of what had happened to the old nobility by the early nineteenth century. To put it briefly, that class was exhausted by the attrition of wars and rebellions which were largely of its own making. Disrupted incomes, actual loss of life (with no replenishment by foreign invasion, as with the Mongols and Manchus in China) and the expense of conspicuous consumption, including of imported goods, had worn them down. Minh Mang thus pushed them aside in 1839, incorporating them into the payments system applied to bureaucrats, albeit at higher rates, and leaving them with little actual land; under the Tu Duc emperor (1848–83) this was finally commuted to a cash payment. The Nguyen period in the years before the French conquest thus witnessed a shift in the class basis of the regime. Its chief support was now the small landowners and rich peasants, upon whom rested the power bloc of royal family and bureaucracy. The unspoken pact was a quite simple one: the locally influential elements effectively agreed to ensure the tax revenue and labour needs of the state apparatus, personified in the emperor, which in any case also ensured their own reproduction, while in turn they were left to run commune affairs without interference and no doubt to their own advantage, whatever the official rules on such matters as division of communal land.

This is not to imply that the new power bloc was any more capable of solving problems than its predecessors, and the pressure on the poor peasants which had increased under the Trinh and Nguyen lords remained unsupportable. According to one estimate there were 105 rebellions under Gia Long and almost 200 under Minh Mang.[69] The reign of the latter, indeed, was marked by serious crises – a rising in 1826–27, then others of minority peoples in 1833 and 1833–35, and an especially serious revolt in the south (1833–35), where the king of Siam took the opportunity to invade. In the nineteenth century as before, peasants, whether Kinh or of the minorities, were subject to tax, forced labour and the abuses of officials. Sometimes this was compounded by natural disasters; thus, in 1854 locusts ravaged part of the Red River delta and the desperate peasants who then rebelled took the name of their non-human tormentors.

The Nguyen imperial system had no way out of its manifest contradictions. The emperors and their senior bureaucrats could give no leads. Despite some reforms, as noted above, their ideas remained highly conservative.[70] The code of Gia Long was little more than a copy of its Chinese counterpart, Confucianism in its most rigid and unyielding form reigned supreme, tolerating no rival. From 1825 measures were taken against Catholic missionaries and converts (who became involved in the southern rising of 1833–35), and Buddhism and Taoism, more popular faiths, also incurred imperial displeasure. It is not surprising that, when some protagonists of 'modernization' who had travelled abroad did emerge in the 1860s, they were unable to get any real hearing.

The Missing Bourgeoisie

Nevertheless, it would be misleading to ascribe the principal blame for the weakness manifested by the imperial regime in face of French encroachments to the reactionary nature of its chief 'feudal' figures, as Vietnamese Communist historians and others have tended to do.[71] There were much more deeply-seated structural and class reasons for the incapacities which became increasingly obvious as foreign gunboats anchored offshore and disgorged troops. As has already been emphasized, radical change would only come about if it had the thrust of a newly rising social class behind it; otherwise the most that could happen was a shift from nobles to smaller landlords and rich peasants as the social base of the regime. Granted, the eighteenth century had seen an extension of the agricultural surface in the south, some area specialization in production of sugar, groundnuts and other crops, and the introduction of new basic food crops like maize into both north and south.[72] But this was no basis for an 'agrarian revolution' which might support others. Productive forces were increased only by using new crops on more land, not by changes of technique; even more crucial, the social relations of production did not change. The nobility were there to gain what they could; then in the nineteenth century the commune displayed its basic contradiction, stabilizing rural life on the one hand – especially in terms of relations with the state – but on the other imprisoning the bulk of its inhabitants behind the bamboo hedge, at the mercy of local petty oligarchs, with only vagabondage, the uncertainties of migration, banditry or rebellion as attempted reliefs. It might even be suggested that it was a particular obstacle to the development of the Vietnamese social formation on the eve of the French invasion that there was no landed nobility, able to play its 'Western' historical roles of either a source of recruits for a rising capitalist class or serving as its opponent and thus aiding the crystallization of that class through struggle (in fact probably both at once).

Nor, conversely, was there any major development of mercantile or manufacturing capital.[73] Granted, partly on the base of the limited agricultural expansion of the eighteenth century, there was an increase of both internal and external trade, and also of manufactures, and hence of urbanization, but in the end its most important consequence may have been the creation of a social scene which could provide a public for the poems of Ho Xuan Huong or Nguyen Du's much-loved story of Kim, Van and Kieu.[74] The relative self-sufficiency of the communes in both agricultural and handicraft production meant that internal trade in staples was limited to such items as iron and salt; as Vu Quoc Thuc has pointed out, there could hardly be said to be a market in rice, when it was produced everywhere.[75] When rice did move, it was basically as tax, or when the state had to relieve famine. Given the general poverty of the peasants, there could be little demand for commodities, and, moreover – at least in the northern heartland – the organization of internal trade discouraged the emergence of big merchants, since a dense network of villages meant frequent markets and the need only to move small quantities over short distances: this was the case with salt, even though the total distance it might cover from its place of production was considerable.[76] As for longer-distance trade, it was mainly in articles for war or conspicuous consumption by the wealthy and vested in the hands of foreigners, particularly Chinese, rather than Vietnamese, or else was a state monopoly. Lastly, movements of prices and currency policy did not contribute to fostering trade. During the eighteenth century mercantile profits were kept low by steadily decreasing prices, the product of the general depression caused by constant wars and rebellions and a shortage of silver for coins.[77] There is no indication of an upturn under the Nguyen, certainly no long secular rise to sustain the development of merchant capital.[78] Even an appropriate monetary system was absent, although the first attempt to introduce a uniform paper currency had come as early as the reign of Ho Quy Ly. In 1760 the Trinh lord rationalized the striking and issue of coins in his territory, but the Nguyen lords were not able to do this; in fact, their debasement of the coinage in the mid-eighteenth century led to speculation by Chinese merchants. They also incorporated Spanish colonial dollars (which arrived from the Philippines) into their currency system.[79] This inability to standardize currency and the tendency to incorporate that of stronger economic forces continued when the Nguyen became emperors. Moreover, they and their advisors seem to have had no real concept of the relationship between prices and currency. Thus, gold and silver coins were assessed only by weight, not buying power, and paper money was introduced in Cao Bang province not to facilitate trade across the border with China but for the 'bullionist' purpose of stopping the northward drain of silver.[80]

Even had merchant capital been able to expand, it would have found considerable obstacles to its development into manufacturing capital, as happened in Western Europe. Under Trinh and Nguyen lords some relatively large concentrations did appear – in mining (though this was largely Chinese) and, more relevantly, in the production of ceramics and sugar, where wage labour was employed.[81] However, these were obviously isolated phenomena. The base from which any putative capitalist manufacturing fraction would have had to develop was much broader and more humble in its control of means of production, the artisans, operating with family labour, apprentices, and maybe a few hired hands in the more affluent cases. Despite the increased urbanization under the rule of the lords, artisan production still in essence meant work within the commune. Since peasant needs and powers of consumption were small, a low level of family specialization sufficed for most purposes, and where land was sufficient there was little pressure to concentrate on non-agricultural production; conversely, poor peasants with insufficient land could not afford to invest in equipment to produce items which most adults could not make for themselves.[82] Where this state of affairs could be transcended, and the specialization of whole villages did occur (in paper-making for example) it was frequent practice in the nineteenth century to limit these only to supplying the imperial court and state apparatus, with payment by 'labour money' rather than an actual price for goods.[83] Again, the most skilled craftspersons were often forced to come and work at court, rather than on their own account: as Woodside puts it, the 'fate of clever artisans in nineteenth century Vietnam was a kind of labour slavery rather than an opportunity to accumulate profits and capital'.[84] Lastly, we must remember the competition from the similar products of south China, imported by the merchants from the same area who already tended to exclude Vietnamese dealers.

In face of these obstacles, artisans and manufacturers might have organized, but insofar as guilds existed they served rather as agents for state control than articulators of class interests. Unlike that of Western (or Japanese) feudalism, the basic structure of the Vietnamese social formation provided no spaces within which a relative autonomy could be enjoyed by the bourgeoisie, and from which its formation as a class for itself could proceed.[85] Without a fully developed bourgeoisie there could be no capitalist class, hence no proletariat; pre-colonial Viet Nam thus lacked both the historical agents of radical social change to which Marxism–Leninism looked.

In lacking a bourgeoisie which might have any real aspirations to become a capitalist class, the Vietnamese social formation of the eighteenth and nineteenth centuries also lacked the class which Stalin had seen as essential for a nation to emerge. This means, first, that nationalism/patriotism was not an ideology of the bourgeoisie and second and consequent on this, did not find expression on the eve of the French conquest through concepts of a nation state.

By the late nineteenth century no class force had emerged in Viet Nam which required such a state as its political expression. Such a process implies a certain form and level of economic development. In a first phase this means a fairly high degree of exchange necessitating internal integration to facilitate the emergence of a 'national' market and permit firm dealings with external suppliers and consumers. In the second phase the bounds of the nation are consolidated on a basis wide enough to meet the demands of the accumulation and reproduction of capital. Although neither of these phases has necessarily to be solely under the control of local 'national' capitalists, it is evident that it is such a class that has an interest in this integration and consolidation and hence in an ideology of nationalism of the 'European' kind. In Viet Nam, as we have seen, internal exchange did not develop to a high degree, and although there were some wealthy merchants involved in external trade these were usually themselves foreigners. Moreover, external exchange could meet demands for luxury goods (which were the bulk of imports) on a sufficiently large scale without calling into question the form of the state, which in fact exercised strong control over it. Even more profoundly, agricultural production experienced no 'revolution' requiring an expansion of markets and providing a basis for capitalist accumulation. On the contrary, although the communes gave a common material base to the formation by dint of their replication in the same shape throughout it, by their very nature they inhibited any development of 'free' labour and commodity production for the market. The lesser landlords and peasants thus remained encapsulated within the communes, while the nobility and bureaucrats were too firmly entrenched in a particular system of extraction of surplus to have any reason to challenge it.

In these historical circumstances, therefore, no bourgeoisie emerged which, in turning itself into a capitalist class, needed a nationalist ideology. There was no occasion to assert that as members of a nation all were equal, a convenient way of cloaking the fact that, in face of noble rivals, an emerging bourgeoisie needs to become more equal than others. Nor did the doctrine emerge that the state's authority derived from its expression of the national will; the Kinh emperor ruled by the mandate of Heaven and expressed the relations of his people with it and with the Earth; ideologically the state was a moral force rather than a secular expression of national aspirations.

The final product of many centuries of pre-colonial Vietnamese history may therefore best be seen as a Kinh nation with a centralized state, but not as a Vietnamese nation state. When the imperial centre was broken and humiliated by the imposition of French rule, it left behind a generally diffused sense of patriotism, which, insofar as it had specific class linkages, was based upon the peasantry not only because of their numbers, but because of its incorporation into their spiritual lives. The peasants had also been deeply involved in resistance to foreign invaders, and it was of great importance that this strong external orientation was basic to the whole phenomenon of national development. This bequeathed to the Vietnamese Communists the extremely ambivalent historical legacy of relations with China. By the time of the French conquest, that power had been simultaneously model and enemy, teacher and exploiter, neighbour and aggressor for more than two thousand years.[86] As Ho and the others found at Geneva, and even more markedly after, such contradictions could not be simply expunged by Marxist–Leninist internationalism.[87]

A second legacy from the past which ran against the current of national unity was regionalism. This found two main expressions. On the one hand, in the mountainous hinterland which extended from the border with China down to just north of Saigon lived the many minority peoples, divided among five linguistic groups (leaving aside Chinese dialects) according to later classification by DRVN experts.[88] Distinct in language, territory, culture and social structure, but lacking a central state to compensate for a relatively low level of economic integration, these may best be termed as nationalities in order to distinguish them from the Kinh.[89] Of course, some of them were either directly incorporated into the Kinh state or tributary to it and shared its resistance to Chinese, Mongol and other invaders. However, that was itself a contradictory relationship which did not necessarily imply a long-term identification.

Leaving aside the considerable differences which existed among people from the centre and the north and even the various provinces, a further, even more important aspect of regionalism was the product of the 'advance to the south'. The changing shape of the whole social formation was recognized by the Gia Long emperor, when he located his new capital at Hue, in the centre, rather than returning to Thang Long (Hanoi) in the Red River valley. He also permitted some administrative decentralization, more particularly a governor-general for the south; the abandonment of this policy by Minh Mang in 1831 was largely responsible for the rebellion two years later. Although high positions in the north continued to be held by southerners, there were also cliques within the bureaucracy based on region. Nevertheless, the consciousness of regional differences ran deeper than rivalries among bureaucratic factions, to include the recognition that the great tidal shift since the late fifteenth century had produced deep and real economic and cultural variations. The Mekong delta in particular was an area which it was difficult to reconcile with the image of what Kinh rural life should be. In 1821 it was commented that:

> This land abounds in swamps, and it is easy for bandits to 'assemble at the sound of a whistle'; moreover, its people do not ordinarily understand techniques of [food] storage, and they do not grow anything other than 'the five cereals.' When they suddenly encounter a year of deficient harvests, it easily produces heterodox creeds.[90]

Although we have already noted the later heterodox creed which produced the tattooed woman in 1940, it must be stressed that these variations by the irony of history were never as great as regional differences in, say, the USA of 1861, although they were compounded and increased by the impact of French colonialism.

Kinh, Thai, Tay, Muong and all other Vietnamese in all parts of the country were to have in common the impact of yet another foreign invader, gradually building up from the mid-nineteenth century. Diverted into Bonapartism, the imperial designs of French capitalism had taken some time to revive after defeat in war. By 1847, however, the combination of trading interests and the naval and military apparatus had sufficiently revived to attempt the forcible penetration of Viet Nam and the whole of what the West called Indochina by firing on ships in the port of Da Nang (Tourane). Such actions could be represented as moves to protect Catholic missionaries and converts, and, by the 1850s, could get a stronger state backing through the imperial longings of another Bonapartism, that of Louis Napoleon. Representing a later, more developed, stage of French capitalism than the merchants and priests of earlier times, it viewed Viet Nam even more greedily.

We have already examined the results of the new imperialism in the previous chapters; above all the creation of new class forces which in time came to make an effective challenge to French rule. What must be emphasized here is that, in attempting to construct a revolutionary terrain upon the basis of pre-colonial Vietnamese history, the Communist leadership faced certain contradictions. Marxist–Leninist orthodoxy led them to seek a national sentiment which could serve as a major driving force in the predicated first stage of the revolution, and also as a base for this among the peasantry. In that sense, doctrine and Vietnamese historical reality were a unity. On the other hand, the Kinh had evolved as a nation without a rising bourgeoisie, thus refuting the received idea of what should have historically occurred. Moreover, the process had not been part of the transformation and overthrow of a 'feudal' system, doctrinally regarded as inimical to the emergence of a nation, but within what might much more accurately have been categorised by the forbidden concept of 'Asiatic mode of production'. Indeed, the centralized state which characterized the pre-colonial formation had been a major factor facilitating the emergence of a Kinh nation.

These deviations of historical reality from doctrine had two consequences. Firstly, in terms of the war of position, as we saw in the last chapter, they left the ICP leaders looking for a national bourgeoisie which was neither a product of pre-colonial history nor of French colonialism. Secondly, and much more positively, the leadership seems to have unconsciously realized that doctrine was pointing them in the wrong direction and this led them to interpret Vietnamese nationalism/patriotism (which they extended to the non-Kinh peoples) in quite a different fashion. For a clear expression of the position which they reached we may turn to Le Duan again, this time to a speech made in August 1957. Commenting upon the first phase of resistance to French rule, led (as he saw it) by the 'patriotic intellectuals', the Communist leader noted that:

...their anti-imperialist spirit and national salvation spirit sprang not mainly from the surviving strength of the feudal regime, but from the spirit of national independence and the millenary culture of these intellectuals and the working masses which developed spontaneously under the royalist banner. Likewise, the modernization movement having a bourgeois democratic tendency and led by the old patriotic intellectuals did not originate from the emerging economic and social basis at a time when the feudal regime in the country was facing bankruptcy and the East shifting from feudalism to bourgeoisie.

Therefore in essence these movements did not reflect the contradiction between imperialism and feudalism, or between imperialism and the economy of the local bourgeoisie which had not yet taken shape, but they mainly showed the contradictions between the spirit of national independence and the aggressive imperialist regime, between the oppression and exploitation by imperialist capital and the toiling people, especially the peasants.[91]

The man who was just then becoming acting General Secretary of the Workers' Party thus gave clear expression to the crucial view of history which the Party needed in order to take position after May 1941. It claimed in fact to be the inheritor of an almost timeless patriotic spirit, which in class terms was in the custody of the masses, rather than of a national bourgeoisie, and which could also be dissociated from the old regime, still characterized as 'feudal.' This was an unorthodox and very partial representation of historical reality. Nevertheless, it gave a tremendous cumulative weight when brought into conjunction with the terrain of class, gender, and ethnic struggle in the fight against first French and then US imperialism.

Notes

1   Le Duan, 'Forward to the Future', in Duan 1977, pp. 527–9.
2   Marr 1981, p. 258. On this theme see also Whitmore 1980.
3   The most prominent colonial scholars were probably Léopold Cadière, Georges and Henri Maspero and Charles Maybon: to these may be added André Masson, a more recent, more derivative but slightly less biased writer. A new approach, based on Marxism, was signalled by Chesneaux 1955 and Le Thanh Khoi 1955, and carried forward in the latter's 1981 book – work on which finished, however, in 1971 (Le Thanh Khoi 1981, p. 448). A non-Marxist, derivative but relatively useful work is Isoart 1961. For those limited to the English language, Buttinger 1958 must be judged in the light of his political commitment to the regime of South Viet Nam (see his own foreword and Chapter 8 of the present work). Hodgkin 1981 is immeasurably superior in its commitment and obviously based on more up-to-date work, including that done in Hanoi. Chapters 2-6 are relevant here. A major work in Vietnamese by a non-Communist is Tran Truong Kim 1964. Special attention should also be drawn to Vu Quoc Thuc 1951, a little known but stimulating work which

remains the most consistent attempt to review Vietnamese history in terms of a unifying theme. Historians in the Democratic Republic (North Viet Nam) produced much original work from 1954 onwards, and I have endeavoured to use this as an important addition and corrective. In that respect I benefited greatly from discussions with staff members of the Institutes of Archeology and Historical Research and the Faculty of History of the University during a visit to Hanoi in March-April 1980. Thanks are especially due to Professors Phan Huy Le, Hong Phong, Van Tao and Van Trong. A major synthesis is the general history edited by the Committee for Vietnamese Social Sciences, *History of Viet Nam:* the first volume covers the pre-colonial period; see *History of Viet Nam* (in Vietnamese) 1971. Useful sketches of certain periods, based on work published in Vietnamese in Hanoi, may be found in Nguyen Khac Vien 1974 and his essay, 'Aperçu historique,' in Vien 1970.

4   Archaeological work reveals a complex culture and class formation, demanding a long period of development under unified rule. See Khoi 1981, pp. 63–7, and also Van Tan 1968 (in Vietnamese), where Van Lang is seen as 'not properly a society with a state' but with 'some elements of a centralized regime' (p. 19).

5   For a recent, detailed discussion of these early kingdoms see Taylor, (unpublished), 1976, ch. 1. For a Vietnamese view see *History of Viet Nam,* vol. I, pp. 31–80.

6   On this see Duy Minh 1963 (in Vietnamese).

7   For a list of risings see Buttinger 1958, pp. 177–8, and for a discussion, pp. 97–9 and 107–8. This author links risings with the upper class and the resistance on a more 'national' basis to the passive resistance of the peasantry. For a different view see Khoi 1981, pp. 111–3.

8   In fact, the Tay, Thai and Muong social formations did begin to move along the same path, developing tribal aristocracies, settled rice cultivation and water-control: see Nguyen Luong Bich 1968 (in Vietnamese).

9   North Vietnamese historians have argued that both the Kinh and the others are equally part of the Vietnamese nation: see Pham Ngoc Lien 1963 (in Vietnamese).

10   Than-Luong 1985, p. 8. By early 1980 Vietnamese historians were tending to deny any borrowings from China, and even to assert the opposite; for example, that wet rice cultivation was taken over by the Han from the Viet (author's discussions in Hanoi).

11   'Marxism and the National Question', in Stalin 1953, vol. 2, p. 307.

12   Ibid.

13   Ibid., p. 313.

14   See ibid., pp. 305–6.

15   'The National Question and Leninism,' in Stalin 1953, vol. 11, p. 351.

16   See Buttinger 1958, pp. 137–41, and Tan 1968, p. 20.

17   See Tan 1968 (in Vietnamese), pp. 20-1, and Nguyen Khac Vien 1974, pp. 32–3.

18   On the Cham and Khmer see Buttinger 1958, pp. 30-8 and passim.

19   See Buttinger 1958, pp. 151–2, and Khoi 1981, pp. 182–92. This episode, not without reason, is given much prominence by North Vietnamese historians: see the official *History of Viet Nam,* pp. 195–211, and Vien 1974, pp. 31–41.

20   For an alternative version of this passage see Truong Buu Lam (ed.) 1967, p. 47.

21   On this see Vien 1974, pp. 44–6, and 'Confucianisme et marxisme au Vietnam' in Vien 1970, especially pp. 204–16, and on popular Buddhism Nguyen Tien Hun 1970, Part II, ch. V.

22   On the mutual permeation of agriculture and religion see further Mus and McAlister 1970, pp. 78–9, and Grivaz 1942, pp. 8–130.

23   This is pointed out in Chesneaux 1955, p. 99.

24   As early as the third quarter of the eleventh century the Ly dynasty were fusing Buddhist themes with the oldest heroic cults; thus, the statue of the Great Buddha put up by the Thanh Tong emperor also signified the reincarnation of Giong, the marvellous boy who had saved his people from foreign invaders. See Taylor 1976, p. 180.

25 The phrase quoted is Buttinger's: see 1958, p. 131.

26 On this literary development see further Vien 1974, pp. 46–9.

27 Its existence is known because it was later substantially incorporated in works which survived: see Vien 1974, p. 49.

28 See Khoi 1981, p. 190.

29 See Van Tan 1968 (in Vietnamese).

30 Stalin 1953, vol. 11, p. 351.

31 Too hasty labelling can distort the presentation of data; thus, for example, Fritjof Tichelman typifies virtually all Asian pre-colonial formations in this way (including Viet Nam) and thus in effect blurs over differences and precludes discussion (see Tichelman 1980, especially Chapter I and pp. 71–84). I prefer to present the characteristics of Viet Nam as I find them, although if pressed I would certainly use the term Asiatic mode, since the feudal model seems quite inappropriate. See also Khoi 1981, pp. 127–38, who finds both terms inappropriate. In recent years Vietnamese Marxist historians have shifted from a blanket use of the term 'feudal' to a more nuanced view of a shift from an Asiatic mode (a term they are still rather reluctant to accept) to a feudalism different from that in Europe, beginning in the fifteenth century. For a valuable summary of their discussions see Phan Huy Le, unpublished, 1986.

32 See Wittfogel 1967, p. 401.

33 See Stalin's 'The Revolution in China and the Tasks of the Comintern' in Stalin 1953, vol. 9, p. 291, and History of the Communist party of Viet Nam: excerpts from Party documents (in Vietnamese) 1979, vol. I, p. 39.

34 At late as the 1930s, villages in north and central Viet Nam, despite many years of the private usurpation of communal land, especially during the colonial period, still averaged 20–25 per cent of their cultivable land in that category: see Table 2.2, p. 31 above.

35 By 1945 the imperial clan was said to number around 10,000: see Lancaster 1961, n. 4, p. 201.

36 For an interesting discussion of the class structure of the minority peoples and their incorporation into the Vietnamese social formation and state see Le Van Lo 1964 (in Vietnamese). The first part of this article is concerned with pre-colonial developments and Lo distinguishes two basic situations regarding the ruling class; Kinh officials were appointed to rule in the highlands and gradually became assimilated as a landholding local aristocracy (among the Nung, for example); or local chiefs were appointed to act for the emperor and this reinforced their emergence as a landholding aristocracy (among the Thai).

37 This is the position of a Soviet historian, M.A. Cheshkov, in Cheshkov 1969, where the concept is employed of a 'State-class'. (The historical period discussed is the fifteenth to eighteenth centuries, but the analysis can be read backwards in this respect.) Cheshkov has been criticised by a North Vietnamese historian, in part along similar lines: see Nguyen Luong Bich 1969 (in Vietnamese). Those who can read Russian might also wish to consult Cheshkov 1967.

38 Bich 1969, p. 44.

39 Vien 1974, p. 26. I have avoided use of his terms, 'domaine' and 'apanage', which in my view give misleading associations with European feudalism.

40 Khoi 1981, p. 178, describes this as the origin of the private estates, but in my view there was already an innate tendency to their creation.

41 These two aspects (moments) of contradiction have given rise to the two predominant interpretations of the communes among modern scholars – the view of Paul Mus and his followers that they were the integrating element in Vietnamese history, the basis of nationhood, and the interpretation, best developed in the work of Vu Quoc Thuc, that the 'communal economy' was essentially static and an obstacle to development. As must be the case with moments of a contradiction, both were of course true.

42 Thuc 1951, pp. 3–50; in general see the whole of Chapters 1 and 2 of the First Part.

43   For further details see Mai Thi Tu and Le Thi Nham Tuyet 1978, pp. 40, 48–9 and 60–7.

44   Data here from a discussion with Professor Hong Phong, Hanoi, March 1980.

45   For discussions of the coming to power of the later Le dynasty (there had been one earlier, in the tenth century) and the achievements of its first eighty years see Khoi 1981, pp. 207–46 and Buttinger 1958, pp. 157–61. For a readily accessible statement of the Communist view, see Vien 1974, pp. 54–62: here Le Loi's insurrection is 'a war at the same time national and popular; with appropriate strategy and tactics' (p. 58). The official Communist *History of Viet Nam* devotes considerable space to Le Loi's uprising (see pp. 239–54) and to the centralization of power in the fifteenth century (pp. 262–84). There is a very full treatment in Whitmore, unpublished, 1968.

46   Tu and Tuyet 1978, pp. 34 and 41–8.

47   Although it is true that the state under the Thai To and Thanh Tong emperors intervened more directly than before in the division of communal land within the commune, in particular fixing the amounts to be given to various ranks and kinds of persons, I find it difficult to attach the significance to this which M.A. Cheshkov does in his article cited above. For him, the state 'was entering directly into relations with the producer with regard to the means of production' (p. 34), thus creating a more unitary relationship between commune members and state apparatus and the basis of the 'State-class'. Particularly given the doubt which may be cast on that hypothetical entity, there does not seem to have been any radical change in social structures and their contradictions.

48   Vien 1974, p. 61.

49   See Dang Phuong Nghi 1969, p. 37, and generally pp. 35–7.

50   Perhaps because in modern times any discussion of the advance to the south must have implications for analysis of the liberation struggle, this theme seems particularly ill-developed in the literature and inclined to be stressed by those opposed to the Communist cause. See, thus, Buttinger 1958, Chapter I passim and pp. 171–5, and the long note 3 in Chapter IV of Buttinger 1967, vol.I, and, for a more philistine account, in which anti-Communism becomes projected onto the Vietnamese as a whole in accusations of 'genocide' and 'colonialism', Fall 1967, pp. 12–16. See also Khoi 1981, pp. 162–5, and Phong Van Dan 1963 and 1964. Brief but useful is Cotter 1968.

51   Estimate by Professor Phan Huy Le, discussion, March 1980.

52   On the popular cult of heroism see Nguyen Tien Hun 1970, Part II, Chapter II. At one point at the end of the 1960s it looked as if historians in the Democratic Republic were about to launch a reassessment of the concepts of patriotism and heroism, when Tran Huy Lieu, then the senior figure among them, actually invited debate on this topic (see Lieu 1969 (in Vietnamese)). In part because of Lieu's death a few months later, but above all because of the central ideological importance for the Party of the patriotism/heroism theme, the articles which followed came down firmly on the side of heroism as a basic part of Viet Nam's national identity. See, for example, Van Tao 1969 and Tran Van Giau 1969 (both in Vietnamese).

53   For details see Le Manh Trinh, 'Dans le Kouang Toung et au Siam' in *Avec L'Oncle Ho* 1972, pp. 210–16.

54   Although it would be a violation of materialism to write the history of pre-colonial Viet Nam in terms of dynasties and their rise and decline, it should be pointed out that the falling-away of imperial families over a period of time was one of the dynamics of that history. Once the enterprise of establishing the new dynasty was past, and the necessary reforms accomplished, bureaucratic routine could take over; the emperor became more and more removed from issues of state unless he made a great effort, and, raised from infancy in the secluded palace amid slaves, eunuchs and concubines, no doubt personally estimable in their own way but by nature with special interests, he could well be attracted more to the senses than to sword and writing-brush. Meanwhile, all around him things fell apart.

55   For details of this gloomy period see Khoi 1981, pp. 245–50, and Buttinger 1958, pp. 162–7.

56   For discussion of the Trinh and Nguyen regimes see Khoi 1981, Chapter VI, Cotter 1968, pp. 18–23, Thuc 1951, pp. 129–37, and especially Nguyen Thanh Nha 1970 and Dang Phuong Nghi 1969.

57   It would appear that it was promotions which were sold, not office itself; entrance to the bureaucracy was still governed by success in examinations (see Khoi 1981, pp. 258–9, though he describes this as sale of office). Nha 1970, pp. 24–6, speaks generally of the sale of titles and duties ('charges'). It should be noted that under the Tran some bureaucratic titles had been sold, without the functions being exercised by the new holder.

58   Some historians have put this development as occurring in the region of Le Thanh Tong: see Woodside 1971, p. 154. Vo Quoc Thong 1952, pp. 21–2, gives an actual date, 1467. This early date seems unlikely, given the Le attempt in the fifteenth century to intervene more closely in communal affairs.

59   On this literary movement see Khoi 1981, pp. 296–300, and Thanh Luong 1955, pp. 29–30.

60   As is to be expected, North Vietnamese historians have paid particular attention to such risings. For a typical discussion see Duy Minh 1965 (in Vietnamese), while the theme runs throughout the official *History of Viet Nam*, vol. I. See also Khoi 1981, pp. 303–9. It should be noted that peasant rebellions are literally characterized by Communist as well as more traditional Vietnamese as 'righteous' (*'nghia'*), thus in the title of the article by Minh – 'Vai tro cua khoi nghia nong dan trong qua trinh phat trien cua dan toc.'

61   This point is made in Nguyen Dong Chi 1964 (in Vietnamese), where the shift is in fact suggested to have occurred by the 1730s and is linked to growing land shortage, attempts to tie the peasants to the land, and discontent at the sale of office. Cheshkov 1969 also postulates a growing gulf between the upper and lower levels of his 'State-class', with the latter providing 'potential ideologues' for popular movements as a result of discontent over income differences, and by the eighteenth century 'not as individuals but as a social stratum' (p.38).

62   On this point see Khoi 1981, p. 314. For the whole Tay Son rebellion (as it is customarily called) and the thirty-year period it inaugurated see the same work, pp. 312–33. Chapters V–VIII of Maybon 1920 are still worth reading, as is Gaultier 1933. Buttinger is weak on this period, preferring to dissolve it into his account of French penetration rather than seeing is as an autonomous part of Vietnamese history: see Buttinger 1958, pp. 175–6 and 233–41. The Vietnamese Communist historians have naturally given Tay Son much attention, almost forty pages (330–68) out of around 400 in the first volume of *History of Viet Nam* for example, and for another extended treatment see Phan Huy Le 1963 (in Vietnamese). See also Hoai Giang 1965, and of particular interest is Nguyen Phan Quang 1962 (both in Vietnamese). Nguyen Khac Vien 1974, pp. 83–93, is a useful accessible statement.

63   Nguyen Phan Quang typifies this as a regression from a first phase of 'revolutionary mobilization' to one of 'feudalization': see Nguyen Phan Quang 1962, especially p. 20.

64   Quang stresses this point: ibid., pp. 13–15.

65   On the Nguyen regime see Khoi 1981, pp. 343–92; Buttinger 1958, Chapter V; and particularly Woodside 1971. For Vietnamese Communist views see *History of Viet Nam*, vol. I, especially pp. 368–86 on the crisis of the 'feudal regime', and Van Tan 1967 (in Vietnamese). For an analysis by a non-Communist Vietnamese historian see Nguyen The Anh 1970 (in Vietnamese).

66   On this, in addition to the above-mentioned sources, especially Woodside, see Jumper and Hue 1962, pp. 17–49.

67   See Ngo Vinh Long 1973, pp. 6–9. Another overly favourable account may be found in Adams and Hancock 1970.

68   Woodside 1971, pp. 137–8.

69 Woodside 1971, p. 135. Long 1973, pp. 31–2, suggests 73 and 234, and over 100 in the period 1848–83.

70 The fullest analysis of this aspect is in Vietnamese, Tran Van Giau 1975. For a summary and discussion in English see the review by 'P.H.' (Phong Hien), *Vietnam Courier*, 43, December 1975, and 44, January 1976.

71 See Van Tan 1969, but also the discussion of the role of the bureaucracy in Buttinger 1958, pp. 286–305.

72 On this see Nha 1970, First Part.

73 See ibid., First Part, Second Chapter, Section II, and Second Part.

74 See ibid., pp. 146–7.

75 Thuc 1951, p. 102.

76 Ibid., pp. 94–5.

77 Dang Phuong Nghi 1969, pp. 64–5.

78 See Thuc 1951, pp. 101–2.

79 Data drawn from Nghi 1969, pp. 102–3.

80 Jumper and Hue 1962, p. 52, and Woodside 1971, pp. 33–4.

81 Nha 1970, p. 107.

82 In this passage I am following a line of argument borrowed from Thuc 1951, pp. 85–7. In general see his discussion on pp. 78–89.

83 Woodside 1971, p. 157. See also his discussion on pp. 31–2.

84 Ibid., p. 32.

85 On this possibility in Western feudal formations see Merrington 1976. I fear that I find my suggestions a better basis for potential explanation than Van Tan 1970 (in Vietnamese), which begs the question by blaming the reactionary policies of the Nguyen dynasty. Khoi 1981, pp. 372–84, has a useful, though untheorized, discussion.

86 For a summing-up in a somewhat similar formula see Chen 1969, pp. 338–9, and the whole discussion on pp. 331–9.

87 Though the opportunity should immediately be taken here to say that I find François Joyaux's emphasis on continuity between imperial and Communist Chinese aims at Geneva exaggerated: see especially Joyaux 1979, pp. 357–9 and 379.

88 See Institute of Minority Studies 1978 (in Vietnamese).

89 The North Vietnamese historian Nguyen Luong Bich in an interesting article distinguishes 'nationality' (*bo toc*) from 'nation' (*dan toc*) as stages in the evolution from clan (*thi toc*) and tribe (*bo lac*), and feels that Viet Nam had reached the last stage before the French conquest. See Bich 1963. However, since he relies on terminological analysis rather than that of social structures, it is not clear what are the essential features of each stage.

90. Quoted in Woodside 1971, p. 96.

91. 'Reassessment of the Leadership of the Vietnamese Proletariat' in Duan nd, pp. 59–60.

5   The August Revolution

In May 1941 the Eighth Plenum of the ICP Central Committee had consolidated a trend which it had begun in mid-1936 and taken position in such a way as to make the weight of Vietnamese history its potent potential ideological weapon. This was not to involve the culmination of history which doctrine suggested, an anti-feudal national democratic revolution in which the Party would play the role of the bourgeoisie, pulling that class in fact behind it. It would not even involve the 'agrarian revolution' against the landlords as a class, only individual collaborators.   It would, however, involve the peasants, the class in Vietnamese history with the most solid continuous existence and therefore the most likely, in face of foreign oppression, to respond to the patriotic message. In building itself a new terrain for struggle, thus, the ICP leadership also created a new contradiction. It turned to a potentially revolutionary class, but not on a class basis; in Vietnamese conditions the needs for national and class liberation were made a unity, but one involved a broad alliance which was inimical to the other.

The new war of position would have to be pushed forward from mid-1941, in continuing conditions of illegality. At the same time, the Party leaders were now more than ever aware of the need for a war of manoeuvre. The world conflagration then in progress, with its immediate results in Indochina, a Vichy administration and Japanese occupation, gave them new opportunities. These were in fact to culminate in the August Revolution of 1945. However, in the preceding four years, upon which the first part of this chapter will focus, the war

113

of manoeuvre took a complex form which would have considerable if not fateful future repercussions. My arguments in that respect run as follows:

- in the period 1941–45 the demands of the war of manoeuvre tended increasingly to create two terrains which were only partially linked, with both involving political struggle but one having a strong military aspect;
- this tendency was reinforced by a geographical separation of activity, with northern and southern centres of gravity;
- activity in the north (Tonkin) involved an alignment towards the border areas of south China and a closer orientation to the Chinese Communist Party.

Before beginning directly to deploy evidence and argument around these themes, however, it seems better to look at what the ICP's enemies were attempting to do during these years. They, after all, still held the initiative until March 1945.

Colonialism in Wartime

Colonial possessions in wartime must always expect extra demands from their masters, and the five parts of Indochina were no exception. However, after the defeat of France, the installation of Admiral Jean Decoux's administration by the Vichy government which served Nazi Germany and the entry of Japanese troops into Tonkin in September 1940 and Cochinchina in July 1941, it was increasingly the needs of Tokyo for labour and raw materials which had to be met.

Given Cochinchina's pre-war status as a world producer, it is not surprising that the basic Japanese demand was for rice. In 1941 585,000 tons were levied, in 1942 973,000, 1,023,000 tons in 1943 and 900,000 in 1944. However, this was not taken from the colony alone; Tonkin, always short of paddy, contributed 130,205 tons (12.7 per cent) in 1943 and 186,130 tons (20.7 per cent) in 1944.[1] As well as other products like jute and coal, the Japanese civil and military representatives expected cash from their French 'allies', as shown in Table 5.1 (between March and August 1945 a further ₽720 million were taken). In theory these piastres were to be exchanged for gold or Japanese yen; in fact they were paid for in virtually worthless 'special yen'.

In face of this situation, the answer of the Decoux administration and the Bank of Indochina was to issue more currency; the amount in circulation rose from ₽42.5million in 1939 to ₽936million in 1945.[2] This, together with the shortage of imported goods in wartime, inevitably meant massive inflation. Taking the cost of living index as 100 at the beginning of 1939, in the last four months of 1943 the official index stood at 339 for a middle level family in Hanoi and 404 for one from the working classes.[3] By June 1945 official figures put the buying power of the worker's piastre in Saigon at 20.2 per cent of its worth in 1939, while in Hanoi it was only 3.3 percent.[4]

114

Table 5.1 Monetary allocations to Japanese forces (million piastres)

1940	6	1943	115
1941	58	1944	360
1942	86	1945	100 (Jan.–March)

Source : Vu Do Thin 1954, p. 37.

The peasants were also under increasing economic pressure. With levies for the Japanese to a large extent taken by the colonial administration in the form of rice, and stockpiles also being built up, payment was fixed in increasingly worthless currency. In order to meet his quota, a peasant had to buy rice himself, and by 1940 the black market price for 100 kilos was ₱350–400, while the luckless seller to the government got ₱25.[5] In addition, due to government pressure to produce cash crops demanded by the Japanese, some land was being taken out of rice production, and increasing quantities of rice were distilled for alcohol which they were using as a substitute fuel. As the war took hold, Allied bombing interfered with coal production in Tonkin and its shipment south, so rice was burned to drive trains and power stations.[6]

Ironically, while economic conditions declined for all classes (though unevenly, workers and peasants as usual suffering the most), social and political circumstances changed more in the period 1941–45 than at any other time under French rule.[7] This was at least true for the urban population, above all the middle strata. The immediate cause of this change was the need for a French response in face of Japanese blandishments offered to Vietnamese nationalism. There was a massive programme for building rural schools, 4,800 in four years, and the number of pupils rose from 450,000 in 1939 to over 700,000 in 1944. In education and elsewhere a much greater use of the *quoc ngu* script was fostered. With French replacements for official posts no longer arriving, high and middle rank jobs held by Vietnamese doubled in the period 1940-44. In a more directly political sense, in May 1943 various professional organizations were given power to nominate to a new Federal Council of Indochina. Even more significant was the emphasis on building organizations, from Boy Scouts to the paramilitary Vanguard Youth in Cochinchina, which provided space for manoeuvre and recruiting grounds for various emerging political forces. True to the semi-fascist themes fostered by the Vichy government in its own part of France, the ideology which such organizations were meant to convey emphasized patriotism and duty; it was part of the whole contradiction of this phase of French colonial policy that patriotism, organizational experience and hope of a responsible job should carry far more weight than simultaneous neo-Confucian exhortations to respect authority. The approach to the peasants, as opposed to educated youth, was best expressed by

115

the replacement of Tonkin village council elections in 1941 with nominations from among those likely to be loyal to France.[8]

Taking Political Position

What were the Communists doing while the colonial rulers attempted to deepen their support, pre-empt nationalism and respond to Japanese pressures?[9] First of all, they had to keep an organizational network in being and attempt to expand it. The distribution of places where Party activists might feel secure was most uneven, and had been reduced by the police actions of September 1939 and late 1940. Despite these blows, there still remained the suburbs and nearby villages of larger cities. The Standing Bureau of the ICP was located in a village on the edge of Hanoi after the Eighth Plenum; capitalizing on existing strength, it was now Party policy to build for itself a stronghold around Hanoi and other cities.[10] Despite continuing police pressure – such that the Hanoi Party Committee had to be re-established seven times between April 1940 and early 1943 – by the latter date the districts north of the city were regarded as a 'security zone' by the ICP.[11] Branches of the various 'salvation' organizations had been set up in most Red River delta provinces. In northern Annam the peasant struggle, including the attempt to seize communal land as in 1930–31, was still continuing.[12] In Cochinchina there were the 'red suburbs' (as the French administrators called them) round Saigon and more directly rural strongholds such as My Tho, where Nguyen An Ninh's work still bore fruit while he was dying in Poulo Condore prison; there was also Cao Lanh to the west, near the Plain of Reeds, already a storm centre in 1930–31. Other contacts were being built up among urban workers; the Party counted eighteen strikes in Hanoi in 1943–44, and there were others at provincial centres like the Nam Dinh textile mill. In Cochinchina official statistics listed 24 strikes between May 1942 and June 1943, and by the end of 1944 the ICP claimed nearly fifty union branches in Saigon–Cholon enterprises and residential organizations in a number of working-class quarters.[13] The need for cadres to carry out this rural and urban organizational work was so great that, from 1943, the Party began to organize escapes and rescues from prisons and detention camps in order to have more struggle hardened comrades at its disposal.[14]

During the war years, the ICP also paid attention to the organization of a particular group which was not in itself a class, women. Thus in September 1941 a conference of cadres in Tonkin called on urban women supporters to use such organizations as savings clubs and knitting groups (proliferating under Vichy sponsorship) as sources of recruits. The conference of the Standing Bureau held in February 1943 again singled out urban areas as a weak spot for the Association of Women for National Salvation and spoke of using cooperatives and literacy classes to extend influence.[15]

Moreover, while continuing to try to organize workers and peasants, the ICP was now committed, at the cost of greatly reducing the radical class content of its programme, to seeking 'national bourgeois' and even landlord allies, since any who did not actively associate with imperialism were welcome. Thus, after only two months of war had passed and eighteen months before the Party actually committed itself to the broadest possible national front, the Sixth Plenum noted that 'Though there are some branches of industry which have the prospect of development in order to supply goods to the war [the] local bourgeoisie...still remain dependent on the French economy.' In consequence, it was expected that, in order to obtain desired reforms or under pressure from 'the mass movement', they would 'move away from the side of the imperialists'.[16]

In any case, the political shift did not markedly occur. In February 1943, the best part of two years after the Viet Minh had been founded, the Standing Bureau of the Party was still complaining that 'In Indochina, there is a lack of a movement for bourgeois national revolution and a youth and student movement. Therefore, the movement for revolution in Indochina is still narrow and has a worker-peasant character more than a fully national one'.[17] It seems that any element of the Vietnamese capitalist class who were radicalized by wartime conditions were attracted to the new government-sponsored organizations, to the more independent ones like the new Great Viet Nam Nationalist Party (Dai Viet Quoc Dan Dang), or to collaboration with the Japanese rather than to the ICP, which could not quickly lose its revolutionary image. Moreover, the social elements at issue as prospective allies were less the Vietnamese capitalists proper than intellectuals and middle strata elements in general, to whose ranks the youth and students mentioned by the Standing Bureau were potential recruits, but who might well prefer to lead them into the alternatives to the ICP just mentioned.

Apart from the problem of expanding on a national basis among class elements which were not necessarily its likely supporters, the ICP in the period 1941–45 experienced other difficulties in taking position politically. On the most basic level, at the time of the 'August Revolution' in 1945 the ICP had still only recruited 5,000 members, including about 1,000 remaining in prison, while the various organizations of the Viet Minh numbered perhaps 70,000.[18] The Party had not yet made a major breakthrough to the peasantry, or was at any rate only just then in process of doing so, in what we shall see to be very extreme circumstances. (This point becomes of particular importance if one views the history of the ICP as involving a shift in class base towards the peasantry, like that of the Chinese Communist Party from around 1930.)[19] The most serious limitation of all, however, was related to the territorial distribution of Party strength. In Chapter 4 emphasis was laid on the shift of the centre of gravity of Vietnamese history southwards, particularly from the early seventeenth century onwards. From data presented in Chapter 2 we can see how French colonialism and the differential impact of capitalism accentuated the economic, social and political variations which inevitably followed that geographical shift of weight. By 1945 this historical process was having a profound effect upon the ICP's fortunes.

It seems certain that, due to the greater openness of ICP activity in Cochinchina in the immediate pre-war years, the police repression of September 1939 was conversely more effective. Similarly, the ill-conceived rising in November 1940 gave the colonial authorities a further chance to shatter Party organization. After this, the location of headquarters in Tonkin and difficulties of communication must have made rebuilding that much more difficult. There is evidence that even the fundamental new line of forming the Viet Minh and national salvation organizations was late in reaching the colony and slow in being carried out.[20] It would seem that the biggest successes were achieved in penetrating the trade union movement (with consequent influence on the strike action noted above) and above all the administration's Vanguard Youth, claimed to be a million strong by mid-1945. Some of the Vanguard's leaders, like Dr Pham Ngoc Thach, later a Deputy Minister in the DRVN, were ICP sympathisers, if not members.[21]

Beyond these factors, the ICP in the south also had a revolutionary rival, the group of Trotskyists who retained an active following in Saigon at least. Even more significant, at least numerically, were the two rural rivals which emerged during the war years. Both were products of the economic and social diversity and complex religious and cultural milieu noted in Chapters 2 and 3 as characterizing Cochinchina and stemming from pre-colonial origins. Reference here is to the Cao Dai and Hoa Hao sects, which by 1945 had developed peasant followings considerably larger than those of the Viet Minh.

Cao Dai (literally in Sino-Vietnamese 'high terrace' or 'high tower') was the Supreme Being which revealed itself in a series of seances to Ngo Van Chieu from 1902 onwards; between then and February 1926, when he was commanded by Cao Dai to reveal to the world the existence of a new religion, Chieu passed on this revelation to a group of converts who were, like himself, colonial officials, or else petty bourgeois and small capitalists by background.[22] So far, the sect appears as a minor attempt by figures representing the intermediate levels of colonial class formation to come to terms with the need to explain their new universe by fusing ancient concerns with spirits with the spiritualism of the West, mixing divination and fortune-telling with table-rapping and the ouija board. However, the new movement rapidly displayed three very important features. First, it built up a large body of doctrine which sought to fuse Confucianism, Buddhism and Christianity into a path to Order, Harmony, Eternal Happiness and Deliverance, a way trodden previously, it was said, by a number of saints, including Joan of Arc, and by Victor Hugo and (later) Winston Churchill. Second, it developed an elaborate hierarchy of adepts, in which mediums played an important part, centred on the great new temple which was built for the faithful in Tay Ninh province, in the north of the colony on the Cambodian border. Third, and basic to these other features, it

118

attracted wealthy supporters – some French through spiritualist circles, but more importantly landowners from the rice plantations of the west, and also many poor peasants from the same area. The class basis of Cao Dai thus was the relationship between big landowner and tenant, now cemented ideologically by the promise that both were equal in seeking the path to righteousness. In more material terms, the rich were offered faithful service, including the free labour which lower adepts were supposed to render higher, the gifts and the levies in kind or cash for the hierarchy and its temples. The poor peasants might hope for plots as tenants, in a situation where many thousands were wandering in search of land and work, either in the Transbassac plantations or in Tay Ninh, where land was bought for settlement. Although such remained the sect's class basis, it did spread also in the 1930s into the other fraction of the peasantry in eastern Cochinchina; in that respect, however, it seems that there it had a significant tendency to schism; for example spawning a separate organization at My Tho.[23]

By the outbreak of the Second World War, Cao Dai may well have numbered 300,000 adherents, and in 1938 it had been recognized as a religion by the colonial administration. The sect's political orientations were another matter.

Pham Cong Tac, an early associate of the founder, had become its second head in 1934, and had turned his mind to secular matters.[24] Contacts were made with Prince Cuong De, claimant to the throne, partner of Phan Boi Chau in his plots and still under Japanese protection; indeed, it was probably the head of the Japanese intelligence in pre-war Indochina who put De and Tac in contact. This commitment to nationalism, albeit of a conservative kind, did not appeal to Admiral Decoux's administration and in May 1941 Tac and the other top leaders of Cao Dai were sent into exile in Madagascar and the Tay Ninh temple was occupied.[25]

A similar fate looked as if it would befall Huynh Phu So, healer, soothsayer, preacher of a purified Buddhism and, in that capacity, founder of the sect named after his native village, Hoa Hao, just before the outbreak of war.[26] Two things are essential to an understanding of the rise and ultimate power of this sect. First, it was solidly based in a long tradition of secret society activity in the region where Hoa Hao village was located, spanning the reaches of the Mekong and Bassac Rivers south of the Cambodian frontier, wild border country under the Nguyen dynasty before the French conquest. At that time it had been home to the Precious Mountain Miraculous Fragrance sect which, continuing as the Religion of Good, was involved in armed resistance to the French and contributed part of the same complex of messianic Buddhism in which the imperial claimant who sparked the risings of 1913 and 1916 found his base. With memories of this movement still strong twenty years later, So made a pilgrimage to one of the holy sites and returned to his village cured of his ailments and became the reincarnation of the Buddha of the Western Peace, who in another manifestation had headed the Miraculous Fragrance sect.

Given this background, and his preaching of a coming millenium with a Buddhist heaven on earth, it is not surprising that So found a following among poor peasants. That is the second crucial point in understanding Hoa Hao – its class roots. With no temples and offerings ('god is not poor' it was said) and a hierarchy of familiar local figures like rich and middle peasants and teachers it could find ready adherence among the peasantry of the middle reaches of the Bassac and Mekong, the transition area between the eastern provinces and the western plantations where the low-yielding 'floating' rice had become established since 1900 and peasant cash cropping petered out (Cao Lanh, in the same area but where Communist links were strong, was significantly an outrider of eastern province tobacco-growing).

It was estimated in 1942 that So already had 40,000 followers, and the colonial authorities suspected him as a possible preacher of nationalism considerably before that.[27] Labelled by them the 'Mad Bonze,' he was first placed in a psychiatric hospital by the Decoux administration, then in May 1941 transferred to house arrest. Nevertheless, as his following grew, his new residence became a place of pilgrimage as, and no doubt the experience of, pressure from the French disposed him more to politics. In October 1942 the Japanese in cooperation with his followers took him away from the French and into their own protection. This event can be taken as marking the beginning of the crucial phase of politicization of both Hoa Hao and Cao Dai. The Japanese occupiers began to cultivate the sects as allies, protecting them from further French reprisals, though Pham Cong Tac remained in exile. What is particularly important is that by the last months of the war the Japanese had begun partly to help, partly to turn a blind eye to, the formation of private armies by the two sects. When the ICP came to make its bid for power in Cochinchina it would have to face the fact that its potential rivals were not merely numerically much stronger but had firepower also.

The situation of the ICP in Cochinchina is given extra point by contrast with events in Tonkin during the war years. There, while the Party's general attempts at organization were continuing, a special nucleus of activity emerged which was ultimately to be the decisive factor in the war of manoeuvre as it moved towards the August Revolution. Once the Democratic Republic which resulted was plunged into war, both that activity and the geographical area upon which it was centred were again to become pivotal. Furthermore, since these involved political forces in southern China and, by extension, the Chinese Communist Party as a whole, they laid the ground for a future relationship of fundamental importance. The activity was, of course, armed struggle and the creation of liberated base areas.

Towards the end of 1938 the future Ho Chi Minh had been sent by the Comintern back to China to make contact with the CCP, now under the uncontested leadership of Mao Tse-tung.[28] It seems probable that the main motivation of the Soviet leadership was to obtain a reliable first-hand report on what the CCP, which since the epic 'Long March' of 1934-35 had had its main base in the remote northern Shensi area, was doing. In December 1936 Mao and his associates, carrying out their version of the Comintern's united front line, had agreed to join with their blood-enemy, Chiang Kai-shek, in resisting Japanese imperialism. In July 1937 the inevitable Japanese attack on China began and thrust deep into the country; in December Nanking, Chiang's capital, was captured. The activities of the CCP thus took on new significance for the world revolution, not to mention Soviet foreign policy (in July–August 1938 and May–September 1939 Soviet forces were to fight bitter local wars against the Japanese on the borders of the part of Manchuria occupied by the latter (Manchukuo)).

Another factor in the equation was the independent position taken by the CCP leaders. In May 1943, when agreeing to the dissolution of the Comintern, they remarked that although their party 'had received much help from the Comintern in its revolutionary struggle...the Chinese Communists had now for a long time been free to decide independently on its policy and put it into effect'.[29] Such independent tendencies had indeed been notable even before the Long March to Shensi and Mao's ascendancy.

The activities which Quoc/Ho began in late 1938 were in fact to lay the foundations for a renewed linkage between the Vietnamese and Chinese Revolutions. After a period with the Communist Eighth Route and New Fourth Armies, Quoc moved to south China. There his Chinese comrades were less strong, but the frontier provinces – Kwangtung, Kwangsi and Yunnan – hosted extensive networks of Vietnamese, employed, for example, on the railways between the two countries. The ICP made efforts to maintain cells there, through which communication could be (somewhat tenuously) made with Mao's headquarters in Yenan.[30] Apparently the Comintern or Quoc himself had informed the ICP Central Committee of his presence in China, and when again forced into illegality in September 1939 it put through a request to the CCP to have him return to his native land. This proved difficult to organize, and in any case it would seem that Quoc preferred to use Chinese territory and the Vietnamese exile community as a base while organizing new moves in the highlands of Tonkin. These were directed towards armed struggle.

We have already noted in Chapter 3 how, in the wake of the Lang Son uprising in June 1940, the ICP Central Committee had decided to create base areas and train armed cadres. This again reinforced the orientation towards the CCP. An extremely interesting development among ICP-aligned intellectuals generally in the late 1930s had been a turning towards work by Chinese Marxists, or at least materialists, in philosophy and history, providing a kind of background to the political and military developments we are now examining.[31] With the Japanese onslaught on China giving much more direct meaning to the menace of fascism, the need for a united front, and hence the policies and experiences of the CCP, had taken on new significance. Symbolically, it was at this time that Dang Xuan Khu took his final revolutionary name, Truong Chinh, meaning 'Long March.' More directly, it was in China that the example was set of a 'national salvation' movement, launched in early 1936 and captured by the CCP just after the Japanese invasion in its 'Ten Great Policies' on 'Anti-Japanese Resistance and National Salvation.' Over the next years a range of national salvation organizations for workers, peasants and others was launched by the CCP, inviting immediate comparison with what the ICP began to do after May 1941.[32]

In the period 1938-39 Vietnamese Communist publications also focused heavily upon the military aspects of the struggle in China.[33] According to one source, the ICP cadres in south China had already sent comrades for guerrilla training in Yenan by the very experienced Chinese in 1938.[34] In June 1940 the Central Committee sent Vo Nguyen Giap (who had already written a piece on the CCP's concept of protracted war) and Pham Van Dong off on the long journey to Mao's headquarters.[35] Stopped short by changing circumstances with the fall of France to Hitler's armies, they instead joined Nguyen Ai Quoc and their other future Politburo colleague, Hoang Van Hoan, near the Vietnamese border. From there they were to journey to Pac Bo the following year for the historic Eighth Plenum.

According to a Kuomintang source, in August 1940 it was agreed to put the ICP under the guidance of the CCP, on behalf of the Comintern.[36] This is not impossible, given that the French Communist Party could no longer act as guide, as was the formal Comintern practice for colonial parties. If it is also true that the ICP was given the task of establishing a United Front for National Independence, this would put an interesting perspective on the creation of the Viet Minh in the following May. In any case, the period 1938-41 witnessed a very significant, though not formalized, coming together of two of the three crucial cases (the other being Korea) in the history of the shift of the world revolution from the West to the East. Having been interrupted in 1927, a linkage was now re-established between the ICP and the CCP which was to have a very important influence on the fortunes of the former up to the Geneva conference and well beyond. Moreover, from 1941 it was to have a significant military aspect, above all in the realm of revolutionary strategy. On his return to his native land, Nguyen Ai Quoc, very soon to assume his better known name, personified this by writing two pamphlets on guerrilla warfare based on his observations in China.[37]

Once installed in the Tonkin highlands Quoc began to write other things, most notably a number of poems about the history and geography of Viet Nam to be used in education classes for local peasants, in which patriotic themes and those of resistance to oppression predominated.[38] Although the wholehearted shift to the national salvation line was fully in accord with his own inclinations and left him free to consolidate his moral authority over the other leaders, he faced the problem that the new approach was not having a great effect in urban areas among the more educated and affluent. When the Standing Bureau of the Party, headed by Party Secretary Truong Chinh, met in February 1943 Ho Chi Minh, as he had now become, was not in Viet Nam. Carrying documents in the new name he had gone back to China in August 1942, presumably to make contact with the CCP and to supervise further training of Vietnamese on that side of the frontier. Arrested by the Kuomintang commander of the Fourth Military Region soon after arrival he stayed in various gaols under hard conditions until September 1943. Aided by Communist sympathisers on the general's staff, he secured his release by agreeing to help organize the Revolutionary League which his captor hoped would group mainly followers of Prince Cuong De and the VNQDD and give political leverage to the Kuomintang, and even more to himself, after the war and the anticipated end of French rule.[39] Since the League did not even join the Viet Minh, probably the most important political result of Ho's last period in China was the contacts he made with agents of the USA, to which we shall return.[40]

Here we should return to the February 1943 meeting of the Standing Bureau, which later Party historians would treat as a turning-point.[41] Truong Chinh and his colleagues, Hoang Quoc Viet and Hoang Van Hoan, were strongly influenced by international events. In June 1941 Nazi Germany had invaded the USSR, bringing the leader of the world Communist movement into the war on the side of Britain and De Gaulle's Free French. In December of the same year Japan's attack on Pearl Harbor brought the USA into the conflict, then the desire in Tokyo to extend its Greater East Asian Co-Prosperity Sphere to the British and Dutch colonies (as well as the Philippines) broadened the Pacific war further. By February 1943 the tide of the German invasion of the Soviet Union had been turned at Stalingrad. Confident now that Japan and the other Axis powers would lose the war, the ICP Standing Bureau looked ahead to the general uprising which must find consummation in the principal towns like Hanoi and Saigon. Probably again influenced by what Mao and the CCP were trying to do in Yenan, Chinh and the Standing Bureau attempted to reach the urban middle strata in particular by publishing a set of 'Theses on Vietnamese Culture' in 1943 and forming a National Salvation Cultural Association.[42] Similarly, in June 1944 the ICP sponsored the creation of the Democratic Party of Viet Nam. If organizations of other classes than the workers and peasants did not already exist to be brought into the Viet Minh they would have to be created.[43]

Developing a War of Manoeuvre

In October 1944 Ho Chi Minh, his health impaired by his imprisonment, returned from China. Whatever the remaining political problems of taking position, he found that a crucial base for an ultimate bid for power had further developed in his absence. This was in the areas of the Tonkin highlands in which units had been maintained since the rising of mid-1940. The local inhabitants were of course minority peoples, and the Party had already profited from its interest in these by being able to disperse some cadres in advance of

123

the French suppressions in late September 1939. Thus its supporters among the Tay and Nung of Cao Bang could shelter Kinh comrades in Tonkin, and the Kor, Hre and Bahnar peoples of the Truong Son mountains could do the same in Annam.[44] In both the Cao Bang and the Bac Son–Vu Nhai bases from May 1941 onwards much educational and propaganda work was done among the minorities; the programme of the Viet Minh, for example, was translated into the Man language in traditional verse form.[45]

In February 1943, at the same time as the Standing Bureau met to review the general progress of the revolutionary movement, the leaders of the two base areas met to coordinate their next moves. The main result was that in August the two were linked by a drive south, led by Vo Nguyen Giap, and one north led by Chu Van Tan, a Nung; these two men were emerging as the military experts of the ICP. Significantly, organizational areas were now being given the names of historic national heroes, like Nguyen Hue, the Tay Son leader.[46] In late 1943, however, French military action put heavy pressure on the Party, especially in Vu Nhai, and the armed units which existed were still only capable of a limited guerrilla war. Something more formidable would be needed to take an offensive, and the embryo of such a force was not created until 22 December 1944, when the Armed Propaganda Company for the Liberation of Viet Nam, comprised of 31 other ranks and three officers, commanded by Vo Nguyen Giap, was set up in Cao Bang.[47]

This very modest beginning raises the issue of the place of armed struggle in the Party's plan at this time, and more generally the strategy by which it hoped to manoeuvre itself to a point from which it could seize power. Thus, it is evident that a close link was seen between military and political activity. In the contribution he had written for the Comintern's basic text on the role of armed struggle in the seizure of power in 1928, Ho had declared that 'In the overall pattern of class struggle, guerilla movements play the role of an auxiliary factor; they cannot of themselves achieve historic objectives, but can only contribute to the solutions provided by another force – the proletariat'.[48] Seven years later, despite his observations in China, Ho's position had not basically changed. The decisive blow in the war of manoeuvre was seen as a general uprising in the urban areas supported by guerrilla activity outside. Making due allowance for Vietnamese conditions, thus, the ICP's doctrine on the final phase of the war of manoeuvre had not changed radically from the 1928 Comintern prescription of an urban general strike and armed insurrection, supported by rural guerrillas. The most important additions had been the idea of preliminary 'partial uprisings' in the rural areas, launched at the Seventh Plenum and confirmed at the Eighth, which noted 'we have the ability to lead a partial uprising in some areas as well as gaining successes through which we take the road to a large general uprising'.[49] At this stage Vietnamese Communist military doctrine contrasted sharply with that evolved by Mao for the Chinese Party, with its emphasis on main force regular armies, surrounding the cities with peasant guerrillas and a protracted war ending in large-scale battles in the field.[50]

The ICP attached more importance to organization in urban areas, since the decisive blow was seen as coming there, rather than by victory on the battlefield. This strategy was to prove correct. The problem for the ICP leaders in December 1944 was, however, to reach the urban areas in order to be able to coordinate the uprising there with rural action. Although reasonably secure in their highland bases in Tonkin they were very remote from Saigon and the south, while the insurrection in centres in Annam would not be decisive. In Tonkin itself, with around 80 per cent of the population living in a radius of less than 150 kilometres from Hanoi, the Party's bases were physically separated even from the bulk of the peasants, not to speak of coordination with cadres in Hanoi and Haiphong. At that conjuncture, on the other hand, events were to begin to move.

The Seizure of Power

The movement in Tonkin was on two levels in the first months of 1945 – the fundamental material level of a threat to people's very existence and the political level which helped to determine what they might do in response. By August a new conjunction of contradictions had emerged which gave ICP leaders their chance to strike.

We have already noted how the two protectorates were always on the margin of hunger, and faced famine if crops failed. In October–November 1944 there was a typhoon in Tonkin and then the rains were late. The shortfall in the immediate harvest was not too drastic (around 7 per cent), but compulsory deliveries took almost 17 percent more, and that made the shortfall catastrophic. With another bad harvest in May 1945, it was calculated that the available rice per head was 11 kilos a month; pre-war consumption had been 26.5 kilos.[51] Moreover, the only mechanism which had acted in the past to provide some rice for sale in the period of 3–4 months after the monsoon, when rice was always short, broke down. Normally, rich peasants with a surplus sold small quantities throughout these months to those in need, but in late 1944 all surplus rice had gone to the government or had been bought up by speculators.[52] The latter even benefited the most when the government belatedly permitted cash payments instead of rice deliveries, since they could sell their rice to those who had none for five times the cash payment, pay cash to the government themselves, and avoid costs of transport to government collecting stations.[53] Lastly, rice could not be brought to Tonkin from Cochinchina, as in the past, since the surplus was reduced there by the compulsory levies and transport was disrupted by war conditions.

In these circumstances the result was simple and drastic: somewhere between half a million and two million people starved to death.[54] Yet at the same time, in the face of French and Japanese intransigence the Tonkin peasants had little alternative but to act for themselves, and particularly from March 1945 this action was led by cadres of the ICP, and generally by Viet Minh members.

In order fully to understand the significance of this, the picture must be widened to take note of developments at the global level of the war. With the Soviet Union on the side of Britain and the USA, the ICP leadership had to modify its positions somewhat. In an analysis issued just after the Japanese attack on Pearl Harbor it was stated that Kuomintang troops would be welcomed in Viet Nam if they came in to fight the Japanese and not as invaders. Economic concessions could even be granted to Britain and the USA by an independent Viet Nam if those powers did not try to help de Gaulle restore French rule.[55] Again, when the Comintern was dissolved in May 1943 to show the new respectability of Stalin, the ICP leadership passed on the decision to its followers with the rationalization that 'the immediate goal of the world revolutionary proletarian class in this period is not to overthrow the imperialist bourgeoisie in general but to overthrow fascism'.[56] It was indeed to be the effects of the Pacific conflict which gave the ICP leaders their opportunity to accelerate their war of manoeuvre.

Under severe pressure from the Allies, early in 1945 the Japanese High Command decided that its forces in Indochina should brush aside the Vichy administration and take direct control, in order to safeguard their last sources of supplies and communication routes.[57] On 9 March this was done, against only sporadic resistance. This coup broke apart the always unstable power bloc between the Decoux regime and the Japanese occupation forces, and the fact that the latter set up a local government for Tonkin and Annam in April under the educationalist and historian Tran Trong Kim did not deceive any patriotic Vietnamese.[58]

One of the decrees of the new government, in June 1945, provided for death penalties for those who, in groups of more than ten, robbed stores of rice and other foodstuffs. This was in response to the movement which had begun immediately after the Japanese coup on 9 March, first of all in Bac Giang province north of the Tonkin delta and then in Bac Ninh closer to Hanoi, then spreading into the southern delta and northern Annam. Led by local Viet Minh activists, the peasants in effect took over village administrations, with or without the support of councils and officials, and confiscated food stocks on French plantations or held by landlords and rich peasants and traders, or even what was already in the hands of the Japanese. The food was then distributed to the needy.[59]

The importance of this movement cannot be too strongly emphasized, for it was the beginning of the ICP's breakthrough to the peasants of the Red River delta. However, it was only part of the Party's new activity after March.[60] On that very day the Standing Bureau met with other leaders and in a three-day conference assessed the situation. Assuming that the Japanese coup would be successful, it was decided that the 'pre-insurrectionary period' was now being entered. General popular struggle was therefore to be launched, centred on the seizure of rice stocks and involving liberation of further areas and extension of guerrilla action. For the civil struggle new slogans were launched: 'Don't let one grain of paddy, cent of tax, recruit or coolie go to the Japanese.' Taking a more distanced stance than in December 1941, it was now held that an Allied landing would help create favourable conditions for a general uprising, but that this must not be made dependent upon such an external factor.[61]

Simultaneous with the Standing Bureau conference, which laid down the new political line, the inter-provincial committee for the unified Cao Bang-Bac Son base (now extended into Lang Son province) decided on an increase of military action. Through March, April and May remaining French garrisons and administrators, who had not been disarmed or interned by the Japanese or had fled into China, were mopped up by the expanding Armed Propaganda units or Viet Minh local forces, first in the highlands, then the midlands and down into the delta and northern Annam. Provincial prisons and prison camps were overrun and cadres freed to resume their work. In Hanoi and other towns propaganda and organizational work was intensified, especially in schools and colleges. Such activity could be extended from the north to Cochinchina, particularly built round a campaign to send money and food as relief to Annam and Tonkin, but in the very different politico-military conditions the actual seizure of local control was not as yet possible there.

Nevertheless, when the Standing Bureau called a Revolutionary Military Conference in April it decided to set up a new 'resistance base' in the colony, along with four in Tonkin and two in Annam.[62] This meant, over the next two months, extending control in the mountains spanning the Tonkin-Annam border, in northern and central Annam, and in north-east Tonkin, centred there on the coal mines. As for the original base areas in the Tonkin highlands, following a further conference in June they were constituted as a Liberated Zone under full control of the Viet Nam National Liberation Committee set up by the Viet Minh National Committee in April, which was in effect now a provisional revolutionary government under Ho Chi Minh.[63] That meant that, in the whole of six provinces and part of four others, a new administrative structure was being set up and new policies implemented. The main policy lines involved confiscation of property from French owners and 'traitors' and its redistribution, along with communal lands, a moratorium on debts, rent reduction, abolition of colonial taxes and forced labour, a limit on working hours, social insurance, achievement of a 'self-supporting economy', universal suffrage, literacy campaigns, and equality among ethnic groups and sexes.[64]

By mid-1945, therefore, the ICP leadership had manoeuvred into a position of considerable strength, solidly in control of a Liberated Zone covering around a third of Tonkin and with firm bases from which to expand and consolidate further, using 5,000 troops who had been organized in May as the

Viet Nam Liberation Army under Vo Nguyen Giap and Chu Van Tan.[65] Nevertheless, the estimated 856,000 people in the Zone comprised only 10 per cent of Tonkin's population, and at least 85 per cent of them were minority peoples.[66] Thus, the last direct move, capitalizing on the anti-famine agitation, had still to be made into the dense Kinh population of the Red River delta, and beyond that the state apparatus had to be seized throughout the country. The Party's opportunity for this came in August 1945. Stunned by the first use of atomic weapons to destroy Hiroshima and Nagasaki, the Japanese power bloc collapsed and surrendered to the Allies. This was on 12 August. From the 13–15 August the ICP held a National Congress of delegates from all over the country, and it was decided to launch the general uprising. A People's Congress held immediately after, representing all elements in the Viet Minh alliance, minority groups and religious communities, endorsed this decision and also ten policies put forward by the Viet Minh National Committee. These substantially repeated those already adopted for the Liberated Zone, but with two significant additions. The first aim was now 'To seize power and establish the Democratic Republic of Viet Nam on the basis of complete independence', and the final one 'To establish friendly relations with the Allies and with the developing nationalist countries, with a view to gaining their sympathy and support'.[67]

Beginning even before the two congresses ended, the ICP and Viet Minh cadres acted. Like the tremors of an earthquake from the Tonkin highlands and delta down through Annam into the Mekong delta the people began to move. In villages and towns administrative buildings were occupied, officials swept aside if they did not join in, Japanese soldiers and those of the Kim government forced to surrender if they resisted (the government had been handed jurisdiction over Cochinchina as well as the protectorates as Japan collapsed). In various ways the actions of demonstrators were combined with those of local defence forces, guerrillas and Liberation Army units to achieve these aims. However, there were significant variations between roughly two halves of the country in the pattern of seizure of power. In Tonkin and northern Annam rural areas were basically seized first, then the urban areas, with Hanoi sandwiched (on 19 August) between such waves of local action. Haiphong and Hue were both taken on 23 August. In southern Annam and Cochinchina, however, the basic pattern was first the seizure of control is Saigon (on 25 August) and other urban centres, then a spreading of the movement out into the rural areas. Later analysis recognized that because of 'many difficulties' in the colony the capacity for local uprisings was only just emerging in mid-August, necessitating moving first in the towns and above all in Saigon, which had a 'decisive' influence.[68] Thus, the different patterns of positioning and manoeuvring in north and south which had emerged since 1939 significantly manifested themselves in August 1945. As we shall see, they were to be greatly compounded within a few months.

128

An Uncertain Grasp

On 26 August the Emperor Bao Dai abdicated in favour of the new government, although he was retained as its advisor, perhaps the ultimate gesture which the ICP made to Viet Nam's history.[69] On 2 September, before an enormous crowd in Hanoi, Ho Chi Minh as President of the Provisional Government of the new Democratic Republic of Viet Nam read its Declaration of Independence.[70] In it, the 1776 Declaration of Independence of the USA was quoted, but there was no reference to the building of socialism.

Yet it remained the case that the now reunited Viet Nam had been freed from colonial rule by a movement led by a Communist Party, the only case of its kind in the history of the world revolutionary movement. The ICP had much of which it could boast. It had positioned itself with skill and pertinacity in face of brutal repression by striking deep roots in the small but sociologically crucial working class, from which it could spread into the peasantry and urban petty bourgeoisie. It had broadened its appeal by playing the theme of the national salvation of an ancient culture (but also by defending the interests of minority peoples), so that it captured, if not an elusive 'national bourgeoisie' then at least many of the better-educated, especially the young. In manoeuvring itself into power the ICP had shown considerable skill in combining political and military means and in using the geography of the country (especially of Tonkin) to its advantage. It had shown a good sense of timing in launching the general uprising to seize the state apparatus. The test of the first year of the new republic would reveal weaknesses which in September 1945 were hidden beneath the aura of success. Nevertheless, the profundity of the Party's triumphant General Uprising in August 1945 must remain one of the axes of the remainder of this study.

The first measures of President Ho's government, in fact, give a rather piecemeal impression. On 1 September, even before independence was formally declared, the Great Viet and other pro-Japanese parties were banned; on 4 September an Independence Fund to which the public could contribute was created; on 6 September a programme for arms production was decreed; on the 7th the poll tax and government monopolies on salt, alcohol and opium were abolished; on the 8th three decrees enjoined a reorganization of the administration of education, the acquiring of literacy by all those aged above eight within a year, and the holding of elections on the basis of adult suffrage within two months.[71] The ICP leaders, who had a very firm grip on the Provisional Government (Ho was also Minister of Foreign Affairs, Vo Nguyen Giap of the Interior, Pham Van Dong of Finance and Chu Van Tan of National Defence), were trying to face up to a situation which demanded rapid action amid great uncertainty.[72] They were trying to consolidate their political dominance and control of state power, to face an appalling financial situation, to come to terms with forces outside Viet Nam, and to carry out the policies laid down at the Viet Minh conference in June. In addition they had to face the

129

continuing famine conditions in Bac Bo (Tonkin).[73] This list of problems gives us one perspective from which to evaluate the work of the new government up to December 1946, when the situation decisively changed.

A second perspective can be drawn from a critical assessment published by Truong Chinh, General Secretary of the ICP (by then formally dissolved) on the first anniversary of the August Revolution. In a series of articles Chinh cited the seizure of power in 1945 as a breakthrough event in Vietnamese history, but made the significant comment that 'the August Revolution did not take on as heroic a character as that of the great revolutions in other countries'.[74] A basic mistake, he felt, lay in not having pushed through the seizure with full determination: 'the error of our revolutionaries consisted in failing to avail themselves of the high tide of the revolutionary movement and of the people's spirit of sacrifice in the decisive hours so as to reduce to a minimum the extent of these shortcomings'.[75] Politically there had been three failures, the incomplete disarmament of the Japanese troops, a 'lack of firmness in the repression of counter-revolutionary elements', and an 'unequal degree of determination throughout the country' which had meant in particular that in Nam Bo (Cochinchina) the Viet Minh leadership had acted out of tune with 'the general line of the Party'.[76] To these had to be added the results of the failure to seize the Bank of Indochina and its assets in August 1945. By the time Chinh wrote his analysis the effects of these errors amounted to a considerable check upon the firmness of the grasp which the Vietnamese Communists had over the politics and economy of their country. Moreover, to them must be added another error, to which he made only very indirect reference, the failure to read correctly the international situation immediately at the end of the war against Japan. Unlike Chinh's direct criticism, which was of local or at most regional cadres, this last factor must be laid at the door of the central ICP leadership, of which he was himself a member.

When the Viet Minh's Provisional Executive Committee took control in Saigon on 25 August 1945 it found itself immediately faced by a rival, the United National Front, composed of the Cao Dai, Hoa Hao, some smaller organizations and the 'Struggle' group of Trotskyists; a second Trotskyist party, the International Communist League (ICL) remained outside. Given that the sects had their own private armies and controlled territory they were formidable rivals, while both the Struggle Group and the ICL had popular support in Saigon–Cholon. The ICP, for its part, had only re-established a committee for Nam Bo in June and for Saigon in July, but it could rely on support from the city's trade unions and Vanguard Youth, which seem to have been closely interrelated.[77] Although sporadic fighting between Viet Minh troops and those of the sects outside Saigon continued, by the end of the first week in September a working agreement between the rival organizations had been patched up, and this enabled the Viet Minh to eliminate the ICL.[78] Some days later it was the turn of the Struggle Group. It should be noted also that the elimination was direct and permanent; leaders like Ta Thu Thau were murdered (in his case in Quang Ngai province on his way back from a trip to Hanoi). Nor was it only the Trotskyists, particularly dangerous from the point of view of the Stalinist ICP, who were thus treated. A great range of political enemies were got rid of, including the veterans Phan Quynh and Bui Quang Chieu – anyone, in short, with a pro-French reputation and/or a political standing and possible following.[79]

The use of such extreme measures by the Nam Bo Viet Minh leadership especially was undoubtedly connected with the crisis they faced in mid-September, with the arrival of British and Indian troops in Saigon whose commander, General Douglas Gracey, rapidly showed himself unsympathetic to the revolutionaries. The ICL tried to organize armed resistance to the new occupiers, but the Viet Minh under Tran Van Giau, veteran Communist and later prolific historian, opposed this. Despite difficulties of communication with Hanoi, in this it undoubtedly reflected the views of Ho Chi Minh's government. There can be little doubt that Ho and some of his immediate associates believed that the United States government would resist a restoration of French colonial administration in Indochina after the end of the war. They had been encouraged in this belief by the American intelligence agents in south China with whom they had deepened relations in March 1945.[80] It is well known that President Roosevelt displayed considerable hostility to British, French and Dutch colonialism, and after his death in April 1945 it might have been expected that his successor, Harry S. Truman, would maintain his attitudes.[81] It was not for nothing that the Vietnamese Declaration of Independence on 2 September quoted that of the USA. But already before Roosevelt's death, and increasingly under Truman, the view of the State Department, that wartime allies should not be alienated and barred from recovering their possessions, prevailed.[82]

At the Potsdam meeting of the major allies in July the original intention of leaving supervision of the Japanese evacuation of Viet Nam to the Kuomintang Chinese under US guidance was modified; this was still to be the pattern north of the sixteenth parallel, but below it the British were to take charge. Unopposed by the Viet Minh forces, and aided by the fact that Japanese troops had also been left by the Viet Minh with their weapons in control of strategic points and were ready to surrender them to him, Gracey moved in his men. On 23 September, with a becoming display of generosity to an old imperial rival, he allowed the French troops and administrators released from Japanese captivity to seize Saigon from the lightly armed Viet Minh: the counter-revolution was underway.[83]

While in Nam Bo the ICP–Viet Minh had only a month in which to try to consolidate their political control before a major crisis arose, in Trung Bo (Annam) and Bac Bo (Tonkin) the situation was quite different. In the old Cochinchina the revolutionaries had the support of most of the Saigon–Cholon working class and other poor and much of the middle strata youth. Outside the capital and its suburbs it was effective in such provincial strongholds as

131

My Tho and Cao Lanh but, further west, whole areas were held by the armed forces of the sects. In the two former protectorates the network of Viet Minh Liberation Committees had spread from the Liberated Zone to almost every district since the middle of August. Upon this basis the Provisional Government, from its seat in Hanoi, could begin to restructure the state apparatus, creating a new terrain on which the Communists could manoeuvre.

That process could be given expression in a new constitution, and on 20 September a drafting committee was set up under President Ho; its six other members included Truong Chinh and two more ICP leaders, but also the former Emperor Bao Dai.[84] In the meantime important measures were taken. With an eye to security, on 13 September decrees were promulgated establishing military tribunals and relating them to the ordinary and security police, the object being to deal with offences 'against the independence of Viet Nam'; informal murder of opponents by local cadres was an inappropriate technique for the new state.[85] Ten days later, as if in recognition of the implicit contradiction between a bureaucratic apparatus fully armed with security powers and popular democracy, Decree 64 established a Special Inspection Committee to review the workings of the administrative machinery and hear complaints from citizens, with power to pass cases on to a Special Tribunal composed of the President, Minister of the Interior and Minister of Justice.[86] As to the nature of the future bureaucracy itself, it is significant that, in mid-December, existing (hence French-trained) civil servants were ordered to remain at their posts.[87]

Given that it was impossible to replace the central bureaucracy with more dedicated nationalists and Communists, it was all the more essential for the ICP leaders to establish an effective presence in the localities. Measures were taken to curb spontaneous action by poor peasants. By early November the Provisional Government was already instructing Provincial Administrative Committees that 'The rice fields and cultivated lands will not be divided, as false news has put about'.[88] On 22 November Decree 63 prescribed Administrative Committees and Peoples Assemblies at village, district and province levels, and also for the three Bo; a further decree a month later extended this system to Hanoi, Haiphong, Saigon and five other municipalities.[89] As we shall see, it was not possible by late November to apply the new system in Nam Bo. But especially as the Democratic Republic came under the stress of war after December 1946, it was to prove the most effective instrument of President Ho's government in Trung Bo and Bac Bo. Not only this, but the impact of the new system was revolutionary in the village context. First of all, it changed age-old units and boundaries. Village communes were grouped together and previous communes were down-graded to hamlets affiliated to remaining ones; according to official sources numbers were reduced to a quarter of previous communes in the Red River delta and a half in the highlands.[90]

This in itself was an enormous change, facilitated no doubt by many communes' loss of population in the famine. Within the villages, the introduction of popular election of Assemblies, which then chose the Administrative Committees (which in turn chose the district and province committees), the principle of service without pay, the obligation of committees to report back and proportional representation in ethnically mixed areas were innovations which threatened to destroy the power of the old oligarchs. Moreover, the old associations and festivals of the tutelary spirits were abolished, and, conversely, it was one of the duties of the new organs to work with the various Patriotic Associations for peasants, youth, women and others, to develop their interests. These would also sponsor new ceremonies and festivals, now honouring Fatherland rather than old gods and spirits. A beginning was made in the revolutionary change of peasant consciousness.[91]

Along with the new administrative structure as an instrument of penetration and change must be taken the policy on education. The decrees of 8 September 1945 did more than enjoin literacy within a year, with fines to be paid for non-compliance; they established free compulsory education in *quoc ngu* script in the primary schools and night schools for peasants and workers. The popular education service which was also created could base itself on the Association for the Dissemination of Quoc Ngu, founded in 1938 and rapidly penetrated by ICP cadres.[92] In further support of the literacy drive the Association was developed with committees at all administrative levels, while there were groups of cadres to control what happened, propagate ideas and prepare manuals.

In terms of the taking hold of the population, however, most stress in the period 1945-46 must be laid on the fight against the famine, which was undoubtedly the major success of the Viet Minh government. Moreover, it is undoubtedly true that a proper understanding of the other actions of that government can only be reached if we keep in mind the fact that throughout the period it could feel the skeletal hand of mass hunger upon its shoulder.

We saw earlier in this chapter that, after the May 1945 harvest in Bac Bo, the available rice was estimated at well under half of the normal supply. During August, as the Viet Minh was seizing power, floods in the Red River valley reached record heights, affecting over 40 per cent of the rice fields and causing a loss of 300,000 tons of rice in the October harvest, around 30 per cent of the regional total.[93] Then, from September to December, drought – often coupled with floods as scourges in Viet Nam – hit the highlands and destroyed half the expected crops, mainly manioc and sweet potatoes, basic foods for the ethnic minorities and essential bridges from the October to the May paddy harvest for the Kinh. All these calamities took place in Bac Bo, but in northern Trung Bo floods also hit. With the total harvest for Bac Bo well under half the average 'tenth month' harvest yield for 1938-43, it was estimated in November that there was enough rice for three months *at a consumption level less than half of normal*, so that massive famine might be expected beginning in February 1946.

Now the government had to take hold. In mid-November a Minister of

Agriculture was appointed, a post previously lacking.[94] A few days later a Central Committee for Rapid and Intensive Production was established. An order was put into effect that all those with unused land must turn it over to anyone willing to till it, and for this purpose all such land had to be declared to village Administration Committees; the same principle was extended to draught animals and implements. First share of any products was to go to the tiller, but the means of production would revert to the owner after the harvest. In addition, especially in urban areas, people were encouraged to grow vegetables and 'dry' crops wherever they could. These measures would take time to have effect, and meanwhile food was brought into the Red River delta from the Bac Bo highlands and southern Trung Bo. Moreover, after 6 March 1946, for reasons which will become clear shortly, it was possible to resume limited imports from Nam Bo. Most important of all, the May 1946 rice harvest was a record, a million tons compared with a 1938–43 annual average of 680,000. By that time secondary crops were being harvested, and in greater quantities than ever before; maize yields were four times the normal, soya beans two and a half, while altogether in 1946 600,000 tons of such 'dry' crops were produced against the usual 250,000 or rather more.[95]

Thus, although many people were hungry in the period February–May 1946, and some no doubt actually starved, the huge disaster which would almost certainly have destroyed the new regime was averted. Good local organization and the mass response of the people (along with deserved luck in the bumper May harvest) accounted for this, while from another perspective the effort involved provided an excellent opportunity for mass mobilization. As an official publication put it at the time:

> The boundaries of villages, the limits of provinces, territorial divisions do not any longer constitute walls which prevent people from being one. At the same time, social preconceptions are disappearing; the rich just as the poor, the intellectual as the worker, each knows that his fate is tied to that of others and of the community at large, that the action which would save his neighbor is the action for his own personal safety.[96]

This social solidarity was not yet permanent, but what had been achieved was a more decisive breakthrough to the rural population than ever before; it may be argued that it was the fight against famine in 1945–46 which secured the final penetration of the peasantry by the Viet Minh and ICP.

In theory, however, the Indochinese Communist Party did not exist after 11 November 1945. To understand why it was formally dissolved we must penetrate more deeply into the politics of the Democratic Republic in 1945–46. The first attempts to build a new state apparatus and to develop education, the fight against famine, were not taking place within a vacuum where the struggle for power had no place. We have already seen that in Nam Bo the French counter-revolution had started only a month after the Viet Minh began to try

134

to take control. Strikes in Saigon–Cholon and urban guerrilla warfare did not tip the balance back, and from the end of September new French troops began to arrive. In the next months they pushed out from the capital of the region, re-occupying provincial and district centres, often against fierce resistance.

Meanwhile, the Provincial Government's position in Bac Bo was not completely secure. As in the south, the situation tended to be determined by a foreign presence, in this case the large number (180-200,000) of Kuomintang troops who from October 1945 stationed themselves at points down to the sixteenth parallel. In theory a liberating force, their presence resembled more an army of occupation. Thus, they effectively brought with them their own set of 'collaborators', since travelling in their baggage train, as it were, came politicians of the old VNQDD and the Viet Nam Revolutionary League.[97] Picking up contacts which they had retained in exile, the two groups emerged respectively around 8,000 and 1,500 strong, as against maybe 70,000 adherents of the Viet Minh in Bac Bo. Nevertheless, these numbers were sufficient to secure each of them control of provincial and district centres along the routes followed by the Chinese troops down to the delta, the Viet Minh's followers moving out into the villages.[98] In Hanoi itself the two nationalist parties waxed impudent and even violent towards the Viet Minh and its government from under the Chinese umbrella. Moreover, the Great Viet party may have been illegal but it was not dissolved and coups were on its mind; in alliance with others it had probably been intending one in August to pre-empt the Viet Minh.[99]

In this situation of induced competition the ICP leaders could either decide to take immediate vigorous action against their rivals or else manoeuvre round them. True to their emphasis since the Eighth Plenum on national unity above all else, after a meeting lasting three days it was announced on 11 November that the ICP was going into voluntary liquidation in order to prove that the Vietnamese Communists 'are always disposed to put the interest of the country above that of classes, and to give up the interests of the Party to serve those of the Vietnamese people'. Those of its more than 20,000 members wishing to pursue their theoretical studies further, it was said, might join the new Association for Marxist Studies. In fact, all this was pure camouflage; there is plenty of evidence to show that, out of the immediate limelight, the Party went on organizing, recruiting and propagandizing just as before.[100]

The first trial of strength among the contestants for national leadership came with the election to the new National Assembly. Hard bargaining among them necessitated postponing this, but polling finally took place on 6 January 1946. Existing evidence makes it somewhat difficult to reconstruct the results, since there is dispute among authorities even over the number of seats to be contested.[101] Two things are certain. First, it was one of those elections noted less for punctilious administration than for high turnouts where such were allowed at all (apparently not in VNQDD and Revolutionary League areas) and vast majorities for some candidates (Ho got 98 percent, Giap 97 percent of votes cast in their constituencies). Second, despite such features, it probably expressed reasonably well the political balance of forces in terms of popular support at the time, at least in Bac Bo and Trung Bo; Nam Bo seems only to have been allocated 18 seats despite having almost a quarter of the population because of the difficulty of holding elections there in a state of war, and only one delegate may have arrived in Hanoi.[102] Likely figures for the different groupings after the election are thus: 'Marxists' and Viet Minh 92; others favourable to or members of the Viet Minh but contesting apart 72; VNQDD and Revolutionary League 48 and Independents 90.[103] On the strength of these figures the VNQDD and Revolutionary League, already granted 70 seats in the pre-election bargaining for which they only had to nominate without contest, found their way into a new National Coalition Government in March. Ho and his lieutenants were apparently still unsure of their grasp on power and yet again opted for a 'national' image. As a result, the new government contained only two known Communists among the twelve full Ministers, three others (Democrat and Socialist) aligned with the Viet Minh, three from the VNQDD, one from the Revolutionary League and three non-party Ministers.[104] Vo Nguyen Giap was one of those dropped, and now began to turn his attention increasingly to military affairs.

The forming of the new government was itself consequent upon a shift in the balance of the struggle with France. As we have seen, this had already taken a military shape in Nam Bo less than two months after the August Revolution and had not gone well for the Viet Minh. As later analysed by a Party historian, there were three main weaknesses. Modern weapons were scarce, as Truong Chinh pointed out in his mid-1946 analysis, because of the failure to disarm the Japanese or seize other stocks. In addition, southern cadres and rank and file had little or no combat experience. Moreover, the bulk of the units (so-called 'divisions') which formed in the rural areas to resist the French were not Viet Minh-controlled, but rather were composed of elements originally organized as paramilitary forces by the Vichy administration or Japanese who now showed a distinct tendency to looting; one 'division' was led by the head of the VNQDD Nam Bo committee.[105] In order to bolster the resistance, Le Duan and Hoang Quoc Viet were sent south to confer with comrades there at a meeting in My Tho on 25 October 1945, thus beginning for the former a close association with the struggle in Nam Bo.[106] Possibly as a result of their report, the Provisional Government launched the 'Southward March'. This was the movement of troops, but it was also an important transfer of political and military cadres south to stiffen organization there; French intelligence sources placed the number involved at around 100.[107] At this time also Tran Van Giau, who had shown himself heavy-handed in dealing with non-Communists and seems to have had no talent for military affairs, was replaced by Nguyen Binh. Under his guidance the original 'divisions' were replaced by 25 regiments.

However, in April 1946, by the time this reorganization was getting underway, President Ho's National Coalition Government had come to terms with the French. After negotiations which had proceeded intermittently since September, on 6 March 1946 an agreement was signed by Ho and a VNQDD representative on the Vietnamese side bringing the Democratic Republic into the new Indochinese Federation and wider French Union; within these groupings the Republic was to be autonomous, including having its own army, but the Declaration of Independence was in effect being forgotten. French troops would be permitted to return to Trung Bo and Bac Bo until 1952. Closely linked with this accord was a second, between France and China, whereby in return for giving up its pre-war extra-territorial rights and other concessions, the former secured Chinese agreement to withdraw the troops stationed north of the sixteenth parallel.[108]

On the very day Ho signed the agreement French ships were waiting off Haiphong to begin landing troops, although they were delayed when recalcitrant Chinese artillerymen fired on them. Given this obvious eagerness to re-establish a colonial presence which was only partially changed by the new form of the proposed French Union, it is apposite to ask why the Communist leaders and other patriots should have been prepared to make the agreement. Some elements of the explanation are already clear. Focusing on the Communists, we have seen that their political dominance was by no means complete and their grasp on the state apparatus not absolutely firm. At the same time, they were centrally involved in the use of that apparatus to fight famine and reduce illiteracy. Militarily they had no hope of beating the French in Nam Bo, only of fighting a long holding action. Finally, by early 1946 they were extremely anxious to be rid of the Chinese occupiers: as Giap put it later, 'We agreed to allow 15,000 French troops to enter the North for a specific period of time in order to boot out 180,000 brutal soldiers of Chiang Kai-shek who declared they would remain here indefinitely.'[109]

The supposed allies had indeed proved a burden. They had exacted a monthly subvention of 60 million piastres, reckoned in Chinese dollars at an artificially high rate for the latter, thus permitting speculation and high profits on the Hong Kong currency market.[110] At a time of hunger in Bac Bo and northern Trung Bo they levied 400 tons of rice per day for their own consumption, and no doubt speculation.[111] To these formal burdens on the Vietnamese population were added pillaging by privates and the more impressive dealings of senior officers; for very many of the occupiers the operation was a business venture. For the Communists, an extra political burden was the protection which the Chinese commanders extended over the VNQDD and Revolutionary League.

To meet these and other expenses the Provisional Government had found a pitiful P1,250,720 in the treasury when it took power in August 1945 – 0.42 per cent of the estimated (colonial) budget expenditure for Indochina for the year.[112] Financing the new Republic thus became a matter of expedients, the launching of the Independence Fund already mentioned with a 'Gold Week' in which women in particular were exhorted to give their jewellery; this raised

370 kilos of gold by one account, worth ₱20 million.[113] Much of this seems to have been used to buy confiscated Japanese arms from the Chinese and generally to keep various of their high-ranking officers happy, since speculation in gold was one of their non-military pastimes.[114]

Such necessities were not the worst of the government's financial concerns. Much more important was the inability to stabilize the currency, and here the key element was the failure to seize the Bank of Indochina, which continued to act as it had always done in the heyday of colonialism. Thus, without any concern for the assets of the new Republic, in November 1945 the Bank unilaterally cancelled its ₱500 notes; only those issued before 9 March 1945 could be redeemed, at 30 percent discount. At a blow, therefore, government reserves, private savings and Chinese currency speculation were threatened. Only under Chinese pressure and with American mediation was the decision reversed.[115] This experience had the effect of starting to push the Provisional Government in the necessary direction of issuing its own currency. This was probably first done in Nam Bo – where the confrontation with the French was direct – at the end of January 1946, possibly clandestinely from My Tho and in connection with a visit by the Minister of Labour in an attempt to reorganize an 'underground' administrative system parallel to that now being re-imposed by the French.[116] As relations with France became more uneasy, it was decided in August to begin to circulate the new dong throughout the country, and in November the National Assembly formally ratified the creation of the new national currency.[117]

In the middle of 1946 the Communists were able to compensate in part for the financial weakness of the government behind which they operated by increasing their political hold over it. With the departure of the Chinese in June, Giap turned his fierce attention on the VNQDD and Revolutionary League. Although these were represented in the government, at the lowest levels relations between them and the Viet Minh–ICP had remained those of mutual abuse and even kidnappings and murder. Communist sources later alleged that the VNQDD was intending to carry out a coup on 12 July.[118] In any event, Giap, as Chairman of the Supreme Council of National Defence, now ordered his forces into action against the two nationalist groupings in Hanoi and elsewhere. With little resistance leaders and followers were imprisoned, shot or driven into exile, including some but not all of the ministers.[119] These moves were partially counterbalanced by the earlier formation, late in May, of yet another broad grouping of pro-independence forces, the National United Front of Viet Nam. This linked the Viet Minh, alongside which it was to operate, with the Democrats, trade unions, Buddhist and Catholic groups, VNQDD and Revolutionary League. In July the new Socialist Party, formed to group non-Communist leftists, also joined.[120]

Although the Communist leaders displayed a surety of touch in directing the Viet Minh and consolidating politically in Bac Bo and Trung Bo, they were much less certain in dealing with France. The continuing guerrilla war required the gaining of time to strengthen the armed forces by negotiation, but the ICP leaders seem genuinely to have felt that the path to national liberation must be through negotiation. They seem to have understood neither the determination of French capitalism to recover its Indochinese assets nor the true countervailing strength of the French left. When Ho Chi Minh and Pham Van Dong led a delegation to a conference in the metropolis in June, after inconclusive discussions at Dalat in April, they certainly behaved as if they could negotiate real autonomy for the Democratic Republic within the French Union and eventual full independence. Yet on 1 June Admiral Thierry D'Argenlieu, Carmelite monk and naval officer in the true tradition of the medieval Christian fighting orders, but also High Commissioner for Indochina, had recognized a declaration by pro-French politicians of an autonomous Republic of Cochinchina within the Union. In the same month a separate administrative zone for the minority peoples in Nam Bo was declared. The principle of divide and rule was obviously far from dead.

Two months of discussion at Fontainebleau yielded no real fruits for Ho. As for the French left, the presence even of Communist Party members in the government meant little, for they supported the idea of the French Union, which it became increasingly clear was not intended to relax the French power bloc's control over the colonies' economies, defence and ability to broaden their foreign relations. President Ho stayed on in France after the others left and secured a so-called 'modus vivendi', signed on 14 September, the main feature of which was a promise to restore confiscated French property and to make future changes in its status only with the agreement of the French Republic.[121]

In the last months of 1946 events moved ineluctably to a final crisis. At the end of October the National Assembly met in Hanoi and endorsed a new government formed by Ho Chi Minh. With the weakening of previous partners since the middle of the year the VNQDD could be left with only one ministry, while the Revolutionary League had none; six Communists, a Democrat and a Socialist outweighed the five non-party members.[122] The Assembly also ratified the new constitution, but this soon proved to be of greater symbolic than practical value. Giap and his military apparatus, in a rather more hard-headed fashion, had been acquiring weapons both within the country and from abroad and setting up repair and even some production facilities.[123] In addition, from about the middle of the year Resistance Committees had been established in the villages of Bac Bo and Trung Bo to organize local forces for guerrilla warfare and self-defence. None of these activities proved to be misplaced. On 23 November, using a dispute over control of customs and armed clashes as an excuse, the French suddenly launched a massive air and naval bombardment of Haiphong, with perhaps 6,000 deaths as a result.[124] The French capitalists, politicians and military men concerned with Indochina had obviously learned nothing from their experience of the Second World War; the colonial clock was to be turned back to the situation, and methods, of 1930–31.

The final rupture came in Hanoi on 19 December when, evidently believing that the capital was scheduled for similar treatment by the French, Ho's government ordered Viet Minh troops into action first. Seven and a half years of full-scale war lay ahead.

The Content of the Revolution

The preceding review of the first seventeen months of the Democratic Republic of Viet Nam gives us a perspective upon the August Revolution. In that respect it can be seen as both a revolution and not a revolution, a contradictory phenomenon. The contradiction lay in this: long years of exploitation by colonial capitalism had given the ICP a chance to take root in the workers, peasants and other poor and from there put itself in a position to take advantage of the Second World War to seize control of the state apparatus and set up the Republic. That was revolutionary but, on the other hand, the strategy which the Party had learned from the Comintern and the objective limits of the class struggle (with the workers, peasants, and others only partially mobilized) had led Ho and his lieutenants into adopting a form of national struggle by a broad united front. That removed the deeper revolutionary content of expropriation of Vietnamese capitalists and landlords (except those actually branded as 'traitors') and radical social change.

Of course, throwing out the French necessarily had radical implications, and these were spontaneously taken up (and programmatically by the International Communist League) in 1945. Thus, in public services and other enterprises originally taken over by the Japanese from American and British owners, or otherwise abandoned, management committees were sometimes set up by the workers in August, and in the next months poor peasants spontaneously occupied land. But this was not in keeping with the 'national democratic' revolution being led by the ICP, and such actions were reversed by the new government. In a speech on Independence Day, 2 September 1945, Vo Nguyen Giap as Interior Minister already promised that foreign and local property would be safe, and eight days later this was backed up by a decree.[125] Only the Hanoi waterworks, Air France radio equipment and a metal works useful for arms repair and manufacture were nationalized. Although land rents were ordered to be decreased by 25 per cent in Bac Bo on 13 November 1945, that would still leave them at 30 percent or more of the total harvest, and the same decree guaranteed landlords that they would be paid. As for urban capitalists, deals in gold and currency during the Chinese occupation opened many avenues for their talents, while shortages of goods throughout the full seventeen months under review were cool water to merchants thirsty for profits; thus, in April 1946, the controlled price of a metre of calico was P10, but on the 'parallel market' it was P25-30.[126]

In the light of this very cautious attitude towards completing the political

140

revolution with a social one, it is easier to understand how the Communist leaders could also believe that a negotiated independence, forgetting the original Declaration, could become possible over a period of years. Imperceptibly, faith in the 'revolutionary' capacities of the 'national bourgeoisie' and even of most landlords – though certainly not the big men of west Cochinchina, like Bui Quang Chieu – grew over into trust in the word of French politicians. Haiphong on 23 November 1946 blew that illusion apart. Moreover, the war that was now beginning would in time involve an even more formidable capitalist power than France. The USA, less than six months after the Second World War ended, was already beginning to look with suspicion at the ambitions of its erstwhile ally, the USSR, in Eastern Europe and elsewhere. In February 1946 George Kennan's celebrated cable to Washington introduced the concept of the 'containment' of the new world power, which he saw as inherently expansive. US military circles quickly picked up the idea; in July the Joint Chiefs of Staff stated their opinion that the Soviet objective was 'world domination'.[127] Less than two weeks after the Haiphong attack, in briefing an emissary to Hanoi, Dean Acheson, the Acting Secretary of State, spoke of Ho Chi Minh's 'clear record as agent [of] international communism'.[128] Not only was the hot breath of a revived French colonialism now beginning to blow against the DRVN in the north as well as the south, but the international chill of the Cold War could also be felt in Hanoi.

Notes

1   Figures from Nguyen Khac Vien 1975, p. 91.
2   Vo Quoc Thuc 1951, p. 219.
3   Ibid., pp. 220–1.
4   Vu Do Thin 1954, p. 31.
5   Ngo Vinh Long 1973, p. 131.
6   Buttinger 1967, Volume I, p. 240.
7   For a discussion of this aspect of the war years see Deviller 1952, pp. 83–8, Woodside 1976, pp. 216–8; and Hammer 1966, pp. 30–3. A generally useful discussion of all aspects of the war years is in McAlister 1969, Part Four.
8   See Woodside 1976, pp. 139–42.
9   For the complex politics of the Japanese occupation see Smith 1978a and Nitz 1983 and 1984.
10 See Do Thinh 1975 (in Vietnamese).
11 Ibid., p. 47, and *History of the August Revolution* 1972, p. 43.
12 *History of the August Revolution* 1972, pp. 38, and 39–40.
13 For this urban activity see ibid., pp. 49–51.
14 Ibid., pp. 61–2.
15 Mai Thi Tu and Le Thi Nham Tuyet 1978, pp. 120–1.
16 'Resolution of the Party Central Committee, 6, 7, 8 November 1939,' *History of the Communist Party of Viet Nam: Excerpts from Party Documents* 1979 (in Vietnamese), pp. 237 and 239.
17 'Party Documents 1939–1945,' p. 385, quoted in Thanh Dam 1975 (in Vietnamese).

18   Elliott, (unpublished), 1976, p. 99.

19   Thus Chesneaux says that 'the war of national liberation against the foreign occupier had at the same time the character of a struggle for the social liberation of the peasantry' and sees this as 'the same fundamental mutation as occurred in China' (Chesneaux 1971, p. 220). Vietnamese Communist scholars seem to have differed with Chesneaux less over his fundamental sociological assumption than over his view that the ICP became interested in a peasant strategy only from May 1941 onwards (see Chesneaux 1971, pp. 219–20, and Tran Van Giau 1972 (in Vietnamese)). Western scholars not on the left also share the assumption: see, for example, Duiker 1976, pp. 283–5.

20   See Woodside 1976, p. 216.

21   Nguyen Khac Vien 1975, p. 99.

22   For basic discussions of Cao Dai see Gobron 1948 (English translation by Pham Xuan Thai 1950); Phan Truong Manh 1950; Thuong Vinh Tanh, Cao Tiep Dao and Pham Cong Tac 1953; Fall 1955; Nguyen Tran Huan 1958; Joan L. Schrock et al. 1966, Chapter 20; Oliver 1976, also Oliver, (unpublished), 1972; Werner, (unpublished), 1976 and 1981; Woodside 1976, especially pp. 183–8; Smith 1970. An important account emanating from the sect itself is Dong Tan (in Vietnamese) 1967 and 1972.

23   Further on the social basis of Cao Dai see Werner, (unpublished), 1976, Chapter II, and for a comparison with areas of Communist strength, pp. 173–9.

24   On the politicization of the sect by Tac see ibid., pp. 188–218. Contrary to his designation in most accounts Tac did not take the title of 'Pope' but first 'Superior' and then 'Supreme Chief' (ibid., p. 186).

25   Specifically on the politics of Cao Dai in this period see Huan 1958, p. 211: Devillers 1952, which remains the standard account of the war years, pp. 88–95; and Duncanson 1968, pp. 150–1.

26   Hoa Hao has attracted less attention by western scholars than Cao Dai, doubtless because it did not incorporate European ideas and personages. A study by a Vietnamese has recently gone far to fill the gap. See Hue-Tam Ho Tai 1983. See also Fall 1955; Schrock et al. 1966, Ch. 23; Duncanson 1968, especially pp. 121–2; Woodside 1976, especially pp. 188–92. For an account from inside the sect see Nguyen Van Hau (in Vietnamese) 1969. A useful discussion of its doctrine is in Popkin 1977, pp. 204–9. The most accessible account of doctrine by the sect itself is *Biography and Teachings of Prophet Huynh-Phu-So* 1966 (text in Vietnamese, French and English).

27   Estimate in Brocheux, (unpublished), 1969, pp. 186–7.

28   Basic sources for what follows are Vu Anh, 'De Kungming à Pac Bo,' in *Avec L'Oncle Ho* 1972, Nguyen Luong Bang, 'Mes Recontres avec l'Oncle Ho', ibid., Chen 1969, pp. 34–5; see also Hodgkin 1981, pp. 296–8; on Mao's ascent to dominance see Rue 1965.

29   Quoted in 'Statement of the Praesidium of the ECCI on the Dissolution of the Communist International', Degras (ed.) 1960 vol. III, p. 480.

30   The best account of this is in Vu Anh, 'De Kungming à Pac Bo'. *Avec l'Oncle Ho* 1972.

31   For details see Marr 1981, pp. 280–1.

32   See Selden 1971, pp. 116–17, and Johnson 1962, pp. 89–90. For the text of the 'Ten Great Policies' see Brandt, Schwartz and Fairbank (eds.) 1959, pp. 242–5.

33   For a list of titles see Marr 1981, n. 88, p. 401.

34   Boudarel 1977, p. 172.

35   On Giap's writing see Marr 1981, p. 278. Further on the proposed mission to Yenan see Boudarel 1977, p. 23, and Giap, 'Ho Chi Minh, Père de l'Armée révolutionnaire du Vietnam,' *Avec l'Oncle Ho* 1972, pp. 283–4.

36   Chen 1969, p. 41. A subsidy to the Vietnamese of 50,000 Chinese dollars a month was also supposed to be part of the arrangement, along with the training of cadres in Yenan.

37   Marr 1981, p. 278.

38   See Marr 1981, pp. 284–5, Woodside 1976, pp. 220–1, and Phan Ngoc Lien 1973 (in Vietnamese) for a different perspective. Quoc had used the same technique when

teaching Vietnamese in Moscow: see Nguyen Khanh Toan, 'En l'URSS avec l'Oncle Ho,' *Avec l'Oncle Ho* 1972, pp. 148–9.

39   See *History of the August Revolution* 1972, pp. 58–60. Devillers 1952, pp. 103–5, varies in details. The most detailed account of this episode is in Chen 1969, Chapter 2.

40   Ho was in contact with the US Office of War Information in south China after his release from gaol, and there was even an attempt to recruit him to work on wartime propaganda in San Francisco: on this see Patti 1980, pp. 50–1.

41   See *Fifty years of activity of the Communist Party of Viet Nam* (in Vietnamese) 1979, pp. 63–4.

42   See Marr 1981, pp. 363–4, especially n. 153, and *History of the August Revolution* 1972, p. 54, for quotations from the 'Theses'.

43   For a different view see *History of the August Revolution* 1972, p. 56.

44   For the first contacts of the ICP in the Truong Son see Ta Xuan Linh 1974b, pp. 15–16.

45   See Vo Nguyen Giap's reminiscences in Vo Nguyen Giap 1975, pp. 119 and 125. For training and educational work generally in the bases see pp. 109–11, and Elliott 1974, pp. 27–30.

46   For these developments see *History of the August Revolution* 1972, pp. 4–7. The most detailed and authoritative account on the Communist side of the development of its early military organization is *History of the Vietnamese People's Army* (in Vietnamese) 1977, Chapters 2 and 3. It should be noted that this official history traces the lineage of the People's Army back to the defence units set up in Nghe An and Ha Tinh provinces in 1930–31 (see pp. 17–31).

47   *History of the Vietnamese People's Army* 1977, pp. 114–18. See also *History of the August Revolution* 1972, pp. 65–6.

48   'The Party's Military Work among the Peasants', Neuberg (ed.) 1970, pp. 264–5. I accept Wollenberg 1970, pp. 22–3, on Ho's authorship.

49   *History of the Communist Party of Viet Nam: Excerpts from Party Documents* 1979, p. 340.

50   See especially Mao Tse-tung 1938a and b, and for the struggle to establish his views within the CCP Rue 1966 *passim*. It should be clear that I disagree strongly with the alternative view of Duiker that after May 1941 the ICP adopted a 'Maoist' strategy based on 'the deliberate use of the peasantry as a major force in the revolution, and the adoption of guerrilla tactics in an attempt to utilize the strength of the rural population to surround the cities peopled by the bourgeoisie and controlled by the colonial power' (Duiker 1976, pp. 284–5).

51   See Hoang Van Duc 1946, p. 4.

52   For a detailed account of the regulatory mechanism see Vu Quoc Thuc 1951, pp. 221–4.

53   Tran Van Mai, 'Who Committed this Crime?,' reprinted in Ngo Vinh Long 1973, p. 226. This short work is the reminiscences of a wealthy man who was involved in some relief work at this time and gives a vivid picture.

54   The first estimate, 5–600,000, is quoted by McAlister 1969, p. 156, and comes from French sources. The second is from Long 1973, p. 130.

55   See *History of the August Revolution* 1972, pp. 36–7.

56   Truong Chinh, 'The question of the dissolution of the Communist International', *Communist Studies*, No. 2, 24 September 1943, reprinted in *Liberation Banners* 1976 (in Vietnamese), Part I, p. 153.

57   For details see Nitz 1983.

58   For developments between 9 March and mid-August see Smith 1978 (a), pp. 286–95.

59   Party historians were later to make a striking historical analogy:
     If in the Russian October Revolution the watchword: 'Peace, bread and land' had been an imperative claim of large masses and had rallied tens of millions of Russian workers and peasants for an uprising to overthrow the Kerensky bourgeois government, in the August Revolution of Viet Nam, the slogans 'National Independence', 'seize paddy

stocks to save the people from starvation' were pressing demands of our masses, which rallied and stimulated the entire Vietnamese people to stand up and overthrow the domination of the Japanese fascists and their agents (*August Revolution* 1972, p. 89).

60   On this activity see ibid., pp. 84–5 and 89–95.

61   Ibid., pp. 72–5. A full Plenum of the Central Committee would normally have been called for such an important discussion, but time did not permit (ibid., p. 72, note). For an English text of the 'Instruction' issued after this conference see *Breaking Our Chains* 1960, pp. 7–17. Text of the slogan from a leaflet in Room 7 of the Museum of the Revolution, Hanoi.

62   For the decisions of this conference see *Breaking Our Chains* 1960, pp. 23–42.

63   For the resolution of the June conference see ibid., pp. 52–7.

64   For a full list see *History of the August Revolution* 1972, p. 99.

65   Ibid., p. 97. There was a third commander, Tran Dang Ninh, a former printer from Tonkin who was to die in October 1955.

66   Statistical data here from McAlister 1969, pp. 159 and 161.

67   For the list of policies see *History of the August Revolution* 1972, pp. 177–8.

68   *History of the August Revolution* 1972, p. 134, *Fifty years of activity...* 1979, p. 75. For further details see pp. 132–5 of the former work and pp. 73–5 of the latter.

69   The last of the Nguyen rulers (although that in name only) did not depart without dignity, expressing 'a certain regret in looking back on Our 20 year-old reign, during which We have been in an impossible position to render any appreciable service to Our country', so that 'We are happy to assume the status of free citizens in an independent country' (abdication speech, in *Vietnam, a New Stage in Her History* 1947, pp. 1 and 2.).

70   Ho Chi Minh 1977, pp. 53–6.

71   See ibid., pp. 178–80; Vo Nhan Tri 1967, p. 110; and Smith 1978 (b), passim.

72   There is not complete clarity about the political composition of this government. One source states that eight of its fifteen members were from the ICP, four from the Democratic Party, with one non-party Catholic and two 'technicians' (Sacks 1959, p. 325, n. 149). A report prepared for the US State Department (by Sacks) in 1949 speaks of six Ministers and three more from the Viet Minh (*Political Alignments of Vietnamese Nationalists* 1949, pp. 76 and 149).

73   With the August Revolution it seems appropriate to begin to use Vietnamese terms instead of colonial ones, thus Bac Bo (Tonkin), Trung Bo (Annam) and Nam Bo (Cochinchina), except where French usage is deliberately followed for political clarity.

74   Truong Chinh 1960, published in facsimile in Fall (ed.) 1963, p. 39. This comment has been deleted from the text published in Truong Chinh 1977.

75   Ibid., p. 43.

76   Ibid., pp. 34–40, passim.

77   Hai Van 1975. The figures given there of 200,000 Vanguard members, 120,000 of whom also belonged to unions, must be greatly inflated (p. 26). A source written much closer to the event gives the more credible figure of around 50,000 Vanguard Youth and Vanguard Women (Mai Van Nguyen (in Vietnamese) 1947, p. 29).

78   For details see Sacks 1959, pp. 153–6.

79   For a detailed account of these political murders from an anti-Communist perspective see Tran Ich Quoc 1958, pp. 88–92. Communist sources avoid specifics and speak in such terms as those quoted from Truong Chinh above: interestingly, he condemns 'extremist' methods in Quang Ngai province (Chinh 1963, p. 40) – some regret may have been felt by ICP leaders in the case of Ta Thu Thau.

80   Patti 1980, pp. 50–1. In March 1945 Ho was contacted by the US Air Ground Aid Section, the role of which was to rescue shot-down airmen, and the next month by Major A. Patti, head of Indochinese operations for the Office of Strategic Services (see Fenn 1973, pp. 65–84, and Patti's own account, Patti 1980, pp. 83–8).

81   On Roosevelt's views see Louis 1977, *passim*.

82 On the question of the Viet Minh's hope for help from the USA see Drachman 1970, pp. 121–2. He argues (pp. 147–58) that the Office of Strategic Services, the main US intelligence organ in contact with the Viet Minh, was acting without liaison with the State Department, and this seems confirmed by Patti's account of his experiences in Hanoi from August until October 1946, when the OSS was officially disbanded. From the same source, it is obvious that Ho's contacts with Patti must have reinforced his view that the new DRVN could work with the USA; Giap, and probably Chinh, were more suspicious (Patti, 1980, Part Three). Further see Warner 1972.

83 The most detailed account of the British role is Rosie 1970. See also Colton, (unpublished), 1969, Chapter IX, and Patti 1980, Chapters 31 and 32. Standard Western sources for the political aspects of the discussion in the remainder of this chapter and the next are Devillers 1952, Lancaster 1961, Hammer 1966 and Buttinger 1967, vol. II. Easily accessible accounts from the Vietnamese Communist side are Nguyen Khac Vien 1975, Chapters VI and VII, and Bui Dinh Thanh 1966.

84 Smith 1978 (b), pp. 575–6.

85 See ibid., pp. 581–2.

86 Ibid., pp. 582–3.

87 Ibid., p. 581.

88 Devillers 1952, p. 184.

89 Smith 1978b, pp. 580–1. and for further discussion Fall 1956, pp. 24–30; Vu Quoc Thong 1952, pp. 295–326; and, from the Communist point of view, Vu Han, 'Les Comités du Peuple' (1946). Detailed discussion of formal structures and powers can also be found in Ginsburgs 1962, but it should be noted that this relies heavily on Soviet sources and so is in a very particular sense secondary.

90 Tran Ngoc Danh 1947, p. 4.

91 As usual, acute remarks on this are to be found in Vu Quoc Thuc 1951, pp. 229–33.

92 Details taken from 'La Lutte contre l'Analphabétisme au Viet Nam' 1946, pp. 19–24.

93 Data drawn from Hoang Van Duc 1946, which is the main basis for this discussion, pp. 4 and 5.

94 The reason for this is unknown, but may be related to disputes among top ICP leaders over policy, especially with regard to measures against landlords: see Smith 1978b, pp. 599–600.

95 Total figures from Doan Trong Truyen and Phan Thanh Vinh 1964, p. 24.

96 Duc 1946, p. 15.

97 Patti 1980 (p. 290 and n. 18, p. 562) says there were never more than 50,000 Chinese present at one time. Further on the VNQDD and Revolutionary League (usually referred to from its Vietnamese name as the Dong Minh Hoi (DMH) in 1945–6 see McAlister 1969, pp. 232–9, and Colton (unpublished) 1969, pp. 443–77; for a Vietnamese anti-Communist view, Duong Chau 1958, pp. 20–23; and for a Communist view Giap 1975, pp. 29–30 and 62–5.

98 Estimates from McAlister 1969, p. 233. The latest Party history seems to suggest that opponents seized these centres in fact during the general August uprising (*Fifty years of activity...*, p. 75).

99 Chau 1958, p. 11. Further on the Dai Viet see Colton (unpublished) 1969, pp. 435–43.

100 Quotations from a communiqué, 11 November 1945, cited in Sacks 1959, p. 158. Membership figures from *Fifty years of activity...* 1979, p. 93. The same source, p. 92, retrospectively admits that the Party continued to control power and consolidate and develop itself.

101 Thus, McAlister 1969, p. 239, speaks of 374, Devillers 1952, p. 200, of 350, Fall 1956, p. 10, of 444 and Smith 1978 b, p. 577, of 329 in the original Election Decree and 70 more added later; I am inclined to accept Smith's figures.

102 McAlister 1969, p. 239.

103 *Political Alignments* 1947, p. 152. To the total of 372 may be added the 17 from Nam

Bo, who did not arrive, leaving another ten seats unfilled for some reason if Smith's figures are accepted, which seems tenable.

104 Ibid., p. 77 and see also p. 150: Vice-Ministers maintained much the same balance.

105 Le Tan Tien 1965, p. 62, see also Hoang Van Dao 1965, p. 237 (both in Vietnamese), and 'A Study on the Evolution of VM Forces in Nam Bo from 1945 to 1953', (unpublished), 1964 (translation of a French intelligence report), pp. 4–6.

106 *History of the Vietnamese People's Army* 1977, vol. I, pp. 195–6 (in Vietnamese).

107 See Vo Nguyen Giap 1975, pp. 38–40; 'Evolution of VM Forces', p. 5; and, for a picture of one of those transferred, the quotation on pp.139–140 of Turley 1975.

108 For further details see Hammer 1966, pp. 153–4. The account of the chief French negotiator, Jean Sainteny, is generally useful for this period, see Sainteny 1953.

109 Giap 1975, p. 102. On relations with the Chinese see also pp. 41–4 and 58–61.

110 There is a good account of this in Smith 1978b, pp. 591–2. See also Chen 1969, p. 138, and generally on the Chinese occupation pp. 15-54.

111 Ibid., p. 3, n. 11.

112 Calculated from figures in Smith 1978b, p. 589.

113 Vo Nhan Tri 1967, p. 110 and Elliott 1975, p. 1. A Note preserved in the Museum of the People's Army in Hanoi lists a total of ₱22,466.30 in cash and ₱429.55 in gold for 7 and 8 September ('Results of a meeting and two "days of gold" beginning on the 7th and ending on 8th September' (in Vietnamese), nd).

114 Smith 1978 (b), pp. 592–3.

115 Tri 1967, p. 109; Smith 1978b, pp. 593–4; Nguyen Ngoc Minh 1966, p.201.

116 Truyen and Vinh 1964, p. 21; Smith 1978 b, p. 595; Limbourg 1956, p. 11 though the date is given there as December 1945. Nguyen Xuan Lai states that the new currency was first issued in southern Trung Bo since the French had not yet re-established control there (Nguyen Xuan Lai 1976, p. 116).

117 Tri 1967, p. 110.

118 Tien 1965, p. 52.

119 One from each party continued to serve. For details of the operations see Colton (unpublished) 1969, pp. 713–17.

120 Devillers 1952, p. 272.

121 For a detailed account of Dalat, Fontainebleau and the modus vivendi see Hammer 1966, pp. 159–74.

122 *Political Alignments of Vietnamese Nationalists* 1949, table on p. 153. The same source, p. 83, speaks of one Revolutionary League minister, as does Hammer 1966, p. 181; Devillers 1952, p. 313, says that neither of the ICP's rivals remained represented. Duiker 1981, n. 4, p. 157, lists 2 DP and only 1 independent.

123 McAlister 1969, pp. 247–55 and 297–305, has a very interesting discussion of the build-up of the Viet Minh forces, based largely on French military archives to which he was given access.

124 For a detailed account see Lanoue 1971a.

125 Smith 1978b, p. 598, citing *Pages of Recent History* (in Vietnamese) (Hanoi, National Salvation Cultural Association, nd), p. 25.

126 Vu Do Thin 1954, p. 50. For views from the Communist side of general economic developments in 1945–6 see Tri 1967, pp. 105–11, and Nguyen Ngoc Minh (ed.) (in Vietnamese) 1966, Chapter II.

127 Leffler 1984, p. 366.

128 Document 81, Porter (ed.) 1979, p. 128.

146

6 The political economy of liberation war to the turning point

From September 1945 until December 1946 the Democratic Republic of Viet Nam had to contend diplomatically with the re-occupation by France of much of its territory, while in Nam Bo it contested this with arms through its Viet Minh surrogate. From the end of 1946 onwards the situation was in a sense simplified: throughout the country the confrontation became one of armed struggle. By mid-March 1947 French forces had consolidated their hold on the main centres of the Red River delta and Ho Chi Minh and his government faded back into the highlands of the Viet Bac from which they had emerged to seize power in August 1945. The ICP leaders now faced a situation without precedent in the history of their movement. Indeed, in order to find such they had to look back to pre-colonial struggles against Chinese and Mongol invaders; it is no accident that, in reviewing the first experiences of war, Truong Chinh was to make reference to such heroes as Tran Hung Dao and the Quang Trung emperor.[1] Putting the issue in terms of the theoretical framework of this study, the comrades now had to find new patterns for their wars of position and manoeuvre so that they might lay out a terrain upon which they could win victory. This and the next chapter will attempt to demonstrate a number of propositions. Thus, my contention is that in the seven and a half years of fighting from December 1946 to July 1954 the ICP leaders:

– successfully mobilized enough people and resources to force the French (and US) governments to negotiate;
– did this at the cost of seeing Nam Bo move out of the main terrain of struggle;

147

- conversely, created an even stronger bond between what happened in Bac Bo and China;
- only belatedly brought the national and social revolutions into line with one another;
- however unwillingly, helped place the Vietnamese Revolution at the centre of the world confrontation between the USA and USSR.

These propositions will be approached from the viewpoint of another, namely that the period from late 1950 until mid-1951 forms a watershed between two distinct phases of the liberation war.

The Consolidation into Zones

In Nam Bo most territory and people were already under French control by the end of 1946. However, there were some bases where the Viet Minh forces could be safe, which they could at times expand, and from which they could always sally forth in units of varying strength. The most important areas were in the Ca Mau peninsula, on the Cambodian border north of Tay Ninh, on the coast of Kien Hoa province south-east of My Tho, and 'Zone C' and 'Zone D' in the rubber plantations north and east of Saigon. In these areas of forest and swamp the ICP had been able to regroup its cadres and could build up a supply infrastructure based on the rice and money levied in surrounding areas. Viet Minh guerrillas, however, were active in many places. Not even Saigon was safe, for there operated notably the famous 'Win or Die' 750th Battalion with its women's section named after the heroine Nguyen Thi Minh Khai, which in June 1948, for example, attacked a meeting of French officers being held in the Majestic Cinema.[2] In southern Trung Bo the Viet Minh had a safe area stretching from behind the port of Nha Trang westwards up into the highlands of Darlac province, and another running along the mountain chain from Quang Ngai province south for about 150 kilometres. In northern Trung Bo nothing the French could do could shake the liberation movement's hold on the coastal strip between Hue and Quang Tri known to the colonial forces as the 'Street without Joy'.

As for the Red River delta of Bac Bo, between April 1949 and May 1950 the French forces waged nine campaigns to clear it. Even then, although they claimed full control, there were 'combat villages' that remained closed to them, like Tan Thuat in Thai Binh province which by mid-1954 was to claim to have been the scene of 657 engagements resulting in the deaths of 857 enemy soldiers.[3] The largest area of the north held by the Viet Minh, although it was only sparsely populated and mostly by minority peoples, was the Viet Bac, where President Ho established his government. Although in the last months of 1947 the French drove along the highways through the mountains and managed to occupy provincial centres and to hold the forts along the Chinese frontier, this region remained the training centre for the Main Force units which the Viet Minh began to develop along with its guerrillas from around September 1947. From there also they could launch their later campaigns, and, in the same secure zone, armaments could be manufactured and repaired.

The French government's necessity was to build a state apparatus for the whole of Viet Nam which would permit both control of internal policies and integration into a wider French Union. The local control was naturally intended to be that of French capitalism, but some cloak of 'national' legitimacy had to be thrown over the colonial nakedness. In the end the formula was the 'Bao Dai solution'. In March 1946 the ex-emperor had been sent on a mission to China in his capacity as advisor to the government of the Democratic Republic, but had never returned. The passage of three more years convinced both the French government and Vietnamese landlords, businessmen and professionals that he was the only possible alternative head of state to Ho Chi Minh. In March 1949 the Elysée Agreements brought Bao Dai back, with that title rather than his old one, to a new Associated State of the French Union which was to have its own army and limited diplomatic representation, even though France was still to control defence and foreign policy. The new State absorbed the supposedly autonomous Republic of Cochinchina, where in any case a provisional government for all Viet Nam had been declared in May 1948.[4]

Bao Dai's reported comment on his new position showed a pleasing realism – 'There is no Bao Dai solution, only a French solution.'[5] Nevertheless, his installation made it possible for him to form a Council of Ministers, initially with him as its President since he could find no suitable collaborator. The new state was thus constructed from the top down and, although its institutions generally remained paper creations, what was on paper is instructive enough. Thus, ordinances promulgated in July 1949 spoke of the 'will of the people' and stated that 'Government must act in accordance with national opinion and not substitute itself in a definitive fashion for the popular will', but the new National Assembly was to be consultative only and its representative element was less than in Cochinchina under direct colonial rule.[6] The various organs of local and central administration, which were created by decree, failed to disguise a power game in which Bao Dai, his Council President of the moment and the French civil and military chiefs manoeuvred more or less warily round one another.[7] As for legislation, this was by ordinance and decree, with execution left to an administration still heavily French, if not in personnel then in training, while often the military were in effect the local administrators. For the same reasons of security, there were numerous local 'fiefs' which were tolerated by the French commanders so long as their chiefs and private armies kept out the Viet Minh. This was particularly true of Nam Bo, where Cao Dai and Hoa Hao warlords controlled large areas west of the Mekong and the latter in particular waxed rich on levies extracted from merchants transporting rice to the Saigon market. French sources in late 1947 reckoned Cao Dai forces at 30,000 men and Hoa Hao at 10,000.[8]

In September 1946 the Cao Dai Supreme Head, Pham Cong Tac, had returned from exile in Madagascar and early the next year he broke definitively with the Viet Minh. The similar action by the Hoa Hao was made irrevocable when, in April 1947, their prophet Huynh Phu So was lured into the Plain of Reeds by Nguyen Binh, the Viet Minh commander, and murdered. By late 1947 the Catholic Bishop Ngo Dinh Thuc, brother of Ngo Dinh Diem, was raising a private army in his diocese of Binh Long.[9] Similarly in Bac Bo, the Catholic bishoprics of Phat Diem and Bui Chu just south of the Red River delta remained autonomous enclaves. In Hanoi, and generally in the delta, the Vietnamese part of the administration was in the hands of the reemerged Great Viet Party which, during the Chinese occupation, had run its own military training courses, attended also by VNQDD members, and now set out to infiltrate the police, army and university.[10]

The Bao Dai solution was thus at once a disguise for a mainly military assertion of power by the French power bloc, which had evolved the formula of the French Union to meet post-war conditions, and an uneasy attempt to balance among rival and basically uncontrollable political forces. Both aspects were expressions of the class forces which lay behind the new state form.

Like its political and administrative structure, the economy of the new Associated State remained a shaky and externally dominated affair. From the end of 1948 money was flowing in for reconstruction under the 'Bourgoin Plan' in the form of reparations for war damages, loans for development and subsidies to rice producers.[11] Despite this, French capitalists remained wary of committing themselves. Indeed, there was something of an exodus of French capital from September 1945 onwards, much of it moving into the African colonies where the metropolitan grip seemed stronger; thus, by late 1950 the Bank of Indochina itself, the giant of the pre-war economy, had only one-eighth of its investments in China, South Asia and Indochina.[12] Rather distant on the horizon there loomed a new presence – US capital. Thus, in July 1946 a new company was formed to exploit the phosphate deposits in the Thai country of Bac Bo, and this had links to the Florida Phosphate Company.[13] On the whole, however, direct US investment was slow to come in – the 30 per cent interest in the new Air Vietnam being exceptional – and the main link remained trade, with rubber accounting for 98 per cent of US purchases between 1946 and 1950.[14] There was, moreover, an important strategic concern, with Saigon being seen in Washington as a vital link in a military transit route through Casablanca to Manila.[15]

Rubber production gives us another angle on the development of the economy after 1946, showing how in uncertain conditions only big capitalists could survive. At the end of the Second World War, there were 956 rubber plantations in Nam Bo, with 884 of them covering less than 250 hectares each and totalling 25 per cent of rubber lands, while the 24 biggest covered 25 per cent. By late 1952 only some 55 of the small and middle-sized plantations had come back into production, averaging less than 70 hectares each and totalling around 0.53 per cent of the land; about one-third of the rubber land in 1945 had been lost to production.[16] Other productive enterprises came only slowly and uncertainly back into operation after the virtual collapse of the economy in 1944–45. Thus, the output of the coal mines was 262,000 tons in 1946, a tenth of the 1939 figure, and in 1949 had only risen to 377,000. The Nam Dinh cotton mills did not get back into business until 1948. The resistance against the French was obviously also a factor: the match factory at Vinh was destroyed by Viet Minh action in 1947 and set up in Saigon at the end of 1948. In less than a year, however, it was supplying all the country's needs, and there were other limited success stories; by 1948 the soap industry, which had developed during the Second World War, was able to export.[17] Basically, these enterprises and most other manufacturing remained French-owned. Nor could the very uneven and moderate revival of business in any way begin to provide work for the influx of migrants into the bigger towns under the control of the Associated State. Table 6.1 shows the magnitude of this movement as the Viet Minh raids and French countersweeps interfered with communications and forced professionals, traders, artisans and skilled workers to move nearer to urban centres where their employment was now concentrated, or made life so wretched for the peasants in particular that they packed up and left the villages.

Table 6.1 Post-war urban growth

	Saigon–Cholon	Haiphong	Hanoi
1943	492,200*	65,400	119,700
1948	1,179,000	142,900	237,100

* 1946 figure
Source : Vu Quoc Thuc 1951, p. 240.

The difficulties facing Vietnamese wishing to enter productive capitalist enterprise in the new Associated State did not mean that there were no business opportunities. Post-war shortages of consumer goods, currency speculation, deals in urban real estate and contracts to supply the armed forces provided opportunities for mercantile capital.[18] The Chinese merchants based in Cholon still controlled the trade in rice, even if they had to pay off the Hoa Hao chiefs to transport it. Such class elements would obviously prefer Bao Dai and even the French to the Viet Minh. So would the landlords, over 6,000 of whom in

Nam Bo, according to a Communist source, fled to Saigon to escape the attention of the Viet Minh guerrillas, for whom they were special targets.[19] Numbers of middle strata intellectuals, some of them nationalists who could not face a long liberation war, also rallied to the new state or at least lived under its umbrella as political neutrals. Often their sympathies were determined by their inability to accept an anti-French struggle led by the ICP and by cadres whom they rejected as illiterates, former servants or political prisoners, 'the incapable, uneducated and dishonest'.[20] The prospect of food or pay where, for many, there was no work or regular income enabled the new state apparatus to recruit Vietnamese to its armed forces to back up the French and other colonial troops, over 200,000 of them by the end of 1953. But none of this gave the 'Bao Dai solution' a mass base, or even anything very effective by way of class support. With the landlords under severe pressure from insurgent tenants and no real formation of productive 'national' capitalists there was no chance of the emergence of solid ruling class interests other than those in France. Hence the fragmented political situation described above.

What was happening on the other side of the necessarily fluid boundary which by 1950 marked off in particular the Viet Minh's Viet Bac zone from the territory controlled by the Associated State? Perhaps the most immediate question for President Ho's government, beyond maintaining sufficient armed strength to contain the French incursions, especially that of late 1947, was how to hold together the area administratively. This was met in two ways. First, by a decree of 1 October 1947, the Administrative Committees and Resistance Committees were amalgamated at their various levels to create Resistance Administrative Committees for villages, districts and provinces.[21] Not only was political administration thus in effect subordinated to military needs, but the whole administrative framework increasingly came to be shaped by the division first into twelve War Zones covering the three regions of the country, then from January 1948 into six Interzones (with another for Saigon–Cholon).[22]

In June 1948 a drive began to strengthen local administration. It was prescribed that Resistance Administration Committees should draw at least a third of their members from poor and middle peasants, but conversely the rest were to be educated people with 'influence'. In 1950–51 'workers and peasants' were reckoned to total 66 per cent of members at this level in Interzone III (basically the Red River delta) and 40 per cent in Interzone I V and lower Trung Bo.[23] On the other hand, in July 1948 a provisional increase in official salaries was granted; the first traces of the contradiction between bureaucratization and popular control were perhaps already beginning to appear.[24]

At the same time, a rationalization of structure was also taking place in the military apparatus. In January and February 1948 new decrees formalized military ranks. (Vo Nguyen Giap was now confirmed as the DRVN's only full general.)[25] This was no doubt a response to needs arising from the earlier creation of Main Force units, but, given that the existence of the state apparatus in general and the whole economic life of the Democratic Republic were increasingly becoming bound to the war effort, it also reinforced the emergence of bureaucratic hierarchies and principles. On the other hand, at the same time as officers were clearly recognized as such, the political apparatus within the armed forces was also being more clearly structured, as the Party realized that the coming greater efforts would require even more devotion and political solidarity among the ranks than before.[26]

The slogan issued by the government on 19 June 1948 to mark the thousandth day of the resistance to the French (reckoned from 23 September 1945) was 'Create Bases and Break Records', thus summing up the need to build up the military effort and to support this with production.[27] To meet the demands which these goals created, in November 1949 a decree was issued making all males of eighteen and over subject to mobilization. The implications of this in class terms were to prove decisive for the development and ultimate success of this resistance war and, indeed, for the first years of the Democratic Republic after its end. The point was that the many more fighters who were to be recruited and trained, and the bulk of the supporting elements who would have to transport their needs, and the food which they would eat, would all have to be drawn from the peasantry. In that respect, it is interesting that a later verdict of the Party was that in the period 1945–49, 'the understanding of the role of the peasantry was insufficient, and the importance of the rural areas in the Resistance was not fully appreciated'.[28]

What evidence there is seems to suggest that the main source of recruits in those first years were urban elements who withdrew to the forest and mountains in face of the French assertion of control at the end of 1946 and beginning of 1947. Indeed, the working-class supporters of the ICP and Viet Minh seem to have played a disproportionate part, consonant with the way in which the Party had positioned itself in the years since 1930. Thus, one important Communist source states that as many as 35 per cent of the 'regular troops' (presumably Main Force units) up to the end of 1949 were drawn from the working class.[29] Combat units of the Saigon–Cholon trade unions and Hanoi workers who first fought the French in September 1945 and December 1946 formed the basis of such later units as the 'Capital' Regiment 112 and the Independence Brigade. Nam Bo rubber workers regrouped to War Zones C and D. Workers from the Hong Gai coal mines likewise formed one of the most active guerrilla units in the Red River delta.[30]

In general, outside the military sphere, one of the pillars of the Democratic Republic was the General Confederation of Labour, launched in July 1946 in Hanoi after preparatory meetings in October 1945 and March 1946 with the old militant Hoang Quoc Viet at its head. Early in 1948 it claimed 168,142 members in the liberated areas – 40.9 per cent of the wage and salary workforce.[31] Already in March 1947 the contribution of the working class was recognized with the promulgation of a Labour Code which provided for such rights as equal pay, paid maternity leave, holidays with pay and accident compensation, but also for basic salaries tied to the cost of living. Beyond these fundamentals, however, the Code contained provisions of potentially wider importance, the right of workers to a share in profits for example, and the institution in all enterprises of over 25 workers of Internal Committees which would supervise such matters as organization of work, pay rates, hiring, discipline, hygiene and safety.[32] This, if implemented, would mean a considerable degree of workers' control.

In addition to workers, the government and Party were concerned to mobilize other parts of the population. Thus the organization of women, for example, had first been expanded by the creation of a new Viet Nam Women's Union in October 1946, which by August 1948 claimed some 1 million members. By the time of the Union's first National Congress in April 1950, the line of the Party Central Committee, however, was that the main organizations for women should be class ones, trade unions and peasant associations, not gender specific.[33] This seems to indicate some doubts concerning the real efficacy of the incorporation of women into the struggle. Moreover, another very important category, youth, was not being mobilized in great numbers; in August 1948 Hoang Quoc Viet reported to a cadres' conference that 80,000 had been brought into new organizations.[34]

In the period 1946-50 there were in fact some ambiguities in the (officially dissolved) ICP's attitude to social struggle and its links to national resistance. Admittedly, Truong Chinh had defined the latter in 1947 as 'a peasant war led by the working class', but his overall emphasis had been different.[35] Above all he spoke of a 'just war', one 'against oppressors and conquerors to safeguard the freedom and independence of the peoples'.[36] The economic, social and political aims of the liberation struggle were not portrayed in class terms, but in terms of 'the entire people' – 'To improve the living standards of the people, to expand their democratic rights – these are two conditions that must be fulfilled if the entire people are to be politically mobilized.'[37] The economy he defined as 'a war economy in form, and a new democratic economy in content', with the object of the latter aspect to 'improve the living standards of the people to enable them to take part enthusiastically in developing the economy and supplying the army and our compatriots'.[38] Such formulations were of course in line with the position taken by the Eighth Plenum in May 1941, when rural class struggle in particular was effectively removed from the ICP's programme. Nor must it be supposed that poor peasants remained unmoved by national themes and could not be persuaded by them to join with workers and other class elements. It had remained an enormously important asset of the ICP that it had put itself at the head of the movement for 'national salvation' and could claim the heroes and heroines of Vietnamese history as its precursors.

By 1950, however, the Party was beginning to be caught in a trap of its own making. Faithful to the precepts of the Comintern, in the name of a United Front it had assumed the existence of a national bourgeoisie which certainly

154

lacked any real historical presence. In such a situation, as we saw in Chapter 3, the ICP leaders had in effect taken class out of Vietnamese history; anyone might be a patriot who was not actually a collaborator with the French and a particularly notorious oppressor. In that respect the Party laid down as its line in 1948 that:

> We must make common cause with the feudal landlords to unify the national resistance front, therefore the slogan of rural revolution cannot be used. We can only carry out land reform on the principle that landlords make concessions, agreeing to this for the sake of their tenants.[39]

Granted, this was partially contradicted a few lines further on in the same document by the statement that the class line to be taken was 'rely on the middle peasants and landless peasants, unite with the rich peasants, isolate landlords, resist French imperialism'. But, in practice, the effect of such theoretical uncertainties was to make any rural reforms intended by the government and Party extremely difficult to implement.

In January 1948, therefore, a Plenum of the Central Committee had decided on a number of measures, including greater efforts to enforce the prescribed rent reduction, equal division of communal lands among needy peasants, and the temporary allocation of land confiscated from French landlords and 'traitors'.[40] In August, however, a very important limit was placed on any attempt to take a class position aligned to the lower strata, when reduction of rents and measures to change land tenure were made subject to the proviso that they 'would not interfere with the interests of the anti-colonial National United Front'.[41] In yet another sphere, that of rural wage labour, landowners had been assured in the same year that the policy on wages would ensure that they would not have to leave land uncultivated 'because of the high cost of labour'.[42]

Rent reduction was understandably not a marked success in the circumstances. Many of the rural notables evidently felt that they could ignore with impunity those limited measures of reform which the government of the Democratic Republic had introduced. Thus, when a decree in July 1949 restated the 25 per cent reduction of rents already made in 1945, and strengthened the machinery for enforcing it, many landlords still either dragged their feet or ignored the measure altogether: for example, it was reported that in Interzones III and IV only 30 per cent complied willingly.[43]

As for land reform, landlords who were not actually traitors were granted compensation for lands used in their absence by local Resistance Administrative Committees, while these bodies were also empowered to take over land spontaneously seized by peasants during the August Revolution.[44] However, this did not mean that there was no redistribution of land in the liberated areas. Taking, for example, Bac Bo and upper Trung Bo, 21.84 per cent of all land eventually transferred was dealt with in the period August 1945 to July 1949. The main source was land owned by French citizens (61.2 per cent of the total in that category), followed by communal lands (31.7 per cent of the total) and landlords' holdings (10.4 per cent of what they finally lost).[45] Figures given in another DRVN source suggest, on the other hand, that actual handing over by local authorities may have been slow. In 3,035 communes only an average of 3.84 hectares had been distributed by mid-1949.[46]

Giving social content to national struggle was not only a question of getting a firm grip upon landlords and rich peasants and satisfying the demands of poor ones. Other spheres and other class interests were also involved. The creation of a reorganized Office of Supply and Transport in February 1948 gives us a clue to the basic concern. The political economy of the liberation war from the point of view of the Democratic Republic was one of supply: of rice to feed soldiers, porters, administrators and state workers; of munitions, medicines and raw materials; of money to pay for the second category. What could not be levied in the territory controlled by the liberation forces had to be imported, either from French-held areas or from abroad. That meant, in terms of the third category, both a supply of the new dong and of the piastres issued by the Bank of Indochina. In April 1948 use of the latter was completely forbidden in liberated areas, but piastres were needed to buy anything outside these, including in places like Bangkok and Hong Kong.

During 1948, then, policy changed. As Truong Chinh emphasized to a conference of cadres of the central administration in January 1949, in the first years of the resistance the practice in enemy-held territory was to seize everthing moveable and bring it back to the liberated zones, and to sabotage what was immovable, like bridges and roads.[47] As the resistance became stabilized territorially, however, in rural areas which were often remote from main urban centres of supply, a more pacific policy of trade had to be adopted. Gradually a whole series of new markets emerged in the rather elastic strips of territory between liberated and French-dominated zones.[48] Here a trade flourished which was at once clandestine, because it was in medicines, raw materials and machinery needed by the government of the Democratic Republic, and known to all, because it was a source of profit to many of the supporters of the 'Bao Dai solution', even though officially the Republic refused to sell such products as tea and coffee.[49] In this way, private trade continued on the revolutionary side of the lines, although a new group of economic cadre also emerged, skilled in extracting a hard bargain from the capitalists.

Another sort of cadre, often the most dedicated and honest, were those involved in collecting taxes and contributions. These took two forms. Outside the areas directly held by the Viet Minh, in places where its guerrillas operated in contention with the French and their allies, levies were made on elements who paid with varying degrees of enthusiasm. Thus, peasants who now had free use of land for which they once paid rent to a landlord who had taken refuge in a town might gladly give rice to the Revolution. Merchants paid less happily – say, ₱5,000 for each lorry allowed to pass, and a levy on their profits. One observer estimated total extractions in Nam Bo at ₱500 million in 1948.[50]

Obviously the amount involved varied greatly, depending on the current political and military balance; Colonel Jean Leroy, overlord of Kien Hoa province in the Mekong delta and leader of the biggest of the private armies, reckoned that at the height of his control he was collecting over P300 million per year and his Viet Minh opponents a mere P151,000.[51]

The taxes and other contributions which could be levied in the fully liberated zones were a much more certain source for President Ho's government. In the period now under review, up to 1950, it seems fair to say that there was little of a tax policy. At various times contributions in kind or cash were more or less willingly extracted, as when in January 1950 all those aged between 18 and 65 were asked to give ten kilos of rice to a 'Public Food Fund'.[52]

Revenue, however, was simply not enough to meet the needs of the state apparatus, and its response was classical, simple and perilous – it issued large amounts of new currency to finance its operations. The result was equally classical, simple and perilous – massive inflation. Table 6.2 shows the trend in Interzones I–IV (Bac Bo and upper Trung Bo); Interzones V (lower Trung Bo) and VI (Nam Bo) had their own budgets. Prices rose 4.4 times in the year 1949-50.[53] In 1948 in the border markets the dong was worth slightly less than a third of a piastre, by 1950 the rate of exchange was 70 dong to a piastre.[54] By 1951, thus, the Democratic Republic was in financial crisis. Insufficient revenue and unwise currency policy compounded the effects of the division of the country into separate territories. In the period 1946–48 there had been little fluctuation in prices; the military effort had not required massive outlays and communication, at least in Bac Bo and northern Trung Bo, was relatively easy for Viet Minh suppliers. In the next years the French pushed their opponents into the mountains in the Viet Bac, clearing the Red River delta of all but guerrilla forces; circulation of commodities became difficult, and the few consumer goods imported from the French-held zones only served to drive prices up further.[55]

Table 6.2 DRVN: budget deficit and currency issue, 1946–50

	1946	1947	1948	1949	1950
Budget deficit (%)	72	73	80	82	77
Currency issue	100	144	171	752	1,914

Sources : Adapted from Vo Nhan Tri 1967, p. 171; Nguyen Ngoc Minh 1966, p. 211.

The cumulation of problems related to the 'political economy' of the liberation war was to lead in 1951 to an attempt by the government of the a firm grip. However, it is important to remind ourselves here that the situation was indeed one of war, and so cannot be understood without examining the evolution of military doctrine and practice. In that respect, the period 1950–51 was to prove a watershed, with developments which strongly reinforced the need to take a firmer social and economic grip.

The Theory and Practice of Liberation War

In order to understand the developments of 1950–51 we must move back in time. As soon as the ICP leaders faced a full war with France, at the end of 1946, they began to theorise its nature. In a series of articles originally published in the main Viet Minh newspaper between March and August 1947, Truong Chinh, the Party's General Secretary, emphasized the need for a protracted war which would combine guerrilla activities with mobile and positional warfare, the last being the task of Main Force units and the first two of a militia organized as either partisans or for defence against enemy offensives. Chinh characterized mobile warfare as being for the purpose of 'annihilating', positional warfare as 'wearing down', and guerrilla action as for both annihilating and wearing down.[56] Further, he discussed three stages in the 'Long-term Resistance', the 'defensive', that of 'equilibrium' and the 'general counter-offensive'.[57] The ICP's chief theoretician recognized that generally the resistance was only in the first stage and stressed that 'genuine independence and unification' could come only with the completion of the third stage when 'we throw all our forces throughout the country into the battle to crush the enemy completely and win back the whole of our territory'.[58]

These ideas are important from the point of view of a number of themes which have emerged from this study. First, they represent a break with the views on manoeuvre and the seizure of power which Ho and the others had basically derived from the Comintern, with the addition of a stronger emphasis on guerrilla warfare and base areas. As we have seen, the August Revolution took a form which, if anything, confirmed the Comintern pattern of general insurrection. This was not a basis, however, for a protracted struggle against enemy armies. Secondly, the new situation of war pushed forward the linkage between the Vietnamese and Chinese Revolutions. The influence of CCP experience and Mao Tse-tung's military writings upon Chinh is evident and indeed inevitable; the only possible model for the ICP leaders was what their Chinese comrades had done and said in fighting the Kuomintang and Japanese.[59] On the other hand, it must not be supposed that Chinh and his associates simply adopted Mao's ideas in their entirety. As good materialists they knew that the realities of the two countries were very different. Significant variations can be seen between Chinh and Mao, which were ultimately to be the basis, as we shall see in later volumes, for the development of a distinct Vietnamese doctrine of revolutionary warfare. In 1947 the issues at stake were already laid

158

down: the use of space, the importance of external support, and the circumstances of the crucial final transition to the general counter-offensive.[60]

Obviously the relative sizes of the two countries meant that a military war of manoeuvre had to make different uses of physical terrain. For Chinh, thus, the appropriate image for the relationship between Viet Minh force and the enemy was 'two combs whose teeth are interlocked'.[61] For Mao the Chinese situation presented a '"jig-saw" pattern', involving larger areas and broad sweeps of encirclement and counter-encirclement.[62] Indeed, for him size was a major asset against the Japanese (as it had been for the CCP against the Kuomintang – witness the Long March to Shensi), giving an opportunity for 'a general rear and vital bases'.[63] Chinh, on the other hand, had to argue against the view that Viet Nam was too small to have base areas; his emphasis was rather upon flexible use of terrain, combining mountains, deltas and 'marshy areas'.[64]

A similar difference marked the attitude towards external assistance to the two struggles. Once again, Mao emphasized China's size, and, though stressing the importance of Soviet support, he was almost certainly also strongly influenced by the experience of the CCP with Stalin and the Comintern. 'Large-scale direct assistance is as yet lacking and will only come in the future,' he wrote, 'but China is progressive and is a big country, and these are the factors enabling her to protract the war and to promote as well as to await international help.'[65] For his Vietnamese comrade, however, the international situation was of much more immediate import and an integral part of strategy; the enemy, wrote Chinh, 'is encircled on our soil, in France, in the French Union and in the world'.[66]

We shall soon turn to the reality of this view, and above all to the special role of China. Here let us note a third variation of view between CCP and ICP leaders. Thus, in mid-1938, Mao had stressed the attainment of absolute military superiority through the proper build-up of the first two stages of the protracted war before launching the general counter-offensive.[67] Chinh, on the other hand, saw the transition as possible even in conditions of only relative superiority.[68] It seems likely that this difference may be explained by the varying degrees of militarization of the two revolutions. Thus, according to Mao, in China 'war is the main form of struggle and the army is the main form of organization'.[69] His Vietnamese comrade put greater emphasis upon political mobilization and its requisite economic, cultural and social reforms.[70]

In direct terms of the war of manoeuvre, of course, the crucial question was the timing of the movement from one stage to another. The containment of the French Viet Bac offensive in October–November 1947 was seen as a turning-point in convincing Viet Minh adherents that a protracted war could be fought and ultimately won.[71] In January 1948 the enlarged Plenum of the ICP Central Committee declared that 'the comparative power of ourselves and the enemy has changed', and saw the war as passing into the stage of equilibrium.[72] The main emphasis, however, remained on guerrilla warfare, with two-thirds of the existing regular forces being broken down into small units for the purpose.[73] Two years later, filled with further confidence, a larger-scale Party conference decided in January 1950 that the time had come to prepare actively for the move to the last phase, the general counter-offensive. In a pamphlet General Giap explained the new line in detail. It is of particular interest that he emphasized both that the new phase would be of long duration and that at its beginning the liberation forces' material strength would still be 'generally inferior to the enemy's', while morale would be superior.[74]

In analysing factors favourable to the new line, Giap referred to the key event in China, the final coming to power of the Communist Party and declaration of the Chinese People's Republic on 1 October 1949. This had great significance for the Vietnamese struggle, since by the end of the year, after the annihilation of the last southern Kuomintang armies, it put the ICP's ally firmly on the northern frontier.

The International Setting of Liberation War

With the main centres of Communist power far away in north China, the Vietnamese leaders had been forced to behave circumspectly with regard to the Kuomintang government of China even after it had withdrawn its troops in mid-1946. A year later President Ho claimed in a foreign press interview that the DRVN was implementing the 'People's Three Principles' of Sun Yat-sen, which 'the French reactionary colonialists' mistook for 'the "class principle" of Karl Marx'.[75] In February 1948 his government even agreed to deny bases to the CCP guerrillas operating in south China, with whom an alliance had been made in August 1947.[76] Naturally, however, the preference was for the CCP, and low-key cooperation continued; the CCP representative in Bangkok helped with arms purchases, for example, and there was mutual assistance along the Yunnan border.[77]

After 1 October 1949 the way was clear for more overt declarations. An important event here was the conference held by the Communist-controlled World Federation of Trade Unions in Peking in November–December. In the keynote speech Liu Shao-ch'i held up the Chinese Revolution as a model for 'the peoples of many colonial and semi-colonial countries in their struggle to win national independence and people's democracy'. The necessary elements were the vanguard party, a national united front based on the worker-peasant alliance, and armed struggle.[78] Speaking later, the chief DRVN representative hailed Liu's address as 'the compass for all workers of Southeast Asia'.[79] Immediately after this international meeting the first national trade union conference was held in the DRVN's Viet Bac area, and there, in addition to the declaration that the recent CCP victory had 'bent the balance of power on the side of the democratic camp' and endorsement of Liu's principles, a more 'Chinese' vocabulary can be noted.[80]

The international situation in which the government of the DRVN had to find its way by the beginning of 1950 had changed much more radically in the last three years than just through the victory of the Chinese Revolution. That was only one milestone on a path for which the old Marxist–Leninist internationalism could scarcely now serve as a guide.

In February 1946, as noted in the last chapter, George Kennan's cable to Washington had introduced the concept of 'containment' of the new Soviet power, which he saw as inherently expansive. Around this core, whatever may have been Kennan's original intentions, the ideology of US hegemony was to crystallize. In March 1947, while requesting funds from Congress to aid the government of Greece against Communist-led rebels, President Truman had laid down his 'doctrine' of the containment of Communism. The following September Andrei Zhdanov, speaking for the Soviet leadership at the founding meeting of the Cominform, which was in some respects to replace the old Comintern, declared that the world had now become 'two camps'. 1948 saw the Communist-led struggle in Viet Nam, Laos and Cambodia joined by other such armed uprisings in India, Burma, Malaya, the Philippines and Indonesia. It is in this context that we must see the first major policy document on Indochina produced by the US Department of State in September of that year, which declared the objective to be 'to assist in the solution of the present impasse which will be mutually satisfactory to the French and Vietnamese peoples, which will result in the termination of the present hostilities, and which will be within the framework of US security'.[81]

In September 1948 the US policy-makers still hoped that nationalism could be prised from the Communist grasp and a group found who could negotiate with the French government, which at the same time would have to be convinced of the folly of seeking a purely military solution. At the international level, however, the military aspect came increasingly to dominate, especially after the Soviet development of an atomic bomb, announced first by the US government in September 1949. On 1 October the foundation of the Chinese People's Republic confirmed the 'loss' of that country to Communism. In April 1950 the Truman Doctrine of containment, which he was to bequeath as a legacy to all following US administrations, took final shape as National Security Council Document 68. Moreover, the need for containment had now been brought to the northern frontier of Bac Bo, and this finally changed the balance of the Washington policy-makers' thinking about Indochina.

In January 1950 first People's China, then the Soviet Union, formally recognized President Ho's government. In return Marxist–Leninist 'internationalism' demanded that the Vietnamese leaders take much more open sides in the global struggle: the report of the Central Committee to the Party's Second Congress in February 1951 was thus to put the DRVN firmly in the camp of 'world peace' and 'democracy' and make a significant link with the

161

struggles of 'colonial and semi-colonial peoples' against US and other imperialisms.[82]

The response of the US government to its adversaries' new moves was to recognize in February 1950 the 'independent' states of Viet Nam, Laos and Cambodia which had been created from Paris as new members of the French Union. On 1 May President Truman approved of aid being given them. The final fateful shift was now in train, with the crystallization of what later came to be known as the 'domino' theory. Thus, in August 1950 the head of a mission to survey the situation reported to Washington that failure in Viet Nam 'will inevitably precipitate balance of [Southeast Asian] mainland into Communist orbit with excellent prospect of similar eventuality in Indonesia and Philippines'.[83] Although this advisor did not see military victory as a long-term solution, two days before Christmas US gifts were given a pronounced military form, when a mutual defence programme was signed.   This new move on the part of one of the two main defining powers of the new Cold War situation was probably inspired by the first major indication of greater closeness between the Chinese and Vietnamese Revolutions. That was the campaign which the first of the DRVN's regular divisions to be formed conducted along the mountainous northern frontier in September-October 1950.[84] Henceforth, with the French garrisons cleared away, contacts between the two Communist regimes could be broadened and Chinese support freely given to the Vietnamese. This was correctly taken by the DRVN leadership to be a turning-point in the whole war.[85]

Building the Base for a Broader War

In a protracted 'people's war' of the Chinese or Vietnamese kind, of course, military success could only be secured upon a firm political and economic terrain. From the beginning of 1950, in fact, the DRVN's government and ruling party had made greater efforts to build such a terrain, with the decision to work towards the general counter-offensive. In February a general mobilization was ordered and more than a dozen conferences of such groups as educationalists, military personnel, youths, peasants, women and cultural personnel were held between February and April. In June-July the mobilization decrees were extended to youths of 16 and men up to 55, and women were urged to join the militia.[86] The training and equipment of five regular divisions was now set in motion, each planned to have around 10,000 men.[87] Together they would comprise the new Main Forces, along with a range of regiments and battalions ordered to act independently, as one element in a threefold division of the fighting forces begun early in 1949. The second and third elements (in which women were often prominent) were the regional forces, which sought to take the offensive and pull the enemy off balance on a more localized basis, and the village guerrillas, who combined defence and limited attack.

This new organizational pattern undoubtedly provided the basis for the tactical flexibility which was to be a marked feature of the struggle by the liberation forces over the next few years. Along with the preparation for a general counter-offensive, however, it demanded many more people. Not only were there eventually to be 75,000 men in the new divisions but in the absence of other forms of transport, massive corps of porters were also needed to supply them – 50,000 to each division. Moreover, the men and women involved in this very heavy work, often in conditions of great hardship, were expected only to serve for 14 days at a time, with seven spent in actual carrying of food and other supplies. This meant mobilizing a fresh contingent of 50,000 per division every fortnight; so campaigns involving, say, three divisions for three months, could mean finding some 450,000 porters, assuming that, during the campaign, two periods were demanded.[88] As the logistics of the resistance forces developed, it became possible to save labour by using specially reinforced bicycles for portage, one of which would carry three porters' loads. However, Bernard Fall still reports the use of 95,000 porters for two divisions in mid-1953, without including the transport of ammunition.[89] Of necessity such burdens had to fall on the peasants, especially the majority of poor cultivators, and this was to have implications for the class basis of the liberation war.

Already by May 1950 President Ho's government was forced once again to face the peasant question. Decrees on debts consolidating previous ones were promulgated, cancelling those contracted before the August Revolution and limiting interest on subsequent ones to a maximum of 18 per cent in cash or 20 per cent in kind; on the opening to peasant use of lands left uncultivated by landlords, even when these were not absentees; the reduction of rents by a quarter was again affirmed.[90]

These decrees were only three among a whole spate which were issued in May 1950, most of them on a single day, and which obviously represent an attempt to consolidate in readiness for the general counter-offensive. Thus, the judicial system was reformed and, more widely, the whole structure of civil authority was regularized, including the incorporation in the relevant decree of a 'Definition of Obligations and Interests'. Significantly, the incomes of civil servants and other government workers (including those called up for labour as porters or on road-building) were now regularized in the form of rice allowances, with 18 common grades ranging from 35 to 53 kilos a month and a further seven levels of bureaucrats rising to a maximum of 72 kilos.[91] This had a double significance: firstly the further reinforcement of hierarchy and of income related directly to position within the state apparatus and, secondly, payment in kind, typifying the war economy and the all-important place which rice took within it as the staple food. As one scholar put it, 'rice became the monetary standard of the Democratic Republic', so that even the price of postage stamps was paid in it.[92]

This package of measures had to be capped, however, by a new political move. In February 1951 the Indochinese Communist Party held its Second Congress, and in doing so rechristened itself the Viet Nam Workers' Party (Dang Lao Dong Viet Nam). Ho Chi Minh and his lieutenants were once more openly exerting their hegemony over the whole revolutionary process in Viet Nam. However, it is significant that a new name was to be adopted, which might continue to imply to non-members some break with the orientations of the past.[93]

The second major significance of the Second Congress may be seen in the way in which it defined the objects of the Workers' Party:

> The founding of the Viet Nam Workers' Party is aimed at reinforcing the leading role of the worker–peasant alliance, uniting the working class more closely with other strata of the working people, and unifying the national and democratic forces under the Party's leadership so as to defeat the imperialists and their stooges, complete national liberation, develop the system of the people's democracy, preserve peace and democracy in the world, and prepare conditions for advancing to socialism.[94]

These were very broad aims. The newly renamed party was not merely asserting a more open control, it was attempting to make a broad and consistent analysis of the situation with a view both to winning final victory over the French power bloc and rebuilding the country afterwards.

At the time of the Second Congress, as we have seen, the Communist leaders believed that the military war of manoeuvre was about to enter its last phase, that of the general counter-offensive by their own forces. This gave the army a central place in the Revolution, both militarily and in class terms. In the latter respect, it was seen as an expression of the bloc of forces aligned in the national struggle:

> It is an integral part of the people, it lives among the people, and draws its strength from the people. On the whole, the social composition of our army reflects the social composition of our nation, the overwhelming majority of its cadres and combatants being of worker and peasant stock. [95]

In February 1951 the task was seen as one of building a 'national, democratic and modern' army, with emphasis laid on 'self-imposed' discipline and on political work to combat 'such bad habits as bureaucracy, formalism, militarism, individual bravado, and claiming rewards for one's services'.[96] It is important to emphasize the stress laid, right since the beginnings of the People's Army, on ideological training.[97] Along with its flexibility in organization and tactics, the effects of such political education were to be a major asset in the coming decisive campaigns.

In that respect, the main appeal in 1951 remained one to national rather than class sentiments, or rather, the two were identified. Thus, in a speech given by Truong Chinh (who had automatically become General Secretary of the

164

Workers' Party) at a Congress of the National United Front (NUF) held a month after the Second Congress of the Party, the question of class struggle was explicitly faced. 'We are involved in class struggle', Chinh argued. 'So long as society is divided into classes, there will be class struggle.' However,

...all strata of our people, all revolutionary classes in our country, are in the same position: they have no other way to safeguard their interest in a reasonable manner than to concentrate their forces on resisting the common enemies. They have no other way of resolving the class antagonisms in the country in a reasonable manner than to join forces and defeat external enemies who have come to invade their country. For us, this war of resistance is an advanced form of national struggle and class struggle.[98]

It is no accident that these remarks were made to the leaders of the NUF, since that organization was to be the major instrument in mass terms for this joining of forces. (To clarify relationships and probably ensure better Communist control the Viet Minh was now to be fused with the Front, rather than existing as a parallel organization.) The tasks of the NUF were defined by the Workers' Party Central Committee as:

...to strengthen unity among the social classes and strata of the people; to seek new allies, particularly in enemy-occupied areas, newly-liberated areas, and regions inhabited predominantly by religious people and ethnic minorities; to consolidate the worker-peasant alliance as a firm basis of the National United Front; to isolate the French colonialists, the US interventionists and their stooges, the Vietnamese traitors; and to mobilize all strata and classes of the people, including still hesitant persons, either to join in, or support, the war resistance, contribute to defeating the aggressors, carry out the policies of the Party, the Front and the Government, and support the people's administration and the people's army.[99]

What we see here, in fact, is a new attempt by the Communist leaders to define the war of position in order to situate themselves more securely. Their position involved an emerging contradiction: necessarily emphasizing the need for national unity in face of a common imperialist enemy, Ho and his lieutenants had also increasingly to face the implications of various class and other contradictions which might lead to disunity. It was somewhere between these moments that they had to situate the Party, navigating it among the shoals of ethnicity, religion and class.

Within Viet Nam itself, ethnic contradictions implied, firstly, those between Chinese and Vietnamese. This became an increasingly delicate matter with the inflow of Chinese aid, when the expression of solidarity between the two peoples became a real necessity but was complicated by the tendency of the new Communist government in Peking to follow its predecessor in regarding all overseas Chinese as under its protection. The Viet Nam–China Friendship Association was part of the National United Front, but, as the Party

165

Central Committee recognized, this did not stop some cadres putting pressure on local Chinese to become citizens (which few had done) or the latter from treating their local Management Associations as separate administrative organs, not under the Resistance Administrative Committees.[100]

Given prominence to the historian's eye by its significance for much later events is the complaint of the Central Committee that Chinese certificates of nationality had been handed out to members of some of the minority peoples who straddled the northern border. The allegiance of the minorities was an especially important question for the Workers' Party. Although it is not necessary to accept the argument of one modern scholar that such support was crucial for survival and ultimate victory, in two respects at least the minority peoples were significant.[101] First, at least in the Viet Bac, the largest area held by the Democratic Republic, they were a majority of the population. It is true, of course, that the government of the Republic would never be firmly established until it could make its writ run in the densely inhabited delta areas of Bac Bo and northern Trung Bo (leaving aside what might happen further south). But, second, the launching points for such manoeuvres, and bases throughout the country, were often in the mountainous areas where the support of local minorities was crucial. Thus, the predominantly Tay province of Tuyen Quang in Bac Bo provided 1,021,138 person-days of labour on the communications network from among its 130,000 people in 1953.[102]

In February 1951, therefore, the Central Committee in its report promised all 'nationalities' full equality and held out the prospect of eventual autonomy for the 'relatively large ethnic minorities' within the Democratic Republic after victory.[103] The possibility of actual secession was described as 'no problem', but it was precisely such separatist feelings that the French were trying to encourage. In March 1948 Admiral Thierry D'Argenlieu had announced the creation of an autonomous Thai federation in north-western Bac Bo, and later semi-autonomous territories had been created for the Tay, Nung and Muong. There were some attempts at social development, in education for example, with a claim of 3,000 Thai pupils being taught for the first time in their own language in 1950, and a special school for advanced pupils from all minorities was opened in Dalat.[104] In Trung Bo the creation of a special Commissariat for the Highland Peoples of South Indochina in May 1946 had led to a special 'autonomous region' centred on Ban Me Thuot, but three of its five provinces contained a strong French military presence.[105] The restoration of Bao Dai as Head of State did not appeal to the chiefs of the minorities, for whom it smacked too much of the old tributary relationship and Kinh domination. As a compromise, the Thai chiefs swore personal allegiance to him without agreeing to incorporation in the new state.[106] A decree in April 1950 ruled the Trung Bo minority region to be a direct Crown Domain, also outside the normal state structure, although in May 1951 a special statute recognized rights to land and education in local languages and promised respect for local customs.[107]

It was to the French, however, and above all to the military, that the minority leaders basically looked. This was undoubtably a continuing problem for the Communists. Probably the greatest single French success was in fomenting a rising of the Hre against Viet Minh cadres in 1949 by playing on suspicion of Kinh settlement.[108] The French footing among the Thai and Meo was also a threat, and by late 1953 there were claimed to be 15,000 anti-Communist guerillas in Interzone II; this was especially serious given the presence of the liberation forces in Laos, a strategy to which we shall turn later.[109] Intense efforts had to be made by Workers' Party cadres to penetrate the Thai provinces, including stirring up lesser chiefs against an overmighty and strongly pro-French rival.[110]

Turning from ethnic groups to religious organizations, we may note that in early 1951 the Communists had not moved any distance towards healing their breach with the Cao Dai and Hoa Hao, so that this remained a permanent weakness for them in Nam Bo. With the Buddhists in general there was no great problem. That faith nominally at least commanded the allegiance of some 80 per cent of Vietnamese, but it had no strong tradition of political activity, although the national congress held in Hue in May 1951, which ratified adherence to the new World Association of Buddhists, was to prove a harbinger of new developments. For the time being, both the Viet Minh and the NUF contained enough priests and other spokesmen for Buddhism to make it easy to claim the faith as part of the national liberation movement. It was the Catholics who were the flies in the religious ointment.

In its report presented in February 1951 the Central Committee of the Workers' Party complained that the French were the real anti-Catholics, and promised freedom of worship (already, in fact, guaranteed in the constitution of the Democratic Republic).[111] Although there were Catholics in Ho's early government, we have already noted that by late 1947 three of the four Vietnamese bishops were staking out their dioceses as armed enclaves.[112] In October 1949 they accepted the 'Bao Dai solution' at the price of continuing to rule autonomous zones, especially in Phat Diem and Bui Chu in the south-west Red River delta. It seems that no less a person than His Holiness Pope Pius XII was enlisted by General de Lattre de Tassigny, supreme French commander in Indochina, to pressure Vietnamese Catholics to rally more wholeheartedly to Bao Dai in 1951.[113] In December 1951 the Bishops in Bac Bo indeed issued a public condemnation of Communism, but probably most immediate among their reasons was a recent (though unsuccessful) attack by the liberation forces on Phat Diem. It is important to note, however, that the most prominent lay Catholic, Ngo Dinh Diem, as a good nationalist remained aloof from Bao Dai and the French. In time, both he and his co-religionists were to prove a real thorn in the Communist flesh; in late 1951, although the Workers' Party preserved its two front organizations, the Association of Catholics for the Resistance and the Association of Catholics for National Salvation, it seems for its part to have decided to move against the Church hierarchy, expelling hitherto tolerated foreign clergy and confiscating property.[114]

In this review of the social and political forces among which the Communists had to position themselves in 1951 and thereafter if they wished to mobilize strength for the eventual general counter-offensive, we have not yet come specifically to class. It goes without saying that the positioning among class forces would be decisive for the future of the Revolution as it had been in the past, and that both ethnic and religious interests were determined by class relations: thus, contradictions between chiefs and subjects were the main axes along which the affiliations of minority groups were decided, while businessmen, professionals, clergy, landlords and rich peasants were the backbone of political catholicism. Before turning more directly to class, however, we should emphasize the position of one more category which was a potentially great social force, which was closely related to class but also analytically distinct – namely women.

As we have had occasion to notice, all Vietnamese women of whatever social background suffered from certain disadvantages and formed therefore a potentially rich recruiting ground for the liberation movement and the Revolution. Such comrades as Nguyen Thi Minh Khai (shot by the French in 1941) had already given all they could, and since September 1945 there had been many others who had joined the war against the French.[115] Although they were not specially singled out in the Central Committee report, the manifesto of the Workers' Party issued after the February 1951 Congress promised that 'Effective help shall be extended to women so as to achieve equality between men and women'.[116] It is with that firm perspective that the discussion in the next chapter must be read, remembering that behind every male worker in the munitions plants of the liberated zones, every man who laboured to grow rice for the national salvation, every fighter of the People's Army, every porter supplying its units, were women who reproduced his labour power, while many produced, fought and carried as well.

Class, State and Party

An important aspect of the Second Congress is that the Communist leaders still displayed no really new view of class forces, their role in the Vietnamese Revolution, and relation to the state. By February 1951 the leadership was, of course, a tight-knit group formed in bitter struggle. Six of the seven full members of the Politburo we have met – Ho, Truong Chinh, Pham Van Dong, Le Duan, Vo Nguyen Giap and Hoang Quoc Viet. The seventh was Nguyen Chi Thanh, son of poor peasants from Annam, ICP member since 1937 and several times in gaol, military commander of central Annam and then in 1950 head of the army's General Political Directorate. The alternate member of the Politburo was a much more shadowy figure, Le Van Luong, possibly a southerner and founder-member of the Party, now head of its key Central Organization Department. In addition to these the Central Committee included 21 other struggle-hardened cadres.[117]

How, first of all, did this revolutionary élite characterize the Revolution itself? Despite its anti-imperialist and anti-feudal nature, it was not a 'bourgeois democratic' revolution, because it was led by the 'proletarian' working class. Nor was it a socialist revolution, 'because its principal task is not yet to establish a dictatorship of the proletariat nor totally destroy the system of capitalist exploitation'.[118] It was a 'people's national democratic revolution'. As to its class basis, according to the report of the Central Committee:

> The power of the Vietnamese revolution is the people, whose essential elements are the working class and the peasantry. The driving forces of the Vietnamese revolution are the working class, peasantry and petty bourgeoisie. The leading class of the Vietnamese revolution is the working class.[119]

In the programme of the Workers' Party which was adopted at the Congress, however, other important elements were added to the 'driving forces' of the Revolution, namely the 'national bourgeoisie', and 'patriotic and progressive personages and landlords'. Along with workers and peasants in the 'basic mass of the people' were grouped 'intellectual workers' belonging 'to various strata of the people, mostly to the petty bourgeoisie'.[120] This shift between one document and the other, with the second significantly intended to be more public, indicates an important ambiguity concerning the real class base of the process of transformation. The broader formulation was consistent with the continuing Marxist–Leninist emphasis on the role of the national bourgeoisie in 'colonial and semi-colonial' countries, with the Workers' Party's own attempted practice as the ICP, and with the perceived need of the Communist leadership to build a broad national basis of support.

However, the most immediate influence was evidently the concept of 'New Democracy' which Mao Tse-tung had developed as part of his creation of a terrain upon which to move to power in China. In November 1948 Liu Shao-ch'i in a pamphlet on *Internationalism and Nationalism* had used almost exactly the same formula as was adopted in the new Workers' Party programme.[121] The point in both the Chinese and Vietnamese cases is that class struggle had in practice been totally subordinated to the anti-imperialist one. With the inclusion of 'patriotic' landlords in the 'driving forces' of the Vietnamese Revolution, even Lenin's combination of anti-imperialist and anti-feudal struggle had in effect been abandoned. A contradiction, not yet perceived by the Workers' Party leadership, now existed between the social implications of such a doctrine and the need to bring to the fore the interests of those elements which were bearing the real brunt of the liberation struggle and on whom any future building of socialism would rest – the male and female workers and poor and middle peasants.

169

The relation between national liberation and socialism was further explored in the ICP Central Committee's report which discussed the stages through which the revolution must pass. Here, in an interesting attempt to place Viet Nam in the context of Cominform discussions, a distinction was drawn by the Central Committee between 'people's democratic countries' (those in Eastern Europe) where 'all the necessary conditions for dictatorship of the proletariat exist' and those, like China and Viet Nam, where only a 'people's democratic dictatorship' could exist.[122] Moreover, China was judged to be more advanced than Viet Nam, having completed its task of liberation and being now engaged in giving 'land to the tiller' and building a 'new democratic' economy and culture. The implications of these concepts of state form and policy will be taken up later, especially in Volume II; here let us rather note the immediately following statement in the Central Committee's report that 'People's democracy is a transitional step toward socialism'. Beginning with Marx – as in his famous observation to Vera Zasulich that a full development of capitalism was perhaps not a necessary stage on the way to socialism in Russia – and intensifying with Lenin and the Bolsheviks, the theorization of necessary stages of class struggle had been crucial in the shift in the main terrain of world revolution from the centre of capitalism to its periphery. In 1951, at a more advanced stage of struggle in a new international conjunction, and looking to the future beyond victory over the French, Vietnamese Communist leadership was required to establish new positions and looked to the writings of Mao Tse-tung for this.

National liberation, then, and the policy of 'land to the tillers' were seen as the necessary steps towards independence, democracy and the building of socialism. However, the last stage was still far off: '...our country's road to socialism is long and winding. To want to transform our society totally and to destroy the system of exploitation of some people by others immediately in one moment is an illusion.'[123] The significance of the last remark is worth emphasizing. It is evident from a close reading of the February 1951 report that there was a 'left' tendency in the Party which, over the years, had been pushing for a much more direct move toward socialism. The Central Committee condemned the manifestation of such views 'in the belief that the people's democratic dictatorship is already at this stage proletarian dictatorship, and in the desire of some cadres to carry out the policy of socialist transformation of the national economy and of socialist construction prematurely'. The leftists, it was alleged, 'want to "skip stages", thinking that the present stage of people's democratic revolution is also a stage of socialist revolution'.[124] These deviations manifested themselves concretely in attempts to win a quick victory by excessive reliance on Main Force units, pressure to confiscate all landlords' holdings and distribute them immediately, and 'the tendency to tail after the masses instead of leading them along the correct path, the tendency to follow the "ultra-leftist" actions of a number of people indiscriminately advocating spontaneous struggles to the detriment of resistance solidarity'.[125] Once again we catch here the echoes of a rural class struggle, which the Party leaders feared it might be unable to contain, and with which it would have to come to terms.

Indirectly the leftists were given their answer in an assurance that radical change would come very soon after national liberation.

After defeating the imperialist aggressors, the people's government will be able to, and must, implement a series of vigorous reforms, based on the wholehearted support of the popular working masses in urban centres and rural areas.[126]

The instrument for these reforms, of course, would be the state, but it was anticipated that its form would change as the stages unfolded. Thus, the manifesto of the Workers' Party issued in March 1951 noted that

...political power in our country is a democratic power of the people, that is, of the workers, peasants, petty bourgeoisie, national bourgeoisie, and patriotic and progressive personages and landlords. The form of this is the People's Democratic Republic. Its content is the people's democratic dictatorship: democratic towards the people, dictatorial towards the imperialist aggressors and traitors.[127]

The last formulation was taken directly from the report of the Central Committee, which in turn had borrowed it from Mao Tse-tung's 1949 work, 'On the People's Democratic Dictatorship'.[128] What is significant is again the very broad class base emphasized in the statement for wide consumption. The report limited 'dictatorial' elements to the working class, peasantry, petty bourgeoisie and national bourgeoisie.

The manifesto went on to speak of consolidating the people's rule, the report passed to a more theoretical point. 'Our people's democratic dictatorship', it said, 'is fulfilling the historic task of the worker–peasant dictatorship.'[129] This was defined as smashing the imperialists and their allies, carrying out land reform and abolishing feudal ownership, developing the national economy, strengthening working-class leadership, consolidating the worker-peasant alliance, and fostering solidarity with the world movement for peace, democracy and socialism. The report envisaged that, after completing these tasks, the people's democratic revolution would develop into the socialist revolution. The people's democratic dictatorship would become a proletarian dictatorship of the more classically Marxist kind.

In the present stage, the people's democratic government was to be based on the principle of democratic centralism, defined as combining coercion by the state apparatus with persuasion by the Party, popular election with respect for hierarchies of administrative authority, and initiatives and demands from below with orders from above.[130] Consolidation of the principle was linked in the Workers' Party manifesto to strengthening the ties 'between the state power and the popular masses', to increasing the participation of workers, peasants and women, to putting a 'genuine People's Democratic constitution' into effect, to solidifying friendly relations with the Soviet Union, China and other People's Democracies, and to strengthening Party leadership at all levels.[131]

The last point raises squarely the issue of the role of the Workers' Party. Again following Marxist–Leninist orthodoxy, it was seen as 'a vanguard army, a general staff, a powerful, clear-sighted, determined, pure and thoroughly revolutionary political party'.[132] This was in the manifesto put out for general consumption after the Second Congress. The Central Committee's report presented there was somewhat less sanguine. The Party had grown enormously since the August Revolution, from 5,000 members then to 20,000 at the end of 1946 and 78,000 a year later.[133] This nearly sixteenfold expansion in just under two and a half years was followed by an almost tenfold increase in the next three years – to 765,000 by the end of 1950.[134] The biggest proportion of members was in Interzone V (lower Trung Bo), 220,000 in a population of some 3.5 million. Recruitment continued even despite the need for clandestine work in French-held territory. Thus, it was reported at a conference of cadres in Ha Dong province in the Red River delta in January 1950 that membership had risen from 2,420 at the end of 1947 to 6,360 at the beginning of 1949 and was currently 10,885.[135]

On the eve of the Second Congress the very large total membership was grouped into 7,900 branches – more than 4,000 in villages, 300 in state plants and most of the rest in the army.[136] Formal organization, however, gave no guarantees as to quality of members. The leaders of the newly renamed Workers' Party were quite sure what sort of people they wanted. Their March manifesto stated that it would be composed

...of the most patriotic, the most enthusiastic, the most revolutionary workers, peasants and intellectual workers. It will be composed of those who are determined to serve the fatherland, to serve the people, to serve labour, who place the overall interests of the country and the people above their own personal interests and who set the example in the War of Resistance and in national construction.[137]

On the other hand, the Central Committee's report in the previous month had spoken of serious faults emerging as a result of the very rapid expansion – 'individualism, bureaucracy, authoritarian attitudes, corruption and loose morals' had appeared.[138]

As to the class elements which had been attracted into the Party, there is only the scantiest evidence for this period. Obviously, the more senior positions would be occupied by people who had joined at an earlier time, probably before the August Revolution, and it seems likely that at that level the situation was typified by the statement that, among 1,315 key state posts, 139 were held by cadres of working class origins, while 351 had been 'working peasants'; the rest must have come from intermediate and upper levels.[139] Doubtless, the Party's rank and file recruits during the mass expansion were basically peasants, although not necessarily drawn from the poorest, as we shall see.

The Central Committee's report set out a number of measures necessary 'to build, strengthen and develop' the Party: training of cadres and members; ideological work, especially criticism and self-criticism and fighting 'rightist' and 'leftist' tendencies; improving organization; carrying out of studies to serve as a basis for policy; and, immediately, the adoption by the Second Congress of a new programme.[140] The last of these tasks was accomplished, but there is reason to believe that, during the next year, the other goals proved more difficult than expected. In late April 1952 the Third Plenum of the Central Committee (the numbering had begun again with the reconstitution as the Workers' Party) resolved that 'Party rectification is our main immediate task'. A stop was set on further recruitment to the Party. Between June 1952 and June 1953, courses were held for 800 senior Party and state officials and 11,380 from lower levels, and also for army officers and ranks with a 'narrower programme', but it is significant that emphasis was still placed on 'the unity of the entire people', rather than on class divisions.[141]

Through the question of the role of the Party, raised like so many others at its Second Congress in February 1951, we come once again to the wider question of the contradiction between the concept of broad national unity as the basis for the resistance struggle, and the need to mobilize on a class basis for the necessary effort to win victory. The resistance was characterized as 'sacred' (indeed, the word employed, *than thanh*, carries the force of 'divine'), and as being directed towards 'national salvation,' and appeals were made to the memories of national heroes and heroines. The Party had become skilled in tapping the centuries-old roots of Vietnamese history, and in arousing the patriotism which had always emerged in times of foreign menaces. Its leaders now had to decide whether they could continue to regard all but a small minority of their compatriots as partaking equally in that tradition. As we shall see in the next chapter, after February 1951 they significantly changed their approach.

Notes

1   Truong Chinh 1960 (originally published 1947), p. 89.
2   'Saigon: From Gia Dinh Citadel to Ho Chi Minh City', 1975, p. 22.
3   Nguyen Hoang, 'Combat Villages', *QDND* , 14 November 1964, p. 2.
4   A full account of events leading up to the creation of the Associated State may be found in Hammer 1966, Chapters 9 and 10. A further important source for the period up to 1954 is Lancaster 1961, and see also Duncanson 1968. Much of the flavour of events from the French point of view can be derived from the three volumes of Lucien Bodard 1963, 1965 and 1967. A translated and abridged version of the first two volumes can be found in Bodard 1967.
5   Quoted in Cheverny 1961, p. 162.
6   Vu Quoc Thong 1952, p. 337. See the whole discussion on pp. 336–52.
7   A formal legal description of the new institutions can be found in Blanchet 1954, Chapters 6 and 7.

8   Catala (unpublished) nd. (but lectures for trainee administrative officers 1947–48), Part 5, unpaginated.

9   Ibid.

10   Nguyen Anh Tuan 1967, pp. 86–8.

11   See Vo Do Thin 1954, pp. 59–60.

12   Lanoue 1971b, pp. 301–3. The Bank had also renegotiated its relationship with the French state apparatus just after the war, buying back the latter's shares for around 500 million francs and selling them to the public for almost three times as much (Buttinger vol. 1 1967, pp. 54–9, n. 76).

13   Lanoue 1971b, pp. 313–16.

14   Ibid., pp. 327 and 321.

15   Leffler 1984, p. 353.

16   *Le Commerce et L'industrie au Vietnam* 1953, p. 51.

17   Data on mining and manufacturing from ibid., pp. 13, 15 and 16.

18   On currency dealing see especially Despuech 1953, Chapters IV and V.

19   Nguyen Khac Vien 1966, p. 52.

20   Article in the journal *Tinh Than* ('The Spirit'), 4 September 1948, quoted in Porter unpublished 1976, p. 204. For a general discussion of intellectuals and landowners in this period see pp. 192–215.

21   Vu Van Hoan 1972, p. 69. Fall 1956, p. 28, dates this development after Ho's government withdrew from Hanoi in December 1946.

22   For details see *History of the Vietnamese People's Army* (in Vietnamese), vol. I 1977, footnote on pp. 309–10 and 333–4. See also Hoan 1972, pp. 68–9.

23   Van Tao 1965 (in Vietnamese), p. 20.

24   Data from *Achievements of the Democratic Republic of Viet Nam* 1949, p. 11.

25   Turley 1975, p. 138 and n. 10.

26   Ibid., pp. 138–9.

27   Fall 1956, p. 49.

28   *Summary History of the Party and Eight Lessons from Its Experience* (in Vietnamese) South Viet Nam (sic): Tien Phong Publishing House, vol. I, 1965), pp. 105–6, quoted in Elliott (unpublished) 1976, p. 119.

29   Vietnam News Agency 1955, p. 7.

30   Ibid., pp. 5, 6 and 7.

31   *Events in Party History* 1979 (in Vietnamese), p. 157. This speaks of 352,069 'workers,' which I take to mean both manual and non-manual.

32   Details from *Achievements of the Democratic Republic...* 1949, p. 17.

33   *Women of Viet-Nam in the struggle for national liberation* 1948, p. 15, and Mai Thi Tu and Le Thi Nham Tuyet 1978, p. 170.

34   Tao 1965 (in Vietnamese), p. 23.

35   Chinh 1960, p. 109.

36   Ibid., p. 107.

37   Ibid., p. 210.

38   Ibid., p. 127.

39   *Situations and Tasks* (in Vietnamese) nd, p. 25. This appears to have been a report prepared by the ICP Central Committee for presentation to a meeting of the National Assembly which was never actually called, and reviews the situation in a number of fields including land reform.

40   Vo Nhan Tri 1967, p. 121, and Nguyen Xuan Lai 1976, p. 61.

41   Lai 1976, p. 63.

42   *Situation and Tasks* nd, p. 25.

43   Lai 1976, p. 64.

44   *Situation and Tasks* nd, p. 26: the last point from Lai 1976, p. 62, with my own gloss.

45   Data calculated from Tran Phuong (ed.) 1968 (in Vietnamese), Table 7 (opposite p. 71),

174

and *Thirty years of Economic and Cultural Development of the Democratic Republic of Viet Nam* 1978 (in Vietnamese), Table 37, p.95.

46 See Lai 1976, p. 63.

47 Tri 1967, p. 118.

48 On this phenomenon see Vu Quoc Thuc 1951, pp. 240–2, though his comparison of this localization of trade with the pre-colonial situation should be treated with care.

49 Tri 1967, pp. 155–6.

50 Despuech 1953, p. 132. Data on this aspect of the Viet Minh political economy are basically found in hostile sources: see Fall 1956, pp. 109–11, Duong Chau 1958, pp. 40–8. and Despuech 1953, pp. 125–6.

51 Leroy 1977, p. 185.

52 For discussions on the anti-Communist side see Fall 1956, pp. 194–5, and Tran Nhu Trang (unpublished), 1972, pp. 225–6; for a pro-Communist discussion, Tri 1967, pp. 170–1.

53 Nguyen Ngoc Minh 1966, table on p. 214.

54 Thuc 1951, p. 243.

55 I follow here the line of argument in Dang Viet Chau 1964 (in Vietnamese), p. 56.

56 Truong Chinh 1960, facsimile edition published in Fall (ed.) 1963, pp. 114–17, 183 note, and 193 and note. The original text has not been available to me, and I do not know the extent, therefore, of the 1960 revisions.

57 Ibid., p. 146. I have followed Fall's note that the label 'defensive' is to be found in the French translation (the English text speaks of 'contention'), finding this more in line with the Maoist doctrine of protracted war. Moreover, in a text written two years later by Truong Chinh the Vietnamese term used for the first stage of the resistance is definitely 'defensive' (*phong ngu*): see Truong Chinh (in Vietnamese) 1949, especially pp. 11–14. The other two stages are characterized as those of 'resistance' and the general counter-offensive.

58 Chinh 1960, p. 154.

59 It is interesting to note that in one place in Chinh 1960 he even uses Mao's famous metaphor of resistance fighters and people as fish and water, without acknowledgement (p. 116).

60 I was prompted to look at these points further by Duiker 1981, p. 130. However, it should be evident that my emphasis is quite different from that of his general verdict that 'Despite some departures from Maoism, Truong Chinh's analysis was a reasonably straightforward application of Maoist doctrine to the revolutionary struggle in Vietnam' (loc. cit.).

61 Chinh 1960, p. 140.

62 Mao 1938b, pp. 145–8.

63 Ibid., pp. 158-9.

64 Chinh 1960, pp. 188–9.

65 Mao 1938b, p. 126.

66 Chinh 1960, p. 143.

67 Mao 1938b, pp. 142–3.

68 Chinh 1960, pp. 152-3.

69 Mao 1938c, p. 221.

70 See particularly Chinh 1960, Chapter 17.

71 *Fifty years of activity of the Communist Party of Viet Nam* 1979 (in Vietnamese), pp. 97–8.

72 Quotation from the Plenum resolution, in *History of The Vietnamese People's Army* 1977 (in Vietnamese), p. 331. See further *Bréve histoire du Parti des Travailleurs du Viet Nam* 1976, p. 49.

73 *Fifty years of activity...* 1979, p. 101.

74 Giap, 'Immediate military tasks for switching to the general counter-offensive,' Porter (ed.) 1979 vol. I, pp. 232 and 233, translated by editor.

75 Quoted in Chen 1969, pp. 176–7.
76 Ibid., pp. 178–9 and 188–9.
77 Ibid., pp. 189 and 193–5.
78 See McLane 1966, pp. 365–6.
79 Chen 1969, p. 218, citing NCNA report, 19 November 1949.
80 See ibid., pp. 229–30.
81 Document 121, Porter 1979, vol. I, p. 178.
82 See 'On the Vietnamese Revolution', Part One in Truong Chinh 1977. The long delay by the USSR in recognizing the Democratic Republic is probably explained by Stalin's concern with the fortunes of the French Communist Party, which during the period of participation in the government (1945–47) had committed itself to the French Union: see further Porter 1980, pp. 229–32.
83 Document 183, Porter 1979, vol. I, p. 274.
84 For details see *History of the People's Army of Viet Nam* 1977, Chapter 7, Part IV, and *Fifty years of activity...* 1979, pp. 103–5 (both in Vietnamese).
85 See *Fifty years ...* 1979, p. 105.
86 Chen 1969, pp. 235–6 and 238.
87 Tanham 1967, p. 42.
88 See O'Ballance 1964, pp. 112–3, and Fall 1956, p. 85–6.
89 Fall 1956, p. 86.
90 Ibid., pp. 65 and 67. For the texts of these decrees and commentary see *The Problem of Agrarian Reform* (in Vietnamese) 1950, vol. II, and *The New Reforms of the Government* (in Vietnamese) 1950.
91 See tables in *The New Reforms...* 1950, pp. 54 and 59.
92 Isoart 1961, pp. 393 and 394.
93 Some Party members also detected this implication: in its report to the Second Congress, presented by Truong Chinh, the Central Committee had to assure them that 'a narrow sentimental standpoint' was not appropriately revolutionary, that '"labour" is a beautiful word' despite the existence of a British Labour Party (*lao dong* can mean both 'labour' and 'workers'), and, most significantly, that with the successes of the Soviet Union attracting the support of many 'intermediate social strata in various countries' the name 'Communist' was no longer necessary to attract 'the masses'. ('On the Vietnamese Revolution' in Truong Chinh 1977, pp. 434–6.)
94 Ibid., pp. 433–4.
95 Chinh 1977, p. 407.
96 Ibid., pp. 407 and 408.
97 On this see Turley 1975, pp. 137–9. One of the first manuals for use in such work was *Political Officers in the Army* , published in Hanoi in 1945.
98 'The Party's Policy Concerning the National United Front', Chinh 1977, p. 458.
99 'On the Vietnamese Revolution', Chinh 1977, pp. 404–5.
100 Ibid., p. 423. See also Fall 1956, pp. 65–7.
101 See McAlister 1967.
102 Ngo Tien Chat 1969 (in Vietnamese), p. 13.
103 'On the Vietnamese Revolution', Chinh 1977, pp. 411–14.
104 Details from Hinnens (unpublished) 1961, pp. 26–8.
105 LaBrie (unpublished) 1971, pp. 48–50.
106 Hinnens (unpublished) 1961, p. 28.
107 LaBrie (unpublished) 1971, pp. 50–52.
108 See Schrock et al. 1966, and the memoirs of the chief French agent among the Hre, Riesen 1957.
109 O'Ballance 1964, pp. 201–2. The Meo prefer to be called Hmong, but the former name is so universal in the literature that I have kept to it.

176

110   See Hinnens (unpublished) 1961, pp. 28–30.
111   'On the Vietnamese Revolution', Chinh 1977, pp. 415–16.
112   For the 1945–46 period see Colton (unpublished) 1969, Chapter XIII.
113   See Nguyen Manh Ha 1967, p. 222. Generally on the Catholics and the liberation struggle see Fall 1956, pp. 68–71, Nguyen Anh Tuan 1967, pp. 33–4, and Tran Tam Tinh 1978, pp. 65–89 and 179–85.
114   Fall 1956, pp. 70–1.
115   For two see Ho Thi Bi 1958, and the story of Nguyen Thi Luong in Burchett 1957, pp. 106–12. See also Tu and Tuyet 1978, pp. 153–68.
116   'Manifesto of the Viet-Nam Lao Dong', in Cole (ed.) 1956, p. 108.
117   There were 19 full and 10 alternate (non-voting) members of the Central Committee. For details see Fall 1956, pp. 42 and 44.
118   'On the Vietnamese Revolution', Chinh 1977, p. 356, amended from the text in Truong Chinh (in Vietnamese) 1956, p. 55. Wherever possible I have checked the 1977 text against the earlier one and amended accordingly, since there has been significant editorial change in the English text; unfortunately this has only been partially possible, since Volume I of Chinh 1956 was published in two parts, of which I have had access only to the first.
119   Chinh 1956, p. 55, and 1977, p. 355.
120   'Platform' of the Lao Dong (Workers') Party, in Cole (ed.) 1956, p. 99.
121   See Kautsky 1956, pp. 12–13, which also draws attention to the similarity between Liu's and the Vietnamese formulations.
122   Chinh 1956, p. 17 and 1977, pp. 312–13. For discussion see Schram 1963, pp. 46–7, and Marcou 1977, pp. 168–72.
123   Chinh 1956, pp. 68–9, and 1977, pp. 369–70.
124   Chinh 1977, p. 444.
125   Ibid., pp. 444, 388–9 and 391–2.
126   Chinh 1956, p. 70, emphasis in the original, and 1977, pp. 371–2. There are significant variations between the 1951 and 1977 texts.
127   Cole (ed.) 1956, p. 100.
128   See Mao Tse-tung 1949. This reference was deleted in the 1977 edition, presumably to reduce the impression of theoretical indebtedness to the Chinese Revolution: see Chinh 1977, p. 372, and 1956, p. 71.
129   Chinh 1956, p. 72, and 1977, p. 373. The 1977 edition adds a note identifying the worker–peasant dictatorship with proletarian dictatorship, presumably to ensure orthodoxy.
130   Chinh 1977, p. 395.
131   Cole (ed.) 1956, p. 101.
132   'Manifesto of the Viet-Nam Lao Dong', ibid., p. 107.
133   *Events in Party History* 1979, vol. II, p. 132 (in Vietnamese).
134   Ibid., p. 228. These figures presumably include members in Laos and Cambodia, which may have in effect represented the odd 65,000 in 1950.
135   *Party Members' Training and Investigation Plan* (in Vietnamese) 1950, p. 1.
136   Ibid.
137   Cole (ed.) 1956, p. 107.
138   Chinh 1977, pp. 440–1.
139   'Din' 1953, p. 4.
140   Chinh 1977, pp. 442–7.
141   'Din' 1953, p. 4. See also Le Van Luong, 'Why must there be Party Rectification?',*ND*, 3 July 1952, and 'The Content of the Task of Party Rectification', *ND* , 17 July 1952, reprinted in *The Sacred Resistance of The Vietnamese People* (in Vietnamese) 1960, vol. 3, pp. 294–5, and 299–303. (I am grateful to Christine White for showing me her extracts from this work).

7 The political economy of liberation war from the turning point

In early 1951 the theoretical presentations by the Workers' Party in its Central Committee report, manifesto and programme in fact still left room for some uncertainty as to how they viewed the situation of various classes in Vietnamese history and thus in the present struggle. At the same time, the Party had to position itself, as it had in other conjunctions, in relation to the different class and other social forces. Indeed, during the first half of 1951, spanning its Second Congress, the Party and its government suffered a very definite setback on the military front, calling into question the speed at which the general counter-offensive could be developed.

The French high command reacted to the loss of control over the Chinese border in late 1950 by attempting to wall in the Red River delta more securely with the 'De Lattre Line' of fortifications. In January 1951 General Giap unleashed his new divisions on their first attempt to break through to the most densely populated areas, and this was followed by another assault in March and a third in May. Despite prodigies of logistics and valour, all three were broken, mainly by massive French use of fire-power, including napalm bombing.[1]

Moreover, 1951 brought the realization that the idea of building up to a general counter-offensive in Nam Bo was probably out of the question in the foreseeable future. As we saw in Chapter 5, the situation there had been quite different from that in the centre and north from the eve of the August Revolution. Starting with a mixture of Viet Minh, VNQDD, Cao Dai, Hoa Hao

178

and Binh Xuyen guerrillas, the resistance to the French had to reorganize with the falling away of the last four during 1946.[2] Under French pressure there was protracted reorganization in 1949, when the division into two types of armed units was applied when it was already being replaced by a threefold system elsewhere. Again, in 1950 the so-called Inter-Regiments were turned into standard Main Force units, but, as shown in Table 7.1, the balance between different types of forces (expressing different combat demands) was by no means the same in the three parts of the country.

Table 7.1 Viet Minh organization balance of military units; 1949 and 1951

| | Main Force Units | | Regional Units | |
	April 1949	June 1951	April 1949	June 1951
Bac Bo	20	78	50	6
Trung Bo	7	21	43	6
Nam Bo	5	18	44	25

Source: Adapted from Tanham 1967, table, p. 49.

These changes were occurring during and in the wake of heavier fighting, starting in late 1949 when Nguyen Binh, the Nam Bo Viet Minh commander, launched his 'Red Days' attacks in Saigon and elsewhere. If these were meant to be a contribution to the evolution of the general counter-offensive they were highly counterproductive, since they were defeated and led to an intensified French response. In face of this, two of the four Main Force Regiments had to be divided into smaller units under provincial control.[3] Probably in November 1951, Nguyen Binh was recalled from his command in the south and was killed in an ambush by Laotian forces fighting for the French on his way north.[4] The Party's Central Committee now took firmer control through a new Directorate which gave the leadership to such disciplined cadres as Le Duan and Le Duc Tho, previously overshadowed by Binh.[5]

Overall, the setbacks in the first half of 1951 had three major results. First, it was already clear that Nam Bo was not going to be a decisive area for military victory in the liberation war. The general counter-offensive, when it did come, would in fact have to be in Bac Bo, where Main Force units could be organized in the Viet Bac sanctuaries and supplied from People's China. Second, for this material reason and because a stronger need was no doubt felt for a good grip on military doctrine, the influence of the Chinese leadership seems to have been strengthened. From Giap's defeats the lesson was drawn that 'One must know strategy', and that 'It is our duty to digest the principles of the great Mao Tse-tung's strategy and to make good use of them by adapting them to the circumstances of the moment and place, and taking into account our own situation in the interior of the country'.[6] Third, there was a reorganization of the Viet Nam People's Army command and field structures and the creation of another division of heavy artillery to meet French firepower.[7]

In November 1951 the military balance again shifted, this time in the DRVN's favour. The French high command launched a major campaign in Hoa Binh province, south-west of the Red River delta, hoping to destroy the liberated area there, rally the Muong people finally to the side of Bao Dai and cut communication between the Viet Bac and other Interzones. In bitter fighting, lasting into January 1952, three of the new divisions, supplied by 150,000 porters and other Main Force units halted and ground away General deLattre de Tassigny's troops.[8] With the advantage of hindsight, it can be said that this was probably the turning-point of the liberation war; the French-led forces were never again able to take the real initiative. Immediately this meant, militarily, that President Ho's government had survived a very real threat; politically it meant that the people's democratic dictatorship, which it claimed to represent, could be consolidated in the next years. By the end of the war in July 1954 the government controlled some 6 million people in liberated zones over which its writ ran sufficiently securely to ensure that policies could be made effective.[9] As far as those policies were concerned, it could also now control their economic lives quite effectively.

The 'People's Democratic Economy' and Class

The main instrument for economic and social control had been set up in 1951, in the months after the Second Congress. In March the First Plenum (new series) of the Central Committee decided on necessary measures of financial reform and reorganization of trade, and in May a series of decrees set up a National Bank, brought in a new currency – the so-called 'Bank-dong' – and rationalized the tax system. In August a new State Trading Service replaced the Office of Supply and Transport. The object of all this was to meet the situation of inadequate revenue and inflation which we noted earlier as prevailing in the territories held by the Democratic Republic by 1950. Taking the latter problem first, we can see from Table 7.2 how the questions of currency supply and prices were gradually brought under control.

It seems evident from these figures that it was less the checks on currency supply and more the increased availability of goods which in the end brought the general price index below the already very inflated 1949 level. No doubt this was in part due to the labour of many small artisans, who in Interzone IV, for example, provided 96 per cent of textile supplies, and whose ingenuity is best expressed by the famous 'Ho Chi Minh sandals' made of old tyres.[10] Above all, however, the decisive factor must have been the increased supplies from the French-held areas and from Communist China. Under the aegis of the State Trading Service, the former, which had stood at only 41 per cent of their 1948 level in 1951, rose more than 23 times by 1954, while the latter expanded over four and a half times between 1952 and 1954.[11] Trade and aid agreements with China were signed in January and November 1950 and July and November 1951. In January 1952 some of the aid was described as 'unconditional'. A further agreement in July 1952, with a supplement in May 1953, was renewed in 1954.[12] The balance of trade with China remained unfavourable, but under the watchful eye of a new Committee for Economic Struggle exports to the enemy zones remained considerably in excess of imports and a useful earner of the harder piastre.

Nevertheless, it must be emphasized that it was state control rather than increased productivity which stabilized prices and created the favourable balance of trade. The political economy of liberation war necessarily had to place questions of supply above provenance; in effect, production on the enemy side of the line had to be regarded as favourably as one's own. And in such circumstances the role of the state was bound to expand: the State Trading Service had a virtual monopoly of trade with China, while its share of commerce with the occupied areas rose from 2.5 per cent in 1952 to 42.4 per cent in 1954.[13]

Table 7.2 Currency supply and prices, DRVN 1949–1954

	1949	1950	1951 (Jan.–May)	1951 (June-Dec.)*	1952	1953	1954
Currency Issue	100	264	178	317	336	152	256
Prices	100	440	464	360	335	115	92

* Control from May by new National Bank.
Source : Nguyen Ngoc Minh 1966, p. 214.

Taxation, however, was the major point of contact between the people's democratic state and its citizens. The reform of May 1951 standardized the previous heterogeneous levies into seven different taxes, the most important of which was a consolidated agricultural tax. This was levied on the total paddy produced, thus encouraging cultivation of secondary food crops and industrial crops, and calculated on a basis of rice available for each member of the household; if this was less than sixty kilos no tax was levied. Rates were progressive, from 6 to 45 per cent, but remissions for 'working peasants' and surcharges on landlords living off rents set the effective amounts at between

4.5 and 51.5 per cent. Rates were also lower in French-held areas – since there the occupiers were also levying taxes – and in the mountainous territories of the minority groups.[14] In the absence of data, it is impossible to estimate the impact of the new tax on different social levels.[15] It is certainly true, however, that it proved to be an effective way of raising state income. In 1952 it represented 77 per cent of total receipts and the budget deficit was reduced to 18 per cent (from 77 per cent in 1950); in 1953 agricultural tax formed 71.2 per cent of state income and there was a budget surplus of 16 per cent.[16]

By the end of the liberation war in mid-1954, therefore, the state apparatus of the people's democratic dictatorship was based upon an economy which, in the modest summation of a later Communist economist 'was insufficient but still guaranteed the supply of food for both the front and the rear lines, and provided each person with nearly 3 metres of cotton fabric [a year]. [17] It must again be stressed – for this was to prove a major concern after the war – that productivity remained low in the liberated areas and supplies were obtained basically by trade: 93 per cent of the credits from the new Central Bank went to finance commerce.[18] With this in mind we may look more closely at the class profile of the Democratic Republic.

In its February 1951 report, the Central Committee of the Workers' Party had defined the workers as the leading class in the Revolution. We will look later at what was happening to those who remained still concentrated in the urban centres under French rule. What must be noted here is that part of the established working class, that most closely aligned with the ICP and its General Confederation of Labour, had uprooted themselves after the end of 1946 and, often literally carrying machinery and other means of production on their backs, had moved into the liberated areas. Many became skilled members of the armed forces. Machine shops, mines, paintworks, textile mills, footwear plants, a match factory, chemical works and in particular munitions plants were also set up, often initially on trade union initiative, and then were absorbed into a state industrial sector. By 1952 there were 36 factories with around 4,000 workers.[19] Another important fraction of the working class was involved in transport. In Interzone V (lower Trung Bo) railway workers actually managed to keep 300 kilometres of line open, in Interzones III and IV (the Red River delta and upper Trung Bo) the General Confederation created enterprise TK4; along with other units during over seven years of war transport workers repaired nearly 2,000 kilometres of road, built more than 1,000 bridges and ran motor launches and ferries on the rivers.[20]

The working class which thus formed in the liberated areas was not large; official figures put its component of state employees at the end of the war at 44,436 workers in production and 17,184 'labourers' (probably mostly construction workers in communications).[21] To these units must be added 200,000 or more (on the basis of 1948 figures) who were employed in private enterprise, in the many small factories and workshops which provided most consumer goods.[22] Workers were necessarily dispersed in face of the menace of French military thrusts and later bombing raids, although by 1953 supplies of anti-aircraft guns from China made it possible to group some plants together.[23] Nor were enterprises large. The munitions plant was probably the biggest, with a reported 600 workers, 15 per cent of them women.[24] There was a coal mine and a paper works with nearly 300 workers each, another paper works with over 200, but apparently only five other state establishments with more than 100.[25] Nevertheless, the workers were highly organized and politically conscious. A high proportion of state workers would have been Party members; one observer reports 50 per cent at the MK munitions plant.[26]

The main organizational force, however, was the Confederation of Labour. This embraced a number of constituent unions, for armaments workers, postal workers, teachers and so on, and claimed 168,142 members in the liberated areas and 37,436 in occupied territory in early 1948, 258,000 members in August 1949 and over 300,000 in late 1953.[27] Given that the 135,000 DRVN state employees would all be counted as members, this figure might be possible. (The dues of members in the occupied areas, Haiphong postal employees for example, were an important source of hard currency.) The Confederation was thus a major political force; its head, Hoang Quoc Viet, himself an old working-class militant as we have seen, was a member of the Politburo and a Vice-President of the National United Front. The main task of the unions was to improve production, both in quantity and quality. On 1 May 1948 the first major 'emulation' movement was launched to increase productivity, and by 1952 this had spread into the private sector; by the end of the war a contribution of around 72 million voluntary 'national salvation work hours' was claimed, along with 45,456 initiatives taken by workers to rationalize production methods.[28] In May 1952 a National Congress of Model Workers and Model Cadres was held, at which two Labour Heroes were nominated – a worker in an explosives plant who had remained active even after being severely mutilated in an explosion, and an engineer who had developed several new weapons. Over the next years 12,466 'model workers', both men and women, were designated by their fellows.[29]

All this activity certainly made the working class a leading force in the resistance struggle and the Revolution, and no doubt also gave it – or at least those in state employment – a relatively privileged position. Thus, the reported wage at the munitions plant was 38 kilos of rice per month for a 48-hour week (with another six hours, political study). A guaranteed supply of 456 kilos of rice per year was obviously a major asset in conditions of war economy, while also important was the annual payment of 12 yards of textiles and four pounds of salt, the former some four times the average consumption and the surpluses of both saleable on the open market.[30]

On the other hand, it must not be supposed that capitalists were particularly disadvantaged in the territories of the Democratic Republic. The 'people's democratic economy' was seen as including five sectors, two of which were the 'private capitalist' for the national bourgeoisie and the 'state capitalist' where they might operate in partnership with the government. (The others were for state ownership, cooperatives, and small private producers and traders.)[31] The Workers' Party manifesto declared that the 'national bourgeoisie has to be encouraged, assisted and guided in its enterprises'.[32] In March 1952, in a joint appeal, the Standing Committee of the National Assembly and the Central Committee of the NUF (within which the capitalists had their own Democratic Party) called on:

> ...industrialists and traders to contribute their efforts and abilities to the building of the national economy, in order to safeguard our independence, to invest their capital in co-operation with the people's organs, on the basis of mutual interests of both parties, capital and labour, as defined by the government policy and that of the National Front, and to establish many trading companies in order to develop exchanges.[33]

As we shall see, when a radical land reform policy was adopted during 1953, the same class elements were assured that it would not adversely affect their interests.

As for the middle strata, they too had an established place in the regime of the people's democratic dictatorship. With certain forms of knowledge at a premium – engineering and medicine in particular – individuals at their upper levels were sure of an honoured place. The educational expansion under the Democratic Republic – one of its most remarkable achievements, with over 680,000 children in school after reorganization in 1950–51, meant many more jobs for teachers, while higher education had also been greatly broadened in both the Democratic University of Viet Nam and new colleges in the Viet Bac for medicine, veterinary science, agriculture, languages, teacher training and public works engineering.[34] These class elements were also well represented in the trade union organization, as was their own Socialist Party as a member of the NUF.

The cohesion of the middle strata, however, was above all maintained by the fact that a major bloc of their members were employees of the state apparatus. Actual officials were periodically reduced in numbers by assigning redundant elements to productive work or the army; in July–September 1951 alone 35,159 were thus dealt with (administrative costs as a part of the budget dropped from 27.8 per cent in 1951 to 16.8 per cent in 1953). Nevertheless, there were still 73,708 state officials at the end of the liberation war compared with the 44,435 productive workers.[35] How many full-time Party employees there were is not known, but in 1953 and 1954 up to 4,000 at a time were sent into the rural areas for rent reduction and land reform campaigns.

A large proportion, though by no means all, of these may be regarded as cadres, the ideological and organizational activists references to whom in the pronouncements of Party and government in these and following years were to provide a sort of bass note in the orchestration of the Revolution. Setters of

184

examples in all things, particularly in the industry, thrift, integrity and uprightness which were extolled as the 'four revolutionary virtues', the cadres were expected to be first in discipline, knowledge and judgement.[36] They had to perform the worst tasks with the least thanks, and to face possible torture, mutilation or death while behind enemy lines with equanimity. They were, in short, a very special element in the revolutionary process. As a sympathetic foreign observer wrote of these men and women in French–occupied territory:

> To preserve the cadres is the first law of life in these villages. For it is they who assist the peasants in hoeing, in teaching new methods, in helping on the dykes, in forming the guerrilla lines. They are the key figures in helping to maintain the local liberation governments, in planning and stimulating the struggles against the puppet regimes.[37]

Moreover, the cadres *knew* that they were special. Often selfless to a degree which an outsider can find admirable but impossible to emulate, they obviously had a sense of corporate identity. Significantly, they could even joke wryly about themselves, mimicking the Party's liking for slogans by numbers in complaining of the '3 manys' and '3 fews' which governed their lives – tasks, responsibilities and reprimands versus powers, material benefits and citations and promotions.[38]

In the contours of the people's democratic dictatorship there thus existed – scarcely yet even semi-formed – a constellation of cadres, bureaucracy in general and state power which could in the future provide the basis for a whole new set of social relations. At the end of 1952 it was older, more conventional class forces which were the basic concern. In December President Ho presaged a new move in his 'Appeal on the Occasion of the Sixth Anniversary of the Nationwide Resistance'. Setting out, as was usual in this annual message, the lines of policy for the coming year, he emphasized that:

> ...the peasants make the biggest contribution to the Resistance and the greatest sacrifice to the Fatherland. Nevertheless they are the poorest people because they have not enough land to till....Reduction of land rent and interest rates which are their legitimate rights cannot be undertaken properly. This is a most unjust situation.[39]

In January 1953 the Central Committee at its Fourth Plenum finally faced squarely the issue of landlord and peasant. At this point Main Force divisions had just completed a new major campaign west to the Laotian frontier, upon the basis of which another was to be fought in April and May 1953 in Laos itself. The high command of the Democratic Republic was now finding its final strategy for the general counter-offensive – broad strokes to force the French to over extend their forces and pull them off balance. In January 1953 the Central Committee also laid down the essential military line:

Our strategic orientation is to exert our efforts in the direction of 'soft' spots, attacking the enemy wherever he is weak, compelling him to scatter his forces. We shall thus create conditions for the liberation of the northern delta.[40]

This had two important implications for current and future policies. First, the change of name from Indochinese Communist Party had not ruled out a grand revolutionary – and hence military - strategy for all three territories. Thus in February 1951 the new Workers' Party, which was now for Vietnamese only, had formed a United Front with the nationalist and Communist-influenced Pathet Lao in Laos and Khmer Issarak in Cambodia. The Party's platform spoke of 'long term cooperation with the peoples of Laos and Cambodia, with a view to bringing about an independent, free, strong and prosperous federation of the states of Viet Nam, Laos and Cambodia, if the three peoples so desire'.[41] The first step would have to be the final military victory implied in the new strategic line. And, let it again be stressed, its second implication was that this could only be achieved by a mighty effort of peasants, who had to fight and carry supplies, produce the rice to feed soldiers and porters, pay taxes, perhaps die themselves or lose family members in the cause of national salvation.

The question was whether anything more tangible than this undoubtedly noble aspiration was being offered in return? Whatever the contribution of other classes, by the end of 1952 the fate of the Revolution came down to the issue of the peasants' livelihood, and that was still bound up with the fate of the landlords and rich peasants. Thus the social relations involved constituted the most basic contour of the revolutionary terrain that had still to be formed. In the name of national salvation, the Party had extended the concept of a patriotic national bourgeoisie to 'patriotic' landlords. We noted earlier the reluctance of most landlords to comply with the decrees on rent reduction. Not only did such foot-dragging now appear to government and Party to be slowing down the whole Revolution, but the conviction was growing that these wealthy class elements – along with rich peasants who were their natural allies – were even more actively inimical to it. As Truong Chinh was to put it in a speech to a national conference of the Party in November 1953:

The further we proceed with necessary democratic policies...the more strongly the feudal landlord class reacts and the more closely it colludes with the imperialists to oppose the resistance and oppose the people's administration.[42]

The pressure on landlords had in fact increased in the period August 1949 to April 1953, when they lost a further 30.8 per cent of all they were to lose in the total process of land reform.[43] Evidence existed by early 1953 that some landlords and rich peasants had transformed their anger at loss of land and pressure to disgorge back-rents and pay more taxes into collaboration with French agents. More generally, they still often behaved like petty despots in

186

their villages; the old colonial circle of notables was still not broken. Often they had even accommodated to the new presence of the Party, Viet Minh and NUF by joining them and leading them locally. Thus, a survey of 22 villages in the Viet Bac and northern Trung Bo showed that in April 1953 landlords made up 13.5 per cent and rich peasants 15 per cent of Party committees; only 3.7 per cent of members were poor peasants, 3.5 per cent were classified as 'petty bourgeois' and 61.4 per cent were middle peasants, many of whom might well take the part of their 'natural' leaders.[44] Moreover, by denouncing the 'feudal landlord class' as if it were a clearly defined entity, the Communist leaders were in danger of disguising how deeply entrenched were their enemies. We saw in Chapter 4 how difficult it is to speak of the existence of a class of real feudal landlords in Vietnamese history, and in Chapter 2 that in the colonial period Tonkin (Bac Bo) and Annam (Trung Bo) were characterized by a mosaic of small holdings, some of them held in combination by single families, giving a chance to rent out part. Outside western Nam Bo we are speaking, therefore, not of big landlords, but of predominantly small ones who faded imperceptibly into rich peasants, and in that sense were much more deeply rooted.

This aspect of rural class relations was to cause the Party and government great problems over the next four years. That followed from the Fourth Plenum's decision in January 1953 that it must move decisively beyond rent and interest reduction, distribution of communal lands and grants of lands confiscated from French and 'traitor' owners for temporary use 'to set up a new system of land ownership in the interest of the working peasant'.[45] Even then, that was not to be undertaken in the coming year. Before campaigning for 'Land to the Tiller', the leadership wanted to press for a final enforcement of the rent reduction decrees, and in so doing test out a new method. Policy was not to be enforced by the local Resistance Administrative Committees alone, but principally through mass mobilization of poor peasants by party cadres. Caution demanded that the first wave of the new movement be confined to 25 villages in Thai Nguyen, Phu Tho and Thanh Hoa provinces, but the principle was established; class struggle and not administrative action was henceforward to be the form of rural change. Intentions in fact ran even beyond involvement of the majority of peasants. As stated in a later survey by Truong Chinh, aims were: to destroy the power of the landlords and make the 'working peasants' the masters; 'to liquidate the system of feudal land expropriation, establish the system of land ownership by working peasants, release land to the tillers and liberate the productive forces in the countryside'; 'to educate the peasants ideologically and politically'; and to 'bind together and reorganize organizations in the countryside, reorganize party branches, peasant associations, the political authorities, militia units, branches of the Vietnamese Youth for National Salvation, of the Union of Vietnamese Women; strengthen and support cadre units'.[46] It was thus intended in every respect to take a firmer grip upon the rural areas.

In March and April the Party was given new instruments for these purposes. In the former month, implicitly recognizing the difficulty of separating landlords from rich peasants and those from middle, the decree on 'The Differentiation of Class Status in the Countryside' was promulgated.[47] This laid down in considerable detail the procedures which were to be followed in determining the place of individuals and households in various classes and strata, a classification which was absolutely necessary for the new mobilization and policies. The decisive question was the way in which family income was secured. Three elements were discerned: the personal work of members; earnings from such activities as stock-raising, fishing and woodcutting; and rents, interest and use of wage labour, the 'dishonest products of exploitation'. If a family derived the principal means for its existence from the last – which in practice was taken as meaning that less than a third of its able-bodied members worked in agriculture themselves or that three-quarters of their land was rented out – then it was categorized as 'landlord'. Families which had members who might otherwise have worked the land themselves but were serving as cadres or in the army were exempted from the implications of this. As for rich peasants, they were defined as also partly living from exploitation, distinguished from middle peasants in that more than a quarter of their income was so derived, but the (male) household head worked himself in agriculture for more than a quarter of the working year, reckoned at 120 days total. The other peasant categories together made up the 'working peasants': the middle stratum, who basically worked on owned or rented land and achieved a subsistence, and the poor, who had to supplement work on land to which they had access by wage labour. At the bottom were landless labourers.

In addition, five other categories were discerned, and an important exception made to those who might have been defined as landlords. The first category was middle strata elements (like cadres, civil servants and professionals), small traders, soldiers, the families of war dead and those unfit to work who had a little land; subject to approval of local peasants, their main occupation was to define their status. Second, 'new rich' peasants, who had emerged since the August Revolution 'thanks to the land reform and through the application throughout the countryside of the principles of democracy, thanks also to the personal efforts which they have made', were also to be favoured above others in their stratum. Paupers, vagrants and clergy comprised the other categories. As for the exception, in line with policy regarding 'national' capitalists which we have noted above, land used for trading and manufacturing installations or dwellings or for growing raw materials was not to be counted in defining landlords, only that rented to peasant tenants.

Finally in surveying the main elements of the population classification decree, its implications for the position of rural women must be noted. These can only be described as conservative, since female labour was not specifically singled out and was regarded as encapsulated within the household. Moreover, while the decree did concern itself with women who changed status by marriage, its implications were discriminatory. Thus, daughters of landlords, rich peasants or 'bourgeois' families who married workers or labourers would get their husband's status 'as soon as they have spent one year providing for their own subsistence by labour'; if they did not work outside the household they remained in their former category, which meant that household labour was not considered to be equal to other forms. Daughters of workers and peasants who had married 'upwards' were allowed three years' grace before reclassification, but apparently could not save themselves by any form of work.[48]

As an instrument, this decree was to have far-reaching effects over the next years of land reform, and we shall see that these were not necessarily positive ones. In keeping with the new strategy of mobilization, it concluded by emphasizing that all matters of doubt were to be put before the 'popular masses'. However, powers of adjudication on matters of fact were not the only ones to be given to the poor and landless. Committees were now set up on all administrative levels to supervise policy implementation; these were responsible to a special Party committee – headed formally by Pham Van Dong but in practice by Truong Chinh – and were drawn from the Peasant Associations (with representation from the Resistance Administrative Committees and NUF), but membership had to be at least two-thirds poor and landless and one-third middle peasants.[49] The Special People's Courts created by decree in April were also to have a majority membership of poor and middle peasants, to be selected by district conferences of peasant delegates and Resistance Administrative Committees and with up to a third drawn from the village where cases might be heard. They were created 'in order to guarantee the application of the agrarian policy, the maintenance of social order, the strengthening of the people's legal authority, and to push the Resistance to victory'.[50] A decree issued on the same day gave them power to impose sentences of up to ten years' imprisonment and confiscation of property for such crimes as illegal collection of rents and more political delictions such as spreading false rumours about the government or collaborating with the French; for more serious offences involving loss of life, the new courts could impose the death penalty. Sentences were subject to review by district and Interzone Resistance Administrative Committees.[51]

Supported by these important new extensions of the state apparatus, Party cadres went into the pilot villages with instruction to 'rely on the poor peasants, unite closely with the middle peasants, neutralize the rich peasants, overthrow traitors, reactionaries and wicked village bullies'.[52] In pursuance of these aims they followed the 'three togethers', living, eating and working with the poor peasants, seeking to 'take root' by 'asking about poverty'. As the poor peasants thus became conscious they would 'string beads' – recruit others – and some could be recruited as activists. At this stage, 'bead-stringing' was extended to middle peasants.[53]   When a sufficiently strong bloc had been created, neutralizing the rich peasants and isolating the landlords and their henchmen (the 'traitors, reactionaries and wicked village bullies'), the local Peasants Association could be reformed to make membership conform to the two-thirds poor, one-third middle formula. Further, the village Party branch itself could be purged; in 22 villages poor peasant membership of Party committees rose from 3.7 percent to 53 per cent, while the middle stratum dropped from 61.4 to 44, 'petty bourgeois' members from 3.5 to 3 per cent, and landlords and rich peasants disappeared.[54] With the levers of power thus firmly in their hands, the cadres and activists could launch 'struggle meetings', at which landlords could be denounced, forced to answer, and arrested if necessary. The codification of reform decrees in April gave the legal basis for the struggle, at this stage still directed to repayment of excess rents and interest (the former now not to exceed more than a third of the crop and with a moratorium on all debts owed to those in French-held territory), to distribution of communal lands, and to confiscation of the land of French citizens and traitors.[55]

Faced with this threat, it is not surprising that the landlords, and some of the rich peasants at least, resisted, finding ingenious ways to disguise their exactions and seeking to roll back the gains of the poor once the cadres had left the village. As Truong Chinh was to put it in his speech to the Party conference in November, 'in the villages where the masses have been mobilized for land rent reduction, the class struggle, far from waning remains difficult and relentless and continues in new forms'. 'We should not forget', he went on, 'that all through history, the nearer their doom, the more strongly an exploiting social class struggles for its survival.'[56] Already in August 1953 the Politburo of the Workers' Party had begun to think again about the form of further campaigns. In the trial one, now ended, problems had arisen not only because of the resistance of the 'haves' but of the unleashed resentment of the 'have-nots'. More landlords had been denounced than had been expected, rich peasants had not merely been 'neutralized' but actually attacked, middle peasants had become confused by their position between poor and rich.[57] This situation was both politically unsettling and harmful to production. Therefore, for the second wave of the rent reduction campaign, to be conducted in 163 villages, it was directed that strong measures should be taken against no more than five landlords in large villages and three in smaller ones, and that others should have a chance to engage in self-criticism and voluntary surrender of ill-gotten gains. Even more important, the class line was changed: the slogan was now not to 'neutralize' the rich peasants but to 'ally' with them.[58]

The meeting of Party cadres and local representatives in November was obviously intended to take the situation further in hand. In the presence of Ho Chi Minh, Truong Chinh, as General Secretary, presented a lengthy report. Listeners were reminded that:

...the present form of our people's national democratic revolution is an anti-imperialist and anti-feudal revolution, a revolution of the broad masses of the people, that is, of the working class, the peasantry, the petty bourgeoisie, the national bourgeoisie and democratic personalities, led by the working class, on the basis of the worker-peasant alliance.

Then, however, a very important gloss was added: 'At present our people's patriotic war is in essence a revolutionary war of the peasants, led by the working class.'[59] In fact, as we have noted, the leadership of the workers rather resembled the relationship of central nervous system to Party brain; now, with the need to base so much effort on peasants' willingness to make sacrifices, the Politburo was even shortcircuiting that connection. This more direct link of Party and peasant, along with the solicitude of the former for 'national' capitalists, is illustrated by the care taken to keep peasant and worker struggles apart in 1953. Thus, it was laid down early in the first rent campaign that techniques of mass mobilization were not to be applied to disputes over wages between workers and employers.[60] As for rural labourers, in August the Politburo forbade further attempts to secure backpayments of wages from any but 'traitors, reactionaries and local despots', and these only for the period since the August Revolution.[61]

With regard to the peasants, by November 1953 the Party leaders had taken an important decision, namely to move into the 'Land to the Tiller' phase at the same time as the rent reduction campaign was being pushed forward, and this was made clear by Chinh.[62] So too was the recognition of earlier mistakes, the underestimation of the role of the peasants in the resistance because of a 'one-sided concept of the policy of broad national unity' and the failure to link land reform with the national struggle 'although we did recognize that possibility theoretically'. There had also, it was noted, been a mechanical copying of Chinese experience. This was inevitable in a situation where the Workers' Party leaders were accustomed to look north for guidelines and help, but Vietnamese circumstances were not a simple reproduction of those in China. Chinh significantly admitted that there the Communist Party had had to cooperate against the Japanese with an organized political force, the Chiang Kai-shek regime, and hence to be more moderate than was necessary for the Workers' Party. The main mistake, however, had been to use 'bureaucratic and high-handed' methods, not clearly realizing that to implement agrarian policy required 'a difficult and ruthless class struggle' in which 'we must achieve broad mobilization of the masses, and follow the masses, and follow the mass line'.[63]

Looking to the future, the General Secretary emphasized the need for a carefully planned and tightly controlled process. It was incorrect to think that:

...to mobilize the masses means to leave them free to do whatever they like, improvising their actions, causing the cadres to give up Party leadership, and causing social disorder, which is not only harmful to the unity necessary for the war of resistance but also not in the interests of the peasants....

Physical violence, unwarranted killing, beating and torture of wicked
191

landlords (which it seems evident had occurred) were 'absolutely forbidden'. Certain 'rightist' ideas (such as fear of disrupting national unity and lack of confidence in the peasant masses) and 'leftist' ones (such as the failure to make distinctions within the landlord class) must be avoided. The tendency of higher cadres to remain '"stuck" in their offices and not to take part in local activities, and hence to become bureaucratic and authoritarian, must be avoided.[64]

Two other points of Chinh's speech are worth emphasis. First, as part of his presentation of land reform as a controlled process, he was careful to distinguish between different areas, pointing out that in French-held territory only rent reduction and control of interest payments were presently feasible. An exception was also made for some liberated areas: those inhabited by the minority peoples, where the land reform could not yet be implemented because of 'complex' land holding (in other words, the strength of local chieftains), low levels of consciousness and organization, and lack of minority cadres.[65] Second, he made a point of underlining the link between land reform and increased production. We have already stressed the problems of supply in the political economy of the liberation war. Rice and other food crops in particular were of utmost concern, and it must be remembered that the most secure areas of the Democratic Republic and the Red River delta from which it could draw clandestine supplies were historically areas of low production and frequent harvest failure. Great efforts had raised rice production considerably in some Viet Bac provinces, but overall in Bac Bo and northern Trung Bo it had not proved possible to do more than restore pre-war levels and then increase the yield 13.6 per cent between 1947 and 1953. In secondary crops, a continuation of the struggle to meet the famine conditions of 1944 – 45 had resulted in an overall increase of 134.4 per cent.[66] Chinh now emphasized that 'an important aim of land reform is to develop agricultural production' and, while recognizing peasants' fears of 'having to pool their land to build collective farms' and rejecting the use of force to make them join organizations, nevertheless advocated 'mutual-aid teams, production teams and village credit cooperatives'.[67] Beyond these were to come gradual mobilizations for the establishment of the higher form – production cooperatives. 'Work exchange' teams collectively performing common tasks like harvesting had been an established feature for some time; by 1949 there were already over 9,500 in Bac Bo and northern Trung Bo, and almost 11,700 in Nam Bo, where they seem to have been emphasized as a way of reaching the peasantry. Production cooperatives were no more than experimental; there were apparently none in the difficult conditions of Nam Bo, 178 in northern Trung Bo, 705 in the Red River delta and only 12 in the Viet Bac.[68] However, it seems that in 1952 a movement was started (by a Catholic activist who became a 'Labour Hero') which was intended to bring the work exchange teams to a higher stage, by basing distribution of income at least partly on work done in teams.[69] This was a further step towards production cooperatives.

At the end of 1953, after Chinh had delivered his report, the next important step was the passing of the Agrarian Reform Law by the National Assembly, which met in late November and early December for the first time since November 1946.[70] Much of the new measure summarized what had been laid down in the decrees of April and May and in resolutions of the Central Committee and Politburo, but shaped these issues now in a new direction – towards the confiscation (without compensation) of the property 'of French colonialists and of other foreign aggressors, of landlords, of Vietnamese traitors and reactionaries and of the cruel rich'. The Vietnamese elements among these were to be left enough land to earn their living as working peasants, but further requisition for other uses remained possible. This was also to be the fate of landlords who had supported the resistance or were at least not known as oppressors, but the bulk of their property was to be expropriated with payment in government bonds at 1.5 per cent interest. In view particularly of the relations between the Workers' Party and the Catholic Church, it is important to note that these measures of confiscation or expropriation applied to both religious lands and the private property of clergy, with sufficient to be retained to maintain buildings and people. Special provision was also made to deal with dispersals of land by real or fictitious sales or other transfers since April 1953 to avoid the effects of land reform. Such recent transfers by landlords were made subject to confiscation or expropriation: rich peasants had to resell at the market price current at the time of transfer, middle peasants were urged to hand over such lands voluntarily to poor ones in return for a state indemnity at the old market price.

In keeping with previous measures, certain exceptions to the loss of property were permitted. Land brought into cultivation within the last three years was not to be touched. Small landowners and rich peasants 'who fight in the ranks or in the service of the resistance' or who had rented out plots because of physical infirmity were exempted from expropriation. So were Vietnamese owners of mechanized rice fields, export and industrial crop plantations and land used for manufacturing and trading purposes. In addition, forests, mines, stretches of water and hydraulic works, land used for public works, municipal land and historic and cultural sites became state property.

On the other side of the coin, the land taken from some was to be given to others, without payment and to be held in perpetuity. Four groups were to have priority: landless peasants and those with insufficient land from which to live; poor artisans, traders and fishers who were also able to work the land; families of dead, sick or wounded resistance fighters, and of cadres and workers in state enterprises if these relatives remained in the rural areas; and unemployed rural workers who had no other source of income. As a measure of conciliation, the families of 'traitors' and 'reactionaries' sentenced to five years' imprisonment or less might receive land, and also families of soldiers serving in the army of the State of Viet Nam headed by Bao Dai.

Implementation of the new law was to begin in the liberated zones and move to others when politically and militarily possible, but minority areas were to be dealt with quite separately. The principle of mass mobilization was again affirmed, but the necessary machinery was changed and formalized somewhat. General direction was to be by Agrarian Reform Committees at central, Interzone and provincial levels. In the villages, Councils of Peasants' Delegates and the executive committees of the Peasants Association were to be in charge, working of course with the cadres. The Councils of Delegates would classify the population in terms of class membership, subject to ratification by the provincial Reform Committee or other authorized body. Special People's Courts were to continue to deal with enemies, but were now charged also with settling problems of class classification and disputes over ownership, made much more important by the new land distributions.

At the end of 1953, with the necessary principles and guidelines laid down in law and an organization which seemed more open to control from the centre, the Democratic Republic was thus ready for its most important attempt at rural change. The peasant recruit to the army or the porter who supplied him could now feel that he or she had some material stake in the war and Revolution, that the age-old insufficiency of land and landlord oppression were finally to be tackled. It is no accident that coinciding with the second rent reduction campaign and leading up to the Party's conference on land reform, a massive political education movement had taken place in the army, stressing that it consisted of 'peasants wearing uniforms'.[71] The way was now prepared for the final phase of the war. However, in order to understand that, it is necessary to look at what had been happening in the last years in the territory held by the rival State of Viet Nam.

The Bao Dai Solution

In June 1953, while the Democratic Republic was carrying out the first trial rent reduction campaign, its rival attempted its own land reform. In two decrees, land abandoned for more than two years was provisionally granted for the use of peasants who had occupied it, while if abandoned for more than three years a right of usufruct and first option on eventual purchase were recognized. In another, land rents were fixed at a maximum of 15 per cent of the crop, and landlords were enjoined to give written leases to tenants granting security for a minimum of five years. More radically, a fourth decree placed limits on the size of holdings: depending on fertility, 12–36 hectares in Bac Bo, 15–45 in Trung Bo and 30–100 in Nam Bo, with extra for families with more than three children.[72]

Plantations were not included – an obvious concession to French interests in rubber and other cash crops – and in practice no Vietnamese landlord had actual cause to worry about these decrees. Either he controlled the local administrative apparatus which was supposed to enforce them (a situation left

194

unchanged by elections in some of the more secure villages in 1953), or else he already had the more pressing concern of having been driven off his land by Viet Minh threats, making land reform a rather academic question. This situation adequately sums up the contradiction which characterized the State of Viet Nam throughout its existence: on the one side the grip of the wealthy made any reform meaningless, or even any effective enforcement of policy not completely in their interests; on the other, their exploitation of the poorer classes meant continuing instability and support for the Viet Minh. Moreover, even if Bao Dai and his ministers had wanted to tackle this question – and there is no evidence that they did – they would have had to deal with the French government and its immediate military presence – 156,000 troops by April 1953 against the 80,000 nominally comprising the regular army of their State, but in fact under French command. (The Democratic Republic was estimated to have 176,000 Main Force and regional troops facing these at that time.)[73] Crucial here was the fact that all the dominant economic nterests remained either French or those of class elements like the western Nam Bo landlords which were very close to them.

For all significant purposes, the economy of this Associated State of the French Union thus remained structurally what it had been in the days of a more pure colonialism, except that its distorted growth was now even further warped by the pressures of war. Some spheres of production managed a measure of revival. The coal mines, for example, were helped by orders to supply Japan – then under US occupation – and also obtained new equipment from the USA; the SFATE silk mill got back into operation in 1951 and trebled production in a year, also using new machinery to expand into artificial fibres. Some industries enjoyed a boom. By supplying small assemblers of bicycle frames, the producers of oxygen and acetylene for welding increased output from 101,000m^3 to 843,000m^3 between 1946 and 1952; the presence of thirsty soldiers no doubt helped greatly to raise beer production from 64,000 hecto-litres in 1946 to 269,400 in 1949. Others never did prosper as before: the match factory shifted from Vinh to Saigon was still producing less than a third of its output before the Second World War in 1952 and sugar production in the same year was less than a sixth of that amount.[74] The overall trend can be seen in Table 7.3: a generally uneven performance, recovery in the first years after the Second World War but an inability to return to pre-war levels, and a serious impact of the national liberation struggle on some products, particularly rice, sugar and timber, which were open to easy guerrilla harassment.[75]

French control of the 'commanding heights' of the economy was main-tained not only through private ownership but also by the fact that the French government supplied massive aid itself (mostly military of course) and was the funnel for US assistance. This was expressed in various ways in the state apparatus. Thus, the access of French business interests was well expressed in the planned membership of the Financial and Economic Council for Nam Bo (which never really functioned), which was supposed to be consulted on all

195

matters of economy and finance, especially the budget, and was to be half French.[76] As for the role of the French officials, the Pau agreement negotiated during the second half of 1950, which was supposed to settle administrative arrangements among the three Associated States of Cambodia, Laos and Viet Nam, in fact left them dominant in all departments.[77]

Table 7.3 Production in French Union territory ('000 tons)

	1939	1946	1947	1948	1949	1950	1951	1952
Rubber	66.6	20.3	38.6	43.9	43.0	47.8	51.5	61.5
Coal	2,615.0	262.0	260.0	359.0	377.0	503.0	625.0	860.0
Sugar	37.7*	5.0	13.4	15.8	8.8	5.4	5.7	5.4
Timber	653.0*	26.1	58.0	117.0	128.0	132.0	149.0	186.0
Rice	3,100.0*	1,575.0	1,662.0	1,330.0	1,550.0	1,570.0	1,614.0	–

* Figures for 1938, 1940 and prewar average respectively.
Source : Adapted from Vu Do Thin 1954, pp. 55-6.

In terms of politics, the situation continued to be as we noted in Chapter 6. The absence of a solid Vietnamese capitalist class and the often thwarted aspirations to equality of Vietnamese upper middle stratum professionals meant a fragmented and feverish vying for what power there was, which matched the general scramble for money and corruption which gave Saigon in particular a special flavour of hedonism and greed.[78] The private armies holding what were in effect autonomous territories continued to exact their own levies: Cao Dai, Hoa Hao, Binh Xuyen and Colonel Leroy ruled such areas in Nam Bo, the Catholic bishops there and in Bac Bo, while the Great Viet Party controlled the governorship of the latter. These very qualified allegiances to the State of Viet Nam were nevertheless a more positive commitment than that of the many who sat on the fence and waited to see who would win the war, while clandestinely many thousands sympathized with, and even actively aided, the Viet Minh, National United Front and Workers' Party.

The last element was of course most obvious among the peasantry, who enlisted in and supplied the guerrilla fighters, but there was also sporadic working-class resistance, especially after a conference of union cadres held in free territory in Bac Bo in February 1948 decided to step up agitation in the French-occupied zones. Suppression of publications and arrests were, of course, standard practices and the Communist-leaning unions suffered in particular. (In early 1948 the DRVN's General Confederation of Labour claimed 37,436 members, 20.6 per cent of the total workforce, in the 'temporarily occupied' areas.)[79] Between 1946 and 1950 the Party reckoned to have

196

lost 71 cadres and 600 members killed and 300 others gaoled from the rubber workers' union alone. Nevertheless, there were strikes over the years (Communist sources estimated 478 in all) in such enterprises as the Saigon docks, Haiphong cement plant, Hon Gai coal mines and the army ordnance repair shops. Bomb throwing, sabotage and execution of 'traitors' also continued in the urban areas.[80]

By mid-1953, however, fence-sitters and fighters were only part of a broad mass of class elements who longed increasingly for peace and resented the French presence which seemed indissolubly linked with war. Nationalist sentiments became stronger, including among the firmly anti-Communist, affecting even those from Nam Bo landlord circles who most often held office as President of the Council of Ministers. This situation was not changed by the appointment in June 1952 of the former head of the political police, a dreaded figure of whom his predecessor is said to have remarked '[Nguyen] Van Tam is not a Vietnamese patriot; he is a French patriot.'[81] Bao Dai, who had appointed him, tended, in face of his difficulties with the nationalists on the one side and the French on the other, to withdraw, preferring to expend his energies on the slaughter of wildlife in the highland forests of his personal domain. Almost symbolically, it was the Binh Xuyen who remained most devoted to his cause, a fusion of (ex-)imperial and criminal interests illustrating the perverted continuity of neo-colonial, colonial and pre-colonial Vietnamese history. This organization, which had already reaped a fortune from Saigon–Cholon gambling and prostitution, got its ultimate reward in April 1954 – control, no less, of the Saigon police force.[82]

In mid-1953 a new conjunction of economics and politics was accelerating this nationalist trend. In May the French government and Bank of Indochina devalued the piastre partly in an attempt to control speculation. This measure may have been justifiable from a strictly fiscal point of view, but it was politically unwise for a Vietnamese government which depended on business support and which the French slapped in the face by giving it only some hours' notice of intent. The new intervention was primarily to help curb inflation, a nemesis which had now gripped the State of Viet Nam as it had the Democratic Republic at an earlier phase. Rising production costs – such as the need to hire guards for rubber plantations – played their part, as did increasing expenditure on the bureaucracy (in that respect, salaries were frozen along with the devaluation, but army expansion continued to push up costs). French price rises increased the cost of imports. The P1,305 million given out as subsidies to rice producers by August 1952 in fact went into personal consumption more than improved techniques. Above all, the economy was afloat on the floodtide of around Fr 675,000 million which the French government had poured into military expenditure by the end of 1952.[83] The effect on the cost of living, according to official figures, is shown in Table 7.4. Between May 1949 and May 1951 the index for the working class had fallen somewhat in both Saigon and Hanoi and risen slightly for the 'middle class' (spanning what in this work are termed capitalists and middle strata), although it should also be noted that the cost of living was more than twice as high in the latter city.[84] In 1952, and particularly with the 1953 devaluation, things began to slide. The government took action to control the situation, fixing prices, ordering shopowners to stay open and to declare their stocks, but with only limited effect. Measures were also taken with more long-term implications, new taxes on imports and bonuses for exports, but these could not rebalance a fundamentally distorted economy; between 1952 and 1953 rice exports fell 30 per cent.[85]

Table 7.4 Cost of living index, 1949–53

| | Working Class | | 'Middle Class' | |
	General	Food	General	Food
Saigon				
1949	100	100	100	100
May 1952	137	134	138	131
September 1953	202	193	208	192
Hanoi				
1949	100	100	100	100
May 1952	107	106	110	102
September 1953	153	155	156	158

Source: Adapted from Vu Do Thin 1954, p. 49.

With these developments as a background, in September 1953 a new political force took centre stage in Nam Bo. A 'Congress of National Union and Peace' was held, at which the leading figure was Ngo Dinh Nhu, head of the Vietnamese Confederation of Christian Workers, which in July 1953 claimed 45,000 members.[86] Grouping together a number of dissident figures, the Congress called for unconditional independence for Viet Nam, administrative and military reform, press freedom, an end to corruption and the immediate summoning of a national assembly.[87] Under this pressure, Bao Dai felt impelled to convene his own National Congress in October. It was carefully packed – the Binh Xuyen having more representatives than the Buddhist organizations – but even then got out of hand; delegates, led by the Democratic Republic's former director of public health, who had just defected, refused to accept membership of the French Union 'in its present form' and demanded a national assembly elected by adult suffrage with the power to approve all treaties with France.[88] Nhu and his associates had obviously had

198

a considerable political impact, and had crystallized forces of some strength – in fact, as we shall see in the remainder of this volume, those which were to provide the main internal block on the further progress of the Vietnamese Revolution after 1954. Nhu was not only a labour leader, but a prominent Catholic intellectual. Among his brothers were Bishop Ngo Dinh Thuc of Vinh Long and Ngo Dinh Diem, probably the best known Catholic layman. Nhu's links included the French Confederation of Christian Workers and the Paris-based 'Économie et Humanisme' group of intellectuals headed by Father Pierre-Joseph Lebret, which specialized in studies of former colonial countries. In September Nhu revealed his social democratic leanings when he declared that 'We are on the way to a Socialist state, a non-marxist state where capital and labour equally exercise control over industry'.[89] What he was in fact doing, however, with his union and his new National Union Movement for Independence, was not preparing the way for any variant of socialism, but rather for the rise to power of his brother Diem, who was well known as both a bitter enemy of the Communists and a nationalist, and who refused to serve Bao Dai because it meant collaborating with the French. At that time Diem was not in Viet Nam. He had left in 1950, visiting Japan and Rome for the Holy Year celebrations, and then, as a result of a chance contact made with a professor from Michigan State University in Japan, had travelled to the USA. There he was taken up by none other than Cardinal Spellman and spent several years living in religious houses in that dignitary's diocese and later in Belgium. The way was now being prepared for his return.[90]

In 1953–54 another political force was gradually emerging, which was to play a crucial role in Diem's rise to power, and also in his fall and death, and then in the further history of his Republic of Viet Nam, the Vietnamese National Army. Following the Elysée Accords of March 1949 it had been the expressed intention to build up the new Associated State's armed forces, and the Military Convention of December 1950 between France and Viet Nam specified the building of four full divisions. That, and the general mobilization begun in 1951, required the training of Vietnamese officers in larger quantities. This process had already begun in 1940 as part of Admiral Decoux's opening of more opportunities to young Vietnamese, and had been stepped up from 1946 onwards. A broadening of the class basis of recruitment from the sons of landowners and officials like Nguyen Van Hinh, whose father served as a President of the Council under Bao Dai and who himself became Chief of Staff, brought in scions of more modest middle strata or petty bourgeois families, such as the later politician–generals Nguyen Van Thieu and Nguyen Cao Ky.[91] By mid–1954 perhaps 1,000 such young men had passed through the National Military Academy at Dalat. Rapid expansion of the army since 1940 had thus created several 'generations' of officers, with different class backgrounds and orientations, a fact which was to be of great importance as they became a growing political factor.

By late 1953 it was official policy to devolve an increasing amount of the fight against the forces of the Democratic Republic and its supporters on to the National Army. This was part of the plan drawn up by General Henri-Eugène Navarre which was adopted in June 1953. The Navarre Plan envisaged intensive campaigns to clear the liberation forces out of the Red River delta and suppress the guerrillas and offensives against other enemy strongholds.[92] It was partially set in train, with landings on the coast of Trung Bo, for example, but a new military reality soon caught up with it. As we saw right at the beginning of this volume, in September the Politburo of the Workers' Party adopted the plans for the Winter-Spring Campaign which was to initiate the last stages of the general counter-offensive. The final results of this, and of its accompanying diplomatic manoeuvres, were also already noted: what was won with great sacrifice at Dien Bien Phu was severely compromised in Geneva. Since the analysis has now looped round on itself, we need to put it back on the international level where it began, both to conclude this chapter and to be ready for the next.

Liberation War and World Revolution

The material contribution which People's China made to the cause of Vietnamese liberation from the beginning of 1950 onwards cannot be denied. Western estimates are of some 40,000 men trained in China, and Chinese military personnel advised and provided technical services in Viet Nam itself.[93] Estimates of supplies coming south vary widely, but one study based on 'carefully selected' sources speaks of monthly averages of 3–500 tons in 1951, around 1,500 tons in 1952, some 3,000 in 1953 and around 4,000 in 1954.[94] US intelligence sources available since that study was written spoke of 4–5,000 tons monthly in June 1953.[95] In April 1954 French intelligence reported Chinese military advisers at Giap's Dien Bien Phu headquarters and at divisional level, and Chinese-run telephone systems and radar-controlled anti-aircraft guns.[96] Perhaps three-quarters of the Chinese military aid consisted of petrol, oil and lubricants, the rest comprising weapons, signals equipment and medical supplies.[97] Another valuable help was a thousand lorries delivered in 1953, a third of which were grouped into special Regiment 16 with a decentralized command structure to meet conditions caused by French bombing – a forerunner of what would be done on a much larger scale later in face of US air attacks.[98]

Yet, despite all these signs of the Chinese leaders' devotion to furthering the cause of world revolution, by mid-1953 this had reached its limits. From late August various spokespersons, including Chou En-lai, had begun to hint that a negotiated settlement in Indochina would be acceptable in Peking. With President Ho's published interview at the end of November this desire could be made fully obvious.[99]

The decisive element for Mao and his lieutenants was not to be found immediately in the Indochinese situation, but in what was concluded in Korea in July 1953 – a bitter three-year war in which China had become involved directly on the battlefield and, despite early successes against troops from the Republic of Korea and the USA, in which it had later suffered very heavy casualties. Moreover, its ally, the Democratic People's Republic of Korea, had been laid waste in the process. Following the outbreak of fighting in June 1950, pressure from the US government had mobilized an eventual maximum of nearly 650,000 US and allied troops to fight against the armies of North Korea and China in the name of the United Nations Organization. The Korean case showed that the US power bloc, whether expressed through Democratic or Republican administrations, was prepared if necessary to intervene in Asia in the most direct way if it seemed necessary for 'containment' or its more militant cousin, 'rollback'. Subsequent events in Viet Nam and Indochina in general thus had more in common with those in Korea than merely the fact that the end of Korea's only war and that of Viet Nam's first shared negotiating time in Geneva in mid-1954.

In February 1952 a staff study presented to the National Security Council in Washington advised the administration that:

> Communist domination of Southeast Asia, whether by means of overt invasion, subversion, or accommodation on the part of the indigenous governments, would be critical to United States security interests. Communist success in this area would spread doubt and fear among other threatened non-communist countries as to the ability of the United States and the United Nations to halt communist aggression elsewhere. It would strengthen the claim that the advance of communism is inexorable and encourage countries vulnerable to Soviet pressure to adopt policies of neutralism or accommodation. Successful overt Chinese Communist aggression in this area, especially if achieved without encountering more than token resistance on the part of the United States or the United Nations, would have critical psychological and political consequences which would probably include the relatively swift alignment of the rest of Asia and thereafter of the Middle East to communism, thereby endangering the stability and security of Europe. Such a communist success might nullify the psychological advantages accruing to the free world by reason of its response to the aggression in Korea.[100]

This indeed established the close relationship between events in Korea and Viet Nam. Although the Eisenhower administration, inaugurated just under a year later, chose not to substantiate Chinese fears by intervening in the latter case militarily, it did succeed, with more than a little help from its Soviet and Chinese antagonists, in achieving the first part of a counter-move. We shall see in the next chapter how it was able to take still more counter-measures in South Viet Nam. The central point to note here is that an enormous price which the Workers' Party leadership had paid for their Marxist–Leninist internationalism was full incorporation by mid-1954 into the confrontation between the US and Soviet power blocs.

201

In the second half of 1953 the Chinese leadership shifted its position on how to conclude the liberation struggle in Viet Nam because it feared direct US intervention. (This fear was shared, of course, by Ho and his comrades.) World confrontation had thus produced a contradiction, since the US government had been supplying military aid to France and the Bao Dai regime through fear of Chinese intervention. In August 1951 a US Military Assistance Advisory Group was established on the spot to facilitate receipt and use of the new supplies. It and its successors were to stay in place until the final precipitous withdrawal of all US personnel in face of the Great Spring Victory in April 1975.[101] By mid-1945 aid was to reach a total of $2,400 million, $1,600 million of it in the form of military supplies.[102]

The Vietnamese Revolution at the End of a Liberation War

Between the end of 1946 and mid-1954 the Vietnamese Communist leaders had been faced with a tremendous task – the building of a whole new revolutionary terrain in a protracted liberation war involving taking new positions amid social struggle and finding new forms of manoeuvre. All this they did, though only, of course, through the willing labour and self-sacrifice of tens of thousands of their compatriots. Moreover, the basis of that willingness had tended to shift, with the period 1950–51 as a watershed. Patriotism did not diminish, but a much stronger social content had to be given to the mobilization of effort, although the leadership only took a firm grasp on this early in 1953.

On an international level, the efforts of leaders and followers in the Vietnamese Revolution in the period 1946–54 had played a very large part in the process, begun in 1920, of shifting the world revolution to the periphery, a process principally located in Asia and which included the triumph of the Chinese Communist Party and the establishment of the Democratic People's Republic of Korea. This participation in world events had two extremely important consequences. Firstly, it linked the Workers' Party and DRVN government directly and intimately to their Chinese counterparts. That in its turn had the side-effect of confirming a trend already apparent since August 1945, namely for the main seat of the struggle to be located in the north of the country. Secondly, the fate of the Vietnamese Revolution now became intimately bound up with the course of the Cold War between the new superpowers, the USA and the USSR, as, indeed, had become the whole future development of the world revolution. It is in particular to the detailed working out of these themes that we must turn in the next chapter.

Notes

1   For accounts see O'Ballance 1964, Chapter IV. This remains the basic military account of the war in a Western language, but it is very inadequate, both because of its anti-Communist bias and its failure to use Vietnamese sources. A useful overview from the perspective of the French is Gras 1981. The collection which includes this piece has much (biased) information in its various essays and excellent illustrations. Some further sense of the fighting, again from a French point of view, can be gained from Fall 1961. Volume I of the official *History of the Vietnamese People's Party* (in Vietnamese) provides much detail on campaigns from the Communist point of view, but is also imbalanced; for example, it devotes only four pages to the battles of January–May 1951 (pp. 432-6). For pictures of the fighting from the viewpoint of the combatants on the side of the liberation forces see Hoang Zuy 1958, Nguyen Huy Thuong 1962, and an account of the famous attack on the Cat Bai airfield outside Haiphong in Burchett 1957, pp. 37–45.

2   In fact, the Binh Xuyen, a sort of mafia based in Saigon, were probably the best forces among the guerrillas at this time: see 'A Study on the Evolution of VM Forces in Nam Bo from 1945 to 1953' (unpublished) 1964, pp. 6 and 8. The VNQDD units had dispersed in mid–1946 after the break with the Viet Minh had led, according to sources linked to the former, to actual fighting: Hoang Van Dao (in Vietnamese) 1965, p. 239.

3   See 'Study on the Evolution of VM Forces' 1964, pp. 11–17, and O'Ballance 1964, pp. 95–100 and 109.

4   For a rather sensationalized account see Bodard 1965, pp. 286–94.

5   Thayer 1975, p. 33; see generally pp. 30–3.

6   Chen 1969, p. 267, citing a radio commentary.

7   O'Ballance 1964, pp. 143–6 and 155–6.

8   See O'Ballance 1964, pp. 161–7; Fall 1961, pp. 47–60; from the Communist side, Huu Mai 1966, pp. 110–18, and *History of the Vietnamese People's Army*, (in Vietnamese), vol. I, 1977, pp. 446–62.

9   This is a rough estimate, based essentially on two pieces of data. First, a report on the rent reduction campaign in 1954 gives a population figure of 5,733,429 for 14 provinces which roughly include the Viet Bac, the original base for the Democratic Republic after December 1946, and the areas into which it had extended its control on a fairly consolidated basis (outside the lower Red River valley and delta, thus) up to Dien Bien Phu. (See 'Achievements of the fourth wave of the mass movement for rent reduction,' *ND*, 13–15 August 1954, p. 2). Some allowance should probably be made for the fact that not all villages in all these provinces would have been under total control. Second, the estimated population of the western provinces later termed the Thai-Meo area was given a few years later as 330,000 (Ginsburgs 1962b, Part 1, p. 226). Again, the writ of the DRVN may not have run over the entire population there, since the French, as we have noted, made efforts to play its minority peoples off against the Viet Minh/NUF. A later Soviet source, which must have been based on an estimate made by cadres in the DRVN, gave an estimate of around 7 million for the population of the liberated areas in mid-1954: see Rastorguyev 1965, p. 70.

10   For artisan production see Vo Nhan Tri 1967, pp. 140–3.

11   Data from ibid., pp. 157 and 158. See also Doan Trong Truyen and Pham Thanh Vinh 1964, pp. 31–5.

12   Chen 1969, pp. 251–72, passim.

13   Tri 1967, pp. 158–9.

14   For discussions see Nguyen Xuan Lai 1976, p. 135, and Tri 1967, pp. 72–3.

15   Fall 1956, pp. 105–6, attempts this in a very hostile discussion, alleging that the main burden fell on the poorer peasants. His anti-Communist zeal, use of sources which are

no longer available but which appear to have been badly translated, and failure even to mention the system of remissions and surcharges do not inspire confidence.

16   Lai 1976, p. 137, and Nguyen Ngoc Minh 1966 (in Vietnamese), p. 218 note. Further on finance in the whole 1945–54 period see Rastorguyev 1965, pp. 10–24, 49–67 and 97–105.

17   Le Chau 1966, p. 56.

18   Lai 1976, p. 124.

19   *The Vietnamese Working Class in the Long Hard War of Resistance 1955*, p. 10. but see below for a total figure for state workers. Generally on manufacturing see Tri 1967, pp. 140–8.

20   Vietnamese Working Class in the Long Hard War, pp. 11–12.

21   Nguyen Cong Binh 1975 (in Vietnamese), p. 14.

22   DRVN Cadres counted 352,069 wage and salary (my gloss) workers of all kinds in the liberated areas in early 1948; see *Events in Party History* 1979, (in Vietnamese), vol. II, p. 157.

23   Fall 1956, p. 102.

24   Starobin 1953, p. 26. The author, a Communist journalist, toured extensively in the area held by the Democratic Republic and gives one of the few inside accounts.

25   Van Tao 1965 (in Vietnamese), p. 21.

26   Starobin 1953, p. 26.

27   *Events in Party History* 1979, vol. II, p. 157; Nguyen Quoc Chao 1953, cited Fall 1956, p. 142. Fall 1956, pp. 140 and 141, is the only readily accessible source which gives any information on union structure, but as usual he contradicts himself, does not give some sources and produces some very unlikely 'facts' such as a special union for the 'Secret Police' (chart, p. 141).

28   Vietnamese Working Class in the Long Hard War , pp. 14 and 15.

29   Ibid., p. 15. See also Fall 1956, pp. 142–3, Starobin 1953, p. 20, and Hoang Quoc Viet 1952, p. 950.

30   Figures from Starobin 1953, p. 26.

31   Truong Chinh 1977, pp. 395–6.

32   Cole (ed.) 1956, p. 102.

33   Quoted in Truyen and Vinh 1964, p. 35.

34   See Nguyen Van Huyen 1961, pp. 16–19; Nguyen Khanh Toan 1965, pp. 14–20, and Fall 1956, pp. 147–8.

35   Tri 1967, p. 175, Lai 1976, p. 137, and Binh 1975, p. 14.

36   For a good example of how they were regarded by the Party leaders, see 'To the 6th Congress of Party Cadres' in Ho Chi Minh 1977.

37   Starobin 1953, p. 23.

38   Hoang Zuy 1958, p. 246.

39   Quoted in White (unpublished) 1981, p. 153. I am indebted to her for allowing me to see two chapters of an early draft of this work.

40   Quoted in 'Contribution to the Study of Dien Bien Phu' 1965, p. 37.

41   Cole (ed.) 1956, p. 105.

42   'Implementing the Land Reform', Chinh 1977, p. 479.

43   Calculated from Tran Phuong (ed.) 1968 (in Vietnamese), Table 7 (opposite p. 71), and *Thirty Years of Economic and Cultural Development of the Democratic Republic of Viet Nam* 1978, (in Vietnamese), Table 32, p. 95.

44   Figures from *ND*, 6–10 October 1953, article reprinted in *The Sacred Resistance of the Vietnamese People* , vol. 4, 1960 (in Vietnamese), cited in White, (unpublished), 1981, p. 175.

45   Resolution quoted in Lai 1976, p. 73.

46   Truong Chinh, 'Rectify Errors and Advance', 1956, pp. 12–13.

47   The most accessible text of this decree is in Cole (ed.) 1956, pp. 139–48, but this is

translated from a French version, not the original Vietnamese. For hostile commentary see Tran Nhu Trang (unpublished), 1972, pp. 242–4.

48 An article published by the President of the Women's Union at this time also discussed the contribution of peasant women in terms of 'family production schemes', thanks to which 'a cordial atmosphere prevails in many peasant families' (Le Thi Xuyen 1953, pp. 6–7).

49 See White (unpublished), 1981, p. 169.

50 'Decree Concerning the Creation of Special People's Courts in the Localities where the Mobilization of the Popular Masses is being Carried Out,' quoted in Mau (unpublished) 1977, pp. 290–1. See also VNA report, 22 May 1953, BBC ES254, 28 May 1953, pp. 23–31.

51 For further discussion see Trang (unpublished) 1972, pp. 248–9, and White (unpublished) 1981, pp. 170–1.

52 'The Policy Line of the Party during this Year's Mass Mobilization,' *ND*, 16–20 June 1953, in *Sacred Resistance*, vol. 4, 1960, p. 67.

53 On this process see White (unpublished) 1981, pp. 167–9.

54 *ND*, 6–10 October 1953, cited in ibid., pp. 175–6.

55 See White (unpublished) 1981, pp. 160–5; Trang (unpublished) 1972, pp. 244–7; and Fall 1956, pp. 125–6.

56 Chinh 1977, pp. 520–1.

57 See Phuong (ed.) 1968 (in Vietnamese), pp. 125–6.

58 Resolution quoted in ibid., pp. 143–4.

59 Chinh 1977, pp. 473–4.

60 'The Spirit of Rural Policy at the Present Time', *ND*, 1–5 June 1953, *Sacred Resistance*, (in Vietnamese), vol. 4, 1960, p. 58.

61 Phuong (ed.) 1968 (in Vietnamese), pp. 99 and 135.

62 See in particular Chinh 1977, pp. 476–7.

63 Ibid., pp. 482–3.

64 Ibid., pp. 530–1, 524, 544–9 and 543.

65 Ibid., pp. 529–30.

66 Lai 1976, pp. 112–3; see also Tri 1967, pp. 138–40.

67 Chinh 1977, pp. 536–8.

68 Tri 1967, p. 138.

69 Fall 1956, pp. 130-1, with some 'reading between the lines.'

70 An incomplete English text can be found in Cole (ed.) 1956, pp. 150–6, and a French one in Chau 1966, pp. 393–402. The official English text, copies of which are rare, is *Agrarian Reform Law* 1955.

71 Le Quang Dao, 'The Army has carried out a successful political rectification', *ND*, 6–15 October 1953, *Sacred Resistance*, vol. 4, 1960, pp. 127–32.

72 Wurfel 1957, pp. 82 and 88–9; Ladejinsky 1961, pp. 158 and 165.

73 Annexes A and B to 'Probable Developments in Indochina through Mid-54,' Document 15 in *PP* I.

74 Data in this paragraph from Lanoue 1971b, pp. 312–13 and 326; *Le Commerce et l'industrie au Vietnam* 1953, pp. 14, 16 and 45–6.

75 Too much significance should probably not be attached to detailed figures, as official sources may have inflated some: thus, another source (*Le Commerce et l'Industrie* 1953, p. 7) gives rubber production as 12,921 tons in 1946, 27,633 in 1948, 33,936 in 1950 and 37,280 in 1951.

76 Vu Quoc Thong 1952, p. 343.

77 For details see Hammer 1966, pp. 277–81.

78 See in particular Bodard 1965, Part I.

79 *Events in Party History* 1979, vol. II, p. 157, with correction.

80 *Vietnamese Working Class* 1955, pp. 16–19. A useful source is 'M.N.' 1967 (in Vietnamese).
81 Quoted in Hammer 1966, p. 282.
82 On the Bao Dai–Binh Xuyen alliance see Schrock et al . 1966, pp. 813–4.
83 Details from Vu Do Thin 1954, pp. 60–8 passim .
84 See tables, ibid., pp. 49 and 156.
85 Ibid., pp. 68 and 57.
86 Lancaster 1961, p. 276, n. 19.
87 Hammer 1966, p. 305.
88 Lancaster 1961, pp. 276–8; Hammer 1966, p. 305.
89 Details on Nhu from Nguyen Anh Tuan 1967, pp. 92–4.
90 For Diem's early years see ibid., pp. 94–8.
91 For detailed discussion of this and other points on the early development of the National Army see Porter (unpublished) 1976, pp. 215–41.
92 On the National Army and its role in these campaigns see O'Ballance 1964, pp. 174–5.
93 Figure from Tanham 1967, p. 63. For Chinese personnel see Chen 1969, pp. 273–4.
94 Chen 1969, p. 276. Tanham 1969, pp. 68–9, gives much smaller totals for the same years, 10–20 tons, 250, 4–600 and 1,500–4,000.
95 Document 15, 'Probable Development in Indochina through mid-1954,' *PP* I, p. 395.
96 Document 29, *PP* I, p. 462.
97 Tanham 1967, p. 68.
98 Ibid., pp. 70–1.
99 For details see Joyaux 1979, pp. 89–91.
100 Document 240, Porter (ed.) 1979, vol. I, pp. 389–90.
101 For further details see Irving 1975, pp. 100–3; Collins 1975, p. 1.
102 Porter (ed.) 1979, vol. I, pp. 500 and 502.

8 Containing the Revolution

This volume has now come to its turning point, the punctuation mark which represents the division of the Vietnamese Revolution into two parts. That was not immediately clear in July 1954, at the end of the Geneva Conference, and it will require a further chapter to show how an apparently temporary setback for the Workers' Party became a determinant factor, ultimately for twenty-one years. This chapter will analyse the first moves in what was, in fact, a battle to contain the Revolution, fought above all by the Eisenhower administration for what they perceived as US interests but involving the governments of the USSR and China in apparently surprising roles. As we have already noted, with the emergence of People's China, the Democratic People's Republic of Korea and the DRVN, the world revolution really did appear to have shifted substantially to the capitalist periphery after the Second World War. This chapter will examine the reality of this in the Vietnamese case in terms of three propositions:

1   The decade after 1945 saw the final subordination of the cause of world Communist revolution to the foreign policy interests of the Soviet and Communist Chinese states.
2   Although those two powers worked together, their interests were by no means identical.
3   The US government, moved by a single vision of a world threat by Communism, was given an opportunity to lay the basis for containment in Viet Nam.

A Question of Allies

In late December 1949 the government of the DRVN formally recognized the Communist newcomer – Mao Tse-tung's government in Peking. The latter responded reciprocally the following month and the government of the USSR seems to have hastened to follow. The main question, of course, must be why the decision-makers in Moscow had not recognized Ho Chi Minh's DRVN much earlier; after all, their Peking allies took more or less the first opportunity.

We do not, of course, have the documentation upon which an answer can be based with any certainty. However, it does not seem appropriate to speak, as Chen does in his important study, of 'indifference and indecision' in Moscow with regard to Vietnamese affairs and Asia in general up to 1950.[1] In fact, contrary to the image prevalent in Washington, Stalin and his lieutenants were not trying to push forward the revolution in all corners of the globe. Thus, in the case of Korea, they were prepared at the end of 1945 to accept continuing US occupation of the southern half and a possible trusteeship of the superpowers over the country after that.[2] Soviet policy, concerned more with 'great power' than world revolutionary interests, consciously gave priority to Eastern Europe and the bloc of satellite countries being developed there, and was not inclined to adventure elsewhere.[3] Thus, despite what has been alleged, there is absolutely no hard evidence that the Conference of the Youth and Students of Southeast Asia Fighting for Freedom and Independence held in Calcutta in February 1948 was used to pass on instructions to go over to armed revolt in India, Burma, Malaya, Indonesia and the Philippines.[4]

The Calcutta conference must in fact be viewed against the background of the report presented by Andrei Zhdanov to the founding meeting of the Cominform in September 1947, which we have already noted. The new Communist Information Bureau had as members only the Soviet and East European parties, and the continuing major orientation of the Moscow leaders to Europe was confirmed in Zhdanov's speech, which devoted only a brief passage to the 'national liberation movement' and did not mention the Chinese comrades at all.[5] When the combative Soviet line of the 'two camps' was applied explicitly to the colonial situation in December it did not follow the doctrine of a very broad class front developed by Mao. Rather, the Leninist combination of anti-imperialist and anti-feudal struggle was retained, while 'in many', but thus not all, countries the united fronts should include the 'petty and middle bourgeoisie'.[6] Moreover, when a new speech by Mao was reported in the Cominform journal in January 1948 its phrasing was modified to remove the very broad united front implications.[7]

Since it was a meeting attended by Asian Communists (although also by others) not long after the Zhdanov speech, the Calcutta conference takes on new significance in this context. Generally its discussions followed the Soviet position and opposed working with bourgeois nationalists, while armed struggle was also endorsed. [8] This last feature seems to have been largely a response to the stress laid by the Viet Minh delegation, described as all army officers.[9] Of particular interest to us are the reported clash between them and the Yugoslavs when the latter criticized their Vietnamese comrades for dissolving the ICP in the name of national interest, and their complaint on the way home at the attempt to impose the Moscow line on them[10] – the Yugoslavs in early 1948 still being a bastion of orthodoxy – and this points up the potential alternative which was by now before the Vietnamese Communists, made clear at the conference by the Chinese delegation's claim that the affinity between their struggle and that of Southeast Asian countries was 'much closer than that between other regions.'[11]

The Chinese leadership persisted in its emphasis on a broad front including the national bourgeoisie. In Liu's November 1949 speech, already mentioned in Chapter 6, he explicitly extended the line to such countries as India, Burma and Viet Nam, describing it as a 'grave mistake' not to make such an alliance.[12] On the other side, at a conference of Soviet specialists on Asia in June 1949 the keynote speaker attacked the national bourgeoisie, specifically naming Jawaharlal Nehru of India and U Nu of Burma.[13] The point is that the experience of the Vietnamese Communist leadership with the 'national bourgeoisies' in other countries (assuming them to be such) substantiated the view in Moscow much more strongly than that of Mao and his followers. Thus, the DRVN government had sought to use the Conference on Asian Relations convened by the Indian nationalists in March–April 1947 to enlist support for its liberation struggle, but had met with a cool reception from Nehru.[14] (Soviet commentary attacked the conference as an attempt by Indian capitalists to create a 'Pan-Asiatic movement'.[15] Similarly, attempts to use Bangkok as a centre for arms purchases met with varying success under different governments of Thailand (Siam again in the period 1946–49), resulting finally in diplomatic recognition of the DRVN but the closure of its agency in the Thai capital in 1950.[16]

By the time the final victory of the CCP in China brought a second major Communist country onto the world scene, the Soviet government had already begun to focus more attention on Asia. One of the prime reasons was, of course, the continuing struggle in Viet Nam, which was now seen as a battleground in the Cold War. Thus, in August 1949 *New Times*, the Moscow-based periodical for foreign audiences, noted that the French aim was 'to convert that country into an operational base for the American military, who are embarking on a new campaign against the democratic movement in Asia and, above all, against people's democratic China'.[17] This is a particularly interesting comment given that US military aid to the State of Viet Nam had not yet begun. Even more important, it enables us to recognize that the constant public policy of the Soviet government was complete support for the CCP's struggle. On the other hand, there continued to be less open differences between the two leaderships concerning appropriate strategies. Furthermore, although we must beware of projecting future conflicts backwards in time, it does seem clear that the accession of Mao and his comrades to state power brought more to the fore rivalries which had in fact begun in the early 1930s when Stalin's line on China had been one of the sources of conflict among CCP leaders, with Mao's emphasis on autonomy eventually triumphing.

The open stance taken in the Cominform's journal, therefore, was one of support for the line taken by Liu Shao-ch'i in November 1949, that the struggle for national independence and people's democracy must be based on Communist Party leadership on Marxist–Leninist principles, with a united front based on the working class and a people's liberation army.[18] Since the June conference of experts, in fact, policy-making circles in Moscow had begun to accept the national bourgeoisie as a necessary part of the united front.[19] Conversely, with the development of land reform in China from mid-1950 the Maoists put less emphasis upon the inclusion of landlords and rich peasants. On the other hand, there are signs that such claims as Liu's in November 1949 that China now provided a model of struggle irked the Soviet leaders, and that this implicit rivalry continued. Thus, in mid-1951 the Cominform journal published an article by a leading Chinese theorist which distinguished between the October Revolution as the 'classic type of revolution in the imperialist countries' and the Chinese as its counterpart for the 'colonial and semi-colonial countries', a doubtless unacceptable claim to equality.[20] It may well have been in direct answer to this that the top Soviet Asian expert, in summing up at the end of a conference in November, noted that the CCP's experience must not be turned 'into a fetish by viewing it as universally applicable to all situations which may arise in the various countries of Asia'.[21]

It is even more significant, however, that the direct reference here was to the CCP's experience with armed struggle based on a regular army. That struggle had been successful; the resort to arms in all the other Asian countries except the three in Indochina had not (and in Cambodia and Laos was entirely dependent upon what happened in Viet Nam). More globally, the policy of the Soviet Union as a world power, as opposed to leader of the world revolution, was caught in a contradiction. So too was that of People's China as a new state on the international scene since October 1949. On the one hand, Mao's government had entered the Korean War in support of an ally (but also to protect its own borders), and the Soviet government had supported it both diplomatically and with massive supplies of arms. Obviously that had contributed greatly to the vision in Washington of a great Communist monolith which must be contained at almost any cost. Hence, in May 1953, the Eisenhower administration even privately threatened to use atomic weapons if the Chinese did not negotiate a truce more expeditiously.[22] The basic point, however, is that these negotiations, in progress since June 1951, had been begun under Soviet influence and formed a major focus of the USSR's world peace campaign, which in its turn had begun early in 1949. Already by then – and this is the other side of the contradiction – Stalin and his advisers had decided that the formation of the North Atlantic Treaty Organization and continuing inferiority in weaponry necessitated a cautious policy on the part of the Soviet state.[23] In April 1952 Stalin, in an interview with American newspaper editors, introduced the concept of 'peaceful coexistence' as a part of Soviet foreign policy.[24]

In March 1953 Stalin died, and his successors had even more need to reduce international tensions to help stabilize their position. Now the possibility of an accord in Viet Nam was brought into the picture. On 4 August, a mere week after the truce was signed in Korea, the Soviet government proposed a five-power conference (of the USSR, People's China, the USA, Britain and France) to resolve tensions in the Far East. On 28 September it extended the list of issues – for example, to include Berlin. Ten days later, Chou En-lai indicated China's acceptance of the idea, but stressed also his government's concern with admission to the United Nations Organization. This made clear the difference between the Soviet Union and People's China, its ally, in their concern for international settlements. The new Communist power was concerned above all with recognition of its place as a force to be contended with in world affairs – particularly, of course, in Asia.[25]

As we saw right at the beginning of this volume, the government of the DRVN had gone along diplomatically with its major allies for reasons of its own, and the diplomatic struggle shifted to Berlin and the four-power conference in January-February 1954. There the USSR succeeded in getting China included in the conference on Korea and Indochina to be held in Geneva, but could not prevent the USA writing an express refusal to recognize the legitimacy of the People's Republic into the final declaration.[26] For its part, the Peking government gave further major indication of its desire to be included in the system of normal relations among sovereign states. In the preamble to a treaty with India signed on 29 April, which recognized the incorporation of Tibet as a region of China, the cornerstones of its foreign policy were declared to be the 'five principles' – mutual respect for territory and sovereignty, mutual non-aggression, mutual non-interference in internal affairs, equality and mutual advantage, and peaceful coexistence.[27]

Taking as our focus the standpoints of the two allies of the DRVN whose actions were to prove so decisive at Geneva, we have now traced them through from the end of the Second World War to the eve of the conference. In terms of the shift of the centre of world revolution to 'the East', we have seen how Soviet and Chinese Communist policy-makers differed in attempting to come to grips with the very new situation created by the DRVN's creation and struggle, the division of Korea and the creation of People's China itself. What should be stressed is not so much the final convergence of Soviet and Chinese views but the radical shift in perspective of both, in which the Korean and Indochinese questions played a major part. Confirming the established trend on the part of the older socialist power, and indicating already a similar direction for its new ally, world revolution and armed struggle went increasingly astray on the very different terrain of peaceful coexistence and the desire for acceptance as a major power. It was against this backdrop that Pham Van Dong, Deputy Prime Minister and Foreign Minister of the DRVN, and his delegation appeared as actors in Geneva at the beginning of May 1954.[28]

The Diplomatic Struggle

On 10 May, Dong put forward the DRVN's proposals. Having already fought unsuccessfully to have delegations from the Pathet Lao and Khmer Issarak admitted to the conference, he now included all three Associated States in his points. These were:

- all 'foreign' troops to be withdrawn to regroupment areas, followed by an agreement on their evacuation;
- conferences to be convened in each country representing the 'governments of both sides' to discuss holding elections and subsequent formation of unified governments;
- the elections to be supervised by local commissions;
- until they were held, the opposing sides to administer areas under their control;
- a ceasefire supervised by mixed commissions of the antagonists, to come into effect after all other proposals;
- no new forces or equipment to be brought into Indochina during the armistice.[29]

The combination of regrouping of French ('foreign') troops with continuing fighting (since the ceasefire was to come last) is a perfect expression of the 'talk and fight' strategy, giving the Communist-led forces every opportunity rapidly to occupy more territory, which they would have the right to administer. From that position of strength they would supervise elections there and bargain for a unified government in which they would no doubt have a dominant place. From that point on, the experience of their comrades in the Eastern European countries a few years earlier provided a good model for the road to power. All these aspects of Dong's proposals were of course evident to the US government and its allies, and henceforth the blocking of them became the main dynamic of the conference. What the DRVN delegation did not anticipate was their allies' role in this operation.

First of all, on 14 May, at a plenary session, V.M. Molotov, Soviet Foreign Minister and head of the delegation, suggested that the eventual ceasefire be supervised by a 'neutral' body from capitalist and communist countries, and on 17 May he proposed to the French delegation that in general the military question should be dealt with first at the conference.[30] By separating the political from the military issue, with the latter bound to be ultimately easier to settle, and by treating it first, the possibility was raised of a solution like the armistice in Korea in July 1953, with in fact no political solution compatible with the Communist hope for control over the whole country ever being reached. Nevertheless, Dong accepted under protest.

With the possibility open of 'compartmentalizing' the various aspects of the negotiations, moves began to separate not only the military and political aspects but the questions of Viet Nam, Laos and Cambodia. It was obvious that the small pro-Communist groups in the last two could only hope for a strengthening of their position as a result of the negotiations if they could be carried along on the DRVN's coat-tails. On 20 May Chou En-lai, the Chinese Premier, confirmed to the British Foreign Secretary, Anthony Eden, that the military and political issues might be separated, and in the same conversation mentioned that the political solutions for each of the three Associated States might be different.[31]

In fact now, less than two weeks after the opening of the conference, their allies were cutting huge chunks of ground out from under the DRVN delegation's feet. On 18 May, at a private dinner, the secretary-general of the Chinese delegation assured senior French representatives that 'We are not here to support the Viet Minh point of view but to make every effort to restore peace', and that China was not encouraging a DRVN offensive into the Red River delta.[32] At another such dinner on the 22nd, Molotov indicated to the head of the US delegation, Bedell Smith, that the USSR would accept separate treatment of Laos and Cambodia as well as a ceasefire, regrouping of troops into separate areas and neutral supervision.[33] On the 27th Chou En-lai, in a closed conference session, made six proposals which did not include elections and put a general ceasefire first.[34] This combination of informal hints to the other side and formal stances running counter to the DRVN's original position made things almost impossible for Dong and his colleagues.

In this situation, with his government's position in Laos and Cambodia crumbling, on 25 May Dong made a proposal on his own country which eventually was to change the shape of the whole settlement. There should be an immediate ceasefire, he suggested, and regroupment of all armed forces into zones to be specified by the conference. This arrangement was to be only temporary, but the zones should be 'relatively extended', have clear boundaries, be economically viable,[35] have possibilities for internal transport and communications and be administratively viable. The way was thus opened for the partition of Viet Nam, and this path became clearer when secret talks began on 10 June between French and Communist Vietnamese representatives (the State of Viet Nam was excluded) concerning the military aspects of a settlement. The Deputy Defence Minister of the Democratic Republic indicated that his government was interested in a temporary 'state' encompassing the country from the Chinese border down to Hue, to exist until elections for the whole country could be held.[36] It would seem that Dong's proposal and the follow-up were a response to the effective defeat on the questions of continuing with the fighting until the political questions were settled and of holding combined military and political talks. Now the attempt was to ensure a firm grip on as much territory as possible once the fighting was over, to serve as a base for political unification. In these circumstances, the north and upper centre of the country were the obvious DRVN base – at least until the French could be eased out of Hanoi and Haiphong.

The military situation in Viet Nam itself during May and June did in fact seem to be going well for the DRVN. On the day before the Indochinese part of the Geneva conference began, the French commander and the remainder of his 16,000 men surrendered at Dien Bien Phu. US intelligence expected that this would have no immediate effect since Giap would have to rest his victorious troops, but in fact within two weeks 33,000 out of 35,000 had been redeployed to the outskirts of the Red River delta.[37] With this back-up, the liberation forces in the delta began to seize those villages not already in their grasp. The French commanders were forced to pull back to Hanoi, Haiphong and the immediately surrounding areas, deserting even the Catholic bishoprics of Phat Diem and Bui Chu by the end of June. In Trung Bo almost all of its north and centre, save a very narrow coastal strip (and parts of that) and areas of its south, were in National United Front hands. In Nam Bo, where the struggle had always been hardest, French intelligence sources had already conceded that, in early 1954, guerrilla action 'had fully recovered its former vitality', with long-established strongholds in the Ca Mau peninsula and elsewhere being consolidated and expanded.[38] It is necessary to emphasize these overall advances in face of the general tendency to focus attention on Dien Bien Phu, which was, after all, remote from major population centres. Although that battle was a famous victory for the People's Army from which nothing can detract, in May–June 1954 the successes were becoming generalized, and the Communist leadership could feel that the final phase of the general counter-offensive was well underway in Viet Nam.[39] The political battle, however, was being lost in Switzerland.

By mid-June that side of the conference seemed to be running aground. At the sixth plenary session on the 9th both Molotov and Chou took a hard line supporting the original proposals of the Democratic Republic and seeming to go back on some of the concessions they had already made in smaller meetings.[40] On 14 June the Korean talks, which had been going on simultaneously, finally collapsed with no political solution. Then, on the 17th, internal French politics came into play. Four days earlier the government of Joseph Laniel had finally given up the struggle and resigned, and the Radical Socialist Party's Pierre Mendès-France was asked to form a new one. In seeking a vote of confidence on the 17th he announced in the National Assembly that he would permit himself four weeks to reach a settlement at Geneva, and then resign if none were achieved; he got his vote of confidence. In this way, the new French government had in effect delivered an ultimatum to the delegates. Since Anthony Eden and the USA's Bedell Smith had already announced that they were leaving the conference, it looked as if only the military talks would continue and no political settlement could be reached.

The Geneva talks had now reached their turning-point. The Vietnamese leaders were learning a bitter lesson – something which will occupy much attention in this study – namely that their revolution was to be given shape not by their people's sacrifices alone, but by decisive intervention from outside. Like inexperienced boxers in an unfamiliar arena, they were losing round after round on points, with no referee to enforce any rules and, worse still, seconds in their corner who had motives of their own.

It seems very likely that the line taken by Molotov and Chou on 9 June had only been a tactic – the switch from soft to hard beloved of police interrogators and diplomats, and probably mostly designed to reassure their Vietnamese allies. In any case, the representatives of the major Communist powers returned to their more conciliatory line in face of the announcements of withdrawal and French ultimatum. On 16 June the Chinese Premier informed Eden that his government was prepared to influence that of the DRVN to withdraw its troops from Laos and Cambodia, and even that China might be prepared to recognize the royal governments in the two countries, despite their anti-Communist stands. On Eden's advice, Chou then met with Georges Bidault, the French Foreign Minister, and proposed an armistice before political negotiations and withdrawal of all troops.[41]

Also on the 16th Molotov suggested a formula for membership of the supervisory commission of neutral nations which would permit its Communist members to be outvoted ('neutrality' was being interpreted to mean a mixture of these and others). He in addition restated his earlier acceptance of holding military talks before political.[42] On 19 June Molotov spoke to Bedell Smith on the subject of Laos and Cambodia, indicating that the USSR saw no objections to separate settlements for them.[43] On 23 June Chou met with Mendès-France himself at the French embassy in Berne. Once again he reaffirmed acceptance of separate military and political settlements, with the former having priority, and offered the recognition of the government of Laos and Cambodia.[44]

With so much ground cut from under his feet by his allies, there was little else that Pham Van Dong could do than make concessions himself. He did so as unobtrusively as possible, however, conceding in a meeting with the Laotian delegation that a separate solution for their country would be acceptable to the DRVN, even with French bases remaining, although he still spoke of a government of 'national union' to include the Pathet Lao.[45] Moreover, in the secret military talks where bargaining was taking place directly between Frenchmen and Vietnamese Communists, the latter were taking a tough line. The contest was over territory, fought with words rather than bullets but no less crucial for both sides than what was still happening in Viet Nam. Indeed, the talking in the Swiss city reflected directly what was happening in the rice-fields of the Red River delta, with the troops of the DRVN gradually eroding the French hold (it was at this time that the Catholic bishoprics were evacuated). The Communist delegates were demanding a demarcation line between the territory to be temporarily held by the DRVN and that of the State of Viet Nam on the thirteenth parallel, well south of Hue, which would give them control of the whole border with Laos and part of the Cambodian border. The French delegation, given full power by Mendès-France to negotiate a ceasefire, insisted on the eighteenth parallel, some 400 kilometres further north. Representatives of the Bao Dai regime did not take part. Since 4 June their State had been formally completely independent, as a result of a last-minute attempt by the French government to meet nationalist stirrings, though it remained an Associated State in the French Union. French delegates still assumed the right to dispose of its future. Moreover, in the absence of its representatives, the French military delegates, who were also in effect discussing political questions, had begun to abandon their previous joint position of refusing to specify a date for elections to result in a unified government. Rather they were offering to accept a period of eighteen months after the armistice, while Dong's lieutenants wanted six.[46]

In the end it was the position of the DRVN which would shift the most, but before that significant developments were to take place far from Geneva. The major figures were now on their travels. Bedell Smith, in fact ill and wishing to give up his brief, had returned to Washington and Anthony Eden also arrived there on 25 June, along with his chief, Prime Minister Winston Churchill. During their discussions with President Eisenhower and his lieutenants progress was made towards setting up what was to become the new South East Asia Treaty Organization (SEATO); steps were thus being taken to contain any new Communist state which might come into existence after Geneva, and any further threat of Communist-led insurrection. For his part, Chou En-lai took a swing through India and Burma, reaffirming the 'five principles' as he went, and ended up in Nanning in southern China, where he met with President Ho from 3-5 July. The details of their talks are not known, but it is very significant that on 9 July during a dinner the French Ambassador to Switzerland was assured by the Chinese Ambassador to the USSR that the results would be 'helpful to [the] French'.[47] Indeed, on the 10th, if an official Vietnamese account twenty-five years later can be taken as authoritative, Chou advised the Workers' Party Central Committee to offer 'fair and reasonable conditions acceptable to the French'; 'time-consuming discussions and prolonged negotiations' should be avoided, he said, so that the USA would be given no chance to sabotage the conference.[48]

Whether Ho and his comrades were convinced of the efficacy of the help they were receiving from their Chinese and Soviet allies is doubtful. Ten days after the Nanning meeting the Central Committee of the Workers' Party held its Sixth Plenum, specially enlarged by the attendance of senior cadres. At this gathering Ho presented a report on 'the new situation and the new tasks'. In it the reference to the recent talks with the Chinese Premier was very brief ('My meeting with Comrade Chou has also been fruitful'), and the assessment of the

Geneva talks so far was cool – 'the Conference...has led to some results'.[49] What is significant is that the veteran Communist leader now located the Vietnamese struggle, not in the context of the long fight for national independence but that of the 'world movement for peace and democracy' led by the USSR and China. In that context the French capitalists diminished in importance, so that *the US imperialists* are not only the enemies of the world's people but are becoming the *main and direct enemy of the Vietnamese, Cambodian and Lao peoples*.[50] Ho then went on to outline the Party's programme over the last nine years: complete independence for the three countries of Indochina; refusal to recognize the French Union; expulsion of all French troops; destruction of 'the puppet administration and armed forces'; confiscation of property of 'imperialists and traitors'; reduction of land rents and interest payments, 'as a step towards agrarian reform'; democracy for the whole nation; and final victory in the liberation war. 'However, in the new situation we cannot maintain the old programme.' Hence:

> We must take a firm hold of the banner of peace to oppose the US imperialists' policy of direct interference in, and prolongation and expansion of, the war in Indochina. Our policy must change in consequence: formerly we confiscated the French imperialists' properties; now, as negotiations are going on, we may in accordance with the principle of equality and mutual benefit, allow the French economic and cultural interests to be preserved in Indochina. Negotiations entail reasonable mutual concessions. Formerly we said we would drive out and wipe out all French aggressive forces; now, in the talks held, we have demanded and the French have accepted, that a date be set for the withdrawal of their troops. In the past, our aim was to wipe out the puppet administration and army with a view to national reunification; now we practice a policy of leniency and seek reunification of the country through nation-wide elections.[51]

'Our previous motto', said Ho, 'was "Resistance to the end". At present, we must put forward a new one: "Peace, Unity, Independence, Democracy".'[52]

With the line thus laid down by the Party's most respected and unchallengeable figure, it is evident that between the Nanning meeting and the Plenum the Politburo had finally come to grips with what had been happening at Geneva. The result was the abandonment of the strategy of fighting and talking, of using military action to manoeuvre into the strongest possible political position. Now the ceasefire would have to come first, followed by further non-violent political struggle, and a much more limited basis for the struggle would have to be accepted. The Vietnamese Communists were paying their dues for belonging to the world movement led by the USSR and, above all in Asia, by People's China. The demands of the foreign policy of these two powers were emphasis on world peace and coexistence, on the avoidance of a general war; the Korean War had failed and brought China into difficulties, the Soviet Union was faced with the possibility of the European Defence Community and a rearmed German Federal Republic. The Indochinese conflict had now become an embarrassment, so all the intangible force of fraternal advice from senior partners and the doubtless unspoken but nevertheless present threat of loss of material help could be turned to changing the minds of the Vietnamese Communist leaders.

When Ho spoke to the Sixth Plenum, events in Geneva were moving again. The senior delegates had returned, ready to pick up the political threads from the hands of the military negotiators, although the US Secretary of State, John Foster Dulles, had sought to pressure friend and foe alike by displaying reluctance to commit his government to further participation.[53] On 14 July it had been announced that Bedell Smith would indeed return.

It would seem that the Chinese delegation had cracked under the pressure of fear that Dulles's intransigence marked a secret deal with Mendès-France to wreck the negotiations, and had passed its alarm on to its ally.[54] On 13 July Chou En-lai followed up the hint given at ambassadorial level four days earlier by talking to Mendès-France about the demarcation line between proposed regroupment zones. Pham Van Dong, he observed, had 'some interesting things to say' to which the French 'should listen attentively'.[55] Less than two hours later, Dong, reportedly showing signs of distress, appeared to see the French Prime Minister and offered to accept a line at the sixteenth parallel – a considerable concession.[56]

The imminent approach of the deadline set by the French Prime Minister on taking office, that a settlement be reached by the 20th, exerted further pressure in mid-July. The last week before this date was thus marked by a flurry of meetings, out of which final agreements emerged. Again, it was the DRVN's allies who gave in; on the afternoon of the 20th Molotov, famed as a hard negotiator, suddenly proposed the seventeenth parallel as the demarcation line. Even more extraordinary, with Mendès-France still holding out for setting no fixed date after the ceasefire for the elections which were to lead to unification, the USA and Britain agreed on eighteen months, and when Dong stuck to his demand for a lapse of only six months, the Soviet Foreign Minister in effect overruled his ally and suggested two years! After this *débâcle* it would seem that anybody could get anything from the Soviet delegate. Half an hour before the final plenary session had been scheduled following the afternoon's events, the Cambodian chief negotiator announced a list of eighteen demands to be met before he would sign. The one actually specified was that proposed limitations on the Royal Government's right to seek foreign military asistance be dropped. At 2 a.m. on 21 July Molotov capitulated, and in the case of Laos also.[57]

About an hour after Molotov's final concession had been made, at another session, the military agreements for the three Indochinese countries were signed, although dated 20 July. On the afternoon of the 21st the delegates, at the eighth and final plenary session, formally took note of these. They had before them another document, the 'Final Declaration': because of objections by the USA, delegates were not asked to sign but to give oral assent (also recognized as binding under international law), but now the USA refused even to do this, and was joined by the State of Viet Nam.[58] For his part, Pham Van Dong also made no direct statement accepting the document, but the DRVN was taken as agreeing and regarded itself as having done so.[59] The position of the State of Viet Nam was clear. Objecting bitterly to both partition and the holding of 'unification' elections, it had also been pushed to the margin of the conference by the French delegation. Its government could scarcely be blamed for its final reaction. As for the USA, the Eisenhower administration had already made it clear that it would not accept the likely final provisions of the Geneva agreements. On 21 July, therefore, Bedell Smith only pledged to refrain from acting against them by using or threatening force, and affirmed that the USA regarded elections supervised by the United Nations Organization as a way to unite 'nations now divided against their will'.[60]

The elections to be held in July 1956 and provided for in the Final Declaration, however, were not to be supervised by the UNO, but by a commission formed of representatives of the same countries that were to provide the International Commission for Supervision and Control which would oversee the armistice and regroupment, and this was one of the USA's points of disagreement. In addition to ratifying the military agreements, the other important statement of the Final Agreement was that 'the military demarcation line is provisional and should not in any way be interpreted as constituting a political or territorial boundary'. Viet Nam was thus to remain one country, temporarily divided between two regimes until mid-1956, after which it was to be united. In the meantime, France and the DRVN undertook to take no reprisals against former opponents. Although it was France which formally made the unification undertaking, it was supposed to be sustained by any successor regime, and we shall examine the consequence of this later. It was another of the USA's objections that no real account had been taken of the situation of the State of Viet Nam, and surviving American hostility to France's colonialism had been bolstered by the arrogance of its delegation towards the Vietnamese and its combination of hectoring and importunity when dealing with the USA itself.[61]

The immediate steps were to follow up the military agreements, the most significant of which were between France and the Democratic Republic. A staged ceasefire was to be followed by regrouping of troops within 300 days to either side of a river which cuts the narrow waist of Viet Nam close to the seventeenth parallel. Any civilians who wished to regroup could also move within 300 days, and were to be allowed to do so freely. French troops were to withdraw and no new foreign troops or weapons and munitions were to be brought into either zone, no new bases were to be allowed, and the zones were not to adhere to any military alliance. The International Commission for Supervision and Control (ICSC), composed of representatives from India, Poland and Canada, with the first as chairman, would 'police' these questions; its decisions or recommendations had to be unanimous.[62]

When the gunfire ceased, lastly in Nam Bo on 11 August 1954, the Communists and other members of the National United Front who had fought so hard and so long might well have had mixed feelings, and might even have felt themselves betrayed. The failure of Pham Van Dong to accept the Geneva agreements in so many words on 21 July might almost have served as a silent protest against what the USSR and People's China had wrought. Although it must remain uncertain whether the liberation struggle could have been carried on to final victory, the military and hence political initiative and drive were certainly with the DRVN in Bac Bo (former Tonkin) and Trung Bo, and gains were being made in Nam Bo, where French intelligence put its lowest estimate of villages under NUF control in most of the region at 60 per cent.[63] With the continued erosion of French Union troops, sooner or later the US government would certainly have had to decide whether or not to intervene with ground forces. That was indeed the risk; the political economy of the Democratic Republic's liberation struggle could not have sustained that effort in 1954, if American troops had intervened in the necessary numbers. When they in fact did so, some ten years later, this was a strain which the Democratic Republic then vested in the north was well able to take, as we shall see in later volumes. It does seem, however, that the least that can be said of the situation in mid-1954 is that, with full backing from its allies, the DRVN could have won further military gains and could thus have been in a better position to bargain in a more prolonged political process.

What were the disadvantages from the DRVN's viewpoint? First of all, it lost control of large amounts of territory in Nam Bo and southern and central Trung Bo and had to abandon those of its supporters who did not move north. It is significant that, in his appeal to the Vietnamese people just after the Geneva conference ended, President Ho, in calling for unity and adherence to the line of the Party and government, made special reference to the need for southern compatriots to 'place national interests above local interests or permanent interests above temporary interests'.[64] Second, the Democratic Republic thus lost its major sources of military and political strength south of the seventeenth parallel and was left to rebuild its supporters' organizations in very uncertain circumstances. Third, it apparently accepted in all good faith that the road to unification and the dominance of the Workers' Party lay through the elections scheduled for July 1956, a drastic narrowing of its own previous combined military and political drive. Finally, even if only tempo-rarily, the country was divided, not by the fluctuating fortunes of opponents' ability to hold territory but by international agreement and with no further chance to use the leverage of liberation war. Although no more people would die or be maimed, at least not openly, it was at the price of allowing the French and their allies to continue to control around 12 million people, almost half the population, and more than half the territory.

Containment in the South

Despite the developments at Geneva, the policy-makers in Washington did not secure all that they wanted. Preparations for the conference, for example, had gone on amidst statements that there should be 'no cease-fire in Indochina prior to victory whether that be by successful military action or clear concession of defeat by the Communists'.[65] The same draft report of a special presidential committee on Southeast Asia, dated 5 April 1954, called, irrespective of military outcomes, for 'tangible evidence of Western strength and determination to defeat Communism; to demonstrate that ultimate victory will be won by the free world; and to secure the affirmative association of Southeast Asian states with these purposes'.[66] Among the measures envisaged were the pact which later became the South East Asia Treaty Organization (SEATO), military missions to train special forces for security work, economic and technical assistance, and encouragement of US private investment.

In time, all of these and much more were to feature in the approach to South Viet Nam. We may most aptly begin with another recommendation of the special advisers, the need to 'promote and support energetic, able and honest indigenous anti-Communist leaders in Southeast Asia in order to provide more effective government in the area'.[67]

It is thus of long-term importance that, at the centre of the South's new state apparatus, was to be a short, pudgy bachelor who talked constantly and never listened, who was a devoted Catholic of a conservative kind, anti-Communist, and nationalist.[68] In early June 1954 Ngo Dinh Diem was called on by Bao Dai to become President of the Council of Ministers. Diem had refused to serve the last emperor and present head of state ever since 1933, on the grounds of his close identification with the French. Now, in the middle of the Geneva talks at which the State of Viet Nam was being humiliated by the colonialists and with a rising nationalism behind him which his brother Nhu was helping to orchestrate, he chose to serve – a decision made easier by Bao Dai's absence on the Riviera. Hard evidence that his candidacy was pushed by the US government, as has often been alleged, is missing: in any case, such pressure was not necessary – in a situation where a person known for integrity and nationalism had to be found to hold the line and such were in very short supply.

In 1949 the State Department's Indochinese intelligence expert had correctly assessed Diem as 'influential and ambitious', anti-Communist but 'violently opposed to French control of Vietnam' and in favour of complete independence.[69] Since then, as we noted earlier, he had also become known in Catholic circles in the USA and had found influential backers there. In mid-1954, therefore, he naturally appeared to have qualities which were valuable to the power bloc and US government, who were dubious about the role of the French at Geneva and in the difficult situation thereafter, and were anxious to find reliable Vietnamese leaders for the South.

221

Containment of the revolution in South Viet Nam involved more, of course, than finding a personage around whom a counter-revolutionary regime could crystallize. Four main tasks in fact had to be performed once that had been achieved. These were:

1   the mobilization of sufficient coercive power and general political control to ensure stability;
2   the development of capacity to enforce governmental decisions;
3   the development of an ideological basis for the regime;
4   stabilization of its economic base.

After seeing how Diem in fact came to power, we shall go on to see how he and his US allies faced these tasks in the period 1954-56, during which the revolution in the South was indeed contained.

On 20 August 1954, after some days of discussion, the National Security Council in Washington issued a basic policy document on Viet Nam. The political needs, it stated, were: complete independence for the State of Viet Nam, now vested territorially in the South, which must be accepted by France; a goverment of national union; and a new democratic constitution removing Bao Dai. The government must be headed, with US and French support, by Diem, whom John Foster Dulles described as having 'the necessary ingredients of success'. Economically the keys would be resettlement of refugees and land reform, while US aid would be especially directed towards 'disassociation of France from levers of command'.[70] The government of Pierre Mendès-France took a different course. Firstly, the interests of French capitalists demanded that, on the one hand, withdrawal of political control from the South would be slow; the independence agreement of 4 June was in fact never formally ratified. On the other hand, good relations had to be maintained if possible with President Ho's government which in October was to take formal possession of Hanoi, but not yet Haiphong, as French troops were gradually withdrawn. Jean Sainteny, chief negotiator of the agreement with the Democratic Republic in March 1946, had been sent back to the North and hoped to secure favourable terms for the preservation of French business interests. True to his remarks at the Sixth Plenum, Ho was willing to consider this; there was even talk of making the Hong Gai coal mines a joint enterprise between the French owners and the state.[71] A second axis of Mendès-France's policy seems to have been the hope that Ho, if encouraged by the Western powers, would become a sort of Southeast Asian Tito and break with the USSR and China, although the French Premier had taken out insurance by having France become one of the signatories of the final agreement setting up SEATO on 8 September.

This move to contain Communism was much more in line with US policy (as with that of Britain, Australia, New Zealand, Pakistan, the Philippines and Thailand, the other signatories), and France was regarded in Washington as an unreliable ally. This was no doubt compounded when Mendès-France agreed to back Diem but equivocated on finally ratifying the independence of the State of Viet Nam, and also insisted that all aid should be channelled through French hands. On 29 October the US government informed Paris that, in future, aid would go direct to the Diem government. On 22 October the National Security Council had decided on a crash aid programme to streamline and improve the State's armed forces, still at this stage to be coordinated with French efforts. Two days later, President Eisenhower sent a personal letter to Diem, in which the US President promised military and economic aid.[72]

By this time Diem was in need of any support he could get. He was opposed by the Vietnamese National Army (VNA) Chief of Staff, General Nguyen Van Hinh, who throughout September and October was busily trying to organize coups.[73] Holding his rank in fact in the French air force, Hinh was very close to the French military mission in Saigon. Conversely, the local US representatives worked to thwart him; particularly active was Colonel Edward Landsdale's Saigon Military Mission (SMM), set up since 1 June to carry out all the illegal, semi-legal and generally shadowy operations which situations such as that in Viet Nam in 1954-55 seem to breed like maggots in an untended wound.[74] Among other things, the SMM channelled US funds to General Trinh Minh The, a Cao Dai maverick who was still fighting both the French and National United Front near Tay Ninh, to persuade him to hold his 3,000 troops ready to come to Diem's aid if necessary. (Lansdale, who had previously helped President Magsaysay to suppress the Communist rebellion in the Philippines, later also arranged the secondment of Filipino officers to train Diem's palace guard.)[75]

In November Bao Dai was prevailed on to summon General Hinh into retirement in France; however, more threatening adversaries remained to challenge Diem. The USA might be behind him, but even the presence of Lansdale's SMM, the US Ambassador and the Military Assistance Advisory Group (MAAG) in Saigon was scant comfort when that city and Cholon were in fact under the control of Le Van Vien's Binh Xuyen. Outside the city, especially in the western provinces, large areas still remained in the hands of Cao Dai and Hoa Hao generals with their 40,000-strong private armies. Among them were characters who seem more suited to a Hollywood film than real life, such as the Hoa Hao's Le Quang Vinh who had cut off a finger to remind him to fight the French and sworn never to cut his hair until the country was united. Such men were also economic potentates: Vinh and another Hoa Hao chief controlled the rice trade from the west, and Vien ran gambling and prostitution in 'his' two cities and had interests in opium, rubber, fish, charcoal, the biggest department store and hotels.[76] Faced with such rivals, there seemed little that sharksuited intellectuals like Diem and Nhu could do; indeed, the warlords even had their representatives among the educated middle strata – the Hoa Hao, for example, running its own Social Democratic Party. Late in September 1954 there was nothing else for Diem than to reinforce this facade of political respectibility by taking representatives of the sects – but not of the Binh Xuyen - into his government.

In Washington, on the other hand, things began to move slowly in Diem's favour. His friends in the USA began to become active and to organize, and they were not inconsiderable figures – Senators Mike Mansfield and John F. Kennedy, Supreme Court Justice William O. Douglas, and Cardinal Spellman. Academic contacts were ensured through Professor Wesley Fishel of Michigan State University. Above all, the question of aid for settling refugees from North Viet Nam provided a focal point for organization at this time. This was primarily a Catholic operation, organized through the International Rescue Committee, to which a special perspective was given by its President, Leo Cherne, and his assistant, Joseph Buttinger (Gustav Richter), both Central European refugees from an earlier Communist advance.[77] The State Department could not fail to take heed of such advocacy, particularly the report submitted by Mansfield in October after a visit to Saigon, in which he described Diem's 'program' as one of 'genuine nationalism' and concerned with eradicating corruption and 'advancing the welfare of the Vietnamese people'.[78]

At the level of possible international support - which meant, in effect, that of the USA – the tide turned for Diem in December 1954. The head of a special investigatory mission to Saigon, General Lawton J. Collins, was against him, raising the question in the middle of that month 'when, if ever, Diem will assert type of leadership that can unify this country and give it a chance of competing with [the] hard, effective unified control of Ho Chi Minh'.[79] The Ambassador to Saigon, however, temporarily working from the Far Eastern section of the State Department, recommended that 'in the lack of more useful alternatives' his superior 'continue to support Diem, because there is no one to take his place who would serve U.S. objectives any better'.[80] This memorandum was part of Dulles's briefing for the tripartite meeting with Mendès-France and Eden in Paris which began on 19 December. Here the French Premier pressed strongly for the replacement of Diem, whose detestation of the colonialists was matched by theirs for him (he was commonly characterized even in official circles as a madman). Bankrupt in ideas and beset by rebellion in Algeria, anxious to transfer its troops, the French government still sought a revamped version of the 'Bao Dai solution', more than ever patently an illusion with that figure now permanently ensconced in Cannes. The US Secretary of State gave his French ally some reason to believe he might yet have his way, stating that his government was open to 'possible alternate solutions', but secured agreement to support Diem for the time being. Significantly referring in passing to Senator Mansfield's report, he also pointed out that:

Even slight chance of success in Vietnam was worth considerable investment. US had also to think of what happened in adjacent countries - in Cambodia, Laos, Thailand and Malaya. US situation was different from that of French. French had an investment in lives and property in Vietnam while ours involved effect that fate of Vietnam would have on rest of Southeast Asia.[81]

In this perspective, Dulles's final verdict after the Paris talks was that 'unless situation clearly appears hopeless and rapidly disintegrating, we have no choice but continue our aid Vietnam and support Diem. There [is] no other suitable leader known to us.'[82] At this point the influence of the Joint Chiefs of Staff and of General Collins reporting from Saigon seems also to have been important.[83] The National Security Council decided that the aid promised to Diem late in October was to be released on 1 January 1955 and should be set at around $500 million. Whatever the reservations, the commitment to Diem had finally been made.

The immediate need for aid was in the military sphere, as well as for the settlement of refugees now moving from the North in their thousands. Diem had been fully aware from his first assumption of office that the army was the key element in his plans for the State of Viet Nam: already in July 1954 he had commented that 'We have 300,000 men in uniform but we do not have a real national army. A national army needs to have complete freedom of action and more particularly an entirely independent nation to serve.'[84] After his experience with General Hinh, however, he knew only too well that he had little control of the armed forces, and that what was needed, therefore, was a complete reorganization. It had already been agreed in December that French forces would be completely withdrawn by 1 July 1955, so it was evident that such a task would be one for US money and advice. In February a joint Training Relations and Instruction Mission was set up, but in the words of a later official historian the local French commander 'never interfered with TRIM operations'.[85]

In order to achieve reorganization, it was the view of the US MAAG that the VNA should be reduced from around 170,000 to 100,000 men (the bulk of the rest of the 300,000 mentioned by Diem were regional and local levies).[86] In May 1955 the MAAG was to propose, and have accepted, a ceiling of 150,000, but in the meantime the original ceiling had played a part in Diem's worst political crisis. In February France ceased payment to the armies of the religious sects, and their commanders began to press for incorporation into the VNA, but as separate units. Diem was against this, and in any case their 40,000 followers would be far too great a proportion of the new smaller army. In addition, the obstinate chief minister refused to countenance continuation of personal territorial control. The sect leaders therefore formed a United Front of Nationalist Forces with the Binh Xuyen, angered in turn by the cancelling of their gambling concessions, and withdrew their members from the government. The last move made no difference, as Diem had ignored them anyway, and the Front's attempt to get Bao Dai to dismiss Diem was blocked by a personal letter from President Eisenhower.[87]

What became crucial was the confrontation of arms. On 28 March a VNA

225

paratroop company seized the Saigon police headquarters from the Binh Xuyen and launched three days of fighting, ending in a French-mediated truce. Fearful now of civil war, Secretary of State Dulles again reconsidered, and under pressure from Collins on 27 April agreed to consider finding another politician to support.[88] The very next day, however, Diem moved again; on that day and on 2–3 May troops loyal to him broke the Binh Xuyen in street fighting and drove them first back into Cholon and then out of the urban area altogether, large areas being burned down in the process.

Meanwhile, on this show of strength, Dulles had cancelled his decision to look for a substitute.[89] In Saigon the military assertion reaped political fruits for Diem. The United Front split, as personal ambition (and probably judicious bribes) caused various sect generals to put careers before principle, leaving the Binh Xuyen to take the blows. Various of the warlords, prompted by Lansdale's SMM, joined Ngo Dinh Nhu in convening a National Revolutionary Congress on 30 April, which demanded the removal of Bao Dai as Head of State, elections to a national assembly and a new constitution. Although some of the sect generals had been particularly active in pushing these demands, which were very much in Diem's interest, he was not a man who cared to be pushed or intended anyone to have power other than himself and his family. On 8 May he announced that all 'wayward' provinces would be recovered – the death knell of the warlords – and later in the month secured a show of popular support through an Estates General of selected local councillors which called on Bao Dai to tranfer all power to Diem until an assembly met in six months to draw up the new constitution.[90]

At this time another triparate meeting was held in Paris. In February the Mendès-France government had collapsed, but its successor inherited the old attitude to Diem; once again he was described by the new Premier as a madman. Nevertheless, in the end the French delegation was forced to go along with Dulles's view that the Vietnamese leader 'showed so much ability that US fails to see that he can be got rid of now'.[91] Although, as a compromise, Dulles acccepted a list of French stipulations (such as retention of Bao Dai), future months were to show that Diem was now strong enough to ignore these, or to carry them out in a way which suited him. In December he in fact ended existing financial and economic agreements with France and shortly after withdrew his new Republic of Viet Nam from the French Union and the franc zone. In making the latter move he brought the piastre automatically into line with the US dollar, and this completed a relationship which we have seen building up since the Geneva agreements.

As part of a containment policy in Viet Nam a ruler had thus been found for the South, who might perhaps be able to stabilize a regime there in opposition to the Communists. Already in July 1955 he refused to enter into negotiations with the Democratic Republic on the holding of elections throughout the country in a year's time, although such talks were prescribed at Geneva. That year was to be spent consolidating his position.

Notes

1   Chen 1969, pp. 337–8.
2   See Cumings 1981, pp. 215–17.
3   Here I follow the basic 'revisionist' line on the origins of the Cold War which has emerged in roughly the last fifteen years: for various points of view see Barnet 1972, Gaddis 1982, and Yergin 1978.
4   See McVey 1958 passim, with summary on p. 24, and McLane 1966, pp. 357–60.
5   See Kautsky 1956, p. 28. For more on the founding of the Cominform see Marcou 1977, Chapter 2.
6   Quoted in Kautsky 1956, p. 30. I do not follow this author's view that this was an 'unambiguous and authoritative statement of the neo-Marxist strategy' by Moscow, indeed, rather the opposite; see ibid., pp. 29–31. Nor do I accept his overall framework of 'left', 'right' and 'neo-Marxist' strategies, (despite the pioneering importance of this work). I prefer to see changes in line as the products over time of the general conditions of the shift in location of the major terrain of world revolution, of the contradictions between the demands of this and those of 'national' state policies, and the contradictions emerging from any concrete application of a particular line.
7   Kautsky 1956, pp 32–3.
8   See McVey 1958, pp. 13–14, although I do not agree that Soviet experts were now tending to accept the Maoist line, as stated above.
9   Ibid., pp. 15–16.
10   Ibid., pp. 15 and 23.
11   Ibid., p. 13.
12   See quotation in ibid., pp. 87–8.
13   McLane 1966, p. 362. See also Colbert 1977, pp. 119–20.
14   See Calvocoressi (ed.) 1952, p. 387; Chen 1969, pp. 175–6; Colbert 1977, pp. 75 and 112–3.
15   Colbert 1977, p. 119.
16   For details see Calvocoressi (ed.) 1952, p. 386, 1953, p. 431.
17   'International Life' column, *New Times* No. 35, 24 August 1949, p. 18.
18   Editorial in *For a Lasting Peace, for a People's Democracy*, 27 January 1950, cited in Chen 1969, p. 221.
19   See Kautsky 1956, pp. 86–95. He does not recognize my following point, and therefore sees the shift as only on the part of the Soviet leadership.
20   Lu Ting-yi, 'The World Significance of the Chinese Revolution,' *For a Lasting Peace, for a People's Democracy*, 29 June 1951, quoted in Chen 1969, p. 223.
21   Quoted in McLane 1966, p. 454; see also Chen 1969, pp. 224–5. Kautsky 1956, pp. 148–51, sees this conference as in fact endorsing 'neo–Maoism,' which could hardly be completely true if it rejected the central doctrine of the necessity of armed struggle.
22   Clubb 1971, p. 396.
23   For details see Marcou 1977, pp. 297–302.
24   Ibid., p. 302.
25   For this paragraph and more detail see Chen 1969, pp. 280–92, and Joyaux 1979, pp. 87–96. Simmons 1975, pp. 87–98, argues that the Soviet leaders deliberately tried to keep China out of the United Nations to ensure its dependence, and also that Peking delayed recognising the DRVN for fear of antagonizing France because of its desire for acceptance.
26   For details see ibid., pp. 96–103.
27   Joyaux 1979, p. 133.
28   It must be emphasised that the following analysis is not intended to provide a general account of the Geneva conference. Such can be found in Bator 1965, Chapters 7–11;

Randle 1969; Joyaux 1979, second and third parts; and Irving 1975, pp. 118–30; and of course in Vol. I of the *Pentagon Papers*, pp. 108–78. For further material on the US side see Glennon et al. (eds.) 1981. Useful for the French side is Devillers and Lacouture 1969, Part II. A major participant's account is Eden 1960, pp. 86–106 and Chapter 6. For a sympathetic evaluation of Chou En-lai's role which emphasises his desire to protect China's southern frontier against possible US involvement see Shao 1986.

29   *PP* I, p. 119.
30   Ibid., pp. 133 and 140.
31   Joyaux 1979, p. 195, and see further Glennon et al. (eds.) 1981, pp. 863–4, 1170–1 and 1174.
32   Joyaux 1979, p. 197.
33   Smith to Department of State, 23 May 1984, Glennon et al. (eds.) 1981, pp. 896-97.
34   Joyaux 1979, pp. 188-90.
35   Randle 1969, p. 232.
36   The source for these talks is Devillers and Lacouture 1969, pp. 233-4. See also Randle 1969, pp. 274–5.
37   See *PP* I, pp. 484 and 121-2.
38   'A Study of the Evolution of VM Forces in Nam Bo from 1945 to 1953' (unpublished) 1964, p. 20.
39   Major studies of the battle from different points of views are: Roy 1965; Fall 1967; 'Contribution to the Study of Dien Bien Phu' 1965; Vo Nguyen Giap, (rev. ed.) 1984; and Burchett (rev. ed.) 1957, Chapter 3. The official Communist account is in *History of the Vietnamese People's Army,* vol. I, 1977 (in Vietnamese), pp. 557–91. See also Doyle, Lipsman, Weiss et al. 1981, pp. 65-78.
40   Randle 1969, pp. 270–1.
41   Ibid., pp. 281 and 336; *PP* I, p. 138; Joyaux 1979, pp. 230–2.
42   Randle 1969, pp. 281–2.
43   *PP* I, p. 138 note.
44   Randle 1969, pp. 304–6; *PP* I, p. 147 and Document 64, pp. 537–8; Joyaux 1979, pp. 239-40.
45   *PP* I, p. 139.
46   Randle 1969, pp. 310-14; *PP* I, pp. 146–7 and Document 69, pp. 541–2.
47   *PP* I, pp. 148–9, and Document 76, p. 549.
48   VNA report, 4 October 1979, BBC 6238, 6 October 1979, pp. A3/9–10; for more details, pp. A3/7–10.
49   'Report to the 6th Plenum of the Viet Nam Workers' Party Central Committee', Ho Chi Minh 1977, p. 176. A favourable account of the Chinese role at Geneva, written by a member of the DRVN delegation who much later defected to China, can be found in Hoang Van Hoan 1979, pp. 13-14. At the same time the new official history of the Vietnamese Party was accusing the Chinese leadership of all sorts of ill-intent in mid-1954, including trying to divide Viet Nam so as to weaken the position of the Workers' Party with a view to the eventual annexation of the three Indochinese countries: see *Fifty years of activity of the Communist Party of Viet Nam* 1979 (in Vietnamese), n. 1, p. 124.
50   'Report to the 6th Plenum', Ho Chi Minh 1977, pp. 172–4 and 175, emphasis in the original.
51   Ibid., pp. 177–8.
52   Ibid., p. 178.
53   Randle 1969, pp. 315–17; *PP* I, pp. 149–53.
54   Joyaux 1979, pp. 276–17; see also *PP* I, p. 153; Randle 1969, p. 319.
55   Unable to communicate directly with the US delegation, the Chinese had indicated their disquiet through the correspondent of the *New York Times*, whom they trusted: see *PP* I, p. 155, and Document 88, pp. 566–67.
56   Randle 1969, pp. 317-8.

57   Ibid., pp. 339-41.
58   See Kahin and Lewis 1967, p. 51 and especially p. 64, note 7. For texts of the various documents see the appendix to Randle 1969.
59   Randle 1969, p. 343, and see also p. 425.
60   Ibid., p. 344.
61   On these points see further Kahin and Lewis 1967, pp. 51–3.
62   Laos and Cambodia had similar provisions on withdrawal of foreign troops, including the French. Laos retained two French bases but would permit no others. Cambodia would allow them only if threatened militarily, in which conditions it also reserved the right to join an alliance, as did Laos. Similarly, both could import weapons if needed. In both of them opponents of the royal regimes were guaranteed reintegration into public life, but in Laos regroupment areas were specified for the Pathet Lao, which was not done for the Khmer Issarak. Given that Cambodia had no border with the territory held by the Democratic Republic, this made King Sihanouk's nationalist, but strongly anti-Communist, regime the more secure of the two. A useful parallel summary of the military and final agreements for the three countries can be found in *PP* I, pp. 270-82. Further for Cambodia see Kiernan 1985, pp. 140–52.
63   *PP* I, p. 258.
64   Ho Chi Minh 1967, p. 273.
65   Document 307, Porter (ed.) 1979, p. 531.
66   Ibid., p. 530.
67   Ibid., p. 532.
68   There are a number of character-sketches of Ngo Dinh Diem, more especially in bourgeois studies, since it is ideologically useful to ascribe the failure of the first phase of US policy in Viet Nam to his personal defects. For two of the better ones see FitzGerald 1972, especially pp. 98-101, and Warner 1964, especially Chapter 5.
69   *Political Alignments of Vietnamese Nationalists* 1949, pp. 56 and 124. The author appears to have been Milton Sachs.
70   For a summary of the 20 August document see *PP* I, pp. 213–4.
71   *PP* I, pp. 222 and 236, and Chaffard 1964, pp. 121 and 124–6.
72   *PP* I, pp. 220–3.
73   For a detailed discussion see Porter (unpublished) 1976, pp. 244–7.
74   One of the most fascinating revelations of the liberated 'Pentagon Papers' is Document 95, 'Lansdale Team's Report on Covert Saigon Mission in 1954 and 1955.'
75   'Lansdale Team's Report', pp. 578 and 582.
76   Like Mafia leaders and other major figures in organized crime in capitalist societies, these individuals have attracted a certain kind of attention from journalists and writers of popular non-fiction: see for example, Darcourt 1977.
77   See Robert Scheer and Warren Hinckle, 'The Vietnam Lobby' in *Vietnam Primer* nd, pp. 24–9, and, for Catholic activities in the refugee field, Scheer's 'Hang Down Your Head Tom Dooley' in the same volume. It should be noted that these are hostile accounts. See also n. 14 in the next chapter.
78   *PP* I, p. 222. See also Devillers and Lacouture 1969, pp. 347–8.
79   *PP* I, p. 226.
80   Ibid., p. 227.
81   Ibid., p. 228; for the Paris discussions generally, see pp. 227–8. In fairness to the Secretary of State, it must be assumed that the style of this quotation is determined by a telegraphic form (this part of the *Papers* does not give detailed references). For other views of French attitudes to Diem see Devillers and Lacouture, n. 11, pp. 341–2, and Bator 1965, pp. 175–80.
82   *PP* I, p. 229.
83   Judgement here must be tentative, as material is missing from the *Pentagon Papers* at this point (p. 229).

84 Quoted in Jumper and Hue 1962, p. 113.
85 Collins 1975, p. 3; see also Eckhardt 1974, pp. 9–14.
86 Figures from Collins 1975, p. 6; see also his Appendix D for detailed figures, where the total is shown at approximately 279,200.
87 *PP* I, p. 230.
88 Ibid., p. 233. According to Lansdale (as reported in ibid., pp. 233–5 passim), the French commander, Ely, was giving at least tacit encouragement to the Binh Xuyen to resist Diem. According to the testimony of Col. Jean Leroy and others in the film 'De Franse Oorlog in Indochina,' 1978, France was giving active encouragement at this time to the sects and Binh Xuyen.
89 *PP* I, p. 234; see also p. 297.
90 Sources for relations among the sects, Binh Xuyen and Diem are: *PP* I, pp. 206–8, 240–55 and 303–5; Duong Chau 1958, pp. 149–57; Fall, 'Religion and Politics' in Fall 1966, first published as 'The Political-Religous Sects of Viet-Nam,' *Pacific Affairs*, vol. 28, no. 3, September 1955.
91 *PP* I, p. 237; see generally pp. 235–9.

9 The consolidation of the southern regime

In April 1956 Ngo Dinh Diem, now President of the Republic of Viet Nam, gave a picture of what he called the 'constant geopolitical facts' to the newly elected National Assembly.

> Placed by its geographical position at the outpost of the Free World, at the confluence of great currents of thought and on one of the great axes of human migration, Viet-Nam is continually exposed to multiple dangers which threaten its political stability. Thus the grave problems which we have to solve now are not transitory or accidental phenomena. The risks of relapsing into anarchy and servitude brought about by internal feudalism or foreign imperialism that lie in wait for all newly emancipated peoples weigh more heavily on our country than on others, because of our geographic position.[1]

Almost a year earlier, a National Intelligence Estimate written in Washington had commented pessimistically that:

> ...it would be extremely difficult, at best, for a Vietnamese government, regardless of its composition, to make progress towards developing a strong, stable, anti-Communist government capable of resolving the basic social, economic and political problems of Vietnam, the special problem arising from the Geneva Agreement and capable of meeting the long-range challenge of the Communists....[2]

Seen in this perspective, Diem had accomplished not a little.

This chapter, thus, will examine his government's moves to resettle refugees and to consolidate the new state apparatus, especially in security terms. We shall also see how its economic base was stabilized. Lastly, we shall look at the reaction of the Workers' Party to these early developments below the seventeenth parallel.

The First Consolidation

In its first year Diem's regime had survived the test of the massive transfers of population in the 300 days after 20 July 1954. The exchange had been most unequal: official figures put it at 888,000 civilians and 190,000 troops moving to the South and 140,000 to the North.[3] French and US ships and planes provided most of the transport southwards and Soviet and Polish ships northwards, and the ways in which the movements were organized provide interesting contrasts. An estimated 544,000 of the refugees who left the Democratic Republic's zone were Catholics, and their Church provided both motivation and organization. The tightly-knit bishoprics and parishes showed their anti-Communist effectiveness once again; Christ and the Virgin Mary were moving south of the seventeenth parallel to escape the godless, the believers were told, and should not go alone. Parish priests were joined in both propaganda and organizational efforts by agents of the International Rescue Committee and Lansdale's SMM.[4] Whole villages packed and left, moved by the strength of community and fear of reprisal which were not nearly as strong among others – for example the Buddhists whom the Confederation of Christian Workers tried to move in a display of ecumenical spirit.[5]

As for the National United Front fighters and supporters in the South, they first regrouped into old-established base areas, in Quang Ngai and Binh Dinh provinces in southern Trong Bo and in Nam Bo the Ca Mau peninsula, the Plain of Reeds and Xuyen Moc east of Saigon.[6] There they cached weapons, tightened up the basic organization they intended to leave in place and then departed, saying goodbye to cadres and comrades who had not chosen, or had been ordered, to go North. The SMM did its best to speed them on their way in a demoralized state by using its special talents in the 'black propaganda' of 'psywar', matched, it seems, by the efforts of NUF agents among returning State of Viet Nam soldiers, many of whom took the opportunity to desert under cover of movement south.[7]

As regards the resettlement of refugees from the North, most available land was in the west of Nam Bo but not accessible to government agents until the end of October 1955 (if then) because NUF units were still regrouping.[8] The new villages were therefore mostly established in Gia Dinh, Bien Hoa, Thu Dau Mot and Cholon provinces surrounding Saigon, usually, it would seem, as relocations of whole northern communities under the parish priests.[9] The object was to provide each family with a house-site, vegetable patch and one hectare of riceland.[10] The biggest scheme was at Cai San, in the upper Ca Mau

232

peninsula, where more than 40,000 were settled with the help of 100 tractors and $10 million from the USA.[11] Although estimates concerning the class composition of the refugees differ, it is evident that non-agricultural elements were more numerous than in the northern population as a whole; 14–15 per cent of the 660,000 settled by the government were working class, petty bourgeois and middle strata elements, and certainly most of the 200,000 who found their own new homes would have been drawn from the same levels, having some resources and family contacts they could use (45,000 were Chinese and 40,000 French citizens, some of the latter journeying on to France).[12] Most of the non-agricultural migrants would have settled in urban areas, above all in Saigon–Cholon, where problems were certainly caused by the lack of jobs for wage workers.[13] As for the cultural impact, memories are still sharp of the sudden fashionability of the woman's traditional *ao dai,* replacing Parisian styles, and of sellers of northern soups crowding southern competitors off the pavements.

By the time the 300 days were up, therefore, Diem and his subordinates could feel a certain satisfaction. A daunting task had been carried out without major economic and social disruption, even though only with massive foreign aid.[14] More positively, the arrival of more than 500,000 Catholics meant a heavy infusion of political support for the Ngo family, just at the time when it was needed; almost symbolically, marauding Binh Xuyen adherents in April and May 1955 robbed some of the new settlers.[15] The new villages were able to be absorbed into the normal provincial administrative structure with some speed, starting with those in Bien Hoa in October 1956 and ending in July 1957.[16] The population of the South had increased in one leap by an estimated 5.5 per cent, a substantial addition of people who had no reason to love the Communists and yet another factor in the long historical process of the differentiation of North and South.[17] The Catholics, and northern refugees in general, were to be one of the main supports of the Diem regime. But such edifices need more than one pillar. Even while still unsure of firm US support and unable to tackle the sects and Binh Xuyen head-on, Diem, or rather his brother Nhu, had begun to build up a political organization. In September 1954 legal authorization was given to the Personalist Revolutionary Labour Party (PRLP), which had Nhu as its secretary-general; with an active membership which was probably never more than 20–25,000 this was to be the élite political leadership.[18] The following month the National Revolutionary Movement was founded, with Diem as leader and Nhu as political advisor. This was intended to be the regime's mass base, but in 1955 its membership was probably only around 10,000.[19] In this early period Nhu experimented with a variety of other more narrowly-based support organizations, such as the Movement for the Defence of Freedom and Honesty, which grouped intellectuals and civil servants of northern origin, or the Citizens Community, formed from southern Catholics.[20]

For the most part, however, in its first period the Diem regime consisted of the state apparatus with little in the way of political buttressing, and even that was shaky. For the first fifteen months during which Diem held office, he was legally only the chief minister of Bao Dai, who had shown himself to be far from friendly, as we have seen. The army, the main instrument of the state, was in poor shape except for the paratroops and a few other units and it would take the MAAG time to train it. Similarly, a group from Michigan State University had undertaken studies of the administrative apparatus with a view to its reform, and in August 1955 began courses at the new National Institute of Administration, but that would obviously take time to yield fruit.[21] In the meantime Diem was dependent at the top bureaucratic level on about 120 senior officials who had received their education and made their careers under the French. Suspicious of him at first, and inclined to protect themselves by doing as little work as possible so that at least they would not attract attention, they were gradually brought under control. A few were purged for corruption or association with the sects, some swung actively to the new regime (one became Vice-President in December 1956). Perhaps the most effective of various techniques, however, was to neutralize them, by bringing in the new, young men popularly labelled 'nephews of the President' to hold the more technical and economic posts and by fostering the National Revolutionary Civil Servants League, formally launched in July 1955 on the basis of an earlier organization of pro-Diem bureaucrats.[22]

There were even more serious defects in the state apparatus left over from French rule. Administrative procedures were cumbersome, and there was no common body of law for a territory which now united the old Cochinchina with part of Annam and Bao Dai's personal highlands domain. This situation was not to be improved, but rather ramified, by the 170 new agencies which Diem was to boast had been set up by October 1957.[23] These were in any case of widely varying significance – from a Commissariat for Agricultural Development to a Police Scientific Laboratory.

With about 80 percent of civil servants concentrated in Saigon, the administrative control of the localities in these early years basically remained in the hands of provincial, district and villages chiefs of the old colonial kind. In July 1956 President Diem even abolished the village council elections which had been established under the French. Typical of his uncertain beginnings had been the first attempt to take a firm grasp in the rural areas, beyond, that is, the sweeps of the army against the sects and Binh Xuyen, which among other successes led to the treacherous seizure of Le Quang Vinh when he came in to parlay. At the end of 1954 Diem took up a suggestion which was backed by Lansdale and largely based on his experience in the Philippines, that teams of Civic Action agents be established, whose task would be to go into the villages and live with the peasants as teachers and organizers of 'self-help' projects to improve agriculture. They would thus function very much like Communist cadres, and like them would also have political and military tasks – in the latter case helping to organize local defence forces. By November 1955 there were some 800 Civic Action agents, organized in teams, but not drawn from a party. Rather, they were mostly seconded civil servants from such ministries as Public Health, Education and the Interior. How many of them were truly happy to go to live with peasants is uncertain; what is more important is that the central ministries with which they had to work were suspicious and uncooperative, as were the Provincial Chiefs. A central organization was never stabilized, and in April–June 1956 the teams were regrouped under military control and effectively disappeared.[24]

What we are discerning as the first period of Diem's rule, the years of consolidation up to the middle of 1956, was not in fact one of effective administrative development. Rather, it was a phase in which enemies were eliminated politically or at least driven underground, and the main instrument was the Campaign of Denunciation of Communist Subversive Activities. This began in May 1955 in the provinces just south of the seventeenth parallel, previously strongholds of the Great Viet Party and now in the fist of Ngo Dinh Can, brother of Diem and Nhu and determined to have full control. What seems thus to have been a local initiative was taken up in Saigon–Cholon, presumably by Nhu; on 10 and 13 July there were demonstrations against the presence of DRVN representatives with the International Commission, and on the 20th an even bigger one to denounce Communism and the Geneva agreements.[25] During the last, a Chinese-owned hotel was attacked, and there seems little doubt that the demonstrators were moved by the general pressures of unemployment and high prices which could be harnessed for whatever political purposes. The next step was to institutionalize the campaign, therefore, in order to make it more controllable, and the Campaign of Denunciation was set up, with a Central Directive Committee headed by the Secretary of State (minister) for Information and Youth. The Campaign was affiliated internationally to the Asian People's Anti-Communist League, based in Manila.[26]

In its next phase the Campaign was directed towards the referendum which Diem had set for October 1955, in which voters were to be called on to decide whether Bao Dai and the State of Viet Nam should go on, or a Republic be set up with Diem as president. This focus should be emphasized, since it shows that the Campaign was far more that anti-Communist; it was, in fact, the major attempt during 1955–56 to build a mass base for the regime. Thus, in ideological terms it tried to take nationalism away from the Communists, who were denounced as 'just another kind of Colonialists, who resemble the old Colonialists in that they wanted to destroy the national spirit of the Vietnamese people'. The appeal was made to the sense of the heroic past which had been so potent a weapon for the ICP/Workers' Party.

As recorded in history the will to fight foreign aggression is nature to our people; it is constantly preserved and developed through long and bloody struggles. Anti-Colonialism was born at the very moment when the first colonialists landed in

235

Vietnam; anti-Communism began to exist also on the day when communist ideology was first introduced into our country by Moscow's adepts. [27]

However, the Campaign repudiated the 'feudalism' of the past, with which it associated Bao Dai. When the referendum favoured Diem and the Republic by a majority of 98.2 per cent of votes cast, it claimed to have been the 'main force that destroyed feudalism in order to establish a truly democratic regime'.[28] With Bao Dai deposed as Head of State and President Diem installed, the 'anti-feudal' element did not disappear. As was reported, in the next phase of Campaign activities from October 1955 to July 1956:

> Within the framework of the anti-Communist campaign, a war was waged against four social vices – vestiges of Colonialism and Feudalism. Houses of prostitution and gambling dens, formerly owned by Feudal rebels, were closed; opium-smoking and excessive drinking, banned.[29]

Politically, of course, this meant the final breaking of the grip of the Binh Xuyen in Saigon–Cholon, since they were the 'Feudal rebels' in this context.

This phase was also directly anti-Communist and involved a consolidation of organization and methods. Cholon, where the Communist cadres seem to have found a working relationship with the Chinese secret societies and which the Campaign regarded as 'the most delicate center', was chosen as a special focus. Particularly interesting is that the new control method of grouping families to watch and be responsible for one another was now introduced.[30] (Denunciation of those acting suspiciously, including by children, was of course a general feature of Campaign activities.) [31] In Cholon a special Sino-Vietnamese Anti-Communist Association was also a useful adjunct to the Campaign.[32]

In February 1956 the Campaign reached a peak with a National Congress of 2,000 delegates described as ex-Communists. Once again, this was timed to coincide with the campaign for elections to the new Constituent Assembly, Diem's next step in consolidating his power. A resolution was passed, calling on President Diem 'to order the Administration[,] the Army and specialized agencies of all levels to more actively participate, in direct co-operation with the people, in the Campaign of Denunciation of Communist Subversive Activities, and prescribe political study as an essential duty of the government personnel'.[33] This prefigured the regime at its height, as we shall see in Volume II. Meanwhile the Campaign was rounded off with its own National Congress of 480 delegates in May 1956. Here it was claimed that in the past year 15,473 Communists had been denounced, 87,454 former Viet Minh (National United Front) supporters had been 'converted' and 5,908 'active agents' had 'rallied'; moreover, 123,840 items of arms and ammunition (presumably counting single cartridges) and 75 tons of documents had been seized.[34] Leaving aside the question of the trustworthiness of exact figures, and of what 'conversion'

236

and 'rallying' really meant (though doubtless many nationalists felt they could now join Diem with good conscience), the regional distribution shown in Table 9.1 is significant. Given in particular the different total populations, the scale of organization and activity was obviously much greater in the central provinces round Hue, and there also the heavy fist of Ngo Dinh Can provoked the most marked efforts. (He was at the same time breaking the hold of the Great Viet Party.) In the central highlands, and the mountainous areas of Can's fief, where the majority belonged to various ethnic minorities, the more scattered population and looser administrative grip told against the Campaign. As can be seen from the proportions of 'surrenders' and was to become clear in the next years, there the Communist cadres could also hide easily.

Table 9.1   RVN: distribution of claimed results of the denunciation campaign (%)

	Family Groups	Meetings & demos.	Denunciations	Surrenders	Communist links broken	Weapons seized
South	47.6	11.9	17.4	83.9	4.16	54.3
Centre	49.5	85.1	82.2	16.1	95.66	44.3
Highlands	2.9	3.0	0.4	–	0.17	1.4
Totals	100.0	100.0	100.0	100.0	100.0	100.0

Source : Calculated from *Achievements of the Campaign of Denunciation of Communist Subversive Activities (First Phase)* 1956, p. 116.

All this activity no doubt bolstered Diem's unwavering resolve to refuse to hold the elections scheduled in the Geneva agreements for July 1956. It is pointless to speculate what might have happened if they had taken place, because one determinant of the politics of the first phase of the Diem regime was that they were never going to be held. By mid-1956 the containment regime had been consolidated in the South. The rule of the Ngo family and its supporters was not yet fully established in all the ramifications it would acquire. Nevertheless, the new constitution which was promulgated on 26 October 1956, the first anniversary of the declaration of the Republic, did at least put in place the state apparatus which the new power bloc needed.

Although the Constituent Assembly elected in March contained a large majority of pro-Diem members, the debates on the new draft constitution in June were not entirely formal. The President did not secure the power to dissolve the National Assembly which he wanted and had to be content with a provision for recourse to a plebiscite in cases where a situation of deadlock existed between executive and legislature.[35] On the other hand, the Diem bloc could feel very satisfied with its new legal instrument. At the ideological level, for example, its first article unequivocally announced the sovereignty of the new 'independent, unified, territorially indivisible Republic' over 'the entire Nation from the Point of Ca Mau to the Gate of Nam Quan'; from a different perspective from that of the Democratic Republic the permanent status of the division at the seventeenth parallel was thus denied.[36]

At the level of political practice, undoubtedly the most important feature of the new constitution was the powers given to the President as chief executive. Article 3 declared that 'the President is vested with the leadership of the Nation', and, although his formal powers were to be comparable to those of any such office in systems where the head of state is also an active executive, they were considerably reinforced by emergency powers. Thus, the President could declare states of emergency in designated areas, sign Orders in Council to deal with them even when the Assembly was not in session and retrospectively seek approval. Even more important for the consolidation of the Diem regime, during the period of the first National Assembly (1956–59) the President was given special powers to decree 'a temporary suspension of the rights of freedom and of circulation and residence, of speech and the press, of assembly and association, and of formation of labour unions and of striking, to meet the legitimate demands of public security and of national defense'. Moreover, the object of such measures was made abundantly clear in Article 7: 'All activities having as their object the direct or indirect propagation or establishment of Communism in whatever form shall be contrary to the principles embodied in the present Constitution.' Although, as we shall see, other measures were to prove quite enough to launch a new campaign against all those labelled 'Communists', so that these special provisions were never in fact invoked, they show quite clearly the intention of the Diem bloc to use the state apparatus to ensure its firm control. With that established as axiomatic, we can go on to examine certain important features of the new counter-revolutionary regime in its first years.

Aspects of the Early Diem Regime

In the period 1954-56 the conjunction of forces in the south of Viet Nam moved with growing momentum towards consolidation of power of the Ngo family and its supporters. This political practice had necessarily to be matched by an ideological one; the chief actors, at least, had to generate some sort of explanation of what they were doing, and use it as one instrument to gain their

238

ends. A virulent anti-Communism was an important part of this, particularly when it came to enlisting the support of the US government, but there was something more. In March 1956 Diem laid out some elements of his view of statecraft in a speech at the inauguration of the new National Assembly:

> The living and unconquerable faith which sustained us through the last two years of heavy trials, the watchful intelligence which kept us from giving in to despair and as a consequence turning to fascism these must also furnish us with the resourcefulness and concentration to foster the growth of the permanent orientation of free men towards a democratic structure suited to the conditions and possibilities of the moment, but built out of a genuine respect for the dignity of the individual, from an ideal conception of community life where the common good takes precedence over the good of the individual, from a pluralism which does not represent either social conservatism or a collection of anarchical contradictions.[37]

The relationship between individualism and the community, and of both to democracy and pluralism, were supposedly expounded in the regime's official doctrine of Personalism.

The source of this ideology for Diem and Nhu was the writings of the French philosopher Emmanuel Mounier, who had founded the journal *Esprit* in 1932. Mounier himself can be characterized as belonging to the left–Catholic stream and accepted many of the economic and communalist propositions of socialism, but his ideas were ultimately ambiguous and the new President and his brothers fostered a Vietnamese version of the ideology which was far from radical in its final effect.[38] Granted, it made reference at times to the importance of labour and the labourer; Diem himself spoke of this sphere as 'the walk of life where human personality is most gravely violated', and his brother Nhu, more of a populist and with trade union links, noted that 'Personalism stresses hard work, and it is the working class, the peasants, who are better able to understand the concept than the intellectuals'.[39] But the Vietnamese version also sought to incorporate elements from Confucianism, scarcely a revolutionary doctrine although Personalism in Viet Nam claimed to be one. Emphasis was placed on *thanh*, defined as 'acute consciousness and clear vision' of duties towards creator, country, one's fellows and oneself, and *tin*, 'sincere and courageous practice of all these duties'.[40] In this way, cultivation of individuality became a concern with virtues which were quite compatible with duty and obedience. Similarly, Personalist doctrine transmuted 'the moral rearmament of the Vietnamese citizen' into a recreation of 'the spiritual cohesion which, many times in history, has saved the Vietnamese race from complete destruction'; it must not be forgotten that ideologically Diem's regime attempted to root itself in a nationalism free from Communist links, claiming this as its special legitimacy.[41]

Finally, in the new state ideology adherence to democracy took on a very special form. As one of its apologists put it:

The problem that confronts a man like President Ngo Dinh Diem, well grounded in traditional administrative principles but also familiar with the Western political system, is therefore one of giving Vietnam a solid moral basis on which to rebuild a strong, healthy, democratic state. To think of the form before the substance is certainly to run into failure. The main concern of President Ngo Dinh Diem therefore is to destroy the sources of demoralization, however powerful, before getting down to the problem of endowing Vietnam with a democratic apparatus in the Western sense of the word.[42]

By mid-1956 it was quite evident that the strong control regarded by the regime as necessary to foster the solid moral basis was to be given priority over any pluralistic bourgeois democracy. In January Presidential Ordinance 6 gave the executive power to detain anyone without trial for up to two years in special camps if that person was considered 'dangerous to national defense or collective security'.[43] By early 1957 the number of political prisoners was reckoned at 7–8,000, while up to 20,000 in all had passed through the camps.[44] As for the chance to discuss such questions, although press censorship was formally ended in February 1956, this did not mean freedom of communications. The government controlled publication licences and supplies of newsprint, while sale of newspapers was a monopoly of the War Veteran's Association, which was headed by the Director-General of Police. If these means of control were not enough, and objectionable material did find its way into the hands of the public, Presidential Decree 13 of 20 February 1956 provided for fines, prison sentences of up to five years and withdrawal of licences in cases of publication of material which could be 'exploited by subversive elements' or otherwise endanger security. In the following month the first prosecution was undertaken.[45]

It is thus clear that Personalism as it had emerged by mid-1956 was a useful cloak for the authoritarianism which was a necessary part of the counter-revolutionary regime of President Diem, which itself claimed to be revolutionary. Further than this, there is bound to be a close relation in any political system between offical ideology and policy. A further means, therefore, by which we can come to grips with the new regime in the South is to see how the Diem government began, in its first years, to tackle the manifold economic and social problems which faced it.

It is not surprising that a leadership which laid such stress ideologically on moral themes should have turned rapidly to matters of social policy. On the other hand, there were good material and political reasons for the 'Anti-Four Vices' campaign launched in late 1955: in attacking gambling, alchoholism, opium-smoking and prostitution, the Diem bloc was also mopping up the remnants of the Binh Xuyen in Saigon-Cholon and giving itself the chance to extend control over the business community.[46] Intervention in the economy as a whole, however, was to prove a much more difficult task.

The Economics of a Counter-revolutionary Regime

It cannot be denied that Diem inherited daunting economic problems in mid-1954. His new state took over a debt of more than ₱8,331 million, legacy of war-spending since 1946, but this was only a surface expression of a truncated colonial economy.[47] The truncation by the seventeenth parallel had split the mines and manufacturing of the North from the rice and rubber production of the South, but its bad effects on the latter should not be exaggerated. Saigon–Cholon had also been a major centre of light industry, and some enterprises moved south in 1954–55. Cochinchina had always been the wealthiest part of French Indochina and this was carried over to the new state; Gross Domestic Product for the whole country was estimated at ₱119,000 million for 1954 and South Vietnam's at ₱72,000 million – 60 per cent of the former total – in the following year.[48] The South potentially had the rice with which to feed itself and to export, and the rubber with which to earn dollars. Yet this was also the expression of the main contradiction of the economy, which was structured in a typically post-colonial fashion, dependent upon exporting raw materials and importing finished goods, hence dominated by commercial rather than manufacturing capital and with a low level of productive forces. Manufacturing represented only 6 per cent of GDP in 1955, with agriculture and commerce at 24 per cent each and the activities of the state apparatus reckoned as more than twice as 'productive' as manufacturing.[49] Imports were intended to satisfy the wants of consumers, largely those of the wealthier, rather than to develop production or change its structure; consumer goods represented 82.9 per cent of imports in 1956, 20 per cent of this textiles, and means of production only 17.1 per cent.[50]

Not only were these the basic structural features of the economy, but we have seen how the war years (1946–54) induced feverish speculation on the one hand and destroyed productivity on the other. United States Operation Mission (USOM) sources in Saigon estimated that almost one fifth of agricultural land had gone out of cultivation.[51] The dislocations of the first year of Diem's rule, especially of the onslaught on the Binh Xuyen and the private armies of the sects, and a poor crop, led to a drop of rice exports in 1955 to below half those in 1954, while in 1956 they were in effect nil. In that year rice represented 40 per cent of all production in agriculture and fishing, but it was left to rubber to provide 86.9 per cent of all exports.[52] As was to be expected prices rose, and here speculation prior to a currency conversion in November 1955 as the new state moved away from the old Indochinese piastre and covert buying of rice by agents for the North also played their part. Between mid-1955 and mid-1956, wholesale prices in Saigon rose 20 per cent over the level in January 1955, and the official cost of living index for workers 25 per cent. In the period January–October 1955 money in circulation rose by 12 per cent and bank deposits by 44 per cent.[53] In six months in 1955 the price of rice is said to have risen from ₱4 a kilo to ₱10 and of meat and fish by 50 per cent.[54]

With Saigon–Cholon now amassing nearly 15 per cent of the South's total population and high unemployment, it is easy to see how crowds could be raised for the demonstrations of the Campaign of Denunciation. In his speech at the opening of the National Assembly in October 1957, President Diem looked back and admitted that as 1955 gave way to 1956 'the economic and monetary situation was none too bright'. Things were now under control, he claimed, 'We have left behind a war economy and are now entering a peace economy.' Merchants, industrialists and middlemen in the rice trade might see their speculative profits reduced, and 'It is true that the restarting of the economy will carry with it many problems pertaining to reconversion, but we must make the necessary effort at adaptation; it is better to work hard for a stable future than to live in a climate of facile but artificial prosperity which may crumble overnight.' [55] What, then, happened to change the situation?

First of all, some very basic measures had been taken to control banking and currency. On the first day of 1955 the National Bank of Viet Nam had come into being. This indispensable institution for a supposedly sovereign state had taken over the issue of currency from the Institute of Issue which had formally replaced the Bank of Indochina in 1952 (symbolic of changing times, advice on drafting the National Bank's statute came from an expert of the Federal Reserve Bank of New York). Foreign exchange could now also be controlled, and in December 1955 the state Commercial Credit of Viet Nam was set up to take over the domestic transactions of the Bank of Indochina which held over half of total deposits. Nine other commercial banks (two French, two British, three Chinese and two Vietnamese (the smallest)) continued to operate.[56] During 1957 two more financial institutions designed to foster economic activity were added to the National Investment Fund already founded in October 1955, the National Agricultural Credit Office (April 1957) and the Industrial Development Centre (October 1957).[57]

Prices dropped 13 per cent between August 1956 and March 1957, but it is doubtful whether the main credit should go to the new financial institutions.[58] Rather, at one level, it was the reassertion of the natural fecundity of the Mekong delta and the west and the industry of their peasants; except in exceptional years, the rice was there if only it could be freely transported, and by late 1956 the rural areas were under control. What went for rice went also for pigs, vegetables, fish and other foods, and for the necessary charcoal for cooking. At another level, the state had played some part in restoring production, particularly in rebuilding the larger hydraulic installations destroyed in the war, such as the Dong Cam dam in Phu Yen province. However, as Diem himself recognized in his address to the National Assembly in October 1957, much was also owed to the voluntary labour of the peasants in restoring roads, bridges, canals and dykes and other construction projects, works valued at a total of ₱93 million.[59]

The early phase during which Diem was confirmed in power was also marked in terms of economic policy by some attempt to tackle the main grievances of the poor and middle peasants. Indeed, this was made virtually a prerequisite of US support, although in this the Americans and French, rivals in so much else, were at one. In December 1954 both General Collins and General Ely urged on Diem the necessity for agrarian reform, and within hours, according to the testimony of US advisors, a meeting of experts was convened.[60] Their work resulted first in two measures – Ordinance 2 of 8 January 1955 and Ordinance 7 of 5 February. The first in fact amended the measures on rents and tenure of June 1953. Tenants were now to receive written contracts for a minimum of five years, and these could be renewed. The previous ceiling on land rents of 15 per cent of the annual crop was made a minimum, and the maximum fixed at 25 per cent, but there was now to be a 12 per cent limit on rents charged by landlords for equipment and animals and a similar maximum for interest on loans. No other payments or services could be demanded from tenants. Village and district committees including peasant representatives were to enforce the new law, with penalties for non-compliance. The second Ordinance put supervision of land left uncultivated by owners temporarily into the hands of village councils (this was made permanent in April 1956). If landlords under this pressure wanted now to lease it out, they must ask less than 15 per cent rent, but could claim tax exemption; if they were absentees, councils could administer the land on their behalf, charging reduced rents.[61]

Table 9.2: Tenant contracts, 1955–57: former Nam Bo

	Established tenants	For abandoned land
Mid-1955	16,200	3,800
End 1955	204,313	72,032
End 1957	502,989	172,086

Source : Adapted from Gittinger 1959, p. 202.

Table 9.2 shows the peasants' response to the new measures in the former Nam Bo, which in total meant that by the end of 1957 an estimated two-thirds of all tenants had signed contracts covering some 1,820,000 hectares, around 22 per cent of this abandoned land.[62] This apparent enthusiasm must be qualified in two very important ways. First, as the Federation of Tenant Farmers' Unions –which claimed to have 250,000 members – pointed out in a petition in April 1956, there was a great difference between having a contract and getting it enforced; moreover, tenants who refused to agree to rents of more than 15 per cent were being illegally evicted. In some localities Tenants'

243

Unions were organizing boycotts of the election of representatives to the enforcement committees, although this was a double-edged sword, permitting province chiefs to nominate their own choices.[63] Even the Catholic settlers at Cai San (where the Vice-President and his family owned land) refused to sign contracts and demonstrated in October 1956. After a confrontation between tenants and troops the government restored the subsistence subsidies it had withdrawn. [64]

The second problem from the the tenants' viewpoint relates closely to the failure of a third of them even to sign contracts. Where landlords had fled between 1946 and 1954, which was a quite general phenomenon except close to the large urban centres and in the sect-controlled areas, no rents had been collected, although the Viet Minh and then the NUF had expected contributions. Often, therefore, even the reimposition of a 15 per cent rent by a returning landlord was greatly resented. We must come back to both these matters, for they are better seen in the context of a later phase of agrarian reform in the South, but it suffices to say here that obviously there were already profound rural contradictions in the first period of the consolidation of the Diem regime.

In the first years of the new Republic of Viet Nam the US presence did not only make itself felt in matters of agrarian reform. Advisors gave their considered opinions on banking, planning and much more. US officers and NCOs multiplied: MAAG was formally limited to 350 men by the Geneva military agreement, so the Temporary Equipment Recovery Mission was created as a cover to increase to 692 men by June 1956.[65] Their task was to organize and train the 150,000-strong regular army, the new Civil Guard in the provinces created in April 1955, and Self Defence Corps for the villages formally established in April 1956.[66] It was not only on the military level, however, that men, and especially money, made themselves felt. The whole edifice of the Republic of Viet Nam, economic, social and political, was held in place by a scaffolding supplied by the US government with a lavishness which only those spending taxpayers' money can truly show.

Table 9.3 shows the scale and proportions of direct aid given by the USA to the Diem regime in its first three years of existence. Two points require emphasis. First, the very high proportion of aid devoted to military expenses, given to a state which was not actually at war, laid the foundations for the increasing militarization of its apparatus, a phenomenon to which we must turn attention in Volume II and which was to lead in time to the overthrow and death of Diem himself. Table 9.4 shows for one year the sort of priorities which were allocated even within the non-military category of economic and technical assistance; suffice it to say further that aid given for developing the police force comprised nearly 70 per cent of the total for public administration and was considerably more than the support given to education. Second, although Washington saw its efforts as an application of the principles first established by Marshall Aid in Europe, the effect on an economy with an essentially

244

colonial structure was not to increase productive forces, but rather its dependence on its external linkages. Something like a half of the state's annual revenue came from aid, allowing it in its turn to spend a similar amount on its military apparatus.[67] Moreover, the Republic of Viet Nam was able even to abandon the responsibility laid on its Cochinchina predecessor in its directly colonial days, that of paying its way by exports; US aid now in effect covered the constantly recurring trade deficit.

Table 9.3: RVN: US aid, 1954–57 ($'000)

Fiscal Year	Military Amount	%	Refugee Amount	%	Economic & Technical amount	%	Totals
1954-55	234,000	73.1	55,800	17.5	29,700	9.33	319,500
1955-56	109,000	55.5	37,000	18.8	50,500	25.7	196,500
1956-57	173,000	67.6	–	–	89,900	32.4	255,900

Source: Adapted from Lindholm 1959a, Table 22, p. 317.

Table 9.4: RVN: Breakdown, economic and technical assistance 1956–57(%)

Transport	34.5	Public administration	10.0
Agriculture and natural resources	18.4	Health and sanitation	7.5
		Education	5.3
Industry and mining	15.8	Other	8.5

Source : Lindholm 1959a, Table 23, pp. 318–19, adapted.

Not only was US aid to the Republic of Viet Nam very large, but it took a very particular shape. Well over 80 per cent of it came in the form of commodities, supplied by the US government under the Commercial Import Program (CIP), happily described by the head of USOM in 1959 during testimony before a US Senate Subcommittee as 'the greatest invention since the wheel'.[68] The Vietnamese government thus received these supplies free of charge and sold them for piastres to licensed importers, who were able to derive substantial profits from the fact that they paid at the official rate of 35 piastres to the dollar, while charging prices much more in line with the illicit rate of exchange (80–100 to the dollar at the end of 1957).[69] If customs revenue is included, it can be seen that some two-thirds of Vietnamese government revenue was generated by the CIP by 1959.[70] Its deeper class impact will be examined in Volume II. Here let it suffice to indicate a number of immediately significant points. First, CIP provided a new sphere for hectic activity by local capitalists; by 1956 over 20,000 import licences had been granted.[71] Second, the great bulk of imports in these early years consisted of consumer goods, and not those needed by the poorer classes and strata but rather such items as cars and textiles. Third, the impact of the CIP on local prices must be seen as contradictory. The view in US aid circles was that 'we were...paying the Vietnamese economy for directing its resources into the military sector', with a primary aim 'to offset the inflationary pressures generated by military expenditures'.[72] By injecting large quantities of consumer goods the Program may have helped to impose some limits on inflation in the first years of the Diem regime, but in the longer term it contributed greatly to the overall militarization, both economically and politically, and also must have had an inflationary effect by permitting a new group of importers to manipulate the domestic markets.

By the latter half of 1956 the US power bloc, working through both public agencies and such private ones as the International Rescue Committee (which became the American Friends of Vietnam), had thus been able to join forces with internal Vietnamese political interests and arrest the further progress of the Communist-led revolution. This had basically been achieved by squeezing out the French, on whom fell the formal responsibility for carrying out the Geneva agreements, and ensuring that Ngo Dinh Diem and his supporters consolidated their control. Two points are important here. In the first place, to focus discussion of this process on such issues as the extent of the responsibility of the US government to support the provisions of the agreements of July 1954, and hence on such matters as the support given to Diem's refusal to hold the elections scheduled in July 1956, is to miss the real point.[73] Diem's government had never been a party to the agreements, and the support of the USA was given only to a very limited extent – accepting 'unification' elections, for example, only if supervised by the United Nations Organization. The reality in Washington was the policy of containing, and if possible reversing, what was seen as the forward movement of world Communist revolution, directed from Moscow. Thus, in its one major assessment of the situation in Viet Nam made in these early years after Geneva, the National Security Council in 1956 directed all US agencies to 'Assist Free Vietnam [sic] to develop a strong, stable, and constitutional government to enable Free Vietnam to assert an increasingly attractive contrast to conditions in the present Communist Zone' and to 'work toward the weakening of the Communists in North and South Vietnam in order to bring about the eventual peaceful reunification of a free and independent Vietnam under anti-Communist leadership'.[74] The main instruments for this policy, as we have seen, were the building up of the armed forces in South Viet Nam and pumping in massive aid.

However, this account of the putting into place of a solidly anti-Communist

246

regime in South Viet Nam, as a follow-up to the division of the country in mid-1954, cannot be complete without considering the impact of the new counter-revolutionary state upon its main opponents. As we shall see, this was sufficiently severe in the period up to mid-1956 to cause serious alarm to the leaders in Hanoi.

Facing New Wars of Position and Manoeuvre

In September 1954 the Politburo of the Workers' Party laid down directives for action during the two years leading up the elections which were expected to result in the reunification of the country.[75] The line taken for the South was that:

> The purpose of our struggle is to force the enemy to abide seriously by the Geneva Agreement, fulfill freedom and democracy, better the people's living conditions, democratize the South Viet Nam Government, and bring reunification, independence and democracy to the entire nation. Our current task is not to overthrow the enemy government as in the last Resistance, but to compel the enemy to apply freedom and democracy, gradually replace the enemy government with our own and create favourable conditions for the reunification of the country in accordance with the Geneva Agreement.[76]

As to the methods to be followed, they were vividly expressed in further directives issued to Party Provincial Commmittees in the east of what was formally a temporary southern zone of Viet Nam:

> The struggle is directed at ensuring that the 'mad buffaloes', i.e. the French imperialists and the warmongering puppets, will leave our country within the next two years. Despite our impatience, we can accomplish this no sooner. The Geneva Agreement holds the buffaloes in leash, the International Cease Fire Convention and the Mixed Commission [sic] being their keepers. We must wake up the masses who are at the base of our organization so that their vigilance will prevent the escape of the buffaloes. We must be patient, firm, long-suffering and flexible. We must be able to caress and cajole our enemies on the one hand, and on the other to beat them with whips if they stray from the straight and narrow path of the Agreement. We must not provoke them by noisy manifestations which might lead them to retaliate against the people. Later on, when the Geneva Agreement is on the point of fulfillment, we will fight more openly for more speedy fulfillment. We gain nothing by being impatient or overbold; we must fight reasonably so as to achieve execution of the Agreement without causing difficulties for the population.[77]

What must be emphasized is that the top Party leadership, despite its unpleasant experience during the actual bargaining at Geneva, apparently took the agreement made there and the capacity of the International Commission for Supervision and Control (ICSC) to enforce them completely seriously.[78] With an exercise of patience, they fully expected to manoeuvre their way to power in a united country in the second half of 1956, with the elections prescribed in the agreements as their means. There is no available indication that they thought the basic agreements might be broken, even though neither the Diem government nor that of the United States had subscribed to them. Crucially, of course, the Vietnamese leaders relied on their Soviet and Chinese comrades to guarantee observance.

Along with the trust shown by the Communist leaders in the honouring of the Geneva Agreements, we must emphasize the means that they expected to be effective. There is further publicly expressed evidence (unlike the remarks on 'mad buffaloes' quoted above) that senior Party cadres expected the French government to ensure that events were conducted properly; the Vice-President of the new Executive Committee for Nam Bo was quoted in December 1954 as saying, 'We signed the agreements with the French, not with Diem's government. The French are responsible for seeing to it that these agreements are implemented.'[79] The buffaloes could be controlled by a Vietnamese version of the stick and the carrot, through vigilance and mass action, since the international agreement favoured the Party; and further the ICSC, composed of Canadian, Polish and Indian members, would be on its side. These assumptions were to prove hideously costly.

It was only later, then, that the leaders of the Party in the South came to feel that in the period 1954—56 'we had illusions of peace and a beautiful dream of the Geneva Agreement for the entire Party and People'.[80] In the meantime the new policy for coming to power in the South had enormous implications for the organization and training of cadres and members. At the top, the former Nam Bo Interregional Directorate was replaced in October 1954 by two Regional Committees based on the divisions existing before July 1954; thus that for Nam Bo under Le Duan covered the central delta and western provinces, and the Committee for Trung Bo under the military commander Nguyen Van Vinh had jurisdiction over the provinces of the east and centre up to the seventeenth parallel (in effect the old Interzone V). By February 1955 the other four members of the Directorate (including Le Duc Tho, a specialist on party organization whom we shall meet again), who along with the two just mentioned were members of the Party Central Committee, had been regrouped with their lesser comrades to the North.[81]

The senior cadres at the top would have had less difficulty in adjusting to the new line than those below them; part of becoming such a person involved acquiring the ability to ingest, digest and pass on the line as decided by Politburo and Central Committee with relative ease. Further down the hierarchy, however, things were not so simple. As a senior cadre who later defected put it, 'Although the Party had much experience in secret activity, here in the South since 1945 Party members in general were experienced only in armed resistance against the French.'[82] The basic problem was thus that of switching from primarily military to solely political action. From late 1954,

248

indeed, what was demanded was special skills in penetrating non-Party structures. Recognizing that this was so, a weeding-out was undertaken. Between late 1954 and the end of 1957 the Party ranks were reduced by this action from around 60,000 to some 15,000. Some of the 45,000 were, of course, regrouped to the North, although it is probable that many of those who went were young NUF supporters who were regarded as likely candidate members rather than the more experienced members. Otherwise, an elaborate procedure of grading members and investigating their past conduct proved very protracted, especially as repression interfered. Nevertheless, it was pushed through; for example, membership in Go Vap and Tan Binh districts of Gia Dinh province – Party strongholds since the 1930s – was reduced from 1,000 to 385.[83]

What were the remaining cadres and ordinary members supposed to do in the years 1954–56? Basically their task was to work through front organizations and infiltrate others. Thus, the new Regional Committees decided to dissolve the old range of 'National Salvation' bodies for peasants, women and so on and create others on a pragmatic basis – mutual work-exchange teams among peasants, social welfare groups, trade unions, students' associations, a Saigon–Cholon Relief Association to help victims of the fighting between Diem's troops and the Binh Xuyen in April and May 1955.[84] A distinction came to be made between so-called 'legal' and 'semi-legal' organizations which seems to have been basically an attempt to separate those more formally constituted, and on a larger scale, from the level of bureaucracy and spread of membership found in, say, a neighbourhood welfare association, which in strict formal terms would be neither legal nor, like the Party itself, illegal. It would seem that, over the next two years, cadres and members did not always grasp the need for this new flexibility. 'Some', it was commented in a organizational document dateable from internal evidence at around mid-1956, 'ask why we have not rallied the people under legal forms alone, and what advantage there is in using semi-legal forms.':

There is the answer to that question. If we used only the legal form, the labour union, for example, the time would come when the enemy would take repressive measures to disperse the union and arrest its leaders. At a single blow, the organization of the Party installed therein is lost and no more activity is possible, at least for a time. But if, in addition to the union, we had other semi-legal forms, such as associations, mutual assistance groups, etc... the Party's activities could continue and struggle progressively to re-establish the union. Thus there is a useful connection between the two forms, and this interference [sic] permits us to maintain, at present, the presence and the activity of the Party, even at the most difficult times.[85]

As for the related question of infiltration into the state apparatus at its lower levels, it was pointed out in 1954 that:

Currently, our slogans used in the South are to strengthen the peace, to work for the triumph of democracy, and to achieve independence and unity. In the present situation the strengthening of the peace demands concrete guarantees of the security of the people's lives and their possessions, and the maintenance of security and order, which will permit the population to earn their living peacefully. To accomplish these tasks we must know how to organize and carry out self-defense, how to make use of the police, the notables, and the self-defense troops to defend ourselves against the bandits who disturb the peace and against violations of the Geneva Agreement. [86]

In the rural areas, therefore, the object was twofold. Firstly, the idea was to 'start with local experiences which will develop into mass movements'. As an example, it was suggested that village youths might be grouped for local defence purposes, with the approval of the notables.

A boxing teacher in a village could assemble a group of young men for classes in anticipation of defending the village. Thus a popular movement could be created little by little until there would be an association of youths for protection of property against bandits. [87]

The Party's aims went much further than the creation of local self-defence groups tolerated by village councils. A second intention was to infiltrate the councils themselves. 'Previously', it was noted, 'our aim was to destroy the councils of notables, and so [we] had placed our men among them for this purpose. We must still introduce our men into the councils, but to serve our own cause.'[88] The class line to be followed is important in view of what was to develop by 1960; in late 1954 it no doubt reflected past experience. Thus, 'great efforts must be made to send agricultural workers and poor peasants to the councils. If they refuse, we will have to send elements of the rich peasantry and of the landowning class, providing they are comrades.' It was felt necessary that these last be of worker or peasant origin, 'or they will be too interested in the question of land and rice paddies'. In the last resort, 'we will have to send to the councils former notables whose activities we can supervise'. These would have to be taught 'the spirit of the Geneva Accords' and 'educated to the point where they see clearly that it is in their own interest to place themselves on the side of the revolution, and so that they will take note of their former faults, amend their ways, and serve the revolution'.[89]

Given these efforts by the Workers' Party in the South, it is scarcely surprising that in June 1956 the Diem regime took the step of abolishing elections to village councils. In the meantime, however, it had to meet a serious challenge in the urban areas, where the Communist policy of setting up front organizations was strongest in 1954–55. As the Party later assessed the situation,

Never in the Revolution in Viet Nam has the political struggle movement in cities been so intense as it was then. The coordination between the movement in cities and that in rural areas was closely maintained.[90]

In the urban areas the thrust took two forms. The working class, especially in Saigon–Cholon, was an obvious target, but penetration of the organized labour movement was far from easy. There were three organizations: Ngo Dinh Nhu's original Confederation of Christian Workers, founded in 1949, which was affiliated to the International Federation of Christian Trade Unions headquartered in Brussels; the Confederation of Vietnamese Workers Unions, formed under French auspices with a reputed agent of the security police as its head who remained there after Geneva; and the Workers' Force, founded in 1953 with the help of the French socialist Force Ouvrière, and the smallest of the three.[91] Communist policy seems to have been agitation among the rank and file rather than an attempt to capture union leadership, which would have exposed cadres to the security apparatus. As it was, the union where they were probably strongest, that of rubber plantation workers, was severely repressed in 1955–56. Nevertheless, particularly during the first half of 1955, Party agents were active in organizing strikes of rubber workers, dockers, bus workers, employees in power plants, bottling plant workers and others employed by the French army. Moreover, students and market traders gave support. Some wage increases were gained, but conversely there were dismissals, pressure on unions, and destruction of workers' houses and evictions in the name of slum clearance.[92]

The other thrust of Communist urban activity in this period involved a much wider class front, with particular emphasis on middle strata professionals and intellectuals. Party cadres were active, for example, behind the movement in support of a free press, since the French censorship system was still in force. Already on 1 August 1954 a big demonstration had been organized in Saigon in support of the Geneva Agreements and to demand the release of political prisoners, and this had been fired on by the police. There were also demonstrations in other towns. As a result the Committee for Defence of Peace and the Geneva Agreements, popularly known as the Saigon–Cholon Peace Committee, was formed; one of its prominent leaders was Nguyen Huu Tho, a lawyer close to the Workers' Party if not actually a member, who had already spent two years in prison for leading the famous demonstration in March 1950 against the US naval presence. In November 1954 the Committee's leaders were arrested, bringing this sort of Party work to an early close, although activity on a wide class base continued sporadically, as with support for the relief of those made homeless by the fighting in Cholon in May 1955 or the scattered campaign for a 'pre-referendum' before that of October 1955, demanding a choice between ex-Emperor Bao Dai and Ho Chi Minh rather than the former and Diem.[93]

All this emphasis on a peaceful struggle must not lead to the conclusion that in the period 1954–56 the Party abandoned all thoughts of armed action. Direct statements on military organization are lacking, but the demands of contingency planning alone would have ensured that some consideration be given to it. Weapons were cached, and some armed units were apparently retained in remote areas like the Plain of Reeds or Death Forest in the Mekong delta.[94] The policy of influencing village self-defence groups was obviously suited to the rapid creation of guerrilla units if needed. Nevertheless, the Party leaders were content to leave armed resistance against the Diem forces to the dissident elements of the Binh Xuyen mafia and Cao Dai and Hoa Hao sects which were still holding out in the countryside.

The sects and Binh Xuyen were by no means natural allies of the Communists. As we saw in Chapter 6, after fighting together against the French from late 1945 until early 1947, the former had deserted the Viet Minh and become its bitter enemies; in 1960 the Party looked back on the Cao Dai as 'our greatest obstacle' during the Resistance and on the Hoa Hao as 'a cruel force which opposed us fiercely'.[95] We have also noted that, after the attack on them by Diem in 1955, some elments of the sects came to terms with the regime. Nevertheless, important groups did not: the Cao Dai leader, Pham Cong Tac, who had returned from exile in 1954, fled again into Cambodia, where he was to die. Sect and Binh Xuyen units continued to roam the less accessible areas and occasionally launch attacks on government forces or resist pressure from them; thus, two relatively large actions were fought by them with success in April and October 1956, and in December 1956 the 'Cao-Thien-Hoa-Binh General Staff' was formed to combine efforts by the sects, Binh Xuyen and dissident Catholics.[96] In 1955–56 the Workers' Party sporadically cooperated with these other enemies of Diem, at least to the extent of announcing various fronts with them.[97]

From mid-1955 onwards a certain shift of emphasis began to appear in the Party's assessment of the situation. The policy was still to seek power through the implementation of the Geneva Agreement, and overtures from Hanoi to the Diem regime continued to be made over the next year. However, Diem's refusal even to begin the talks on elections scheduled in July 1955 and then the build-up of his government's Denunciation Campaign to its peak in the first months of 1956 gave food for thought. People, it was later admitted, 'began to worry about the Party policy line'.[98] The first indication of shift of emphasis came with the Eighth Plenum of the Central Committee of the Workers' Party in August 1955, when it was decided to form a new Fatherland Front, which was duly brought into being at the Third Congress of the National United Front in September.[99]

The task which the Plenum set 'the whole Party and the whole of our people' was to create 'a broad front', comprised of 'all forces for the nation, democracy and peace, from North and South'.[100] As Truong Chinh, the Party's General Secretary, emphasized in his speech to the NUF Congress, the Communists were once more searching for 'the greatest possible unity', as they had done ever since 1936. Comparing the present meeting with the one which in 1284 had united the people against the Mongol invaders, with the congress held just before the August Revolution, and with the 1951 meeting which had created the NUF itself, he likened the 'clique that betrays the country and harms the people' to others under the Tran and Le dynasties which had collaborated with foreigners. However, 'the Ngo Dinh Diem clique of today is all the more unable to attain the sinister goal, more particularly as our people have never been so politically conscious as they are today'.[101]

It is extremely significant that, at this conjuncture, faced with a failing policy in the South and in a situation where the class circumstances in the two halves of the country were moving even further apart, the top leaders of the Party should have chosen to appeal to the dense web of Vietnamese national history in terms of patriotism rather than of class, of 'Fatherland' rather than of socialism. Once again, as in the period 1941–51, the struggle was to be one which elements of all classes could share. As Chinh said of the programme of the new Front, now being adopted:

> ...the ten main points included therein are in accordance with the aspirations of the entire people, and they take into account the interests of all strata, of all parties and groups. Not only do they take into account the interests of the labouring masses but also that of the upper sections of Vietnamese society.[102]

We must therefore examine the class implications of the new programme.

The positions to be taken by the Fatherland Front, as they had been worked out by the preparatory committee under the veteran labour leader Hoang Quoc Viet, are interesting both as a reflection of current experience in the North (as we shall see in the next chapter) and as the expression of a realization of the existence of different conditions in the South.[103] Thus, one state apparatus was to be created for the whole country, capped by a National Assembly generally elected under supervision of the ICSC, but with a *coalition* government, representing various class, ethnic, regional and political interests, reverting in that sense to the situation at the very beginning of the Democratic Republic in 1945 and indeed implying less of a Communist presence. In addition, it was promised that local councils and executives would have powers to apply special measures provided these were not in conflict with general laws; this was particularly important from the point of view of the highland minorities. Also significant as a transitional device was the idea of gradually building up a unified army. From a more directly class perspective, the workers, first of all, were promised an 8-10 hour working day, a minimum wage, effective guarantees of the right to work and progressive introduction of labour protection and social assistance measures. None of this, of course, would have been impossible within a fairly advanced capitalist economy. In terms of agrarian reform, the important feature was the expressed intention to extend this to the South by rent reduction and redistribution of land from big owners to poor and landless peasants. However, this was not to follow the pattern in the North which was then being applied: the land taken over was all to be bought 'at a fair and reasonable price'. More similar to the policy in the North, Vietnamese capitalists were guaranteed a place alongside state and cooperative manufacturing and commercial sectors provided their enterprises were judged to be useful to the national economy. Repeating a line which had failed in the North, even foreign enterprises were to be protected and helped so long as they met the needs of the local market and gave up colonial privileges. Foreign trade was to be developed on the principles of equality and reciprocity, with a special place for France.

From these points we can see how cautious was the face which the Workers' Party was presenting to the world, and especially to Vietnamese patriots. The country was certainly to be unified, both politically and economically. The perspective in the latter respect was one of the re-establishment of normal economic exchange, then reconstruction of the national economy and a planned development as an advanced industrial country. But within this process, as we can see, there was ample room in the foreseeable future for private capital, both local and foreign; socialism was pushed well into the background. It is impossible to say how far this was a conscious attempt to woo a putative 'national bourgeoisie' in the South; certainly that element must have been present. The basic position taken, however, was in line with what was being done in the North in late 1955, before the crisis of 1956–57 forced a reappraisal. The launching of the building of a socialist base in the North in late 1957, which we shall examine in the next volume, along with developments in the South, in fact were to render the Fatherland Front an inadequate instrument for the handling of events in the latter. However, its programme is interesting in that it reveals that already, just over a year after the division of the country at the seventeenth parallel, the Workers' Party leaders felt that the rebuilding of a revolutionary terrain in the South demanded a line which was directed to national rather than class appeals, like the Viet Minh line of 1941–51.

Although the formation of the new Front was the first attempt to come to terms with what seemed to be an increasingly unfavourable terrain, the adjustment by the Party continued to broaden and deepen. Looking back on the period of peaceful struggle for unification, the Nam Bo regional leadership was later to diagnose its prime error as a failure to realize that the South was 'still a colony with many feudalist influences'. In consequence, 'we did not consider either the main principle of Marxism–Leninism concerning revolutions in colonies and semi-colonies or our Party's policy to work out appropriate plans for the situation'. There were 'illusions of peace', and 'what we did then separated us from our Party's revolutionary strategic policy which had been worked out when the Party had been formed'.[104]

This recognition of deviation from tried and true revolutionary doctrine (an implicit criticism which reached to the very top of the Party) came at a time

254

when the armed struggle had again been resumed. By the time the new Fatherland Front was launched, in the first period, Ngo Dinh Diem had consolidated his political control and was soon to ratify it with his referendum and assumption of the Presidency. He had also begun the Campaign of Denunciation, which was principally (though not exclusively) a campaign against the Communists and their supporters. The revolution which they sought had thus been effectively contained, and by April 1956 it was to become obvious that President Ho and his comrades were having to think again about the creation of a new terrain for struggle below the seventeenth parallel. Counterposed to this was the serious situation facing the Communist leaders in the new North; there, by the time the Fatherland Front celebrated its first anniversary, they were embroiled in a political crisis of some magnitude.

Notes

1   Ngo Dinh Diem 1957, p. 14.
2   *PP* I, p. 266.
3   See ibid., p. 290, and *Operation Exodus* nd, pp. 4 and 5. Murti 1964, p. 224, gives 129,900 moving north, 86,900 combatants and 43,000 cadres, ex-prisoners-of-war and family members; his figures presumably came from ICSC sources.
4   For the latter's efforts see 'Lansdale Team's Report on Covert Saigon Mission in 1954 and 1955,' *PP* I, pp. 576 and 577. Devillers and Lacouture 1969, p. 335, deny that the name of the Virgin was invoked. See also Tran Tam Tinh 1978, pp. 91–105. The statistic is from ibid., and includes 809 clergy, 71.8 per cent of the total compared with the laity's 60.9 per cent (Table, p. 102).
5   *Operation Exodus*, p.8.
6   See Murti 1964, p. 224: 70,000, more than half, came from Trung Bo.
7   'Lansdale Team's Report', *PP* I pp. 579 and 581, and Collins 1975, p.9.
8   *Operation Exodus*, p. 21.
9   Ibid., pp. 23–4. Although obviously biased, this work is a useful source of detail. See also Part Two of Lindholm (ed.) 1959.
10 *Operation Exodus*, p. 21.
11 See Fall, 'The Birth of Insurgency' in Fall 1966, pp. 180–1 (first published in a longer version as 'South Viet-Nam's Internal Problems', *Pacific Affairs*, vol. 31, no. 3, September 1958); 'Administrative Planning for the Cai San Resettlement Project' and 'The Cai San Tractor Loans' in Montgomery nd. An official account may be found in *Cai San: une expérience de réforme agraire et de réimplantation dans le 'Grenier à riz' de la République de Viet-Nam* nd.
12 *PP* I, p. 290, and *Operation Exodus* , p. 20.
13 *Operation Exodus*, p. 30. Official unemployment figures for the two cities in March 1955 were 56,000 (Ton Vy 1968, p. 5). The same source suggests a rise to 100,000 by August.
14 Altogether in the period 1954–58 the aid organization Catholic Relief Services distributed supplies worth $38,323,927 (*VNP* 1,372, 7 October 1959, p. IX).
15 *Operation Exodus*, p. 21.
16 Ibid., pp. 44 and 46.
17 Population estimate, ibid., p. 50.
18 See Donnell (unpublished) 1964, p. 229 note 6 and pp. 231–2, and Appendix A for the PRLP Charter.
19 Donnell (unpublished) 1964, p. 238, and Nguyen Anh Tuan 1967, p. 140.

20   Tuan 1967, p. 142–3.
21   See Scigliano and Fox 1965, pp. 30–9.
22   On Diem's early relations with the senior bureaucrats see Jumper 1957a, especially pp. 53–5 and 56–7, and on the origins of the Civil Servants League, Joiner and Jumper 1963, p. 206.
23   Speech at the opening of the National Assembly, 7 October 1957, Ngo Dinh Diem 1957, p. 26.
24   Ginter (unpublished) 1972, pp. 160–2; *PP* I, pp. 308–10. The latter source is primarily a quoted account by Lansdale which differs in some details from Ginter's, based in turn on a Michigan State University Vietnam Advisory Group 'Report on the Organization of the Special Commissariat for Civic Action,' dated June 1957, which I have not seen.
25   *Achievements of the Campaign of Denunciation of Communist Subversive Activities (First Phase)* 1956, pp. 59–61. For a description of the demonstrations from another point of view see Murti 1964, pp. 157–60.
26   *Achievements* 1956, pp. 95–7. Despite the bias of this report, it is a valuable source, particularly for assessing the Campaign's aims. For more objective discussion see Thayer (unpublished) 1977, pp. 263–70.
27   *Achievements* 1956, p. 41. This theme of the Communists as foreign tools was not new, nor was it confined to Vietnamese writers: see Tran Van Tung 1951 and Das 1951.
28   *Achievements*, p. 68.
29   Ibid., p. 75.
30   Ibid., pp. 53 and 73–4.
31   See Ibid., pp. 78 and 81, for the singling out for special praise of a twelve-year-old girl who denounced the assistant secretary of a Workers' Party village committee.
32   Ibid., pp. 95–7.
33   Ibid., pp. 121–2. See also pp. 81–3 and the Congress declaration, pp. 87–9.
34   Ibid., p. 17.
35   Such situations were not explicitly recognized. For the discussion of the draft see Donnell (unpublished) 1964, pp. 303–6, and Grant 1958, pp. 441–4 and 449. Grant's article also provides detailed commentary on the new constitution, as does Corley 1961.
36   The official English text of the constitution was published as Supplement A to *The Times of Viet Nam*, 27 October 1956. An alternative source is *News from Viet-Nam* (published by the Vietnamese Embassy in Washington, DC), 'Special Edition. The Constitution of the Republic of Viet-Nam,' 17 November 1956.
37   Diem 1957, p. 11.
38   For general discussions of Personalism see Donnell 1961 and unpublished 1964, pp. 81–93.
39   Diem 1957, p. 12, and quoted in *PP* I, p. 301.
40   Diem 1957, p. 19: see the discussion in Donnell (unpublished) 1964, pp. 21–43 and 459–60.
41   Quotations from Diem 1957, p. 24. Those wishing a further selection of Diem's speeches and writings can consult Ngo Dinh Diem 1962, itself a culling from the eight-volume collection in Vietnamese of the same name.
42   Phuc Thien 1956, pp. 9–10, quoted in Donnell (unpublished) 1964, p. 26.
43   'The Birth of Insurgency' in Fall 1966, p. 171, note 5, and Grant 1958, p. 458.
44   Grant 1958, p. 458, and *PP* I, p. 311. These are conservative estimates.
45   For the whole issue of press freedom see Grant 1958, pp. 458–62.
46   For the campaign see Donnell 1959 and (unpublished) 1964, pp. 34–6.
47   Debt figure from Huyn Van Lang 1959, p. 307.
48   Cole 1959, n. 97, p. 189.
49   Ibid., Table 9, p. 180.
50   Ibid., Table 12, p. 188.

51   Wurfel 1957, p. 86. Communist sources gave much higher estimates, drops in area, for example, of rice in Cochinchina by 31.7 per cent and of rubber by 39 per cent, of riceland in Annam by no less than 90.5 per cent and of sugar by 80.7 per cent. Agricultural production was reckoned to have fallen commensurately, and that of charcoal by an average for the two areas of nearly 85 per cent and of salt by 99.6 per cent in Cochinchina and 41.3 per cent in Annam. (See Limbourg 1956, p. 89.)
52   Cole 1959, pp. 180–1, and calculation from Trued 1960, table, n. 4, p. 251.
53   Schiff 1959, pp. 275–7.
54   Limbourg 1956, p. 90.
55   Diem 1957, pp. 27–9.
56   In fact, the private Banque Française de l'Asie now shared the operations of the Commercial Credit. Data here from Schiff 1959, pp. 260 and 267.
57   Slusser 1959, p. 271, and see also Nguyen Duy Xuan 1959; Nguyen Truong 1974, p. 6.
58   Schiff 1959, p. 278.
59   Ngo Dinh Diem 1957, p. 33.
60   Gittinger 1959, p. 200; see also Wurfel 1957, pp. 82–3.
61   Gittinger 1959, p. 201, and Wurfel 1957, pp.83–5.
62   Gittinger 1959, p. 203, area given there as 4.5m. acres, with 1 million abandoned.
63   Wurfel 1957, pp. 85–6, and Porter (unpublished) 1976, pp. 298–302, for more on the Unions.
64   Porter (unpublished) 1976, n. 53, p. 308, and Scigliano 1964, p. 123.
65   Collins 1975, p. 7.
66   Ibid., pp. 9–10.
67   On these points see Lindholm 1959, pp. 320–1, and Tra Van Kien 1959, pp. 325–6.
68   *Situation in Vietnam*   (Hearings before the Subcommittee on State Department Organization and Public Affairs of the US Senate Committee on Foreign Relations, 86th Congress, 1st Session, July 30 and 31,1959), p. 203.
69   Lang 1959, pp. 296–7.
70   Porter (unpublished) 1976, p. 252.
71   Ibid., p. 256.
72   Interview with Leland Barrows, former head of US aid, quoted in Porter (unpublished) 1976, pp. 251 and 265.
73   See, for example, Kahin and Lewis 1967, pp. 80–3; Randle 1969 Part III, treats the legal aspects exhaustively.
74   Quoted in *PP* I, p. 267.
75   For discussion see Thayer (unpublished) 1977, pp. 77–82.
76   'Situation in SVN since the Restoration of Peace to Date' (unpublished) nd. The considerable use to which this document will be put in the next pages requires comment upon its nature. It is an English translation supplied to Jeffrey Race by the US Embassy in Saigon, but too late for use in his own book. I have not had access to the Vietnamese text used by Thayer (for his discussion of it see Thayer (unpublished) 1977, n 59, pp. 70–1). As always with a supposed Communist document coming from such a source, doubt must be raised about authenticity. This becomes particularly important in this case, since there are obvious errors and anachronisms in the English, particularly references to 'COSVN' (Central Office for South Viet Nam) as directing Workers' Party operations, although in this period it did not yet exist (this is recognized in a letter to Race from the Embassy, 4 August 1971, also in the Race Collection). However, from the style and content of the document I would take it to be genuine, and a most important analysis, probably by the Nam Bo Regional Committee of the Party. Obvious mistakes I consider to be the result of using rather low-level translators who were inclined to wish to please their employers by reinforcing the idea that from the beginning the revolution in the South was closely controlled from the North and therefore interpolated a particular phraseology.

77   'Translation of Lao Dong Party Document aquired [sic] on November 29, 1954, in Saigon–Cholon area', mimeo., nd, p. 3, Document 29 in collection 'Captured Documents and Interrogation Reports' 1968. Although no Vietnamese texts are available, I am satisfied that these documents are genuine. On this see also Thayer (unpublished) 1977, n. 41, pp. 579, discussing another edition.

78   This remains a more than usually conjectural remark, given available evidence.

79   *Le Monde* , 16 December 1954, quoted in Devillers and Lacouture 1969, p.387.

80   'Situation in SVN', p. 31.

81   Thayer 1975, pp. 34–5; *Fifty years of activity of the Communist Party of Viet Nam* 1979, (in Vietnamese) pp. 142–3 .

82   Vo Van An (pseudonym), quoted in Race 1972, p. 38.

83   'Situation in SVN', pp. 25 and 26. For further discussion see Thayer (unpublished) 1977, pp. 83–8.

84   'Situation in SVN', p. 21.

85   'Plan for Strengthening the Organisms [sic]', nd., Document 201 in 'Captured Documents', p. 7. It is probable that the language of legality and semi-legality is the result primarily of two years' experience of the Diem regime, and that the functional distinction made above was of more significance to the Regional Committees in 1954.

86   Document 29, (op. cit. note 77 above) p. 4.

87   Ibid., p. 5.

88   Ibid., p. 6.

89   Ibid., pp. 6–7 *passim* .

90   'Situation', p. 23.

91   Material on the labour movement in the South after mid-1954 (or on the whole country after 1945) is very scanty. Here I have more or less followed Hendry (unpublished) 1960, pp. 106–7, and Porter (unpublished) 1976, n. 21, p. 299. In Hendry's sample of enterprises, union membership was marked by a tendency towards unskilled, female and Hoa workers; this raises fascinating questions and may, for example, help to explain the ability of the non-Communist union 'bosses' to retain their grip, but the sample is far too small to serve as a basis for answers.

92   'Situation in SVN', pp. 7 and 16. See also Ton Vy 1968, p. 13.

93   Data in this paragraph drawn from Burchett 1965, pp. 120–1; Devillers and Lacouture 1969, pp. 385–7 (these authors speak of the *Movement* for the Defence of Peace, founded in April 1954); and Chaffard 1964, p. 40. For further discussion see Thayer unpub. 1977, pp. 100–5.

94   On this see Vo Van An, as reported in Race 1972, p. 35. In my view, An's evidence must be treated with more care than accorded to it by Race, since as a defector he would have an interest in appearing to support the American view that the Party had always been concerned with fomenting armed struggle. Thus he stated (Race 1972, p. 36) that in 1955 the Party had some 6,000 armed men who could have joined the Binh Xuyen, and that cadres were later reprimanded for their 'mechanical interpretation' of the Geneva Agreement because they did not do so. Thayer (unpublished) 1977, pp. 92–5, suggests a total of around 1,000 armed men at this time.

95   'Situation', p. 2.

96   Ta Xuan Linh 1974a, pp. 21–22. The Catholic element must have been small, and possibly was recruited from dissidents at Cai San settlement area, near which the Hoa Hao had scored its success in October (see ibid., and 'Situation in SVN', pp. 20 and 21).

97   See Thayer (unpublished) 1977, pp. 105–12, 145–52 and 170–4.

98   'Situation in SVN', p. 15. For details of the attempted negotiations see Murti 1964, Chapter XII.

99   Thayer (unpublished) 1977, sees the DRVN National Assembly session in March as giving the Workers' Party leaders the opportunity to present a reassessment; see pp. 124–33. They may in part have revealed the beginnings of such when Giap, for example, spoke of elections only coming 'when peace is consolidated' (ibid., p. 132).

100 'Communiqué of the 8th Plenum of the Central Committee of the Viet Nam Workers' Party,' *ND*, 22 August 1955, p. 1.

101 *Viet-Nam Fatherland Front and the Struggle for National Unity* 1956, pp. 50–1 and 53.

102 Ibid., p. 55.

103 The following discussion is based on Pham Van Dong's report to the Fifth Session of the National Assembly held in September 1955, in ibid., pp. 37–45, also available in Pham Vam Dong 1977, and Limbourg 1956, pp. 91–2.

104 'Situation in SVN', p. 31.

10 Crisis in the north

When the sounds of battle died away north of the seventeenth parallel in late July 1954, the Workers' Party Politburo and Central Committee could count themselves victorious. What territory they did not already control soon passed to them, although Hanoi itself did not witness their victorious entry until early October, when the French troops withdrew to their enclave in Haiphong. President Ho was thus not faced by the challenge that had to be met by Chief Minister Diem, that of establishing a basic political control; those elements which might have resisted, especially Catholics, were instead moving in their thousands to the South. Cadres could penetrate all areas, backed up if necessary by troops of the People's Army or local forces. Probably the only places where this was a delicate exercise was in some of the mountain strongholds of the Meo and Thai, many of whose chiefs had backed the French in the liberation war; the former in particular had sold opium to the colonial army, which had then passed it on to the Binh Xuyen in Cholon, and arms had been left behind with them and the others as the French pulled out after the Geneva agreements. Also left in place were two sabotage groups, organized by Colonel Lansdale and his team and trained in the Philippines, who were smuggled into the North in February–March and April 1955 just in time 'to beat the Geneva deadline'.[1] The extent to which they might gain local support remained an open question.

Immediately more serious was the question of establishing an effective Party-controlled state apparatus, asserting control over that left behind by the withdrawing regime by extending the administration that had existed in the previously liberated zones. Among the refugees who passed to the South were some 7,300 civil servants and, although Communist sources claimed that a similar number remained, they also recognized that in mid-1954 the operations of 70 out of 131 administrative services handed over by the French and State of Viet Nam authorities were in effect paralysed; no telephones operated, for example, outside the two main cities.[2] Most crucially, cadres whose experience was of the political economy of the liberation war were now being called upon to organize the rehabilitation of an economy grossly distorted by that struggle, something for which their talents were not necessarily fitted.

Such a situation was basically difficult enough. It was in fact to be turned into a crisis by the end of 1956 as a result of three major circumstances. First, and most basic, was the nature of the political structure, expressed through Party and state apparatus, which the Communist leaders extended throughout the North after mid-1954. Here it is convenient to crystallize my views by contrasting them with those of Douglas Pike, that the liberation war against French rule 'facilitated immensely' the emergence of political integration and 'the development of a modern governmental system' by the DRVN, so that it 'emerged from the forced development process [sic] as a modern state, crudely hewn perhaps, but with two to three decades compressed into five [sic] years'.[3] As is hopefully clear from Chapters 6 and 7, I see the seven and a half years of liberation war not as a period of 'development' but as marked by a just sufficient holding in place of the apparatus required to mobilize the supplies and labour power needed. Granted, following the Party's Second Congress in February 1951, there was an increased effort to take firmer control, but that established only a minimal structure. As we shall see, it was put severely to the test by the need to take a grip on the economy of the North after the Geneva agreements.

Moreover – and this is the second circumstance basic to the following analysis – the DRVN government in its 'regroupment zone' immediately had to face the application of the most important single measure taken to facilitate the mobilization of effort needed for the war - namely land reform, which was overtaken by the Geneva settlement. This, as we shall see, was to prove even more divisive in peacetime than it might have been with the immediate pressure of unity in war. Indeed, such unity in a broader sense provides the background to our third important circumstance in 1954–56. Mobilization of effort upon a broad patriotic basis since 1941 had brought not only landlords and rich peasants but also middle strata intellectuals and capitalists into the revolutionary bloc. During 1956 the intellectuals in particular began to fall away from the Party, and this raised the spectre for the leadership of a potential political expression of rural and other discontents.

The developments which give meaning to those generalizations will form the content of this chapter. Its first focus must be upon the economic measures which had to be taken as soon as the Workers' Party and DRVN government extended their formal control over the new North.

Crisis and Rehabilitation

By mid-1954 the economy of Bac Bo and northern Trung Bo had suffered a serious decline in productive forces as a direct or indirect effect of the fighting. An area of riceland estimated at between 138,800 and 143,000 hectares, some 7 per cent of the total, had gone out of cultivation, mostly in so-called 'white zones' where the French Army had followed a shoot-on-sight policy.[4] On the surface, this was not a large proportion, but it must be remembered that what had now become the 'northern regroupment zone' of the new Viet Nam had always been a rice-deficit area in the colonial period, needing to import annually from Cochinchina. Hence, any decline in production whilst the new 'southern regroupment zone' was politically unstable and under continuing French and increasing US influence was a serious threat. In fact, with the fear of being shot in their fields removed, the peasants soon moved to restore production; it is reported that some 38 per cent of abandoned land was back in production after one month.[5] By 1957 nearly 90 per cent was to be restored.[6] A bigger problem was the destruction of hydraulic works and hence irrigation systems, which were much more difficult to repair. By July 1954 French bombing had caused serious damage to eight major systems, covering 252,000 hectares, and tens of thousands of metres of small-scale earthworks had been breached.[7] The peasants knew well how vital such works were and responded to mobilization for their repair; by the beginning of 1955 over 95 per cent of the land in major projects was back under controlled irrigation, and in a year 2.68 million workdays were given for that purpose and 6 million for the repair of 2,750 kilometres of flood protection dykes.[8]

This hard labour, however, came too late to save the new northern regime from the threat of famine, bringing with it high food prices in the urban markets. This should be seen in the context of the decline of the non-agricultural economic sectors by mid-1954. There, the effects of the war were compounded by French owners and others stripping out machinery and taking away stocks of raw materials and goods for sale as they moved south. It was estimated that, after the ceasefire, there was a rundown of 2,000 million francs of fixed capital in Hanoi and Haiphong, the main manufacturing centres.[9] In the port city, 29 of the 30 French-owned factories pulled out, leaving the cement works which was running at only 56 per cent capacity. When the negotiations concerning joint state–private ownership which we have already noted failed, the management sold equipment as scrap or shipped it out and ran down supplies. The same thing happened in the coal mines; the state bought little more than a shell for a promised delivery of a million tons of coal over fifteen years in March 1955.[10] By mid-1954, it has been estimated, the output of modern industries such as these had dropped to a mere 1.5 per cent of the total for manufacturing and agriculture in the new North, compared with 10 per cent in 1939.[11] During the 300 days it dropped even lower. The result was of course unemployment, threatening above all the estimated 140,000 paid employees and 55,000 petty bourgeois people who had lived directly or indirectly off the French army.[12]

The colonial economies of Bac and Trung Bo had, of course, always lived much more from commerce and petty production than the activities of modern plants. Inflation and shortages had hit French, Chinese and Kinh merchants, handicraft producers and small traders before Geneva, and after it many of the big men and some of the small fled south. In December 1954 Hanoi was left with an unproductive mixture of 6,000 shopkeepers, 8,900 street-traders, (1,200 of them selling soup), 4,000 artisans (including almost 900 tailors) and 20,000 workers. What stocks remained for sale showed similar distortions; thus supplies of alcoholic beverages totalled 140,000 litres, but those of fuel only 30,000.[13] In any case, had there been more goods to distribute they could scarcely have found their way much beyond the two big cities, since in the second half of 1954 the whole of the North could only boast 917 lorries and 959 other vehicles, and bombing and sabotage had severed all the railways.[14] Some further sabotage was apparently carried out during 1955 by the teams left in place by Lansdale's group, which had also contaminated the oil supply of the Hanoi bus company before leaving for the South, thus hoping to ensure the gradual seizing-up of vehicle engines.[15]

In a situation in which there was only a three months' supply of rice and less than one month's of cloth and kerosene in Hanoi, it is scarcely surprising that speculators moved in to seek profits.[16] As a later Party commentator put it, 'as soon as peace was recovered, many commercial enterprise owners spent a great deal of money to grab all available merchandise to hoard'; sources of supplies were found by journeying into the provinces and by buying from those who were packing to leave for the South and from the state shops.[17]

The problem, however, went deeper even than this capitalist reaction. In the second half of 1954 there was a basic structural distortion in the whole pricing system of the newly created North Viet Nam. The possibility of this had been recognized at the Sixth Plenum of the Central Committee in July 1954, when it was resolved that the Party should 'urgently take hold of pricing policy in the former free zones, likewise in the newly liberated zones, so as to guarantee the development of production and to avoid a situation of really excessive price differences between the newly-liberated zones and former free zones to avoid losses to the people and a bad influence on production'.[18] The problem was that the relative shortage of consumer goods in the areas long controlled by the Democratic Republic meant considerable price differences between these and the areas just taken over: thus cloth in the former cost Ð1,350 per metre compared with Ð495 in the latter, sugar Ð2,900 per kilo as opposed to Ð570, and kerosene Ð1,630 per litre compared with Ð300.[19] Inevitably, therefore, such commodities began to flow into the old free zones, creating shortage in the others. The government began to unify prices, generally on the basis of the higher ones prevailing in the older freed areas; rice prices in particular were allowed to go up in the newly liberated areas so that the essential commodity would not be drained off; they stabilized for a time at a general price of Ð260 per kilo from original differences of Ð340 in older liberated areas and Ð150 in newer.[20]

In December 1954, however, natural disaster struck, as so often in North Viet Nam. Floods hit crops, and in the next months the threat of famine and real hunger began to stalk the land. The price of rice jumped in the stricken areas and the urban centres to Ð700 per kilo, and in Nghe An to Ð1,000.[21] The general shortage of manufactured articles also pushed up their prices. Measures had to be taken. Rationing of rice was introduced, with control of its price on the still-permitted supplementary free market, with price controls also for the staples – salt, sugar, cotton goods, kerosene and paper (the last as a 'staple' providing an illustration of the government's concern with literacy and education). Production was encouraged and imports from fraternal countries, especially China, were increased. Curbs were placed on the activities of private traders. Taxes on stocks of goods and incomes reduced the profiteering from the higher prices on the market to which consumers had to resort in the absence of a large number of state stores (which accounted for 19.8 per cent of retail trade in 1955). Private firms and shops had to register with the authorities, and the number of those dealing in rice and salt was limited; some were in fact ordered to become state agents.[22] With the help of 150,000 tons of Burmese rice imported at the cost of the Soviet Union, the price of rice finally levelled off at Ð300–350, while the peak season price of maize in 1955 reaching Ð360 a kilo, up from Ð200 at the end of 1954; during 1955 the cost of a metre of cotton cloth rose to Ð3,700.[23] In the big urban centres the authorities had met the immediate situation with a series of emergency relief measures. Thus, during 1955 the Hanoi Labour Commission managed to find jobs for 23,000 of the 39,000 who were actively seeking work, including, it claimed, all specialized workers. Housing was found for the poorest workers, special restaurants opened and some relief payments given. Emphasis was placed on opening cooperative stores, first in provinces around the capital then further afield; prices in these were on the whole 20 per cent below those on the free market.[24]

With the state forced to intervene in the economy out of immediate necessity, irrespective of doctrine, in late 1955 nature struck again. A typhoon hit the coastal provinces in September, then drought followed, and, beginning in December, an unusually severe cold spell. The measures adopted during 1955 once more served to carry the population through without famine, if at a continuing level of poor feeding and scarcity for the majority, but ominous signs appeared of lack of competence on the part of some cadres. In Nam Dinh province they bought rice on behalf of the state at the price fixed for that of good quality irrespective of its actual worth, while merchants thus took the opportunity to sell poor quality rice to the cadres at the higher price and sell the best on the free market for an even greater profit.[25]

It seems fair to say, in fact, that during the first eighteen months of the existence of the new North Viet Nam, the Workers' Party and the state apparatus it directed were able to intervene only partially in the workings of the economy, and often on an emergency basis. Party economists retrospectively characterized the period until the end of 1957 as one of rehabilitation, but this was on a somewhat piecemeal basis until the first annual plan of 1956, and even beyond it. The Party leadership knew well that not everything could be done at once: thus, in its key policy resolution in September 1954 the Politburo described the restoration and development of agriculture as 'the fundamental problem' and noted that 'at the present moment, an industrial construction plan on a large scale and in a short time appears impossible'.[26] The work in the agricultural sector would be 'the basis for the improvement of the people's livelihood, a guarantee for the people's food, for economic prosperity, for securing the flow of goods'.[27] Talk in 1955 was of expanding the area able to bear two rice crops so as to cover the existing annual deficit of around 200,000 tons and produce a surplus of 2-300,000 for export.[28] According to official figures, it could be calculated that in 1956 a surplus of well over 400,000 tons was achieved, but this was working on the basis of a rice ration of 250 kilos per head, only 10 kilos above what French colonial experts regarded as adequate.[29]

It was later claimed that, by mid-1956, the total cultivated surface for rice had increased 24 per cent over that of 1939, production per head 43 per cent, yield per hectare 36 per cent and consumption 13.25 per cent.[30] Taking these figures at face value, it is important that they had been achieved by a peasantry still working in individual households, with credits for agriculture increasing three times in the period 1955–57 but starting from a baseline of only 2.1 per cent of government credits in the period 1951–54.[31] It seems evident that the rehabilitation of agriculture was thus basically the result of peasant initiative, with little effective government assistance. Moreover, that initiative was demonstrated in other crops in addition to rice, and it seems probable that the avoidance of widespread hunger was a result of the expansion of production of maize, potatoes, manioc and beans. On the other hand, to compare production of these in 1956 with levels in 1939 and to note that these were respectively twice, five and a half times, three and three-quarter times and nearly twice as high is very misleading.[32] This growth can more meaningfully be compared not with production in 1939, but with the efforts made in 1946, when maize production, for example, increased four times over the pre-war level.[33] This implies, therefore, that the period 1954–56 must be seen as a recovery from a considerable decline during the liberation war rather than a huge increase in a short span over colonial production; that had already been achieved after the August Revolution.

Outside agriculture, a modest degree of rehabilitation could also be hoped for in the period from mid-1954 till the end of 1957. At its meeting in September 1954 the Politburo had not taken an ambitious approach to manufacturing. The immediate object, it had resolved, was to 'restore and construct a certain number of enterprises or workshops for the production of consumer goods, for the restoration of the means of communication and transport, enterprises which require little capital but which permit the resolution of the urgent problems relevant to the living conditions of the population'.[34] In fact, however, early attention had to be paid to a number of industries not very immediately related to living standards, which it had been hoped might continue to be run as joint state–private or even foreign-owned enterprises. This especially applied to the cement works at Haiphong, the coal mines and the Nam Dinh textile mill. The first was rebuilt with aid from the USSR between August and November 1955 and then began operating 24 hours per day with three shifts of 2,000 workers each; in this way, in 1956 it attained 61 per cent of its 1939 production, which had dropped to 56 per cent by the time of the ceasefire.[35] The mines at Hong Gai and elsewhere, stripped of their new American equipment before the handover to the state, had to be put painfully back into operation almost entirely by human musclepower. Similarly, the cotton mills could only begin to run at full production after a gift from China of 500 automatic looms early in 1957.[36] New equipment from China also went to the paper mill which had operated in the liberated areas up to July 1954 and was now relocated in Thai Nguyen province.[37] In this period, also, some new modern state-owned plants were opened, the most important being the Hanoi Mechanical Works, built with Soviet aid between December 1955 and August 1957.[38]

In the period 1954–57, therefore, rehabilitation and reconstruction implied the emergence of a state sector of modern industry, defined by scale and complexity of the productive process and by mechanization (implied if not, as in the case of the coal-mines, yet actual). This left much manufacturing production to the private industrial and artisan sectors: in 1955 the state sector accounted for 12 per cent of the total. With total production in the 'modern' sector officially reckoned at 20.2 per cent and artisan production at 71.2 per cent of the total, that left private industrial enterprises responsible for 8.2 per cent of modern production and 16.8 per cent of the total.[39] As with the state sector, the government's policy was formed under pressure of reconstruction, the need to ensure supplies from them – especially of consumer goods – while at the same time controlling profits and directing them away from market speculation. The basic notion, therefore, was that of 'security in return for extra work', with the former ensured through state contracts to supply materials and take products. At the same time, production began to be rationalized by regrouping companies in such fields as soap, paper, glass and office furniture. State control was exerted through the contract system, pricing policies, and the application by the state's National Bank of differential interest rates.[40]

Petty production of consumer goods and trade had formed an important part of the colonial economy and inevitably continued to do so after the Geneva agreements. This was recognized at the Eighth Plenum of the Central Committee in August 1955, which resolved that it was necessary to 'bestow great attention on artisan and small industry, aid them to recover and develop, for they provide merchandise for millions of people and supply tens of thousands of workers'.[41] In fact, as with the peasants, their intrinsic class enterprise had already impelled them into restoring their businesses in order to take advantage of a ready market for anything they could provide. In Hanoi the number of petty bourgeois enterprises rose from 1,552 in January 1955, employing some 4,000 people, to 4,000 in December, employing 18,500.[42] Official estimates for the whole North were 24,000 workshops in late 1954, 53,000 in 1955 and almost 60,000 in 1956.[43] State policy towards this sector, as part of the rehabilitation of the economy, was very similar to that adopted towards capitalist industry and trade. Thus again 'security in return for extra work' meant ensured supplies (including, it would appear, provision of these on credit without security) and delivery contracts. Profits at a 'reasonable' level were also tolerated, in the case of petty producers with the hope of attracting investment in their enterprises by the wealthier merchants in an attempt to turn them into 'producers'. The small businesses were likewise encouraged to group themselves to form a basis for expansion and training of new artisans.[44]

In order to bring the products of state, capitalist or petty bourgeois enterprises to the market and thus make them into proper commodities, two more sectors had to be restored after July 1954 – namely transport and the distributive system, both of them severely damaged by the liberation war. In the former, priority was given to the restoration of the railway lines from Hanoi to the Chinese frontier and the port facilities at Haiphong. Four months' intense labour by volunteers and others brought the former back into service in February 1955 with the help of locomotives supplied by China.[45] Haiphong port was functioning again by May 1955, but continued to suffer from the effects of uncontrolled silting over recent years until the arrival of a Soviet dredger in 1956, which in fourteen months cleared 5.5 million cubic metres.[46] By early 1957 it was claimed that handling capacity was up from 800 tons per week under the French to 2,000. With the North's major port thus back to high capacity, exports rose from 15,600 tons in 1955 to 352,500 in 1957, and imports from 181,500 tons to 401,300.[47]

As for the organization of transport, the railways, already a state concern under the French, passed automatically to the Democratic Republic in mid-1954. In 1957 they handled 50.2 per cent of cargo measured in tons per kilometre and 29.5 per cent in tonnage alone.[48] This implies that a considerable amount of traffic was still left to private road and water concerns, particularly over shorter distances. As with manufacturing, the policy here was to encourage the grouping of enterprises according to the principle of the 'three unities' – vehicle movement, division of merchandise handling and charges. Private firms were also brought into the planning of such questions as the restoration of communications and distribution of goods.[49]

Turning to the actual merchandising of commodities, we have already noted the extensions of control over private traders necessitated by the crisis conditions of 1955 and reinforced early in 1956. In August 1955 the Eighth Plenum defined the task as:

> ...to turn the commerce that served imperialism, aggressive war and a handful of city residents into a commerce that will serve the people's livelihood and production; to restore and develop commerce on the basis of strengthening state-operated trade which must prevail in the market; and at the same time to develop steadily buying and selling cooperatives wherever land reform has been carried out.[50]

To further these policies state participation in wholesale trade was extended from 28.1 per cent in 1955 to 52.6 per cent in 1957, and in retail trade from 19.8 per cent to 25.8 per cent.[51] At this early stage wholesale trade was the crucial link, because it meant control of supplies to retailers, but the fact that actual deliveries to consumers were left largely in the hands of the private dealers was an important indicator of the limited capacities of the state. The 906 state stores were thus not yet the dominant element in 1957, even though their number had almost doubled in two years.[52] Similarly, cooperative outlets for retail trade increased from 174 in 1955 to 1,042 in 1957, but their share of trade, minute in the former year (0.3 per cent) was still only 5.5 per cent in the latter.[53] With state 'and cooperative outlets controlling 31.3 per cent of retail trade in 1957, 59.9 per cent was left in private hands (down, however, from 79.9 per cent in 1955), while the remaining 8.8 per cent was now controlled by joint 'state capitalist' enterprises.[54]

Finally in this part of our discussion, attention must be drawn to the role of foreign aid in the rehabilitation of the economy of North Viet Nam in the period 1955–57. References made in the last few pages have already shown the importance of the fraternal assistance from China, the Soviet Union and some other 'socialist' countries such as Czechoslovakia. This was formalized in the case of the two major allies in July 1955, with China undertaking to supply goods and equipment worth US$325 million and the USSR a total worth US$150 million.[55] In terms of the relative weight of the two, it should be noted that trade with China was growing most rapidly in these years – exports to that country by 170.5 per cent and imports from it by 30.6 per cent.[56]

Land Reform: The Northern Regime Put to the Test

The developments outlined above were very far from a launching of policies intended to begin the building of socialism in the new North, and that for two reasons. First, the Workers' Party leadership believed that such a move would be premature; the pressing demand was for reconstruction after a very destructive war and the ensuring of minimal standards of existence for the mass of the population. As has been suggested above, that work in itself

268

probably led the Party and government to go further in taking control of the economy than had been the original intention. One effect of this was that issues of class conflict were at least implicitly raised, running counter to the general emphasis, since the Eighth Plenum of 1941, on national unity. The implications of this will be developed further in Volume II. Here let us note that a second reason for not yet squarely raising the question of a socialist North was that such an entity, at least until mid-1956, was still not part of the problematic of Viet Nam's future as seen by the Party. In its view, the area north of the seventeenth parallel was only the 'northern regroupment zone' envisaged in the Geneva agreements, something to be superseded in July 1956, when the holding of nation wide elections, to result in reunification, would open the issue of a building of socialism throughout the whole country.

As we saw in the previous chapter, that scenario was not to be enacted and a very different future was to be opened up for the Party. What we must concentrate on here is the more immediate question of the direct major hangover from the war, the land reform campaigns in the North and their effects on the period 1954-57. As will be shown, this had a very definite relation to the question of what policy was to be adopted towards the South. It also had an important bearing on the whole process of reconstruction just discussed. Land reform, by reason of its' being a class struggle, in fact put the Communist regime to a severe test and revealed weaknesses which it would carry over into any attempt to build a socialist system in either the whole or, as proved to be the case, a part of Viet Nam.

The Geneva negotiations which resulted in the supposedly shortlived partition of the country were spanned by the fifth wave of the rent reduction campaign in the areas held by the Democratic Republic and the first wave of land reform, lasting from May to September 1954. The latter wave was on a modest scale, involving only 53 villages.[57] As it came to an end, the Politburo held its meeting to lay down policy lines for the new situation, and its general political position was that now the anti-feudal and national united front must be broadened to 'win over the majority, isolate the minority, consolidate peace and achieve unification'.[58] Given that Truong Chinh, the General Secretary of the Workers' Party, had in November the previous year portrayed the coming land reform as a class struggle in the rural areas, as we saw in Chapter 7, it was evident that the end of the contest of arms had implications for the class basis of future policies, including that of land reform. The continued emphasis on a broad front in the new situation gradually brought to the fore the contradiction between the theme of national unity, as perceived by the Party, and class interest, so that a definite tension within its ranks can be seen arising by March 1955. In the meantime, in the period October 1954 to January 1955, the second wave of land reform took place in 210 villages in the old liberated areas, while the sixth wave of rent reduction extended this on a limited basis into those newly under control. In February–June 1955 an important step forward extended wave seven of rent reduction and wave three of land reform into the

Red River delta.[59] Now those landlords and rich peasants who had stayed longest under the protection of French arms began to find their incomes and property threatened.

During the period of activity in the delta the Party line took an important turn, but the inherent contradiction became more apparent also. In February the South East Asia Treaty Organization came formally into being and John Foster Dulles, the US Secretary of State, journeyed to Saigon afterwards to show the flag on behalf of the Diem regime to which he was becoming increasingly committed. The response of the Seventh Plenum of the Workers' Party Central Committee, held the following month, was to take a defensive posture. Emphasis was now placed on land reform as a means of consolidating the position of the Democratic Republic in the North, 'while also paying attention to the South'. In February *Nhan Dan*, the Party newspaper, had described land reform as 'an effective preparation for the free general election to unify the country', and also noted that 'only through land reform can we train the people in economics and politics, quickly restore agricultural production and create conditions for industrial and commercial development'.[60] This view was shared, it may be supposed, by all tendencies in the Party, but the same editorial made reference to the need to avoid 'leftist errors'.[61] Conversely, at the Seventh Plenum criticism of the 'rightism' which had been vouchsafed since the Geneva agreements was strongly expressed.[62] Since this was the code word always used when opposing a class line advocating a broad class front (as 'leftism' indicated opposition to a class line emphasizing the interests of workers and peasants), we may see here continuing uncertainty in face of the need to come to terms with the situation in the South and simultaneously push through land reform.

It is in fact evident that pressures were coming from different sides in the Party. Thus, on the one hand the National Congress of the National United Front, meeting in the second week of January, had called for the formation of a new organization on an even broader basis.[63] On the other, beginning at the same time, meetings of cadres were being held at which there were 'recountings of suffering' in the past at the hands of landlords. A significantly high proportion of these cadres, who were to take part in future waves of land reform and were now being firmly reminded that such were to be seen as moments of class struggle, were drawn from the lowest social levels in the rural areas; thus it was reported that 2,331 out of 6,093 involved in three provinces had actually been landlords' servants, and even that some 4,600 of their family members had died at the oppressors' hands.[64]

Against this we can set the amendments made to the decree on 'The Differentiation of Class Status in the Countryside' in March 1955, two years after its first promulgation, and to the Agrarian Reform Law in May. The tendency in both cases was to make things easier for the better-off rural elements. In the former amendments, the basic intention was to broaden the criteria for classification by including the number of days in the year actually worked on their land by the peasants and the number of days during which they rented land. A significant proviso was that state employees could automatically claim credit for 120 days' work, thus preventing them being classified as landlords or rich peasants in their home villages, which in some cases, by other criteria, they were.[65] Similarly, although the amendments to the Law were primarily intended to meet a number of new situations now arising with the extension of rent reduction and land reform into the previously French-held areas, such as in villages mainly composed of artisans and traders, some modifications were significant in direct class terms. For example, the status of landlords returning to their villages from urban places of refuge was carefully defined in ways which permitted those who did not resume collection of rents after having abandoned it, and those who could claim to be supported by relatives, to escape classification as landlords.[66] It was made easier for merchants and manufacturers living in urban areas who also owned rural land to establish their class status with regard to the latter property.[67] In addition, the rights of religious establishments to retain enough land for their upkeep and of clergy to be given plots if they had themselves worked on the land in the past were confirmed.

While it might be going too far to speak of the emergence of factions within the Workers' Party in the first months of 1955, it certainly seems correct to say that the issue of land reform had produced different tendencies, and that these found their main location at different levels of the Party and state apparatus. Those who saw the campaigns and mass mobilization as a class struggle against 'feudal' landlords found their main strength in the central Land Reform Committee, headed in effect by Truong Chinh and Ho Viet Thang, the Deputy Minister of Agriculture, and in its subordinate committees and cadres. Significantly, in the name of the worker–peasant alliance – the General Confederation of Labour, headed by Hoang Quoc Viet, was also involved, supplying some of the land reform cadres.[68] In NUF circles, grouped alongside the Party and at the level of government and legislature, the sentiment was in favour of maximum unity and thus against exacerbated class struggle – although no doubt also against 'cruel' and pro-French landlords. It is significant, given that the latter tendency seems to have lost out at the Plenum in March, that President Ho himself gave strong indication of his dissatisfaction at this result. In face of the line taken against 'rightism' he complained in his closing speech that the meeting was 'not carefully prepared', and declared that 'today as never before, solidarity within the Party is important, especially between responsible cadres'.[69]

During 1955, 21,679 cadres of all levels were detached from their normal positions in the state apparatus and sent to join those already at the village level and others seconded by the Party and unions to carry out final rent reduction campaigns and complete land reform; the last and biggest wave of the latter lasted from December 1955 to July 1956.[70] The methods of mobilization which were used were the same as those described in Chapter 7, the 'three togethers,' 'asking about poverty' and so on. The objectives were also as before, to put both means of production and political control in the villages in the hands of the 'working peasants' (former middle and poor and landless labourers) and also to put them into the dominant position in local Party branches. However, in line with the tighter control which we have seen introduced in August 1953, the guidelines issued after the Seventh Plenum in March 1955 did attempt to impose some limits on mass action.[71] (It must be remembered that even the proponents of rural class struggle against the landlords wanted a *controlled* struggle.) Thus, no more public denunciation sessions were to be held against local landlords, and only those believed guilty of serious crimes were to be brought before the People's Courts. More was left to administrative action by the local Agrarian Reform Committee, working with the cadres.

In the first half of 1955 the leadership, and hence by direction the rank and file of the Party, were in a self-critical mood – usually an indication of uncertainty in an adverse situation. Thus, it was admitted that there had been a failure to understand the strength of the USA and a misplaced faith in the French government's providing surety for the implementation of the Geneva agreements. In the same analysis this was linked with a number of failings in driving home the attack on the class enemy, since the present injunction in the North was 'entirely overthrow the landlord class'. Instead, cadres had hesitated to make the objective of land reform clear in the newly liberated areas for fear of causing panic among landlords and had brought too many of them into the united front without sufficient discrimination. Fearing that 'it would adversely affect unity in the cities', comrades had neglected to discuss landlord crimes with civil servants and businessmen.[72]

In August 1955 the Eighth Plenum of the Central Committee met in the knowledge that the government of Ngo Dinh Diem in the South had no intention of opening negotiations which would lead to elections in the next year. This gave special significance to the retention of the formula 'consolidate the North while paying attention to the South', since the former activity was beginning to appear to be the only one of which the Party could be sure. On the eve of the Central Committee's meeting *Nhan Dan* commented sternly on certain comrades who 'think it would be all right to carry out land reform rather slowly, that it is necessary to concentrate all efforts on unification and that consolidation of the North is in contradiction with the struggle for unification'.[73] Further, the Plenum stressed the need to extend mobilization for land reform into a hunt for spies and counter-revolutionaries.[74]

This theme became particularly strong during the first half of 1955 and sprang from the consolidation of the Diem regime in the South with US support; it was now alleged that landlords were acting as agents of the imperialists and their lackeys, particularly in carrying out sabotage.[75] Given the presence in the North of underground groups which had been given that mission, such a fear was not entirely without foundation. The effect was to create a very heightened atmosphere of class struggle, putting landlords and their associates in the position of having to hope that they would be classified as 'patriotic' elements spared from the full force of cadre-inspired popular wrath. What evidence there is seems to suggest that the status of 'resistance landlords' was only grudgingly granted; thus, in the so-called Left Bank Zone 117 of these were recognized in a total of 745 villages – that is, around one for every six villages.[76]

On the other hand, although the emphasis on class war continued, the concept of broad national unity in face of the problem of the South was able to coexist with it, since in September 1955 the founding conference of the new Fatherland Front was held. The task of this, yet another of the Party's broad-based adjuncts, was to campaign for reunification. Its significance for the struggle in the South has already been discussed. To be noted here is that the way in which it was presented was far from a framework of class struggle. Rather:

> We propose that all political parties, all people's organizations and all representa-tive personalities in the two zones, establish contact and exchange ideas on the Programme of the Front and on the task of unifying our homeland. We may have different political ideas and opinions, but if all of us share the common aspirations for the peace, unity, independence, democracy and prosperity of our country, we can after thorough democratic discussion arrive at unity of purpose and consequently act as one man in carrying out the whole programme or specific tasks of the Front.[77]

Particularly given the active participation of Hoang Quoc Viet and Truong Chinh, both advocates of class struggle, in the founding conference (the former headed the committee which drafted its basic discussion document), the creation of this new organization for the broadest grouping of patriotic Vietnamese is significant. It shows that already by September 1955, not much more than a year after Geneva, developments in the two 'zones' into which the country was supposedly temporarily divided had gone far enough to permit in effect the emergence of two quite different class strategies. Towards the end of 1955, as the last big wave of land reform, covering more than half the total villages in the lowlands and midlands, got under way in the North, the National Peasant Liaison Committee addressed a letter to cadres in the field stressing landlords' links with sabotage and the difficulties which might be expected. President Ho in a speech to cadres, however, took the opportunity to stress the need for correct classification and the avoidance of physical abuse of those who were denounced.[78] In an article entitled 'Consolidate and Broaden the Antifeudal Front', the Party newspaper also emphasized the need to implement a correct class line in the rural areas.[79]

Nevertheless, when the cadres moved into action throughout 1955 and in the first half of 1956 they went as if to a battle; indeed, on 10 December 1955, at the beginning of the final wave of land reform, a letter from the executive of the Central Committee exhorted them to treat it as a 'Dien Bien Phu against feudalism in the North'.[80] At this conjuncture the dominant tendency in the Party saw the whole operation as intending to break the power of the 'feudal' landlord class, which had for centuries exploited the peasants and more recently collaborated with the French.

By the time the last wave was halfway through, it is evident that its effects were causing the leadership to think again. At the Ninth Plenum of the Central Committee in April 1956 the issue of necessary self-criticism was stressed. Although the main task of the Plenum was to consider the implications of Nikita Khrushchev's denunciation of Stalin at the Twentieth Congress of the Soviet Communist Party, it seems likely that part of the self-criticism was directed at land reform; two weeks later, on the anniversary of the victory at Dien Bien Phu, a number of Party members imprisoned during that movement were released.[81] What was evidently a debate within Party circles showed through in the press. Thus, within a few days articles in *Nhan Dan* first blamed cadres for 'still leaning to the right' then admitted that errors had been committed, such as treating rich peasants like landlords and discriminating against children of the latter.[82] After the elapse of another six weeks, rethinking had gone far enough to reject one of the main reasons for carrying out land reform as a bitter class struggle. In an article looking forward to the completion of the whole operation in the lowlands and midlands it was admitted that 'At the beginning of wave 5 we overestimated the enemy...we took some cases of unexpected enemy sabotage in a number of places as representing the general situation'.[83]

In mid-August, with the land reform completed, President Ho himself dramatically confirmed that the Party leadership was critically assessing the whole experience. On the 18th was published his 'Letter of Chairman Ho to Agricultural Compatriots in the Countryside and Cadres on the Occasion of the Fundamental Success of Land Reform in the North'. In this Ho recognized that:

Land Reform is a class struggle against feudalism, an earth-shaking, decisive, hard revolution. Still, because the opposing enemy has carried out insane sabotage; because some of our cadres do not yet firmly grasp the policies, do not yet correctly practice the mass line; because the leadership of the Party Central Committee and government has had concrete deficiencies, in urging inspection – this is why land reform has caused deficiencies and mistakes in the tasks of achieving rural unity, attacking the enemy, the question of reorganization, in agricultural tax policies, etc.[84]

As a result, he went on, 'It is necessary to rectify weak points, such as not relying completely on the poor and landless peasants, not uniting closely with the middle peasants, and not truly allying with the rich peasants'. Along with this failure properly to carry out the class line had gone incorrect classifications and improper treatment of landlords – those who had worked for the resistance and helped the Revolution, or had children serving as cadres or soldiers must be protected. People had been wrongfully deprived of their Party membership. The President and Party Chairman now called for a 'resolute and planned' rectification of errors.

Although he had maintained the position that land reform had been a class struggle, Ho had also admitted publicly that something had gone wrong. The question is, what? A detailed answer was given by another very senior figure, Vo Nguyen Giap, on 29 October.[85] Speaking with all the authority of 'the victor of Dien Bien Phu, and significantly to a public meeting in Hanoi, he listed a formidable range of indictments against those who had conducted the land reform campaign, accusing them of a series of 'leftist' errors. In the most general terms, there had been a neglect, Giap said, of the overall demands of the Revolution, the need to broaden the anti-feudal front and the National United Front. Cadres 'have neglected the endeavour in the anti-feudal struggle, separated land reform from the Resistance and from revolution – there were even places where these were made to contradict one another'. The full significance of this somewhat opaque statement will be discussed shortly. Immediately it would be better to review the range of Giap's criticisms.

In the most general terms, therefore, these continued with the comments that cadres had taken a simplistic view of the task of consolidating the North and had taken lightly the task of winning the South and the demands it would make. Giap then made some important comments on the implementation of the Party's class line. Here, he said, those guilty of 'leftism' had correctly relied on the poor and destitute peasants, although because of mistakes even some of these had been attacked. The policy of uniting with the middle peasants had been neglected, and their interests even damaged. An alliance with rich peasants had not been sought and they had, in fact, been attacked and treated almost as if they were landlords. As for the landlord class, this had been destroyed but it had been wrong to attack indiscriminately without implementing a policy of differentiation among individuals. Adequate consideration had not been paid to those (and their families) who had given meritorious service during the resistance, or to those who had family members serving in the armed forces or as cadres, while there had been discrimination against children of landlords. In this central passage of his speech Giap then turned to the way in which the cadres had conducted their activities, which he characterized as lacking proper control in various ways; significantly, he admitted that innocent people had been treated unjustly. These actions 'led to widening of the scope of attack to attacking the enemy indiscriminately and to the widespread use of overly-repressive measures'.

Then followed two comments on specific groups of the population. First, 'in areas where a large number of religious people live' – meaning places where there remained concentrations of Catholics – the scope of the attack on landlords had been too wide and 'the policy of respecting freedom of religion, freedom of worship' had not been correctly implemented. (This comment takes on extra significance if it was correct, as reported by Hanoi radio, that in 1,022 villages in the last wave of land reform, more than 60 per cent of those involved were wholly or partly Catholic.)[86] Further, said Giap, the activists 'in areas of ethnic minorities attacked too widely the upper strata and did not respect or even violated the values and customs of the locality'.[87]

Finally in this part of his speech, the Minister of Defence turned his attention to the effects of the land reform campaign on the local Party and other organizations. Here, he suggested, the proper political criteria had not been used: rather, the test of 'backgroundism' – treating class origins as decisive – had been applied. Moreover, in reforming those judged guilty of errors, comrades responsible for leftist extremes had not used education as their principal means but rather had been marked by 'discipline, purging, punishment and dissolving organizations, and even using hounding measures for putting the organizations in the right order'.[88]

From the comments of Ho and Giap we can see that, in the opinion of the Party leadership, which had met in the Tenth Plenum of the Central Committee in September to review the situation, two things in particular had gone wrong in the land reform campaign. The class struggle in the rural areas had gone out of control, and the organization and morale of the Party itself had been severely damaged. Although both judgements were undoubtedly true, it is also important to make a link between the two, something about which the Party was less explicit. There had indeed been a class struggle in the villages, and this had shaken them to their riceroots. Although probably not now frequently exposed to mass denunciation meetings (which had officially been discontinued), landlords, rich peasants and even middle peasants had been subjected to abuse and sometimes physical mishandling; this is established by the need of the Party leadership to forbid it.[89] Not only had land been seized from those accused of being landlords, but also livestock, tools, houses and even spare clothes, furniture and pots and pans. Thousands had been imprisoned while an unknown (and unknowable) number had actually been executed.[90] Beyond this, many more, particularly family members of those accused of being landlords, had been subjected to boycotts and various forms of prejudiced treatment.

We have seen that Giap referred to discrimination against the children of landlords in his public address of 29 October, and already in August an article in *Nhan Dan* had attempted to clarify this issue by distinguishing between the period of mobilization, when 'it would not be useful to the struggle movement and to one's own person if one visits relatives who have been classified as family of landlords', and now, at the end of the campaign, when the families of imprisoned landlords might be visited, provided they were not under house arrest.[91]

The point of all this is that, as President Ho rather obliquely recognized in his open letter and Giap more directly in his speech, the land reform cadres had pushed the concept of 'landlord' beyond its boundaries, which had been redrawn to incorporate rich, middle and even, according to Giap, poor peasants. Indeed, it would appear that in practice the land reform activists had introduced an entirely new category of suspect persons, those 'connected with landlords', usage of which was condemned in the Party newspaper as early as May.[92] All of this was an expression of a real sociological problem, namely how to draw hard and fast lines around a class of 'feudal' landlords most of whose members in fact held little land, given the conditions of delta rice-growing, and who were difficult to separate from rich or even middle peasants. Even with the use of other criteria for assignments to a class, like the number of days worked in the year added by the amendments of March 1955, it was difficult, with the best will in the world, to separate the landlord class from the rest. Moreover, the will of many cadres and activists was not the best in the world. Urged on to the class war, taught to link landlords with sabotage and treachery, drawn themselves often from the poorest rural elements, they no doubt very often allowed zeal to outweigh methodical evaluation, and the People's Courts may well sometimes have preferred the certainty of a death sentence to the chance of a wrongdoer escaping. Nor should we forget that even small landlords and rich peasants can be, and had been, extremely oppressive in their own petty ways and had thus in numerous cases earned genuine popular ire.

This broadening and deepening of the class struggle could only have had an adverse effect on rural organization. The system of land reform committees had in effect replaced other hierarchies; Giap referred pointedly to this when he remarked that 'serious errors' had been committed, in that organizations which were in charge of land reform, 'organized as one system from top to bottom, have gradually overshadowed the powers of local Party committees and local government'.[93] The crucial question, of course, was what had happened to the Party's local organization during the land reform campaign, since all other organs in the villages were meant to be permeated by, and under the direction of, Party cadres and members.

It had always been recognized that land reform and local Party organization were closely related matters. Thus, an article in the main theoretical journal in March 1956 linked the rural movement with organizational development and especially with the education of cadres and members. Land reform was portrayed as a change to 'purify the Party ranks and increase their firm stability daily'; it must be used as 'a school for the practical study of the continuing education and thought reform of cadres and Party members'.[94] Moreover, the class basis of the Party was now being changed, with members being recruited from among the poor peasants and in 'exceptional circumstances', 'outstanding elements' of the middle stratum. The object was to recruit between 10 and 20 new members in each village during the period of mass mobilization, but the article cautioned against doing this mechanically 'for the sake of fulfilling the recruitment quota'.[95]

Only a month after this was published, at the Ninth Plenum of the Central Committee, which was also attended by non-members, alarm was expressed at the state of the Party. As usual after a Plenum, the press in the following weeks took up the themes laid down by the leadership and applied them. Thus, in an editorial at the end of May *Nhan Dan* pointed out two common errors in the fourth step of land reform work in the villages – namely reorganization. These were the making of incorrect evaluations of Party branches and a 'lack of caution in reforming and disciplining Party members'.[96] Stress was in fact laid on education as a way of correcting errors, rather than expulsion from the Party.

Such self-criticisms and exhortations were only the froth on the surface of a boiling cauldron. As the Tenth Plenum was to recognize in September and Giap to make public in his speech, the Party in the rural areas had been effectively shaking itself to pieces for more than two years. War upon the landlord class had turned into a war within its own ranks. In part this was by design, at least of the 'leftists', who evidently felt that the land reform campaign must be coupled with a purging of the Party's ranks in readiness for new tasks ahead. This meant more, however, than just winnowing out individuals who lacked competence and zeal; rather, the intention was a complete shift in the Party's class basis. The base in the rural areas was to be shifted downwards, as it were, from the middle peasants and even rich peasants and landlords to the poor and landless. This design of Truong Chinh and his supporters was a logical extension of Party policy since the Second Congress of February 1951, which marked the realization that the major burden of the liberation war must be borne by the mass of the peasantry. But this need gave rise to a deep contradiction within the Party's ranks: the burden of fighting and carrying supplies rested on the poorest, but local leadership was in the hands of the better-off, sometimes of the actually wealthy. Ever since May 1941 the Party had appealed to all patriots in the name of national unity, and love of the Fatherland apparently respected no barriers of class or strata; certainly that was how the leadership of the Party saw it. That being so, any apparently true supporter of the resistance could join its ranks. With that policy in force, the old structure of the village commune asserted itself; what was more natural than that respected figures, and even some who were not respected but had local power, should become ICP and then Workers' Party branch office-holders and committee members? Kinship ties, respect for age, even tenancy could ensure support in the ranks of the Party, as they had ensured hierarchy under the French and before.

Attention has already been drawn to this phenomenon when discussing the first rent reduction campaigns in Chapter 7. The point is that, with the adding of land reform in mid-1954, a new contradiction intersected and interpenetrated that within the ranks of the Party. The launching of a class war against the landlords, which inexorably drew into itself rich and middle peasants as targets of cadre action, meant also war within the ranks of the Party, as the boosting of poor and landless peasant representation came to imply not just a turnover of personnel but a purge in the name of class 'backgroundism' – sometimes involving actual deaths – of those who had previously controlled local branches. This could only have a catastrophic effect. It meant that the Party's local organization practically ceased to function in many areas, and was replaced, as remarked by Giap, by the pyramid of land committees. Thus, in Bac Ninh province only 26 out of Party branch committees had members actually participating in land reform and in the Left Bank region none from its 25 committees.[97] This reflected an even more serious problem from the leadership's point of view, the collapse of morale on the part of many hitherto active members. The reminder had to go out that 'If the fish muddy the waters, the egret gets fat' – internal dissension could only profit the Party's enemies.[98]

Giap's remarks on 29 October concerning the fault of cadres in bringing land reform, the resistance and the Revolution in contradiction with one another now become clearer. Rich and middle peasants, and even landlords, had rallied to the patriotic struggle and had thus been adopted by the Party as part of the revolution, since the two had been taken as one since at least May 1941. They had run the local Resistance Administrative Committees and Party branches, openly in the liberated areas, clandestinely where the French still ruled; members of their families had served as soldiers and cadres. No doubt among them were some of those who evaded rent and interest reduction until the campaign to enforce this was initiated in 1953 and was extended into land reform in 1954. With the added pressure to change the basis of the rural Party the squeeze began, and there is reason to believe that the struggle was worst where the Party had for long been strongest. An article in *Nhan Dan*, for example, noted that:

> The province of Nghe-an has had Party and mass organizations since 1930. However, the land reform has committed many grave mistakes, particularly it has attacked many Party organizations, improperly punished many cadres and old Party members.[99]

In face of the organizational collapse and demoralization in the Party ranks prevailing in at least some provinces, the leadership had to act. The contradictory views which had prevailed for two years and which had put even Ho on the losing side for a time were now finally argued out, under pressure, as we shall see, of growing political unrest outside the Party. At the Central Committee's Tenth Plenum, held before Giap made his speech, it was recognized that 'serious errors' of a 'widespread and prolonged' nature had been committed 'against the policy of the Party, against the principles and statutes of a party following Marxist–Leninist doctrine, against the legal regime of a people's democratic state'.

The mistakes not only limited the victory in the past but also caused damage to the organs of the Party, of government, of the mass organizations, caused harmful effects to the policy of the Party's Front in the countryside as well as the cities, greatly affected the sentiments and everyday life of our people, made the situation in the countryside tense, affected the spirit of unity and enthusiasm in the Party and amongst the people, the task of consolidating the North, the struggle undertaken for the achievement of the unification of our country.[100]

So serious was the situation that, against all custom, the losers had to pay a public price. Even the inner circle, the eight-man Politburo, was affected. Leading figures from the 'leftist' tendency were downgraded. Ho Viet Thang was expelled from the Central Committee; Le Van Luong, Director of the Party's Central Organization Department, was forced to resign that post, was expelled from the Politburo and downgraded to alternate membership of the Central Committee; Hoang Quoc Viet was forced to leave the Politburo. Much more dramatically, Truong Chinh himself was stripped of his office as Party General Secretary and formally replaced by Ho Chi Minh.[101] In the following week, decrees of the Government Council ordered that People's Courts should be abolished, forbade illegal arrests and transferred the handling of accused offenders from the village to the district level in most cases. Agrarian reform committees at central and regional levels were henceforward to be mere study bodies, without executive powers, and all were to be responsible to normal administrative organs. In an attempt to undo the harm already done by the effectively autonomous structure controlled by the radicals, those unjustly imprisoned were amnestied and rehabilitated, disputed assessments of property leading to possibly incorrect class classification were to be reviewed, and improper seizure of church lands and other abuses of the rights of religious and ethnic minority groups were to be corrected.[102]

These measures were too late to forestall a three-day peasant rising beginning on 13 November, in Quynh Luu district of Nghe An province. There had already been disturbances involving clashes with security forces and deaths in that province and in Thanh Hoa in January 1955, caused by Catholics who felt they were being held back from moving south.[103] In November 1956 Catholic peasants in Nghe An still aggrieved at this, and by what they saw as unjust land seizures, attacked cadres and security forces and for a time took control of four villages. Army units had to be brought in to restore order, with some resulting deaths.[104] Although it seems probable that this was the most serious affair, Truong Chinh himself later acknowledged at least one other problem with Catholics, in Nam Dinh province, where 'agitators stirred up a number of war-wounded to disturb the peace'.[105]

It was in an atmosphere of heightened tension, thus, that the Party prepared itself for the Rectification of Errors Campaign, which was to last for the greater part of 1957. Directives were laid down by the Central Committee, with the class line 'completely rely on the poor peasants, unite closely with the middle

280

peasants, ally with the rich peasants, take preventive measures against a resurgence of the landlords'.[106] Nevertheless, the most significant anticipated struggle from our point of view was not that against the landlords who might once more lift their heads but within the ranks of the Party, as the 'new' cadres and members who had led the purge of the 'old' now faced their rehabilitated and possibly vengeful rivals.

As the released prisoners, estimated by most sources at 12,000 in number, began to journey back to their villages, anxiety on the part of the previously dominant radicals proved well-founded. Once more, many areas plunged into bitter struggle, as the old members sought revenge by purging their opponents in turn. As a previously cited article noted, during Rectification in Nghe An province:

> The incorrect conceptions which were not corrected at the provincial meeting have affected meetings in the district and village levels. There were villages which forced those who committed mistakes during land reform to appear before a meeting for denunciation. There were villages where beating of hard-core elements took place in the meeting or their expulsion from the meeting. In many villages that prejudice has badly affected the improvement of organization. The phenomenon of removing hard-core elements from leading organizations in villages happened in many places.[107]

According to figures in the same source, 1,839 poor peasant and landless labourer individuals had been put on village committees during the land reform campaign itself and 900 of the 1,162 expelled during Rectification were drawn from that group. In the perception of the Party, however, the contradiction between old and new members was not the most profound; more damaging were those between old members who had forgotten their comradeship in the long struggle against the French and had instead clashed with one another, a division which went to the absolute heart of the Party.[108]

The Rectification Campaign was also evidently plagued by the uncertainties of cadres faced with a most delicate task, namely redressing grievances without further splitting the ranks. It would appear that they often fell back on such bureaucratic expedients as referring tricky decisions to their superior, or simply ordering peasants to do things without carefully explaining the policy of the Party and government.[109] Sometimes they even backed up their authority with squads of militia.[110] In these circumstances, it is scarcely surprising that the complaint was passed down from the top that cadres did not realize that proper documentation of cases was itself a part of the class struggle and that 'Party branch committees have preconceived ideas, relying more on their own feelings than on the basis of facts; they cannot assemble adequate opinions from the masses'.[111] At the end of the Rectification Campaign, therefore, the Party leadership's rather cautious summation was that 'After eight months of ceaseless efforts, we have carried out relatively well the policy of rectification of errors of the Party and Government in the rural areas', but it was admitted that cadres were tired and anxious to complete their work. In addition, the comment was made that 'socialist awakening is not yet acceptably upheld among Party members in the rural areas'.[112]

With a longer perspective, Truong Chinh gave a more complete survey of the efforts at correction in his report to a National Congress of the National United Front in March 1958.[113] Rectification had been carried out in 3,501 villages – all, that is, but a few in Thai Nguyen, Ha Tinh and Bac Ninh provinces. Prisoners had been released, expelled Party members reinstated and previous office-holders restored to their functions. Class status classifications had been reviewed. As to property, almost half the land (in terms of value) had been returned to those from whom it had been wrongfully taken, along with 38.5 per cent of the animals transferred and 64.6 per cent of the houses, with partial compensation for a further 17.7 per cent.[114] In addition Chinh reported that land had been restored to religious communities which had been improperly deprived of it. Further government assistance had been given to veterans and the families of war dead.

The former General Secretary's summation was not entirely positive. Along with the rest, some 'dangerous individuals' had been released from prison, while some Party members had been reinstated without really deserving it. Some cadres had been so upset by their experiences that they had refused to resume work. The restitution of property had been characterized by cases which were either too high in amount or too low, and work had gone slowly. In undertaking further tasks, care would have to be shown to follow strictly the Party's class line and prevent landlords from emerging again, while the audience was exhorted not to 'throw cold water on the masses'.

The last comment becomes more significant when placed in the context of what happened to the rural class struggle during Rectification. In material terms, the experience of the peasantry in the period 1954–57 may best be considered in the next volume. Here let us note that the radicals, though chastened, had evidently not entirely abandoned their position after the Tenth Plenum. Thus Truong Chinh, who apparently remained Deputy Director of the Central Land Reform Committee, continued to give authoritative pronouncements on agrarian questions, as in March 1958, and still placed weight on the role of the 'masses'. Even in the month following his loss of his most important office he had remained somewhat unrepentant. Thus, on the one hand he acknowledged that mistakes had been made, attempting an explanation:

We had gained an enormous victory in the Resistance and we had also just begun the period of moving forward towards socialism. Our country is adjacent to China, which had made giant steps towards socialism. Such a situation, on the one hand, created an atmosphere of victorious intoxication, cadres gave vent to subjectivism and self complacency, on the other hand, it included shallow thinking, a desire to advance hurriedly to socialism and the achievement of the country's unification. In that situation the leadership, particularly organizations (the Land Reform Committees at various levels, the committees of [various] bodies, the Central Organization Department) were induced to commit grave errors.[115]

At the same time, Chinh described the land reform as 'a revolution', asserting firmly that 'A peaceful land reform equal to an exercise in offering up land is an illusion'.[116] As we shall see in Volume II, the question of inequalities within the peasantry and the possibilities for struggle were by no means resolved. Here it seems preferable to set the events of the land reform and rectification campaigns in a wider economic and political setting.

Before attempting that, however, there is one further topic related to land reform upon which comment is unavoidable. In face of assertions by authors such as Hoang Van Chi that what was done in the DRVN was only a direct copy of Chinese policies, some brief comparative remarks must be made.[117] First, and most generally, it is obvious that, given the overall similarities of agriculture and rural classes in North Viet Nam and South China, land reform was bound to take the same broad shape. This came through most markedly in the attempts to define class and strata, where it seems obvious that the Vietnamese cadres borrowed directly from Chinese formulations. Second, the methods used in the villages of the DRVN were obviously modelled upon the Chinese; even the terminology was the same. It seems likely that Chinese advisers were active, even at that level. Certainly pictures of Mao Tse-tung were displayed along with slogans wishing him a long life, which seems to indicate a Chinese presence.[118] Organizationally however, and third, the overall impression is that the Vietnamese leaders attempted to operate a tighter structure than their allies: there was no central Land Reform Committee in China, and peasant associations rather than local committees directed reform in the villages. Fourth, in the DRVN more attention seems to have been paid to the special categories of cadres and state employees, soldiers and women. Finally, and of the greatest importance, Chinese advisers directly involved in the DRVN apparently did not bother to warn their Vietnamese comrades of the errors which had been committed in their own country. What had finally to be rectified during almost two years in North Viet Nam had already to a high degree occurred in China, above all in the period of the 'Great Deviation', in 1947–48.

The Regime in Crisis, 1956–57

From the above account and analysis, it seems no exaggeration to describe the period 1956–57 as one of crisis for the Workers' Party and its government in the North. As we have seen, faced from July 1954 with the necessity to restore the economy and bring it to the point at which it could minimally provide for the basic livelihood of the people – which already implied an advance beyond colonial levels – within two years the leadership found itself confronted by widespread discontent, not only among class elements which felt themselves under pressure but also in the ranks of the local Party and other organizations which were essential instruments for any agrarian policy. Moreover – and this is where the situation became really serious – problems were not confined to the rural areas which, it must be remembered, contained the vast bulk of the population; they also spread to he urban nerve-centres, where they translated themselves into direct political pressure on the Party.

With little effort of the imagination it can be supposed that all the new disruptions of peasant life, already beginning in 1953, must have had an effect on rural production. Moreover, as can be seen from Table 10.1, 1956 was particularly bad for floods and 1957 bad for drought. Official figures later admitted a drop of 7.5 per cent in food production from 1956 to 1957 (1955 = 100; 1956 = 120.1; 1957 = 111.1), and specifically in the case of paddy of 4.2 per cent, with a 7 per cent fall in per capita production.[119] Again it must be pointed out that for the rice-deficient North *any* drop in production must mean a tightening of belts for some, especially in the urban areas, and a generally adverse effect on the economy.

However, the problem in 1956–57 stemming from shortages was less the prices of basic food than those of consumer goods. The peak season prices of rice and maize actually fell according to official figures from 1955–56 and on into 1957, as the system of government control was extended to cover all agricultural products, although that did not mean that there was enough of these foodstuffs on the controlled market to make it unnecessary to buy at the higher prices on the free market. As prices began to rise from October 1956, it was basic consumer goods which caused the pinch: in 1956 pipe tobacco, for example, had cost Ð3–4,000 a kilo on the controlled market and Ð20–30,000 on the free market but insufficiency of supply pushed the latter's price up to Ð60,000 in 1957.[120] Where necessities could be bought only from private traders they could charge much more than the controlled price: thus, a metre of poplin sold for Ð3,640 officially in May 1957 and Ð6,000 on the free market, a tube of aspirin for Ð700 and Ð3,000 respectively. This situation also prevailed for all but the most basic foodstuffs. In 1957 a kilo of pork cost Ð2,500 on the controlled market and Ð4,500 on the free, a kilo of raw sugar Ð1,300 and Ð2,500–3,000, prices which must be viewed in the context of the setting of the basic monthly wage Ð21,000 in December 1955.[121] Under these circumstances it is scarcely surprising that between 1955 and 1957 despite the rapid inroads of the state in this sphere, private wholesale trade grew by 8.4 per cent, and private retail trade by 28.2 per cent.[122]

What had caused these price rises and growing differentials? The principal explanation is, of course, the low level of consumer goods production, which was then compounded by other, conjunctural factors. Firstly, more money was in circulation, with small wage increases in November 1956, heavy government expenditure on construction and, above all, the issue of more currency, with an increase in circulation of 31.2 per cent in 1955–56.[123] Conversely, goods were scarcer, with imports kept down and stocks held over from French Union days exhausted. A third factor was the new purchases by those peasants who had got something by way of cash and saleable items from the distribution of 'landlord' property. The most important factor, however, was undoubtedly the activities of the private traders, who moved in to buy up commodities produced, or at least bought wholesale, by state enterprises (especially textiles and pharmaceuticals) and sell them retail, and also forestalled the state purchasers in seeking out foodstuffs like pork and sugar in the rural areas.[124] The government's answer was a decree against speculation in April 1957 and the launching of a Party campaign to combat this abuse. State control of retail trade was pushed forward, with the result, as noted earlier, that by the end of 1957 public enterprises covered just over a quarter of the total trade and cooperatives 5.5 per cent more (14.3 per cent by another count). Prices on the free market were increasingly fixed by the state and the system of using private traders as its agents was extended to textiles, medicines, tobacco and cigarrettes, tea, meat and some agricultural products. From July 1957 prices, which officially had risen overall 10.2 per cent between January and May, began to drop, although they were not really to stabilize until 1958.[125]

Table 10.1 DRVN: Impact of drought and flood, 1955–57

| | Hectares affected by: | | |
| | Drought | | Flood |
	May season	October season	October season
1955	135,300	130,300	34,500
1956	145,300	141,100	174,630
1957	138,800	273,400	52,000

Source: Ha Ke Tan 1964 (in Vietnamese), p. 47.

Private traders were not the only class force against which measures had to be taken by state apparatus and Party in 1956–57. While their threat was economic, at the same time there were political confrontations with forces outside the ranks of the Party. Moreover, there emerged a serious tension among its militants additional to that between 'old' and 'new' members in the rural areas. This concurrence and interpenetration of contradictions served to call even further into question the Party's grip on affairs.

One of the political confrontations of late 1956 has already been mentioned since it arose directly from the land reform campaign, namely that with the Catholics. What must be emphasized here is that the Quynh Luu rising was only the most dramatic manifestation of a broader political problem for the

Northern regime, namely the continuing presence of some 846,500 adherents of a church which had been passionately anti-Communist during the liberation struggle.[126] Although those who had not immediately chosen to move south may well have been less antipathetic to the new government than those who left during the 300 days, it was to be expected that they would view it with suspicion, and if they were provoked to resist its policies their concentration in Hanoi, Nam Dinh, Ninh Binh and Nghe An provinces could give them extra solidarity.

Party and government therefore proceeded very carefully from July 1954 onwards. A new Liaison Committee of Patriotic and Peaceloving Catholics with its own periodical was created. The nomination of new bishops to replace those who had left was officially accepted, and the Bui Chu and Phat Diem seminaries re-opened.[127] In June 1955 a 'Decree Concerning the Problem of Religion' guaranteed religious rights and recognized the authority of the Vatican in internal church affairs, but denied any special autonomy to religious communities and forbade them to propagandize against government policies.[128] The further consolidation of the status of church lands in the same decree, along lines already mentioned above, however, brings out by implication the class side of the Catholic question. The Church was a landlord and among its adherents were its tenants, often rich and middle peasants, and other individual landlords. Its total landholdings were not a large part of cultivated land taken overall – 1.3 per cent according to Communist sources – but they were concentrated in a few provinces, like the Church's adherents.[129] Moreover, it is likely that during the 300 days its holdings in effect increased, since some of the refugees must have handed their land over to the local parish to hold in trust or even as an outright gift. With the land reform therefore threatening both the Church as an institution and many of its adherents, the chance of opposition acquiring a religious colouration was strong and, as we have seen, became actual.

Access to French education and culture meant that Catholic families had produced many bureaucrats, professionals, teachers, journalists and other members of the middle strata. More generally, such class elements had imbibed the European concepts of democracy and legality in their bourgeois form. In 1955–56 this provided a second impulse to opposition, coming from a significant number of intellectuals, in particular professional artists, writers, and musicians. Under the influence of the emerging stresses of land reform, these began to voice doubts concerning the workings of the system.

The first signs of unrest may have emerged among artists and writers attached to the Arts and Letters Department of the People's Army. The Party had long known the importance of the arts in expressing its policy and rallying support, and the firmly established existence of such a body in the ranks of the military is therefore not surprising. According to one source some thirty of the intellectuals involved drafted, and perhaps sent, a resolution to the Central Committee sometime in 1955 calling for an end to Politburo control over arts and letters in the army. They also prepared a draft 'Outline Policy' which would permit them to form an arts and letters association within the army and remove direct control over them by the military hierarchy.[130]

The immediate response was apparently the arrest of one of the leaders of the group, but this did not silence critical talk more generally. The same source says it was being argued that the Party 'can supply expert leadership in fighting the enemy, but now is the period for constructive work. The Party can no longer lead, but should give way to the intellectuals.'[131] A sense of corporate identity as a social category was probably asserting itself and was likely to be spurred on by the Party's talk in late 1956 of creating a new intelligentsia drawn from 'the old lower class'.[132] Moreover, the intellectuals may well have denied the Party a monopoly on patriotism, even if the story is itself apocryphal that Phan Khoi, who was to emerge as one of the most prominent of the critics, had spoken to friends of how, like sugar in coffee, the sweetness of patriotism offset the bitterness of Party leadership and preserved the dignity of the intellectuals.[133]

Criticism by the intellectuals found public voice in a series of collections of fictional pieces and essays which appeared in March 1956 as the *Spring Selection of Literary Works*, with later Summer and Autumn volumes. The writers were taking advantage of the willingness of the Central Committee, aware of stresses appearing in the Party ranks because of land reform, to try to bring discussion into the open: no doubt it was influenced by the new 'Hundred Flowers' policy being adopted at this time in China. We have already noted the stress laid on necessary self-criticism at the Ninth Plenum in April. Apparently the ideas expressed in the first *Selection* caused considerable debate in a special series of study meetings called by the Writers and Artists Association.[134] Attacks on contributors were vigorously rebutted by Phan Khoi, in an article entitled 'Criticism of the Leadership in the Field of Arts and Letters', and others.[135] However, comments were by no means directed only at the Northern literary establishment. Other topics which were exposed were the sufferings of families of those imprisoned during land reform and the deficiencies of state shops. The attribution of direct responsibility to the Party was generally avoided, but, if sources are accurate, in August 1956 the *Summer Selection* contained a poem calling on 'You, who defeated invaders' to turn against 'these villains who shame our Fatherland'.[136] It would need little imagination to apply the latter appellation to cadres and other functionaries.

In September the critics extended their activity with the appearance on the 20th of a new periodical, *Nhan Van* ('Popular Literature'), under the editorship of Phan Khoi. This achieved five issues, and its fate was probably sealed when the Quynh Luu rising occurred between the fourth and fifth. An apophthegm to Communism as 'the most wonderful ideal of mankind' in what proved to be its last appearance did not save the journal from an order by the Hanoi Administrative Committee on 18 December forbidding its further publication or circulation.[137]

While *Nhan Van* was still appearing, however, critical comments on current developments had taken a more political tone. In the last days of October the Central Committee of the Fatherland Front held a National Congress, and Nguyen Manh Tuong, the Deputy Chairman of the Association of Vietnamese Lawyers, took the occasion to voice his disquiet. His theme was basically the need for the rule of law: even where there was no doubt of the guilt of an accused person, it was necessary to assume innocence; judges must be independent; if respect had been shown in the past months for legality, fewer mistakes would have been made; the most serious comment of all from the point of view of political power, was that the National Assembly lacked the ability to control the government.[138] Tuong was brave, and also either lucky or possessed of good political judgement, for the tide was in fact running with him.

Already between May and August a series of 33 'People's Conferences' had been sponsored by the Party, the most important of them at the end, in Hanoi. There the audience had heard the Vice-Chairman of the Administrative Committee, for example, confess that some cadres and police had committed errors which prejudiced democratic freedoms, while criticisms had been voiced of bureaucratic working methods.[139] Capping these meetings, the communiqué issued by the Tenth Plenum of the Central Committee spoke of the 'development of democratic practice, guaranteeing of democratic liberties, and strengthening of democratic legality', while at the same Congress at which Tuong spoke, held immediately after, the representative of the Democratic Party spoke of the need for reorganization on the basis of fully developed democratic liberties.[140] At the same time, Vo Nguyen Giap himself made reference to the issue of democracy in his address to the citizens of Hanoi. 'Popular power', he said, 'is one of the essential core elements guaranteeing the victory of the resistance and completing the foundations for the antifeudal revolutionary task in the North'.

In past years, in face of the difficult and complex situations of the resistance, and in the period which immediately followed the restoration of peace, limitation of democracy to a certain extent was correct and necessary, in accordance with the needs of the patriotic war, the maintenance of order and security. However, in the recent period there have been numerous failings in the building of our popular democratic power; the democratic rights of the people were not fully realized, we did not pay attention to the guarantees of the system of democratic legality, particularly in land reform, in putting organization into good order, controlling households, etc.[141]

The comments of Nguyen Manh Tuong had effectively put into political terms what had been implicit in the criticisms of the intellectuals – the demand for more freedom, for guarantees of legality, for democratic controls over Party and government or at least over their cadres. How widespread such demands might have become had there been any means of making them known beyond a small urban reading public it is impossible to tell. (A circulation of 6,000 has been claimed for *Nhan Van*.)[142] Certainly many of the more politically conscious peasants must have wished to see an end to cadres' highhandedness and ignoring of proper legal procedures.

The critics, however, were caught in a contradiction. They gained an immediate resonance, including within the Party itself, because they could appeal to a whole body of ideas which were far more widely spread among the educated than Marxism–Leninism and to which the Party had itself paid lip-service, especially in periods like that of the Popular Front government in France from 1936 to 1939. Moreover, around the Party was a whole penumbra composed of people who were not themselves Communists but had been attracted to the liberation movement by the appeal to all patriots and democrats. These provided a natural following for the critics, as well as many of their number. Phan Khoi is typical, an elderly intellectual, grandson of the Governor of Hanoi who had committed suicide in face of the French occupation in 1883, himself the last survivor of Phan Chu Trinh's 1907 scholar's movement. Having disputed with Party intellectuals on such matters as materialism and idealism in the 1930s, he found the ICP's appeal to patriotism after May 1941 more acceptable and became well-known for his support of the Viet Minh and readiness to share in the privations of the liberated areas rather than live under French rule.[143] In 1956 his son was editor of the journal of the Fatherland Front. Prominent too were other 'democratic personalities' like Nguyen Huu Dang, Minister of Culture in the early days of the Democratic Republic, or Tran Duc Thao, professor in the Hanoi University Institute of Pedagogy. The other moment of the critics' contradiction at the end of 1956, however, was precisely that their base was on the margins of the Party. By the time Tuong gave his speech, Giap had already pre-empted the themes of past breaches of legality and new resolves to do better on behalf of the Workers' Party leadership and the critics themselves had, it would seem, no voice in those circles.

The Workers' Party leaders had brought much of the trouble on themselves by grouping such a broad front of middle strata elements around their organization. President Ho and the others were thus caught in a contradiction of their own. For a long time they had chosen to surround the Party with front organizations which ensured the support of elements in the middle strata like the now-critical intellectuals, 'national' capitalists and 'patriotic' landlords. Moreover, in these early years the new regime in the North felt that it could not do without their services in restoring economic activity and consolidating itself there. In terms of the Party's own rural organization, we have already seen that the landlord's influence had penetrated deeply and that the Central Committee was worried by the extension of the landlords' influence into the urban bureaucracy and the army through family members; hence the desire of the Party radicals for example to inform civil servants about the objects of land reform and of the moderates to protect 'patriotic' landlords from reprisals. In late 1956 and early 1957, therefore, there was a danger that the statements of the critics might have found a broader audience and set off a wider series of shock waves which would not have overthrown the regime, but would have shaken it badly.

In this situation, the Party's tactics were to admit errors, and in fact to introduce itself some of the themes taken up by the critics. More directly, on 14 December 1956 a Presidential Decree guaranteed freedom of the press within certain limits (no attacks were permitted, for example, on unification of the country), while early in January draft laws were published providing rights of association, assembly and personal freedom and regulating the conditions of arrest and temporary detention.[144] Throughout 1957 the approach remained conciliatory, probably typified by the publication in June of a translation of Mao Tse-tung's new piece 'On the Correct Handling of Contradictions Among the People'.[145] In February the Second National Congress on Arts and Literature was addressed by Truong Chinh on 'Striving for a popular arts and letters under the flag of patriotism and socialism.' Speaking on behalf of the Party, Chinh emphasized that the correct path for intellectuals was one of 'serving the fatherland, the people and the truth'. A cultural revolution was needed, which would combine socialist content with a national form. Marxism–Leninism must be studied, and all 'patriotic-progressive' writers and artists grouped into a broad front under Party leadership. Mistakes had been made, but were now being corrected.[146] During subsequent discussions eleven speakers referred to the problem of criticism and ideological struggle, and at the end of the Congress a new Writers and Artists Union was formed, with some of the critics, like Van Cao, musician and poet and author of the National Anthem, on its executive. This ensured publication of work by the critics in the new magazine, *Van* ('Literature') which was launched in May. At the beginning of 1958 the Politburo was drastically to change its approach, but that development is better left to a later part of this study.

Here it should be stressed that the Workers' Party leadership and its government weathered their crisis in 1956–57. Indeed, no impression should be left that they could have failed to do so. The travails of land reform and rectification certainly brought on political crisis and economic problems. A swing to a radical class policy and cadres' heavyhandedness in applying it in a situation where class lines were not as clearly drawn as was assumed, and particularly not in the ranks of the Party itself, brought widespread demoralization and anger. However, the absence of clear class divisions in the history of the Party since mid-1941 also meant that there was no firm social bloc aligned against it. Although any assertion of bourgeois democratic rights and of such political principles as the supremacy of the legislature over the executive might be argued to have a class content which could only ultimately favour the capitalists, there is no evidence that the critics had any real links with the merchants who were busy at the end of 1956 trying to turn a fast, high profit, even though this was later to be hinted by Party spokesmen.[147]

There was also no organized force to give articulation to protests and demands, only some artists and intellectuals whose contacts were outside the Party more than at its heart. Such middle strata individuals had no links with the peasants or workers, merely some influence over students at the University of Hanoi and secondary schools in the capital. The only potential mass support might in fact have come from the Catholics, but there is no direct evidence of intellectuals drawing inspiration from Catholic doctrine as such. In fact, the Party must have benefited from the failure of the two forces directly to come together, for each lacked what the other might have provided. The two could thus be faced separately. The Catholics had a potential mass base in certain provinces but lacked any overall leadership willing to give voice to general demands. The dissident intellectuals had no mass base. The Party leadership could bring into play its history as the rallier of all patriotic forces, its victory over the French and not least of all its ability to use the state apparatus to control critics.

The point of the 1956–57 crisis was thus not that the Workers' Party was likely to lose its grip, but that it proved to be much less tight than one moment of a major contradiction – a Communist Party with a very cohesive leadership which was recently victorious in a great liberation war - might have led us to expect. The other moment, of course, the 'patriotic' united front policy, was exactly how the leadership had chosen to fight the war but resulted in a far from cohesive mass base.

Nevertheless, the Workers' Party leadership had received a stern warning. With the Rectification Campaign under way in the 'northern regroupment zone' and the conflict with the intellectuals continuing – signs that the policy of consolidation as the first task there was proving unexpectedly difficult to execute – Ho and the others were being reminded that a long, difficult road lay ahead and that the Revolution would remain extremely complex until the country was again one. At that time under pressure from several directions, they were not to know that what they were consolidating was to become a socialist North Viet Nam which would experience a separate existence for another eighteen and a half years. On the other hand, we can now see that a fundamental shift in the shape of the revolutionary terrain was beginning in the years 1954–56. This was as a result of two developments, one long foreseen by the Party leadership (indeed in a sense planned) and the other unforeseen. Long before they came to hold office in the Democratic Republic, Ho and the others had envisaged socialism as their goal. What they had not intended was that it would be realized in a truncated country, with half of the national democratic stage of the Revolution still to be completed and potentially in isolation from its counterparts in Laos and Cambodia. Now in their first phase of really holding state power in peacetime (the period August 1945 to December 1946 having been qualified in various ways), the Workers' Party leaders were finding both that the problems of using that power were very complex and that the need to continue the liberation struggle while dealing with them greatly compounded the difficulties. The two developments, taken together, had shifted the whole trajectory of the Vietnamese Revolution which the Party had come to lead in the name of the workers and peasants and then all patriots.

Notes

1 See 'Lansdale Team's Report on Covert Saigon Mission in 1954 and 1955,' Document 95 *PP* I, pp. 578, 580, 581 and 583. Statement on French policy based on evidence of former Lieutenant Sassi and Colonel Trinquier, in 'De Franse oorlog in Indochina', television documentary, 1978. At the end of the war, French-organized guerrilla groups among the Thai and Meo totalled around 3,600 effectives, at least 1,000 of them from the latter nationality: see Trinquier 1981, p. 270.

2 Estimate for refugees from Jumper 1957, p. 186; other data from Vo Nguyen Giap 1955, pp. 13–14, and Le Chau 1966, p. 272.

3 Pike 1978, pp. 89 and 90.

4 Estimates from Limbourg 1956, p. 47, and Vo Nhan Tri 1967, p. 213; Chau 1966, p. 191, says 140,000 hectares.

5 Limbourg 1956, p. 47.

6 Chau 1966, p. 191.

7 Area taken from Limburg 1956, p. 48. Tri 1967, p. 213, suggests 320,200 hectares, but this seems rather high if the total under irrigation schemes in 1939 was 326,000ha. (Chau 1966, p. 192). Not all systems were damaged.

8 Chau 1966, p. 192, and Limbourg 1956, p. 48.

9 Limbourg 1956, p. 18.

10 Details from Burchett 1957, pp. 189–91 and 194–8; Chau 1966, pp. 227–S8.

11 Chau 1966, p. 225.

12 Ibid., p. 239.

13 Limbourg 1956, p. 30.

14 Tri 1967, p. 237.

15 'Lansdale Team's Report', p. 579.

16 Nguyen Thuong Hoa 1962 (in Vietnamese), p. 23.

17 Van Loc 1960, p. 2.

18 Quoted in Hoa 1962, p. 64.

19 Ibid., pp. 63–4.

20 Ibid., p. 65.

21 Ibid.

22 Data from ibid., pp. 64–5, and Tri 1967, pp. 239, 241 and 247.

23 Hoa 1962, p. 66.

24 Data from *Public Welfare and Standard of Living in North Vietnam* 1958, pp. 16–25 *passim*.

25 Pham Van Kinh, 'Shortcomings in trade in Nam Dinh province in the matter of acquisition of paddy,' *ND*, 23 January 1956, p. 2.

26 Quoted in Chau 1966, pp. 226–7.

27 Quoted in Pham Hung nd, p. 156.

28 Limbourg 1956, p. 53.

29 See Chau 1966, p. 139.

30 Ibid., p. 139. Somewhat different figures may be calculated from a table in Tri 1967, p. 215, namely 24.2, 39.4 and 39.6 per cent for the first three factors.

31 Chau 1966, p. 205.
32 Tri 1967, table, p. 216.
33 See above p. 134.
34 Quoted in Tri 1967, p. 220.
35 Chau 1966, p. 228. For description of the start-up in the cement works and mines see Burchett 1957, pp. 200–2 and 212.
36 Shabad 1958, p. 44.
37 Burchett 1957, pp. 204–6.
38 Chau 1966, p. 229. On revival of existing and starting of new enterprises see also Limbourg 1956, pp. 40–4.
39 Based on data in Chau 1966, p. 230 and Table XLVII, p. 237.
40 For discussion see Limbourg 1956, p. 23, and Hoa 1962 (in Vietnamese), p. 25. These points, and others made in this section, will be picked up again in Chapter 2 of my second volume.
41 Quoted in Tri 1967, p. 225.
42 *Public Welfare and Standard of Living* 1958, p. 22. Limbourg 1956, p. 24, suggests a growth in such enterprises of 3.36 times between January and September.
43 Shabad 1958, p. 40. It should be noted that this article is based primarily upon Soviet sources.
44 See discussion in Hoa 1962 (in Vietnamese), p. 25, and Vo Nhan Tri 1967, p. 226.
45 Tri 1967, p. 233, and Shabad 1958, p. 49. For an account by a woman worker on the line see Burchett 1957, pp. 109-12.
46 Shabad 1958, p. 50; Hanoi Radio report, 26 February 1957, BBC ES256, 7 March 1957, p. 44.
47 Tri 1967, p. 235.
48 Ibid., p. 237.
49 Ibid., pp. 237–8.
50 Quoted in Hoa 1962 (in Vietnamese), p. 24.
51 Ibid., p. 25, also Tri 1967, p. 239.
52 Hoa 1962, p. 25, also Tri 1967, p. 240.
53 Figures from Hoa 1962, p. 25; Le Chau 1966, Table XVII, p. 164, gives 4.3 per cent for 1957. Tri 1967, p. 241, speaks of 56 cooperatives in 1955 and 169 in 1957, each with an average of five outlets.
54 Data from Tri 1967, pp. 241 and 243. A rather different division can be seen in Chau 1966, Table XVII.
55 Shabad 1958, p. 51, values reckoned at official rates of exchange. Fraternal aid took other forms; thus, by late 1956 Soviet experts had treated 43,000 malaria and 28,000 trachoma cases and trained 250 doctors to handle these; VNA report, 9 November 1956, BBC ES 242, 22 November 1956, p. 15.
56 Tri 1967, p. 262.
57 White (unpublished) 1981, p. 240. A pilot land reform wave had been held in six villages in Thai Nguyen province from December 1953 to March 1954 (ibid., pp. 225–6).
58 Tran Phuong (ed.) 1968 (in Vietnamese), pp. 105 and 145.
59 For a useful tabulation of the various waves see Moise 1983, pp. 186–7.
60 Editorial, 'Develop strengths, correct errors, firmly complete a successful Wave 7 of Rent Reduction and Wave 3 of Land Reform,' *ND*, 11 February 1955, p. 1.
61 Ibid., p. 4.
62 See also White (unpublished) 1981, pp. 265–8.
63 Hanoi radio reports, 11 and 12 January 1955, BBC 423, 19 January 1955, pp. 38–40. See also White (unpublished) 1981, pp. 259–61.
64 Nguyen Van, 'Strongly support class hatred, clearly recognize the glorious task of fulfilling mass mobilization, rent reduction and a victorious land reform,' *ND*, 8 February 1955, p. 2.

65   For details see Chau 1966, pp. 134–5, and general discussion Moise, (unpublished) 1977, pp. 316-20. This passage does not appear in the book version.

66   For the text of the amendments see Chau 1966, pp. 402–5.

67   See Moise (unpublished), pp. 327–9.

68   Van Tao and Dinh Thu Cuc (in Vietnamese) 1974, p. 174.

69   Ho Chi Minh 1962, vol. IV, pp. 68 and 70.

70   Figure from Tao and Cuc 1974, p. 174, where a further unclear reference to 'cadres recruited from outside' is taken to mean from Party and unions.

71   'The situation and tasks before us,' *ND,* 22 March 1955, p. 2. See also VNA report, 4 April 1955, BBC 447, 13 April 1955, p. 49. White (unpublished) 1981, pp. 243–4, suggests that the guidelines and amendments stemmed from the Politburo meeting of September 1954; perhaps they were held over until the following March because of the debates in Party circles.

72   Tran Cao, 'Party Activity: taking stock of mistaken thought,' *ND,* 14 June 1955, p. 3. The last point was obviously regarded as important: thus, on at least one occasion Ho Viet Thang himself had spoken to civil servants on the subject of land reform as class struggle ('The righteous nature of our Land Reform', *ND,* 6 April 1955, p. 2), and according to a (hostile) witness officials were sent to the villages to observe (Hoang Van Chi 1964, p. 188).

73   Chien Huu, 'Urgently complete Land Reform in the North precisely according to plan', *ND,* 12 August 1955, p. 3.

74   Generally on the Eighth Plenum see White (unpublished) 1981, pp. 281–6.

75   On this theme see ibid., pp. 268–9.

76   'Smash [literally spill] the whole landlord class gradually, making distinctions', *ND,* 23 July 1956, p. 2; number of villages from Moise 1983, p. 186, and see further his note 11, p. 213.

77   *Viet-Nam Fatherland Front and the Struggle for National Unity* 1956, pp. 29–30.

78   'Letter to Land Reform cadres engaged in the recapitulation of Wave 4', *ND,* 18 December 1955, p. 1.

79   'Consolidate and broaden the anti-feudal front', *ND,* 22 and 23 December 1955, p. 2.

80   'Letter from the Executive of the Central Committee of the Viet Nam Workers' Party to all Land Reform Cadres', *ND,* 14 December 1955, p. 1.

81   White (unpublished) 1981, pp. 304–6.

82   Hoang Ba Son, 'The victorious forward stride of Wave 5 of Land Reform in Ta Ngan Region', *ND,* 14 May 1956, p. 2, and 'Strengthen and broaden the anti-feudal front', *ND,* 18 May 1956, p. 2.

83   'Complete and recapitulate Land Reform Wave 5 Well', *ND,* 27 June 1956, editorial, p. 1: see also White (unpublished) 1981, pp. 311–2.

84   'Letter of Chairman Ho to agricultural compatriots in the rural areas and cadres on the occasion of the fundamental success of Land Reform in the North', *ND,* 18 August 1956, p. 1. There is an English version in Ho Chi Minh 1967.

85   'Text of a speech by Comrade Vo Nguyen Giap at a meeting of the people of the capital, 29–10–56', *ND,* 31 October 1956, p. 2. What appears at first sight to be a long quotation from the same section of this very important document can be found in Nguyen Khac Vien 1970, pp. 90–4. Those who cannot read Vietnamese should be warned, however, that this passage is heavily edited and interpolated with Vien's own text without any indication of the fact.

86   VNA Report, 13 August 1956, BBC 588, 21 August 1956, p. 45.

87   This presumably refers to minority peoples, like the Tho of Thanh Hoa province, living outside the highlands proper north and west of the Red River delta, since land reform was only extended to the latter after the Sixteenth Plenum in April 1959.

88   The translation here of *truy buc* as 'hound' requires special comment. The original is a

compound word, made up of *truy*, to chase, and *buc*, to oppress, to pressure. Fortunately, there is an English word which does contain both connotations.

89   Hostile accounts, especially that of Hoang Van Chi 1964, give the impression that methods did not change or that things became worse in the land reform campaigns than in the rent reductions (see, for example, pp. 196–7). It is noticeable, however, that the examples of mass action he actually quotes are not of the now-banned denunciation meetings (pp. 199–200 and 206–8).

90   The controversy around the question of deaths has probably been the single most prominent feature of discussion of the land reform so far, and has been characterized by all the heat without illuminating light which partisanship generates. It is somewhat rash, therefore, to venture into this subject, but some comments are unavoidable. Anti-Communist writers speak of around 50,000 executions (Turner 1975, p. 143) and estimate total deaths at 'hundreds of thousands' (Honey 1962, p. 8) or around half a million (Chi 1964, pp. 72 and 205). The more sympathetic Gareth Porter estimates between 800 and 2,500 executions (Porter 1972, p. 55). The estimates (they are no more on the part of anyone) by the anti-Communists seem to me too high for three basic reasons: first, their ideological impulse obviously overrides any other; second, it is difficult to accept that peasants who had in very many cases fought heroically against the French would have failed to resist in a far more widespread fashion than the evidence indicates (even the critics can find only one limited rebellion, for which see below); third, deaths in the order of half a million would have been in the range of the famine of 1944–45 and caused social breakdown beyond any which can be established for this period. It also seems particularly significant that anti-Communist circles closer in both place and time to the events gave much lower estimates for deaths during Land Reform – 15,000 according to the head of the US Mission in Saigon, speaking at a National Land Reform Congress there in July 1959; it is also worth noting that his figure for those imprisoned (12,000) coincides with Communist sources (see *VNP* 1,274, 1 July 1959 (evening edition), p. III). On the other hand, Porter's estimates seem somewhat low, given the picture of the struggle in the villages which can be built up from the Communist press itself and the evident alarm felt by the leadership by the time of the Tenth Plenum. (In addition, I take into account the response by Porter's adversaries in *The Human Cost of Communism in Vietnam II. The Myth of No Bloodbath* 1973. Though reluctant to side with people of the ilk of Daniel E. Teodoru and Hoang Van Chi, I feel that some of their comments on Porter's uncritical use of sources have strength.) Probably the most sensible discussion by someone who cannot be accused of being a Communist sympathiser is in Moise 1983, pp. 217–22; he estimates the number of executions at 'almost certainly' between 3,000 and 15,000 and expresses an inclination to c. 5,000 (p. 222). (See also Moise (unpublished) 1976, pp. 73–8.) If one is to get into this unpleasant kind of 'numbers game', my own 'guesstimate' would be 4,900 executions. This is reached by taking as base data the number of villages involved in rent reduction and land reform, 3,653, and the 'quota' to be accused of serious crimes fixed after the first wave of rent reduction, namely 4–5 in large villages and 1–3 in small. I assume that a third of the villages could be classified as large. My estimate of executions is then fixed by on the one hand assuming that one out of three were put to death in small villages and one out of five in large (Chi 1964, p. 196, alleges that there was a minimum quota of five death sentences per village). At least this method exposes its procedure, which writers like Turner and Chi do not. It is of interest that a quite different source, Ho Chi Minh, estimated in an interview in March 1959 that 'perhaps 10,000' had been executed (Utrecht 1973, p. 220: I am grateful to Ad Spijkers for bringing this to my attention).

91   'Some opinions concerning relations with the families of landlords,' *ND*, 21 May 1956, p. 2.

92   Le Thach Son, 'Further consolidate the unified bloc of the labouring peasants', *ND*, 21 May 1956, p. 2.

93   'Text of a speech', p. 2.

94   Le Van Luong 1956 (in Vietnamese), pp. 18 and 20.

95   Ibid., p. 22.

96   'Complete well the task of re-establishing organizations in the village in Wave 5 of Land Reform', *ND*, 29 May 1956, p. 1.

97   'Some urgent problems of summation in the task of reorganizing villages', *ND*, 6 July 1956, p. 2.; Huu Buc, 'Some experiences in reorganizing village branches in stage 4,' *ND*, 6 July 1956, p. 2.

98   'Party Activity', *ND*, 30 October 1956, p. 3.

99   Quynh Son and The Quy, 'The Nghe-an Provincial Committee leads in rectifying errors,' *ND*, 27 March 1957, p. 2. This passage is an example of Hoang Van Chi's distorted translation: compare Chi 1964, p. 225.

100 Quoted in Giap, 'Text of a Speech', p. 2.

101 'Communiqué of the 10th Plenum of the Central Committee of the Viet Nam Workers' Party concerning the implementation of discipline regarding comrade members of the Central Committee who have committed errors in the matter of guiding the task of land reform and revamping of organization' and 'Communiqué of the 10th Plenum of the Central Committee of the Viet Nam Workers' Party concerning the replacement of the General Secretary of the Central Committee,' *ND*, 30 October 1956, p. 1.

102 See 'Decree of the Government Council concerning some concretization of policy on rectification of errors, Land Reform and organizational restructuring,' *ND*, 7 November 1956, p. 1: and Chaffard 1964, pp. 141–2.

103 See Murti 1964, pp. 75–9; Moise (unpublished) 1977, pp. 313–15, and, for contemporary Communist accounts, Vo Dung, 'It was the American imperialists and their lackeys who instigated the riots and caused the coerced movement [south] in Luu-my (Nghe-an),' *ND*, 23 February 1955, p. 4, and 'The two ringleaders who led the disturbance in Luu-my (Tru-son-Nghe-an) have already admitted their crime before the International Commission,' *ND*, 24 February 1955, p. 3.

104 See Chau 1966, pp. 151–3. and, for details from the Government side, Hanoi Radio report, 20 November 1956, BBC 616, 27 November 1956, pp. 23–4. Leaders of the rioters received prison sentences ranging up to fifteen years; for the trial see VNA report, 30 April 1957, BBC 661, 7 May 1957, pp. 42–3.

105 Truong Chinh (in Vietnamese) 1958, p. 30.

106 'Go further to the heart of the general line of the Party in the rural areas' 1957 (in Vietnamese), p. 1.

107 Son and Quy, 'The Nghe-an Provincial Committee', p. 2.

108 On this see editorial 'Enthusiastically struggle for a victorious fulfillment of Wave 2 of Rectification of Errors,' *ND*, 25 March 1957, pp. 1 and 4.

109 Editorial, 'The comrade cadres rectifying errors still have to make further efforts,' *ND*, 18 May 1957, p. 1.

110 See 'B.T.', 'Overcome some behaviour which is harmful to rectification,' *ND*, 14 June 1957, p. 2.

111 'V.N.', 'For what reason is the question of reclassification in the village of Van-duong dragging on for three months?,' *ND*, 7 May 1957, p. 2.

112 Editorial, 'Uphold the consistent spirit of enthusiastic struggle of Party members in the rural areas,' *ND*, 12 August, 1957, p. 1.

113 Chinh 1958 (in Vietnamese), pp. 50–5 *passim*.

114 Chau 1966, p. 155, in citing this passage has misread it. The figures are for proportions restored so far of what had been adjudged wrongly seized, not as he suggests, the total proportion of everything seized adjudged to have been wrongly taken. I take the version

summarised in the following paragraph on trust from Chau, pp. 156–7, not having had time to complete my check of the original text in Hanoi.

115 Truong Chinh 1956b (in Vietnamese), p. 17.
116 Ibid., p. 11. It should be noted that Chinh's demotion did not stop him making authoritative pronouncements on behalf of the Party, the day after its announcement, for example, to a meeting of the Central Committee of the Fatherland Front (VNA report, 1 November 1956, BBC 611, 8 November 1956, p. 33).
117 See Chi 1964, *passim*. This view is described in Moise's directly comparative work, 1983, p. 234, as 'simple nonsense'. For further discussion on China see Wong 1973 and Shue 1980.
118 Such is clear in a photograph taken in 'a Catholic village in the delta', published in the Dutch magazine *Katholieke Illustratie*, no. 27, 2 July 1955, pp. 1252–3 (I am again grateful to Ad Spijkers for bringing this to my attention).
119 See Chau 1966, Table XXXIII, p. 213, and p. 148.
120 Le Hoang 1964 (in Vietnamese), p. 64, and Chau 1966, p. 207.
121 Tri 1967, p. 242, and Chau 1966, p. 207.
122 Tri 1967, p. 243.
123 Ibid., p. 253.
124 Ibid., pp. 241–3.
125 Ibid., pp. 247–8; VNA report, 25 January 1958, BBC ES303, 6 February 1958, p. 36.
126 Figure from Tran Tam Tinh 1978, table, p. 202.
127 See VNA report, 9 March 1955, BBC 440, 17 March 1955, pp. 41–2; VNA report, 4 April, 1955, BBC 447, 13 April 1955, p. 50; VNA report, 27 March 1956, BBC 548, 4 April 1956, p. 38; VNA report, 14 June 1956, BBC 571, 21 June 1956, p. 35; and VNA report, 2 July 1956, BBC 576, 10 July 1956, p. 28. According to one source the Vatican deliberately nominated new bishops hostile to the Democratic Republic; see Tran Tam Tinh 1978, pp. 202–3.
128 The text may be found in *ND*, 4 July 1955, p. 1.
129 Figure from table in Nguyen Xuan Lai 1976, p. 96.
130 Nhu Phong 1962, p. 57, citing *Van Nghe* 11, April 1958, pp. 106 and 79. Given the importance of this whole phenomenon of intellectual resistance, it is most unfortunate that the major sources are all militant anti-Communists like Phong.
131 Phong 1962, p. 57, citing *Van Nghe* 13, June 1958, p. 17.
132 VNA report, 16 December 1956, BBC 623, 20 December 1956, p. 24.
133 Hoang Van Chi 1964, p. 229. For Phan Khoi's role in the 1920s and '30s see Woodside 1976, Chapter 3, *passim*.
134 Chi 1964, pp. 229–31; Hoa Mai (ed.) 1958, pp. 14–15.
135 This essay is reprinted in Mai (ed.) 1958, pp. 357, and see also the extract there from Tran Dan's 'Victory is Certain', pp. 21–7. These Saigon reprints seem to be the only source for this material.
136 See Chi 1964, p. 233.
137 Mai (ed.) 1958, pp. 109 and 167–68. See also Phong 1962, pp. 58–60.
138 On this speech see *The Human Cost of Communism II* 1973, pp. 7–8 and 45–6, and Chau 1966, pp. 142–4. Hoang Van Chi 1958 gives what he claims is a full translation of the speech. I have preferred here to follow the summary in Do Van Chang, 'Some opinions concerning law and the rule of law,' *ND*, 20 December 1956, p. 3.
139 VNA reports, 2, 3 and 4 August 1956, BBC 585, 9 August 1956, p. 34; VNA reports, 8 and 9 August 1956, BBC 587, 16 August 1956, p. 36; VNA report, 12 September 1956, BBC 596, 18 September 1956, p. 32.
140 VNA report, 20 October 1956, and Hanoi Radio report, 31 October 1956, BBC 610, 6 November 1956, pp. 41 and 42.
141 'Text of a Speech', p. 4.

142   Mai (ed.) 1958, p. 18.
143   For the dispute on materialism in 1933 see *Events in Party History*, vol. I (in Vietnamese) 1976, pp. 303–6.
144   VNA report, 16 December 1956, BBC 623, 20 December 1956, pp. 23–24; VNA report, 12 January 1957, BBC 630, 17 January 1957, p. 29.
145   *ND*, 28 June 1957, pp. 3 and 4.
146   See VNA reports, 21, 22 and 23 February 1957, BBC 642, 4 March 1957, pp. 30–1; VNA reports, 25, 26 and 27 February 1957, BBC 643, 5 March, 1957, p. 31; also Phong 1962, pp. 61–2.
147   See, for example, Van Loc 1960, p. 2.

11   An interrupted revolution

This volume began by raising the question of the containment of the Vietnamese Revolution in the mid-1950s, initially at the Geneva Conference in mid-1954. It then looped back in time – in Chapter 4 very far back – and moved forward gradually to return to its initial question, going on to spell it out in detail, and show how by the end of 1956 the scission of country and revolution had been temporarily consolidated. Its conclusion thus is that the division of Viet Nam by imposed international agreement split apart the whole revolutionary process which had been in train since the mid-1920s and had taken on its real thrust with the founding of the Communist Party in February 1930. The Party in its newer form was left to face Janus-like towards a North already experiencing the strains of separate existence and a South where its presence was critically diminished.

Obviously, much of the weight of this study has so far lain with one of the major themes raised at its beginning, the importance of the international context of the Vietnamese Revolution. That theme will constantly recur in coming volumes, and, particularly in Volume III, will be joined by another, the issue of how to build socialist systems in countries which up to the point of successful revolutionary seizures of power have been part of the capitalist periphery. Seen in this way, that problem is inseparable from the matter of international linkages, since in this study the historical significance of the Vietnamese Revolution is taken as above all because it formed a major part of the shift of the world revolution anticipated by Lenin and the Bolsheviks from the developed 'West' to the underdeveloped 'East', quite contrary to the predictions of Marx and Engels. This involved major revisions of Marxist theory – above all the introduction of the proposition that, in the conditions of modern imperialism, countries such as Russia, China, or even colonies like those in Indochina could be 'weak links' in the capitalist chain. Further, despite their low level of development in capitalist terms, successful revolutionaries there could go on to build socialism.

The evolution of such doctrines was, of course, part of the emergence of Marxism–Leninism, above all as consolidated by Stalin, as the dominant theory of world revolution. Again, many passages in this volume have been devoted to showing how that body of ideas influenced the Vietnamese Communist leaders and the consequences of such influence. Apart from the inspirational message that an anti-imperialist revolution was indeed possible in their country and its neighbours, the 'received ideas' with which the leaders were imbued which had the greatest long-term influence were doubtless those of conducting their struggle in two stages, first the 'national democratic' then the 'socialist', and the doctrine of necessary leadership by a 'vanguard' party.

That leadership was initially to be directed principally towards the seizure of power from French colonialism, central to which was the taking of control of the state apparatus. Again, the greater part of this volume has been devoted to analysing this process up to the point at which the Workers' Party's seizure of power was more or less consolidated in the North but its struggle thrust backwards in the South. Given the latter situation, much of the remaining volumes will be devoted to exploring that theme further. However, from this point on, another will be opened up alongside it – namely what the Party (especially its leaders) chose, or were forced, to do once in power in the North. Anticipating the account, it may be briefly noted that the crucial decision came in late 1957, when it was resolved to go ahead with building socialism in half the country and not to wait until power had also been seized in the South. As we shall also see, just over a year later, in January 1959, the Central Committee of the Workers' Party was to take the momentous decision to support a policy of armed counter-blows by comrades in the South against the repression of the Diem regime.

In the more theoretical terms adopted in this study, that was to be a resumption of an active war of manoeuvre. Thus, I have attempted to conceptualize the seizure of state power, as involving the active creation and organization by a revolutionary leadership of a terrain of struggle across which they hope to move to victory. In part, this is a terrain in the normal sense, a territory established by political decisions (for example, emphasis on urban or rural struggle) and often military ones also, as we have seen clearly in both the lead-up to the August Revolution and the adoption of a protracted war strategy against the French armies. In another sense, more metaphorically, the terrain of social struggle has boundaries like the physical one, this time defined by the structures of power – above all the state apparatus – on the other side. These

300

set the limits within which revolutionaries have to build up their own power until strong enough to shift the boundaries in their own favour. This idea of movement should remind us of the further postulate of two necessary wars which have to be fought across the terrain. The war of position indeed plays a major part in defining it because it serves politically to mobilize the social forces which, in another sense of the terrain, form its actual substance.

One of the most important assertions of this study is that a terrain of revolutionary struggle does not form spontaneously. This is not to deny the vital self-mobilization of workers, peasants, radical intellectuals, women, youth, and ethnic minorities, to mention the key groups in the Vietnamese Revolution. But it is to assert, now with the foregoing analysis to support the statement, that shape has to be given by some sort of leadership, however problematic and even dangerous this may be from the point of view of democracy.[1] Beyond this, a terrain of social struggle is *selectively* constructed: it never contains all alienated elements, and even in the greatest revolutionary upsurges only a minority are in fact actively involved, though supporters may be very numerous.

The central point is that, in order to fight a successful war of position which will ensure them a sufficient critical mass of active followers and supporters, the leaders have to find ideological themes which will attract adherents, what I have metaphorically termed contours across the terrain. These have to be sufficiently powerful as mobilizers to ensure, firstly, enough support to prevent the revolutionary movement being suppressed and secondly, its successful seizure of power. In the Vietnamese case, as we have seen, the contours followed were partially those indicated by Marxist–Leninist doctrine: namely socialism and internationalism. However, from deep historical experience another could be drawn – the theme of patriotism. We have seen how, over time, by shifting emphasis among these, partly by luck and partly by good judgement the Vietnamese Marxist–Leninists were able to find their indispensable mass base. This in turn permitted a successful political and military war of manoeuvre, by which they first seized power in the unusual circumstances of August 1945 and then, over another nine years, learned painfully how they might at any rate liberate half of the country.

Steps Across a Terrain

Viewed in the perspective of the above, we can see the first decade of the Party's existence as marked by a search for position, with shifts which were determined by both internal and external factors. Its very origins early in 1930 sprang from a coming together of class elements – workers, a ravaged peasantry, a new group of intellectuals – which were the creations of colonialism and the Comintern's Marxist–Leninist doctrine relayed primarily through the future Ho Chi Minh. In its first eighteen months the struggle within the country almost destroyed the Party, as the uprising by peasants and others in 1930–31 evoked a most violent French response. The next years involved a painful reconstruction of an organization, necessarily relying on outside leadership and support and with extra weight thus given to people, ideas and instructions emanating from Moscow or its extensions. Vital strongpoints were established in some areas, such as the Saigon suburbs, but the taking of position and development of a social terrain of struggle under real Party control came only from mid-1936, with the advent to power of the Popular Front in France. Again, a decisive internal shift was propelled by outside developments. That was true in another sense, for the new French government was itself partly an expression of changed Comintern policy, with its emphasis on anti-Fascist unity and 'national salvation'. Particularly as the ICP developed this theme along with those of class and other social struggle, a line which culminated in May 1941 and the Eighth Plenum decisions, it found it could get a wide response.

This process involved the Party intellectuals' discovery of Viet Nam's history, its potential importance as a usable instrument. Relating to the pre-colonial past through a concept of 'feudalism' which disguised as much as it revealed, they paid tribute to doctrinal orthodoxy while at the same time asserting a heterodox nationalism quite divorced from its supposed avatars, a bourgeoisie which in fact had never really existed. Above all, a centuries-old sense of national identity, which had rather crystallized around a centralized state expressing quite different class interests, found its most revolutionary form through a patriotism associated above all with the peasants.

Again, the imported concept of feudalism had not proved a false guide when it led to stress on that class, however misleading it might have been concerning the nature of the landlords. This is an important case in point when we return to the question of external influences. In that respect, the essence of the matter is that the Vietnamese struggle always had a deep historical reality of its own, rooted back in the pre-colonial epoch. It was not merely some blind and automatic extension of happenings outside the country, and this must be emphasized in respect of the importance laid throughout this study on international linkages. Economically Viet Nam was of course subordinated to France from the late nineteenth century and thus in a sense became part of its capitalist economy. After mid-1954 the South was to be in some ways a typical post-colonial economy (though with the important additional factor of very large US aid of a peculiar kind). Nevertheless, the social relations and struggle engendered by such systems found very particular expressions, not matched even in the neighbouring Laos and Cambodia, and gave an opportunity for the ICP/Workers' Party to position itself. Politically and ideologically, too, Vietnamese history and the way in which it was popularly regarded, the patriotic symbols which it provided for use by a revolutionary movement, were quite distinct. None of the impinging external factors would have been sufficient to generate and give shape to the Communist-led Revolution had they not been able to articulate with these internal particularities. Thus, for example, the impingement of the Second World War certainly created a situation in which three decisive events occurred in six years – the outlawing of the ICP in September 1939, the Eighth Plenum in May 1941 and the August 1945 seizure of power – but none of these would have been possible had not the necessary internal conditions also existed.

However, all this is not to suggest, as Huynh Kim Khanh seems to do, that Marxism–Leninism and its bearer, the Comintern, were necessarily dubious influences upon some purer, indigenous phenomenon. The Vietnamese Revolution, including its aspects of *national* liberation, is quite simply impossible to imagine unless external elements of certain kinds had come together in a positive fashion with internal ones. The doctrine, after all, did draw attention to crucial spheres of social struggle which other ideological positions ignored: how else are we to explain the success of the ICP compared with others like the VNQDD? The concept of a two-stage revolution, however problematic in other respects, did permit a shift of tactical emphasis at different times from class to national struggle. Basically, Marxism–Leninism in the 1930s and early 1940s proved flexible (or ambiguous) enough to permit the Communist leaders to fight the first campaigns of their war of position and even to launch a war of manoeuvre which would bring them in time to state power.[2]

As noted above, what I am characterizing as 'wars' of a special kind were profoundly influenced by the events of 1939–45, which constituted a war in the more generally used sense. That period, and above all May 1941 onwards, can be seen as a second period in the history of the ICP, shorter than the first principally because the wars of position and manoeuvre took on a different character and so led rapidly to a decisive event, the August Revolution. Again, this would be incomprehensible unless due weight was given to external factors. This meant not merely the impact of the Second World War, particularly the Japanese occupation of Indochina, but also the new alignment to China and the Chinese Communist Party. That had begun, in fact, as we have seen, even before the war and was facilitated by Stalin's dissolution of the Comintern in May 1943. Moreover, this development was closely linked to another of great significance for the future; the beginnings of the emergence of a double terrain of struggle, the northern centred in the highland bases and the southern centred principally in Saigon and the Mekong delta. These, in turn, had deep historical roots, going back to the seventeenth century.

With the crucial upsurge of August 1945 and the first seizure of state power as a watershed, the years 1946–56 constituted a third phase in the development of the Vietnamese Revolution, one in which terrain, position and manoeuvre all changed profoundly. The first of these continued to develop two aspects, each social as well as geographical, with the decisive part of the anti-French war of liberation taking place in the north. Again, that involved an increasing Chinese influence. Decisively too in the north (Bac Bo) mass support was mobilized for the Party's struggle, but only belatedly in terms of a social revolution involving, above all, radical land reform and a general transformation of rural class relations. With this positioning finally possible after the Party's Second Congress in February 1951, the war of manoeuvre could be pushed to a decisive point.

Nevertheless, the form which that took, combining military and political action, with the latter primarily diplomatic in nature, was very significant. First, from the internal point of view, the stage of general counter-offensive was never actually reached and, at base, the Democratic Republic was approaching the limits of its capacities.[3] Second, in venturing on to external seas for which they had no proper charts the Workers' Party leaders were forced to rely on other pilots, namely their Soviet and Chinese allies. By taking the line that led then to Geneva, therefore, they finally placed their revolution in a position of subordination not basically to other revolutionary leadership but to other conductors of foreign policy. Reason of state thus became the determining factor rather than furtherance of global struggle against imperialism. The foreign policy concerns of the leaderships in Peking and Moscow might well have diverged since October 1949, but neither of them looked unequivocally to that goal.

This inability to rely on old mentors was made absolutely crucial by the fact that the conditions of the emerging Cold War since early 1946 had brought the Indochinese struggle to the centre of that global confrontation between the power blocs of the USA and USSR. Of all the issues discussed throughout this study this is the single most important, for two reasons. First, it lies at the heart of the major historical issues which were raised in Chapter 1 and to which all subsequent discussion has directly or indirectly referred, namely the transfer of the location of world revolution from the centre to the periphery of the world capitalist system.

Here the basic question might be raised of the validity of a concept of 'world revolution,' and the dangers of imposing this on twentieth century history since 1917 in a reificatory way. As I see it, the answer to this is provided by a more fundamental taking of position. If modern history is to be 'read' as marked profoundly, and even with a determining effect, by the expansion of capitalism from its heartland in such a way as to create a world system, however uneven its structure, then since the Bolshevik seizure of power in Russia a reaction and struggle against this on a similar, though equally if not still more uneven, scale can be posited. It then becomes central to our precise understanding of that unevenness to comprehend the shift in location to such countries as China, Korea and Viet Nam. Second, in all three cases, but pre-eminently in Viet Nam because of the nature and duration of US intervention in its Revolution, the global confrontation between the US and Soviet power blocs had an effect upon every single aspect of struggle, whether it be to achieve the liberation of the whole country from foreign control or to build a socialist system there.

Immediately, of course, in the period 1945–56 the question was how the

USA, as the newly dominant world power, would react to the appearance on the scene of the DRVN as the first Communist-controlled successor to a colonial power. In the circumstances of the Cold War and the emergence of the doctrine of containment there was little question that the decision of the Democratic Truman administration, sustained by the Republican one of Eisenhower, was to intervene on the side of the French power bloc when it attempted to restore its control. When the French political and economic system could no longer sustain the effort, the USA had to take the centre stage, first of all in Geneva. When that proved a major success, keeping half of Viet Nam, most of Laos and all Cambodia out of Communist hands, containment in the first of these had to be ensured by stabilizing a strongly counter-revolutionary regime in the South. This was done by sponsoring the consolidation of a new power bloc centred on the Ngo family and ensuring it political control, the capacity to coerce and enforce state decisions and an economic base which was stable at least in the short term.

In the DRVN, now unwillingly limited to the North, the Party had to watch its supporters below the seventeenth parallel being systematically rooted out, with a decreasing prospect of nationwide elections intervening in mid-1956 to reverse the process. Above the dividing line, the state apparatus and structure of political control were sufficient to ensure that no ultimate challenge could be made to Party hegemony, but they were no more than adequate for immediate purposes. Left by the intervention of peace to carry out land reform not as an act of wartime mobilization but as a first step in a social transformation which in time would lead to socialism, President Ho and his lieutenants found this a trying and divisive experience at all social levels. The tensions that followed in effect dissolved the bloc of class and other elements which had formed during the war of position since at least mid-1941. Peasants and workers were in effect cut loose, many intellectuals were disaffected, new organizational efforts had to be made to retain a hold on women, young people and minorities.

These last points must be picked up and expanded in the first two chapters of the next volume. In order to round off this one, the cue must be taken from the last point made above. Having reviewed this volume's treatment of the first thirty years of the Vietnamese Revolution by looking at it in terms of period and process, we should now look at it from another angle, that of class and social grouping.

The Social Content of the Revolution

How then are we to typify overall the social content of the revolutionary process in Viet Nam during its first thirty years? First, we have to remember that too close a Marxist–Leninist emphasis on class would obscure the vital roles played by social groups with other bases, women, youth and ethnic minorities, though these have also been viewed in terms of class. Second, to extend a point made earlier about spontaneous mobilization, a terrain of social struggle in a revolutionary form has to be *created*. In the Vietnamese case, the most important social characteristic is that the creation of a revolutionary terrain involved a shift from a working class base to something very much broader.

According to Marxist–Leninist orthodoxy, from the moment the Communist Party took command, in the name of the workers, the revolution would assume a socialist perspective. This is no place to debate the Marxist assumption that only the working class under capitalism has the potentiality to find its way forward into a socialist future. Even if this is untrue (and I am no longer sure), the Party leaders believed it to be true and acted as if it were. They received from the Comintern both that idea and the one that theirs was the vanguard party of the proletariat, which it would bring into alliance with the peasantry, in the leading role, around which nucleus would then be built a broader class front. We have seen particularly in Chapter 2 how intellectuals, even if from other classes, were 'proletarianized' and brought by the Party into conjunction with a working class which in the late 1920s and early 1930s was not large but potentially militant, and above all situated sociologically and geographically in a way which permitted instant access to the peasants and non-agricultural petty bourgeoisie. Immediate substance could thus be given to theory; practice was not divorced from principle as it came to be in the experience of the Chinese Communist Party after 1927. But there is no doubt that the ICP and its successor did move away, both sociologically and in practice, from its original stance.

In May 1941 the ICP leadership could still claim that a quarter of the Party's members were 'proletarians,' and 70 per cent peasants and 'petty bourgeois'. (The other 5 per cent, interestingly counted separately, were women.)[4] Assuming these figures to be accurate, they bring out the central contradiction which followed from the place of the working class and 'its' party in the Vietnamese class struggle. It was strong enough in the crucial first decade of the ICP's taking position to give it a base from which it could never be dislodged; a 25 per cent worker membership is a very respectable figure in a colonial social formation. However, on the other hand, the place of the working class in the Vietnamese social formation in the 1930s was characterized by a profound sociological contradiction: it was strong enough to give a foundation to the Party's efforts, but by no means able to provide the raw material for building the whole edifice of the revolution. The basic question of numbers alone would have determined this, but there was also a more profound qualitative factor. As we have seen, workers, peasants and petty bourgeoisie were so interpenetrated that to move the first politically meant necessarily shifting the others. Moreover, the struggles of women, youth and minority nationalities were developing at the same time.

The Vietnamese liberation struggle which took shape between 1930 and

1945 was thus not a 'workers' revolution', and its orientation towards their class was in practice, if not in theory, becoming less. The main weight of the Party membership, and hence of its activity, lay elsewhere by the end of the Second World War and this had been determined not only by the sociological reality of Viet Nam's class structure, which we have seen could still permit a leading role for the working class, but also by the conscious policy of the ICP leadership. That, in its turn, had been determined by the adherence to another doctrine transmitted by the Comintern, which laid down a policy of alliance as the correct one in colonial and 'semi-colonial' situations and moreover prescribed a strategy of stages in which immediate aims were not even socialist in nature, but 'democratic' and 'anti-feudal'.[5] The Party leaders had turned increasingly since 1936 to petty bourgeois, middle strata and even more affluent elements, from May 1941 and the Eighth Plenum, in fact, anyone who was anti-French and not a big landlord. Both in terms of numbers of recruits and of programmes, this set limits upon the extent to which the workers and their interests would directly influence what the ICP set out to do.

Indeed, if we see the class conjunction in mid-1941 in terms of interest and programme, it is clear that it was not the working class which was hegemonic at that point, nor, for that matter, was it the peasantry or any other class, but the Party itself. In binding together elements of very diverse classes, the ICP shifted the weight in the contradictory relationship between itself and the working class towards its own autonomy of action. Moreover, as has frequently been evidenced in the preceding text, when we speak of 'Party' we in fact usually speak of its leaders. In fighting their war of position these had served as a vanguard– perhaps general staff would be a better metaphor here – in the full and sincere belief that no gap could appear between Party and working class. This had meant that the implicit assumption reigned that nothing the leadership did could fail to be a direct expression of the latter's interest. If the Central Committee decided that there should be a majority of new recruits to the struggle from other classes, that the fight should first be against the French and landlords in the name of patriotism and democracy, with socialism deferred to a later stage, then that must be what the workers wanted. No doubt the class-conscious elements indeed wanted to eliminate French colonialism and its local allies; no suggestion is intended here that any real divergence of interest between Party and class emerged at any time during the period covered by this volume. But the phenomenon had implications which were very important indeed for the continuing trajectory of the revolution, above all seen in terms of socialist transformation.

Thus, the first part of this study suggests, and the remainder will seek to show, that in class terms the Party leadership proved capable of only a limited and mechanical form of analysis of the social forces with which they had to grapple. Thus, from the ICP's beginning but especially from 1936, the doctrine that in colonial situations the 'national bourgeoisie' could play a progressive role in the struggle became an imperative. Where such a class element existed, even if only weakly and scarcely able to act as a political force, it had to be proclaimed to be important and presented with a suitable organization of its own – the Democratic Party, when none other could be found. Again, although Vietnamese patriotism was a vitally important historical force, which had to be incorporated into any revolutionary process, and although it can be said finally to have come into the hands of workers, peasants and revolutionary intellectuals, it did so in a way which treated it as a doctrine lacking essential class content. As the resolution of the Eighth Plenum put it, 'The responsibility for fighting the French and driving out the Japanese is not solely that of the proletariat and peasantry, but a common responsibility of the whole people of Indochina.'[6] This not only submerged the differences between Viet Nam, Laos and Cambodia, but in effect took any class content out of nationalist struggle. This was not only a major revision of orthodox doctrine (though following the Comintern line), but also made it more difficult to understand the Revolution as a process of social transformation all the while it was held to be dominated by the patriotic imperative.

It can be argued, thus, that as the ideas taken over by the ICP leadership from the Comintern's version of Marxism–Leninism became a material force through Party-induced social action they came into conflict with the class realities of the Vietnamese workers and peasants. Class emancipation became absorbed into national liberation, which was held to be a necessarily anterior, and in a sense a superior, struggle. Nevertheless, in practice the improvement of the conditions of life of peasants and workers was always an aim of the Party and of its Democratic Republic after August 1945, and much was achieved.

Looking forward to future volumes of this work, we may suggest that, in various ways, this question of the relation between forms of struggle was to recur again decisively in South Viet Nam between 1956 and 1975. Again, the acceptance of the concept of 'revolutionary' capitalists and landlords, especially the latter, which was the result of allowing a concept of patriotism to override that of class, had already led to grave problems in the North between 1954 and 1956. Belatedly broadening the base of the Revolution, in order to defeat the French, a turn to the peasants had become necessary. Fuller measures were taken from 1953 to relieve debt and rent burdens and, above all, to redistribute land, directly contrary to the class interests of the landlords and rich peasants who had hitherto often been accepted as patriots. Moreover, the Party itself was severely damaged in the resulting upheavals, particularly because many of its own cadres were drawn from the very classes and strata now under attack. The effects of this were made much worse by the imposition of another class concept taken over from Comintern doctrine and of the most dubious worth in the Vietnamese rural context, that of 'feudalism'. This often meant a search for a clearly definable landlord class which was arbitrarily broadened to make it a real presence by including rich and even middle peasants.

Nevertheless, land reform in the North was not a 'major error', as it has been

308

portrayed by Douglas Pike, with 'radical agrarian institutional change' draining off cadres' energy and popular support. Nor was it 'an historic strategic blunder' not to have concentrated on developing an organization in the South which was capable of launching a second August Revolution against the Diem regime.[7] Both issues, of course, lie at the heart of the dilemma which faced the leaders of the Workers' Party by the end of 1956 – the effects of the division of the Revolution into two parts and its containment in the South. If this volume has succeeded in its task it should have fully brought out this dilemma, but even more importantly, it should have shown that the Vietnamese Revolution was not a simplistic matter of leaders' errors. Nor can it just be said in a similar vein, as William Duiker does, that 'of all the revolutions ... the Vietnamese revolution was, above all, an act of human will'.[8] Like the Bolshevik Revolution which split open the front of world capitalism in 1917, the Chinese one which was the major expression of the shift of the world revolution to the periphery, and the Korean struggle which paralleled it in many respects, the Vietnamese upheaval was the product of, and was formed by, extremely complex interactions of internal class and other social forces with external ones. Human volition and leaders' decisions played their parts, but only within determining structures and contradictions of great intricacy. Specifically, radical agrarian change in North Viet Nam and the comparative falling away of revolutionary effort in the South and its (temporary) containment by 1956 were historical necessities, not avoidable blunders. Generally, the displacement of world revolution to the periphery, of which the Vietnamese is one of the major cases, was part of the logic of world history in the twentieth century, not something which could be willed by Josef Stalin, Mao Tse-tung, Kim Il-sung or Ho Chi Minh. This is the basic approach taken by the present volume and such will continue to be the basis of its successors.

Notes

1   Those familiar with history will recognize here the classical debate between Lenin and Rosa Luxemburg, though it is an oversimplification to put the latter simply on the side of 'spontaneity,' and Lenin's position shifted over time. For a useful discussion see Geras 1976, Chapter 3.

2   For another more sanguine view of the Comintern's influence see Rousset 1984, especially pp. 322–33. I differ from him because he seems to wish to exculpate the Vietnamese, at least in this period, from some charge of 'Stalinism' defined rather narrowly (see pp. 321–2 and especially n. 2). I do not see any need to make excuses for them or defend them in this way. Their revolutionary struggle was necessary in every sense. That did not free them, however, from the contradiction inherent in Marxist–Leninist theory and practice as a whole, and not just the Stalinist variant, that between its obvious efficacy as a doctrine of the revolutionary seizure of power and its obvious grave flaws when it comes to democracy and popular control, which Rousset raises as a problem above all for the post-1975 period, which is much too late (ibid., pp. 338–42). My subsequent volumes will investigate this issue more deeply.

3   This seems a better way of making the point than to speak of 'exhaustion' or 'war weariness', as some others have done; there is no real evidence that the mass of the DRVN's supporters were becoming demobilized in the way such expressions suggest. For the best exposition of the 'weariness' point of view see Thayer (unpublished) 1977, pp. 45–8.

4   *History of the Communist Party of Viet Nam: Excerpts from Party documents* (in Vietnamese), vol. I, 1979, p. 341.

5   To say this is not to be in a posture of theoretical deviation, abandoning Marxist materialism. Determination by Comintern *ideas* does not constitute an idealist explanation, since such a direction could only be given in a concrete *class* situation in which the workers were strong enough to give an indispensable initial boost to the Party but action could be 'displaced' if recruitment and associated goals were consciously directed to other, more numerous classes. For more on the displacement of class action see Post 1978 and 1981, where this serves as an extended theme.

6   *History of the Communist Party ... Excerpts from Party documents* (in Vietnamese) p. 327.

7   Pike 1978, p. 91.

8   Duiker 1981, p. 322.

Bibliography

There is always a basic decision to be made when compiling a bibliography, namely whether to attempt to list every item of which one knows which appears relevant or to include only those works which have been directly used. It seems more in keeping with the spirit of this undertaking to follow the latter course. If a major purpose is to show what can be done in the present state of our knowledge and thus to encourage further research, comment and criticism, it follows that part of the first and last of these activities will be the discovery of new sources and the bringing to the general notice of those which I should have used and missed. Hence, I have not included, for example, any of the tantalising titles in Vietnamese (such as *Classes and class struggle in Vietnamese society* by Nam Moc (Hanoi, Nha Xuat Ban Su That, 1956) which I found in the catalogue of the library of the Institute for Information in the Social Sciences in Hanoi in April 1980 but did not have time to consult. Those who want a list of these can contact me. For others the following may suffice, at least as a starting-point.

Works in Western Languages and Russian

Achievements of the Campaign of Denunciation of Communist Subversive Activities (First Phase) (1956), Saigon, People's Directive Committee for the Campaign of Denunciation of Communist Subversive Activities.

311

Adams, John and Nancy Hancock (1970), 'Land and Economy in Traditional Vietnam', *Journal of South East Asian Studies*, vol. I, no. 2.

Agrarian Reform Law (1955), Hanoi, Foreign Languages Publishing House.

Ambrose, Stephen E. (1980), *Rise to Globalism* , Harmondsworth, Penguin.

Anderson, Perry (1977), 'The Antinomies of Antonio Gramsci', *New Left Review* 100, November 1976–January 1977.

Anh Van and Jacqueline Roussel (1947), *Mouvements nationaux et lutte de classes au Viet-Nam* , Paris, Publications de la IVe Internationale.

Avec l'Oncle Ho, (1972) Hanoi, Editions en Langues Etrangères.

Avineri, Shlomo (ed.) (1969), *Karl Marx on Colonialism and Modernization*, Garden City, Anchor Books.

Barnet, Richard J. (1972), *Roots of War* , Harmondsworth, Penguin.

Bator, Victor (1965), *Vietnam: A Diplomatic Tragedy* , London, Faber and Faber.

Bergman, Arlene Eisen (1975), *Women of Viet Nam* , San Francisco, Peoples Press, revised edition.

Berman, Larry (1984a), 'Waiting for Smoking Guns: Presidential Decision-making and the Vietnam War, 1965–67' in Braestrup (ed.) *Vietnam as History* .

Berman, Larry (1984b), 'Commentary: On Betts and Schandler' in Braestrup (ed.) *Vietnam as History* .

Bernal, Martin (1981), 'The Nghe-Tinh Soviet Movement 1930–931', *Past & Present* 92, August.

Bernard, Paul (1934), *Le Problème économique indochinois,* Paris, Nouvelles Editions Latines.

Biography and Teaching of Prophet Huynh-Phu-So (1966), Saigon, Central Committee for the Diffusion of Hoa Hao Buddhism. (text in Vietnamese, French and English).

Blanchet, M. Th. (1954), *La Naissance de l'Etat Associé de Viet-Nam* , Paris, Génin.

Bodard, Lucien (1963, 1965, 1967), *La Guerre d'Indochine, l'Enlissement, L'Humiliation* and *l'Aventure* Paris, Gallimard. The first two volumes translated and abridged (1967) as *The Quicksand War*, London, Faber and Faber.

Boudarel, Georges (1977), *Giap* , Paris, Editions Atlas.

Boudarel, Georges (1981), 'L'extrême-gauche asiatique et le mouvement national vietnamien' in Pierre Brocheux (ed.), *Histoire de l'Asie du sud-est: révoltes, réformes, révolutions*, Lille, Presses Universitaires de Lille.

Braestrup, Peter (ed.) (1984), *Vietnam as History* , Washington DC, Wilson Center.

Brandt, Conrad, Benjamin Schwartz and John K. Fairbank (eds.) (1952), *A Documentary History of Chinese Communism* , Cambridge (Mass.), Harvard University Press.

Breaking our Chains (1960), Hanoi, Foreign Languages Publishing House.

312

Brève histoire du Parti des Travailleurs du Viet Nam (1930–1975) (1976), Hanoi, Editions en Langues Etrangères.

Brocheux, Pierre (1975), 'Le Prolétariat des plantations d'hévéas au Vietnam meridional', *Le Mouvement Social* 90, January–March.

Brocheux, Pierre (1977), 'L'Implantation du movement communiste en Indochine française: le cas du Nghe-Tinh (1930–1931)', *Revue d'histoire moderne et contemporaine*, January–March.

Brötel, Dieter (1971), *Franzosischer Imperialismus in Vietnam*, Freiburg imB., Atlantis Verlag.

Bui Dinh Thanh (1966), 'The first year of Resistance in South-Vietnam 1945–1946', *Vietnamese Studies*, 7, *Pages of History (1945–1954)*.

Burchett, Wilfred (1957), *North of the Seventeenth Parallel*, (rev. edn.), Hanoi, Red River Publishing House.

Butterfield, Fox (1983), 'The New Vietnam Scholarship', *New York Times Sunday Magazine* , 13 February.

Buttinger, Joseph (1958), *The Smaller Dragon* , New York, Praeger.

Buttinger, Joseph (1967) *Vietnam: A Dragon Embattled* , vol. I, *From Colonialism to the Vietminh*, vol. II, *Vietnam at War*, London, Pall Mall Press.

Cady, John F. (1954), *The Roots of French Imperialism in Eastern Asia*, Ithaca, Cornell University Press.

Cai San: une expérience de réforme agraire et de réimplantation dans le 'Grenier à riz' de le République de Viet-Nam, (nd), Saigon, State Secretariat for Information.

Calvocoressi, P. (ed.) (1952), *Survey of International Affairs 1947–1948*, London, Oxford University Press.

Calvocoressi, P. (ed.) (1953), *Survey of International Affairs 1949-1950*, London, Oxford University Press.

Carr, E.H. (1966), *The Bolshevik Revolution 1917–1923*, Vols. One and Three, Harmondsworth, Penguin.

Carrère d'Encausse, Hélène, and Stuart R. Schram (1969), *Marxism and Asia*, London, Allen Lane.

Chaffard, Georges (1964), *Indochine: dix ans d'indépendance* , Paris, Calmann-Lévy.

Chen, King C. (1969), *Vietnam and China, 1938–1954,* Princeton, Princeton University Press.

Cheshkov, M.A. (1967), *Ocheri istorii feodal' nogo V' etnama* ('Outline History of Vietnamese Feudalism'), Moscow, Nauka.

Cheshkov (Tchechkov), M.A. (1969), 'La Classe dirigeante du Vietnam Précolonial', *La Pensée* 144, March–April.

Chesneaux, Jean (1955), *Contribution à l'histoire de la nation viêtnamienne*, Paris, Editions Sociales.

Chesneaux, Jean (1971a), 'L'implantation des intérêts coloniaux au Vietnam et ses rapports avec l'économie traditionnelle' in Chesneaux, Boudarel and Hémery (eds.) *Tradition et Révolution au Vietnam*.

Chesneaux, Jean (1971b), 'Les Fondements historiques du Communisme Vietnamien' in Chesneaux, Boudarel and Hémery (eds.) *Tradition et Révolution au Vietnam* .

Chesneaux, Jean, Georges Boudarel and Daniel Hémery (eds.) (1971), *Tradition et Révolution au Vietnam* , Paris, Editions Anthropos.

Cheverny, J. (1961), *Eloges du colonialisme*, Paris, Julliard.

Chu Van Tan (1974), 'Reminiscences on the Army for National Salvation', Ithaca, Cornell University, mimeo.

Claudin, Fernando (1975), *The Communist Movement: from Comintern to Cominform*, Harmondsworth, Penguin Books.

Clubb, O. Edmund (1971), *China and Russia* , New York, Columbia University Press.

Colbert, Evelyn (1977), *Southeast Asia in International Politics 1941-1956*, Ithaca, Cornell University Press.

Cole, Allan B., (ed.) (1956), *Conflict in Indochina and International Repercussions*, Ithaca, Cornell University Press.

Cole, David G. (1959), 'Economic Setting' in Lindhom (ed.) *Vietnam: The First Five Years*.

Collins, James L. (1975), *The Development and Training of the South Vietnamese Army, 1950–1972* , Washington, DC, Department of the Army.

Le Commerce et l'industrie au Vietnam (1953), Saigon, Eros.

Contribution à l'histoire des mouvements politiques de l'Indochine Française. Documents, (1930–34), Hanoi, Gouvernment Générale de l'Indochine, 5 vols.

'Contribution to the Study of Dien Bien Phu' (1965), *Vietnamese Studies* 3, March.

Corley, Francis J. (1961), 'The President in the Constitution of the Republic of Viet-Nam', *Pacific Affairs*, vol. 34, no. 2, Summer.

Cotter, Michael G. (1968), 'Towards a Social History of the Vietnamese Southward Movement', *Journal of Southeast Asian History*, vol. 9, no. 1, March.

Cumings, Bruce (1981), *The Origins of the Korean War*, Princeton, Princeton University Press.

Dang Phuong Nghi (1969), *Les Institutions publiques du Viet-Nam au XVIIIe siècle*, Paris, Ecole Française d'Extrême Orient.

Darcourt, Pierre (1977), *Bay Vien: le Maître de Cholon*, Paris, Librairie Hachette.

Das, S.R. Mohan (1951), *Ho Chi Minh, nationalist or Soviet agent ?* Bombay, Democratic Research Service.

Degras, Jane (ed.) (1960), *The Communist International 1919–1943* : *Documents*, vols. II and III, London, Oxford University Press.

Despuech, Jacques (1953), *Le traffic des piastres*, Paris, Deux Rives.

Deux Victoires de la Révolution Vietnamienne (1946), Paris, Information Service of the DRVN.

Devillers, Philippe (1952), *Histoire du Viet Nam de 1940 à 1952*, Paris, Editions du Seuil.

Devillers, Philippe and Jean Lacouture (1969), *End of a War* , London, Pall Mall Press, revised version of *La Fin d' une guerre*, Paris, Editions du Seuil, 1960.

Dimitrov, Georgi (1935), *The United Front Against Fascism* , New York, New Century.

'Din' (1953), 'We are sure of Final Victory (Letter from Vietnam)', *For A Lasting Peace, For a People's Democracy,* 34 (250), 21 August.

Doan Trong Truyen and Pham Thanh Vinh (1964), *Building an Independent National Economy in Vietnam*, Hanoi, Foreign Languages Publishing House.

Donnell, John C. (1959), 'National Renovation Campaigns in South Viet Nam', *Pacific Affairs*, vol. 32, no. 1, March.

Donnell, John C. (1961), 'Personalism in Vietnam' in Fishel (ed.) *Problems of Freedom* .

Dornhorst, Robert (1977), 'The Communist Parties of Western Europe: The Origin of the National Roads to Socialism', *Revolutionary Communist* no. 6, April.

Doyle, Edward, Samuel Lipsman *et al.* (1981), *The Vietnam Experience: Setting the Stage,* Boston, Boston Publishing Company.

Drachman, Edward R. (1970), *United States Policy Toward Vietnam 1940–1945*, Rutherford (NJ), Fairleigh Dickinson Press.

Duiker, William J. (1973), 'The Red Soviets of Nghe-Tinh: An Early Communist Rebellion in Vietnam', *Journal of Southeast Asian Studies,* vol. 4, no. 2, September.

Duiker, William J. (1975), 'The Comintern and Vietnamese Communism', Athens (Ohio), Ohio University Center for International Studies, mimeo.

Duiker, William J. (1975) , 'Building the United Front: The Rise of Communism in Vietnam, 1925–1954' in Joseph J. Zasloff and MacAlister Brown (eds.) *Communism in Indochina* .

Duiker, William J. (1976), *The Rise of Nationalism in Vietnam, (1900–1941)*, Ithaca, Cornell University Press.

Duiker, William J. (1981) *The Communist Road to Power in Viet Nam*, Boulder, Westview Press.

Dumarest, André (1935), *La Formation des classes sociales en pays annamite* Lyons, Imprimerie P. Ferréol.

Duncanson, Dennis J. (1968), *Government and Revolution in Vietnam* , London, Oxford University Press.

Duncanson, Dennis J. (1974), 'Ho Chi Minh in Hong Kong, 1931–32', *China Quarterly* , 57, January–March.

Duong Chau (1958), *The Seventeenth Parallel* , Saigon, Cong Dan.

Duong Dinh Khue (1976), *La Littérature populaire vietnamienne*, Brussels, Thanh Long.

Eckhardt, George S. (1974), *Command and Control, 1950–1969,* Washington, DC, Department of the Army.

Eden, Anthony (Lord Avon) (1960), *The Memoirs of Sir Anthony Eden. Full Circle*, London, Cassell.

Elliott, Mai (1974), 'Translator's Introduction' to Chu Van Tan, 'Reminiscences on the Army for National Salvation'.

Elliott, Mai (1975), 'Translator's Introduction' to Vo Nguyen Giap 'Unforgettable Months and Years'.

Fall, Bernard (1955), 'Religious Sects of Viet-Nam', *Pacific Affairs* , vol. 28, no. 3, September.

Fall, Bernard (1956), 'The Viet Minh Regime', (rev. edn.), New York, Institute of Pacific Relations, mimeo.

Fall, Bernard (1961), *Street Without Joy*, Harrisburg (Penn.), Stackpole.

Fall, Bernard (ed.) (1963), *Primer for Revolt* , New York, Praeger.

Fall, Bernard (1966), *Viet Nam Witness* 1953–66, London, Pall Mall Press.

Fall, Bernard (1967), *Hell in a Very Small Place* , London, Pall Mall Press.

Fegan, Brian (1982), 'The Social History of a Central Luzon Barrio', in Alfred W. McCoy and Ed. C. de Jesus (eds.), *Philippine Social History*, Quezon City, Anteneo de Manila University Press.

Fenn, Charles (1973), *Ho Chi Minh*, New York, Charles Scribner's Sons.

Fishel, Wesley R. (ed.) (1961), *Problems of Freedom* , New York, Free Press.

FitzGerald, Frances (1972), *Fire in the Lake* , Boston, Little, Brown.

Five Years of the Implementation of the Geneva Agreements in Viet Nam, Hanoi, Vietnam Peace Committee, 1959.

Gaddis, John Lewis (1982), *Strategies of Containment*, London, Oxford University Press.

Gaultier, Marcel (1933),*Gia-Long* , Saigon, SILIC Ardin.

Geras, Norman (1976), *The Legacy of Rosa Luxemburg*, London, New Left Books.

Ginsburgs, George (1962a), 'Local Government and Administration in North Vietnam, 1945–1954', *The China Quarterly* 10.

Ginsburgs, George (1962b), 'Local Government and Administration in the Democratic Republic of Vietnam since 1954', Part 1, *China Quarterly* , 12.

Gittinger, J. Price (1959), 'Agrarian Reform' in Lindholm (ed.) *Vietnam: The First Five Years*.

Glennon, John P., *et al.* (eds.) (1981), *Foreign Relations of the United States*, vol. 6, *The Geneva Conference*, Washington DC, Government Printing Office.

Gobron, Gabriel (1948), *Histoire du Caodaisme*, Paris, Dervy (English translation by Pham Xuan Thai, *History and Philosophy of Caodaism*, Saigon, Tu Hai, 1950).

Goudal, J. (1937), *Problèmes du travail en Indochine*, Geneva, International Labour Office.

Gourou, Pierre (1936),*Les Paysans du Delta Tonkinois* , Paris, Ecole Française d'Extrème Orient.

Gourou, Pierre (1945), *Land Utilization in French Indochina*, New York, Institute of Pacific Relations.

Grant, J.A.C. (1958), 'The Viet Nam Constitution of 1956', *The American Political Science Review*, vol. 52, no. 2, June.

Gras, Yves (1981), 'Les grandes phases', in Philippe Héduy (ed.) *La Guerre d'Indochine*.

Grivaz, Raymond (1942), *Aspects sociaux et économiques du sentiment réligieux en pays annamite*, Paris, Domat-Montchréstien.

Hai Van (1975), 'The August 1945 Revolution in Saigon',*Vietnam Courier*, 40, September.

Hammer, Ellen J. (1966), *The Struggle for Indochina 1940–1955*, Stanford, Stanford University Press.

Héduy, Philippe (ed.) (1981), *La Guerre d'Indochine*, Paris, Société de Production Littéraire.

Hémery, Daniel (1975), *Révolutionnaires vietnamiens et pouvoir colonial en Indochine*, Paris, Maspero.

Hémery, Daniel (1977) , 'Aux origines des guerres d'indépendance vietnamiennes: pouvoir colonial et phénomène communiste en Indochine avant la Seconde Guerre mondiale', *Le Mouvement Social* 101, October–December.

Henry, Yves (1932), *L'Economie agricole de l'Indochine* , Hanoi, Gouvernement Général de l'Indochine.

A Heroic People: memoirs from the Revolution, (2nd edn.), Hanoi, Foreign Languages Publishing House, 1965.

History of the August Revolution, Hanoi, Foreign Languages Publishing House, (1972).

'The History of the Vietnamese Workers' and Trade Union Movement (1860–1945)', *The Vietnamese Trade Unions*, nos. 1–6, 1976 and no. 1, 1977.

Hoa Mai (ed.) (1958), *The 'Nhan-van' Affair*, Saigon, np.

Hoang Quoc Viet (1952), 'Vietnam Kämpft und arbeitet', *Die Länder der Volksdemokratie*, no. 167.

Hoang Van Chi (1958), *The New Class of North Vietnam* , Saigon, Cong Dan.

Hoang Van Chi (1964), *From Colonialism to Communism*, New York, Praeger.

Hoang Van Duc (1946), 'Comment la Révolution a triomphé de la famine', in *Deux Victoires de la Révolution Vietnamienne*.

Hoang Van Hoan (1979), 'Distortion of Facts About Militant Friendship Between Viet Nam and China is Impermissible', *Beijing Review*, 49, 7 December.

Hoang Zuy (1958), 'Face au bataillon de Corée' in *Les Premiers jours de notre Combat*.

Hoare, Quintin, and Geoffrey Nowell Smith (eds.) (1971), *Selections from the Prison Notebooks of Antonio Gramsci*, London, Lawrence and Wishart.

Ho Chi Minh (1967), *On Revolution*, ed. Bernard Fall, New York, Praeger.

Ho Chi Minh (1970), 'The Party's Military Work among the Peasants' in Neuberg (ed.), *Armed Insurrection.*

Ho Chi Minh (1977), *Selected Writings*, Hanoi, Foreign Languages Publishing House.

Hodgkin, Thomas (1981), *Vietnam: the Revolutionary Path*, London, Macmillan.

Honey, P.J. (1962), 'Introduction' in Honey (ed.), *North Vietnam Today*, New York, Praeger.

Ho Thi Bi (1958), 'Une mère combattante' in *Les Premiers jours de notre Combat.*

Hue-Tam Ho Tai (1983), *Millenarianism and Peasant Politics in Vietnam*, Cambridge (Mass.), Harvard University Press.

The Human Cost of Communism in Vietnam – II. The Myth of No Bloodbath. Hearing before the Subcommittee to Investigate the Administration of the Internal Security Act and other Internal Laws of the Committee on the Judiciary, United States Senate, Ninety-third Congress, First Session, 5 Jan., 1973, Washington, DC, Government Printing Office,1973.

Huu Mai (1966), 'De Lattre De Tassigny's Failure', *Vietnamese Studies*, 7, *Pages of History (1945-1954).*

Huynh Kim Khanh (1971), 'The Vietnamese August Revolution Reinterpreted', *Journal of Asian Studies*, vol. 30, no. 4, August.

Huynh Kim Khanh (1982), *Vietnamese Communism 1925–1945*, Ithaca, Cornell University Press.

Huynh Van Phuong (1935), *La piastre et la classe ouvrière*, Saigon, Imprimerie Testelin.

Huyn Van Lang (1959), 'Commentary' on Pierre Hunt and 'The Foreign Exchange Policy of Viet-Nam' in Lindholm (ed.) *Viet-Nam: The First Five Years.*

Irving, R.A.M. (1975), *The First Indochina War*, London, Croom Helm.

Isoart, Paul (1961), *Le phénomène national Viêtnamien*, Paris, Librairie Général de Droit et de Jurisprudence.

Johnson, Chalmers (1962), *Peasant Nationalism and Communist Power*, Stanford, Stanford University Press.

Joiner, Charles A., and Roy Jumper (1963), 'Organising Bureaucrats: South Viet-Nam's National Revolutionary Civil Servants' League', *Asian Survey*, vol. 3, no. 4, April.

Joyaux, François (1979), *La Chine et le réglement du premier conflit d'Indochine*, Paris, Publications de la Sorbonne.

Jumper, Roy (1957a), 'Mandarin Bureaucracy and Politics in South Viet Nam', *Pacific Affairs* , vol. 30, no. 1, March.

Jumper, Roy (1957b), 'Problems of Public Administration in South Viet Nam', *Far Eastern Survey,* vol. 26, no. 12, December.

Jumper, Roy, and Nguyen Thi Hue (1962), 'Notes on the Political and Administrative History of Viet Nam, 1802–1962', Saigon, Michigan State University Vietnam Advisory Group, mimeo.

Kahin, George McT. and John W. Lewis (1967), *The United States in Vietnam*, New York, Dial Press.

Karnow, Stanley (1986), *Vietnam: A History* , Harmondsworth, Penguin.

Kautsky, John H. (1956), *Moscow and the Communist Party of India*, Cambridge (Mass.) and New York, Technology Press and John Wiley & Sons.

Kelly, Gail P. (1984), 'The Presentation of Indigenous Society in the Schools of French West Africa and Indochina 1918–1938', *Comparative Studies in Society and History*, vol. 26, no. 3, July.

Kiernan, Ben (1985), *How Pol Pot Came to Power*, London, Verso.

Lacouture, Jean (1968), *Ho Chi Minh*, New York, Random House.

Ladejinsky, Wolf (1961), 'Agrarian Reform in the Republic of Vietnam' in Fishel (ed.), *Problems of Freedom*.

Lancaster, Donald (1961), *The Emancipation of French Indochina*, London, Oxford University Press.

Landau, Bruce (1977), 'Lenin and the Bolshevik Party', *Revolutionary Communist*, 6, April.

Lanoue, Henri (1971a), 'Comment a débuté la guerre du Vietnam: Le massacre de Haiphong' in Chesneaux, Boudarel and Hémery (ed.) *Tradition et Révolution au Vietnam*.

Lanoue, Henri (1971b), 'L'Empire économique américaine', in Chesneaux, Boudarel and Hémery (ed.) *Tradition et Révolution au Vietnam*.

Le Chau (1966), *Le Viet Nam socialiste*, Paris, Maspero.

Le Duan (nd), *On the Socialist Revolution in Vietnam*, Hanoi, Foreign Languages Publishing House, vol. 1.

Le Duan (1977), *Selected Writings*, Hanoi, Foreign Languages Publishing House.

Leffler, Melvyn P. (1984), 'The American Concept of National Security and the Beginnings of the Cold War (1945–48)', *American Historical Review*, vol. 89, no. 2, April.

Le Manh Trinh (1972), 'Dans le Kouang Toung et au Siam' in *Avec l'Oncle Ho*.

Lenin, V.I. (1920), 'Report of the Commission on the National and Colonial Questions' in Lenin, *Collected Works*, vol. 31.

Lenin, V.I. (1923), 'Better Fewer But Better' in Lenin, *Collected Works*, vol. 33.

Lenin, V.I. (1966), *Collected Works*, Moscow, Progress Publishers.

Leroy, Jean (1977), *Fils de la rizière*, Editions Robert Laffont.

Le Thanh Khoi (1955), *Le Vietnam: histoire et civilisation*, Paris, Editions de Minuit.

Le Thanh Khoi (1981), *Histoire du Viet Nam des Origines à 1858*, Paris, Sudestasie.

Le Thi Xuyen (1953), 'Vietnamese Women in the Struggle to Defend Their Own Interests', *Vietnam Information* 17, 1 May.

Limbourg, Michel (1956), *L'Economie actuelle du Viet–Nam démocratique*, Hanoi, Editions en Langues Etrangères.

Lindholm, Richard W., (ed.) (1959), *Viet-Nam: The First Five Years*, East (Lansing, Michigan State University.

Lindholm, Richard W., (1959a), 'American Aid and Its Financial Impact' in Lindholm (ed.) *Viet-Nam: The First Five Years*.

Lindholm, Richard W., (1959b) 'Commentary' on David G. Cole, 'Economic Setting', in Lindholm (ed.) *Viet-Nam: The First Five Years*.

Louis, Wm Roger (1977), *Imperialism at Bay*, London, Oxford University Press.

Lulei, Wilfried (1979), *Die Nationalen Einheitsfront Organisationen in Vietnam*, Berlin, Akademie-Verlag.

'La Lutte contre l'Analphabétisme au Viet Nam' in *Deux victoires de la Révolution Vietnamienne*, 1946.

McAlister, Jr., John T. (1967), 'Mountain Minorities and the Viet Minh: A Key to the Indochina war' in Peter Kundstadter (ed.), *Southeast Asian Tribes, Minorities and Nations*, vol. 2, Princeton, Princeton University Press.

McAlister, Jr., John T. (1969), *Viet-Nam: The Origins of Revolution*, London, Allen Lane The Penguin Press.

McLane, Charles B. (1958), *Soviet Policy and the Chinese Communists 1931–1946*, New York, Columbia University Press.

McLane, Charles B. (1966), *Soviet Strategies in Southeast Asia*, Princeton, Princeton University Press.

McVey, Ruth (1958), 'The Calcutta Conference and the Southeast Asian Upprisings', Ithaca, Cornell South East Asia Programme, mimeo.

Mai Thi Tu and Le Thi Nham Tuyet (1978), *Women in Viet Nam*, Hanoi, Foreign Languages Publishing House.

Mao Tse-tung (1938a), 'Problems of Strategy in the Guerrilla War Against Japan', in Mao, *Selected Works*, Vol. II.

Mao Tse-tung (1938b), 'On Protracted War', in Mao, *Selected Works*, Vol. II.

Mao Tse-tung (1938c), 'Problems of War and Strategy', in Mao, *Selected Works*, Vol. II.

Mao Tse-tung (1949), 'On the People's Democratic Dictatorship', in Mao, *Selected Works*, Vol. IV.

Mao Tse-tung (1962), 'Speech at the Tenth Plenum of the Eighth Central Committee' in Schram (ed.) (1974).

Mao Tse-tung (1961), *Selected Works of Mao Tse-tung*, Peking, Foreign Languages Press, vol. IV.

Mao Tse-tung (1965), *Selected Works of Mao Tse-tung*, Peking, Foreign Languages Pres, vol. II.

Marchese, Stelio (1971), *Le Origini della Rivoluzione vietnamista (1895–1930)*, Florence, La Nuova Italia.

Marcou, Lilly (1977), *Le Kominform*, Paris, Presses de la Fondation Nationale des Sciences Politiques.

Marr, David G. (1971), *Vietnamese Anticolonialism*, Berkeley and Los Angeles, University of California Press.

Marr, David G. (1981), *Vietnamese Tradition on Trial*, Berkeley and Los Angeles, University of California Press.

Marvel, W. Macy (1975), 'Drift and Intrigue: United States Relations with the Viet Minh (1945)', *Millennium*, vol. IV, no. 1.

Marx, Karl, and Friedrich Engels (1960), *The First Indian War of Independence*, Moscow, Foreign Languages Publishing House.

Maybon, Charles (1920), *Histoire Moderne du Pays D'Annam (1591–1820)*, Paris, Librairie Plon.

Merrington, John (1976), 'Town and Country in the Transition to Capitalism' in Rodney Hilton *et al.*, *The Transition from Feudalism to Capitalism*, London, New Left Books.

'Minh Khai' (1975), *Vietnam Courier*, 35, April.

Mkhitarian, S.A. (1967), *Rabochi Klass i National'no Osvoboditel'-noe Dvizhenie vo Vietname, 1885–1930* 'The Working Class and the National–Liberation Movement in Vietnam 1885–1939', Moscow, Nauka.

Moise, Edwin E. (1976), 'Land Reform and Land Reform Errors in North Vietnam', *Pacific Affairs*, vol. 49, no. 1. Spring.

Moise, Edwin E. (1983), *Land Reform in China and North Vietnam*, Chapel Hill, University of North Carolina Press.

Montgomery, John D. (nd), *Cases in Vietnamese Administration*, Saigon (?), Michigan State University Vietnam Advisory Group.

Mortimer, Edward (1984), *The Rise of the French Communist Party 1920–1947*, London, Faber and Faber.

Murray, Martin J. (1980), *The Development of Capitalism in Colonial Indochina*, Berkeley and Los Angeles, University of California Press.

Murti, B.S.N. (1964), *Vietnam Divided*, London, Asia Publishing House.

Mus, Paul (1952), *Sociologie d'une guerre*, Paris, Editions de Seuil.

Mus, Paul and John T. McAlister, Jr. (1970), *The Vietnamese and their Revolution*, New York, Harper and Row.

Neuberg, A. (ed.) (1970), *Armed Insurrection*, London, New Left Books.

Ngo Dinh Diem (1957), *President Ngo Dinh Diem on Democracy*, Saigon, Presidency of the Republic of Vietnam Press Office.

Ngo Dinh Diem (1962), *La Voie de La Juste Cause*, Saigon, Service de Presse de la Présidence de la République du Viet-Nam.

Ngo Vinh Long (1973), *Before the Revolution*, Cambridge (Mass.), MIT Press.

Ngo Vinh Long (1978), 'The Indochinese Communist Party and Peasant Rebellion in Central Viet Nam 1930–1931', *Bulletin of Concerned Asian Scholars*, vol. 10, no. 4, October–December.

Nguyen Anh Tuan (1967), *Les Forces politiques au Sud Viet-Nam depuis les accords de Genève 1954*, Louvain, Faculty of Economic, Social and Political Sciences of the Catholic University.

Nguyen Duy Xuan (1959), 'Commentary' on Slusser, in Lindholm (ed.) *Viet-Nam: The First Five Years*.

Nguyen Huy Thuong (1962), *The Frontier campaign. Memoirs*, Hanoi, Foreign Languages Publishing House.

Nguyen Khac Vien (1966), 'The Peasant Struggle (1954–1960)', *Vietnamese Studies*, 8, *South Viet Nam 1954–1956*.

Nguyen Khac Vien (1970), *Expériences vietnamiennes*, Paris, Editions sociales.

Nguyen Khac Vien (1974), *Histoire du Vietnam*, Paris, Editions sociales.

Nguyen Khac Vien (1975), *The Long Resistance (1858–1975)*, Hanoi, Foreign Languages Publishing House.

Nguyen Khanh Toan (1965), *Twenty Years' Development of Education in the Democratic Republic of Vietnam*, Hanoi, Ministry of Education.

Nguyen Khanh Toan (1972), 'En URSS avec l'Oncle Ho' in *Avec l'Oncle Ho*.

Nguyen Luong Bang (1972), 'Mes Rencontres avec l'Oncle Ho' in *Avec l'Oncle Ho*.

Nguyen Manh Ha (1967), *L'Eglise et le Tiers Monde*, Paris, Editions de Cerf.

Nguyen Ngoc Minh (1966), 'The Birth of an Independent Currency', *Vietnamese Studies* 7, *Pages of History 1945–54*.

Nguyen Quoc Chao (1953), 'Profsoyuzi V'etnama v Borba natsionalniyu nesavisimost' ('Vietnamese unions and the national liberation struggle'), *Sovietskii Profsoyuzi*, December.

Nguyen Thanh Nha (1970), *Tableau économique du Vietnam au XVII et XVIII Siècles*, Paris, Editions Cujas.

Nguyen Tien Hun (1970), *Dörfliche Kulte im traditionellen Vietnam*, Munich, Verlag UNI Druck.

Nguyen Tran Huan (1958), 'Histoire d'une secte réligieuse au Vietnam: le Caodaisme', *Revue de synthèse*, 3rd series, nos. 11–12.

Nguyen Truong (1974), *The role of public enterprise in national development in South Vietnam*, Singapore, Regional Institute of Higher Education and Development.

Nguyen Van Huyen (1961), *Sixteen Years Development of National Education in the Democratic Republic of Vietnam* , Hanoi, Foreign Languages Publishing House.

Nguyen Xuan Lai (1976), 'The First Resistance (1945–54)' in *Vietnamese Studies* 44, *Economic Policy and National Liberation War*.

Nhu Phong (1962), 'Intellectuals, Writers and Artists', *China Quarterly*, 9.

Nitz, Kiyoko Kurusu (1983), 'Japanese Military Policy towards French Indochina during the Second World War: the Road to the *Maigo Sakusen*', *Journal of Southeast Asian Studies*, vol. 14, no. 2, September.

Nitz, Kiyoko Kurusu (1984), 'Independence Without Nationalists? The Japanese and Vietnamese Nationalism During the Japanese Period (1940–45', *Journal of Southeast Asian Studies*, vol. 15, no. 1, March.

O'Ballance, Edgar (1964), *The Indochina War (1945–54)* London, Faber and Faber.

Oliver, Victor L. (1976), *Caodai Spiritism*, Leiden, E.J. Brill.

Operation Exodus (nd), Saigon, Directorate General of Information,.

'Orgwald' (1933), 'Tactical and Organisational Questions of the Communist Parties of Indochina and India: Questions and Answers', *Pan Pacific Worker*, July.

Osborne, Milton E. (1969), *The French Presence in Cochin China and Cambodia* , Ithaca, Cornell University Press.

Osborne, Milton E. (1974), 'Continuity and Motivation in the Vietnamese Revolution: New Light from the 1930's', *Pacific Affairs* , vol. 47, no.1, Spring.

Patti, Archimedes L.A. (1980), *Why Viet Nam?*, Berkeley and Los Angeles, University of California Press.

The Pentagon Papers (1971), vol. I, Gravel Edition, Boston, Beacon Press.

Pham Hung (nd), 'Accelerating the Development of Agricultural Production All-Sidedly, Vigorously and Steadily to Make It a Basis for Socialist Industrialisation', in *Third National Congress of the Viet Nam Workers' Party, Documents*, vol. III, Hanoi, Foreign Languages Publishing House.

Pham Van Dong (1977), *Selected Writings*, Hanoi, Foreign Languages Publishing House.

Phan Thanh Son (1971), 'Le Mouvement ouvrier vietnamien de 1920 à 1930' in Chesneaux *et al.*

Phan Truong Manh (1950), *La voie du Salut Caodaïque*, Saigon, Imprimerie Ly-Cong-Quan.

Phong Van Dan (1963, 1964), 'La Formation territoriale du Viet Nam', *Revue du Sud-est Asiatique*, nos. 4 and 2.

Phuc Thien (1956), *President Ngo Dinh Diem's Political Philosophy*, Saigon, Horizons Magazine.

Pike, Douglas (1978), *History of Vietnamese Communism 1925–76*, Stanford, Hoover Institution Press.

Political Alignments of Vietnamese Nationalists (1949), Washington DC, State Department Office of Intelligence Research.

Popkin, Samuel L. (1976), 'Corporatism and Colonialism: The Political Economy of Rural Change in Vietnam', *Comparative Politics*, vol. 8, no. 3, April.

Popkin, Samuel L. (1977), *The Rational Peasant*, Berkeley and Los Angeles, University of California Press.

Porter, Gareth D. (1972), 'The Myth of the Bloodbath: North Vietnam's land reform reconsidered', Ithaca, Cornell University International Relations of East Asia Project, mimeo.

Porter, Gareth D. (ed.) (1979), *Vietnam: the Definitive Documentation of Human Decisions* , vol. 1, London, Heyden and Son.

Porter, Gareth D. (1980), 'Vietnam and the Socialist Camp: Center or Periphery?' in Turley (ed.)*Vietnamese Communism in Comparative Perspective*.

Post, Ken (1978), *Arise Ye Starvelings*, The Hague, Martinus Nijhoff.

Post, Ken (1981), *Strike the Iron*, Atlantic Highlands, NJ, Humanities Press, and The Hague, Institute of Social Studies.

Post, Ken, and Phil Wright (1989), *Socialism and Underdevelopment*, London, Routledge.

Les Premiers jours de notre Combat, Hanoi, Editions en Langues Etrangères, 1958.

Public Welfare and Standard of Living in North Vietnam, New York, JPRS Report no. 702, 1958.

Race, Jeffrey (1972), *War Comes to Long An*, Berkeley and Los Angeles, University of California Press.

Rageau, Christine Pasquet (1970), *Ho Chi Minh*, Paris, Editions universitaires.

Rambo, Terry A. (1973), 'A Comparison of peasant systems of Northern and Southern Viet-Nam', Carbondale, Southern Illinois University Center for Vietnamese Studies, mimeo.

Randle, Robert F. (1969), *Geneva 1954*, Princeton, Princeton University Press.

Rastorguyev, V.S. (1965), *Finance and Credit in the Democratic Republic of Vietnam*, Moscow, Publishing House for Finance, original in Russian, JPRS Scholarly Book Translation Services, no. 618, nd.

Riesen, René (1957), *Jungle Mission*, London, Hutchinson.

Robequain, Charles (1944), *The Economic Development of French Indo-China*, London, Oxford University Press.

Rosie, George (1970), *The British in Vietnam*, London, Panther Books.

Rousset, Pierre (1975), *Le Parti Communiste vietnamien*, (2nd edn.), Paris, Maspero.

Rousset, Pierre (1978), *Communisme et nationalisme vietnamien*, Paris, Editions Galilée.

Rousset, Pierre (1984), 'The Peculiarities of Vietnamese Communism' in Tariq Ali (ed.), *The Stalinist Legacy*, Harmondsworth, Penguin.

Roy, Jules (1965), *The Battle of Dien Bien Phu*, London, Faber and Faber.

Rue, John (1965), *Mao Tse-tung in Opposition*, Stanford, Stanford University Press.

Sacks, I. Milton (1959), 'Marxism in Viet Nam', in Frank N. Trager (ed.), *Marxism in Southeast Asia*, Stanford, Stanford University Press.

Sacks, I. Milton (1949) (anonymously), *Political Alignments of Vietnamese Nationalists*, qv.

'Saigon: From Gia Dinh Citadel to Ho Chi Minh City', *Vietnam Courier*, 37, June, 1975.

Sainteny, Jean (1953), *Histoire d'Une Paix Manquée: Indochine 1945–1947*, Paris, Amiot-Dumont.

Sansom, L. (1970), *The Economics of Insurgency in the Mekong Delta of Vietnam*, Cambridge (Mass.), MIT Press.

Sassoon, Anne Showstack (1980), *Gramsci's Politics*, London, Croom Helm.

Scheer, Robert (nd), 'Hang Down Your Head Tom Dooley' in *Vietnam Primer*, San Francisco, Ramparts Press.

Scheer, Robert and Warren Hinckle (nd), 'The Vietnam Lobby', in *Vietnam Primer*, qv.

Schiff, Frank W. (1959), 'Monetary Reorganization and the Emergence of Central Banking' in Lindholm (ed.) *Viet-Nam: The First Five Years.*

Schram, Stuart R. (1963), *The Political Thought of Mao Tse-tung*, New York, Praeger.

Schrock, Joan L. *et al.* (1966), *Minority Groups in the Republic of Viet Nam*, Washington DC, Department of the Army.

Scigliano, Robert (1964), *South Vietnam: Nation Under Stress*, Boston, Houghton Mifflin.

Scigliano, Robert and Guy H. Fox (1965), *Technical Assistance in Vietnam*, New York, Praeger.

Scott, James C. (1976), *The Moral Economy of the Peasant*, New Haven, Yale University Press.

Selden, Mark (1971), *The Yenan Way in Revolutionary China*, Cambridge (Mass.), Harvard University Press.

Shabad, Theodore (1958), 'Economic Development in North Vietnam', *Pacific Affairs*, vol. 31, no. 1, March.

Shao Kuo-kang (1986), 'Zhou Enlai's Diplomacy and the Neutralisation of Indo-China 1954–55', *China Quarterly*, 107, September.

Shue, Vivienne (1980), *Peasant China in Transition*, Berkeley, University of California Press.

Simmons, Robert R. (1975), *The Strained Alliance*, New York, The Free Press.

Slusser, Robert H. (1959), 'Early Steps Toward an Industrial Development Bank' in Lindholm (ed.) *Viet-Nam: The First Five Years.*

Smith, Ralph (1968), *Viet-Nam and the West*, London, Heinemann.

Smith, Ralph (1969), 'Bui Quang Chieu and the Constitutionalist Party in French Cochin-china', *Modern Asian Studies*, vol. 3, no. 2, April.

Smith, Ralph (1970), 'An Introduction to Caodaisme: Origins and Early History', *Bulletin of School of Oriental and African Studies*, 33.

Smith, Ralph (1972), 'The Vietnamese Elite of French Cochinchina 1943', *Modern Asian Studies*, vol. 6, no. 4, October.

Smith, Ralph (1978a), 'The Japanese Period in Indochina and the Coup of 9 March 1945', *Journal of Southeast Asian Studies*, vol. 9, no. 2, September.

Smith, Ralph (1978b), 'The Work of the Provisional Government of Vietnam, August–December 1945', *Modern Asian Studies*, vol. 12, no. 4, October.

Smith, Ralph (1983), *An International History of the Vietnam War*, vol. I, *Revolution Versus Containment 1955–61*, London, Macmillan.

Smith, Ralph (1985), *An International History of the Vietnam War*, vol. II, *The Struggle for South-East Asia 1961–65*, London, Macmillan.

Smith, Ralph (1984), 'The Vietnam War', *History Today*, 34, October.

'Special Edition. The Constitution of the Republic of Viet-Nam', *News from Viet-Nam* , Washington DC, Vietnamese Embassy, 17 November, 1956.

Stalin, J.V. (1936), 'Marxism and the National Question' in Stalin, *Marxism and the National and Colonial Question* .

Stalin, J.V. (1936), *Marxism and the National and Colonial Question*, London, Lawrence and Wishart.

Stalin, J.V. (1953), 'Questions of the Chinese Revolution' in Stalin, *Works*, vol. 9.

Stalin, J.V. (1953), 'The Revolution in China and the Tasks of the Comintern' in Stalin, *Works*, vol. 9.

Stalin, J.V. (1953), 'The National Question and Leninism' in Stalin, *Works*, vol. 11.

Stalin, J.V. (1953), *Works*, London, Lawrence and Wishart.

Starobin, Joseph R. (1953), *Viet-Nam Fights for Freedom*, London, Lawrence and Wishart.

Taboulet, George (1955, 1956), *La Geste française en Indochine*, (2 vols.), Paris, Maisonneuve.

Tanham, George K. (1967), *Communist Revolutionary Warfare* (rev. edn.), New York, Praeger.

Ta Xuan Linh (1974a), 'How Armed Struggle Began in South Viet Nam', *Vietnam Courier* , 22, March.

Ta Xuan Linh (1974b), 'Armed Uprisings by Ethnic Minorities Along the Truong Son', *Vietnam Courier*, 28, September.

Taylor, Keith (1976), 'The Rise of Dai Viet and the establishment of Thang-long' in Kenneth R. Hall and John K. Whitmore (eds.), *Explorations in Early Southeast Asian History*, Ann Arbor, University of Michigan Center for Southeast Asian Studies.

Thanh-Luong (1955), *A short history of Vietnam*, Hanoi, Foreign Languages Publishing House.

Thayer, Carlyle A. (1975), 'Southern Vietnamese Revolutionary Organizations and the Vietnam Workers' Party: Continuity and Change 1954–1974' in Zasloff and Brown (eds.) *Communism in Indochina*.

Thompson, Virginia (1937), *French Indochina*, London, Allen and Unwin.

Thuong Vinh Thanh, Cao Tiep Dap and Pham Cong Tac (1953), *La Constitution religieuse du Caodaisme* (text also in Vietnamese), Paris, Dervy.

Tichelman, Fritjof (1980), *The Social Evolution of Indonesia: the Asiatic Mode of Production and Its Legacy*, The Hague, Martinus Nijhoff.

Ton Vy (1968), 'Les ouvrières au Sud-Vietnam, de 1954 à 1965', *La Pensée*, 138, March–April.

Tran Huy Lieu (1960), *Les Soviets du Nghe-Tinh de 1930–31 au Viet-Nam*, Hanoi, Foreign Languages Publishing House.

Tran Ich Quoc (1958), *The Fatherland Front, a Vietnamese communist tactic*, Saigon, np.

Tran Ngoc Danh (1947), *Two Years' Achievement of the Viet Nam Nationalist Government*, Paris, Vietnam Information Service.

Tran Tam Tinh (1978), *Dieu et César*, Paris, Sudestasie.

Tran Van Kien (1959), 'Commentary' on Lindholm, in Lindholm (ed.) *Viet-Nam: The First Five Years* .

Tran Van Mai (1973), 'Who Committed this Crime?' in Ngo Vinh Long, *Before the Revolution* .

Tran Van Tung (1951), *Le Viet-Nam au Combat: Nationalisme contre Communisme*, Paris, Editions de la Belle Page.

Trinquier, Roger (1981), 'Le fin des maquis thais' in Philippe Héduy (ed.) *La Guerre d'Indochine*.

Trued, M.N. (1960), 'South Viet-Nam's Industrial Development Center', *Pacific Affairs*, vol. 33, no. 3, September.

Truong Buu Lam (1967), *Patterns of Vietnamese Response to Foreign Intervention, 1858–1900*, New Haven, Yale University Press.

Truong Buu Lam (1973), 'Japan and the Disruption of the Vietnamese Nationalist Movement' in Walter F. Vella (ed.), *Aspects of Vietnamese History*, Honolulu, University of Hawaii Press.

Truong Chinh (1960), *The Resistance Will Win*, (rev. edn.), Hanoi, Foreign Languages Publishing House, facsimile edition in Fall (ed.) 1963.

Truong Chinh (1962), *The August Revolution*, Hanoi, Foreign Languages Publishing House, fascimile edition in Fall (ed.) 1963.

Truong Chinh (1977), *Selected Writings*, Hanoi, Foreign Languages Publishing House.

Truong Chinh and Vo Nguyen Giap (1974), *The Peasant Question (1937–1938)*, Ithaca, Cornell University Southeast Asia Program, Department of Asian Studies.

Turley, William S. (1975), 'The Political Role and Development of the People's Army of Vietnam' in Zasloff and Brown (eds.).

Turley, William S. (ed.) (1980), *Vietnamese Communism in Comparative Perspective*, Boulder, Westview Press.

Turner, Robert F. (1975),*Vietnamese Communism* , Stanford, Hoover Institution Press.

Utrecht, Ernst (1973), 'Interview with Ho Chi Minh', *Journal of Contemporary Asia* , vol. 7, no. 2.

Van Loc (1960), 'State–Private Jointly Operated Commercial Enterprises', *Thoi Moi* , 2 August 1960, JPRS 5,893.

Vietnam, A New Stage in her History , Bangkok, Vietnam News, 1947.

Viet-Nam Fatherland Front and the Struggle for National Unity, Hanoi, Foreign Languages Publishing House, 1956.

The Vietnamese working class in the long hard war of resistance, Hanoi, Foreign Languages Publishing House, 1955.

Vlastos, Stephen (1984), 'Teaching the Vietnam War: Objectivity in the Classroom?', *Bulletin of Concerned Asian Scholars*, vol. 16, no. 4.

Vo Nguyen Giap (1955), *On the Implementation of the Geneva Agreements*, Hanoi, Foreign Languages Publishing House.

Vo Nguyen Giap (1961), *People's War, People' Army*, Hanoi, Foreign Languages Publishing House.

Vo Nguyen Giap (1972), 'Ho Chi Minh, Père de l'Armée révolutionaire du Viet Nam' in *Avec l'Oncle Ho.*

Vo Nguyen Giap (1975), 'Unforgettable Months and Years', Ithaca, Cornell University, mimeo.

Vo Nguyen Giap (1978), *Unforgettable Days*, Hanoi, Foreign Languages Publishing House.

Vo Nguyen Giap (1984), *Dien Bien Phu*, (rev. edn.), Hanoi, Foreign Languages Publishing House.

Vo Nhan Tri (1967), *Croissance économique de la République démocratique du Viet Nam*, Hanoi, Editions en Langues Etrangères.

Vu Anh (1972), 'De Kunming à Pac Bo' in *Avec l'Oncle Ho.*

Vu Can (1967), 'With the Nam Dinh Weavers', *Vietnamese Studies* 10, *Vietnamese Women* .

Vu Do Thin (1954), *Evolution économique du Viet Nam*, vol. 1 *Monnaie et salaires*, Paris, Librairie Générale de Droit et de Jurisprudence.

Vu Han (1946), 'Les Comités du Peuple' in Walter R. Stephen, Vu Han and Xuan Ngoc, *Quelques aspects du Viet Nam Nouveau* , Hanoi, Editions de l'office d'information de la République Démocratique du Viet Nam.

Vu Quoc Thong (1952), 'La Décentralisation administrative au Viet Nam', Saigon, Presses Universitaires du Viet Nam, second edition, mimeo.

Vu Quoc Thuc, 'L'Economie communaliste du Viet Nam', Hanoi, Presses Universitaires du Viet Nam, mimeo. (1951).

Vu Van Hoan (1972), 'Les Organes Locaux du Pouvoir d'Etat' in *Aperçu sur les institutions de la République Démocratique du Viet Nam*, Hanoi, Editions en Langues Etrangères.

Warner, Denis (1964), *The Last Confucian* , Harmondsworth, Penguin Books.

Warner, Geoffrey (1972), 'The United States and Vietnam', *International Affairs*, July and October.

Werner, Jayne Susan (1981), *Peasant Politics and Religious Sectarianism* : *Peasant and Priest in the Cao Dai in Viet Nam,* New Haven, Yale University Southeast Asia Studies.

Whitmore, John K. (1980), 'Communism and History in Vietnam' in Turley (ed.) *Vietnamese Communism in Comparative Perspective* .

Wittfogel, Karl A. (1957), *Oriental Despotism* , New Haven, Yale University Press.

Wollenberg, Erich (1970), 'How We Wrote *Armed Insurrection*' in Neuberg (ed.) *Armed Insurrection* .

Women of Viet-Nam in the struggle for national liberation, Paris, Union of Viet-Nam Women in France, 1948.

Wong, John (1973), *Land Reform in the People's Republic of China* , New York, Praeger.

Woodside, Alexander B. (1971), *Vietnam and the Chinese Model* , Cambridge (Mass.), Harvard University Press.

Woodside, Alexander B. (1976), *Community and Revolution in Modern Vietnam*, Boston, Houghton Mifflin.

Wurfel, David (1957), 'Agrarian Reform in the Republic of Vietnam', *Far Eastern Survey*, vol. 26, no. 6, June.

Yergin, Daniel (1978), *Shattered Peace*, Boston, Houghton Mifflin.

Zasloff, Joseph J. and MacAllister Brown (eds.) (1975), *Communism in Indochina*, Lexington (Mass.), D.C. Heath and Co.

Works in Vietnamese

Cao Van Bien (1979), *The Vietnamese Working Class in the Period 1936–1939*, Hanoi, Nha Xuat Ban Khoa Hoc Xa Hoi.

Dang Viet Chau (1964), 'Some Problems concerning Price Policy', *HT*, 4.

Dong Tan (1967, 1972), *History of the great path of Cao Dai for the relief of the people in the three eras*, vol. I. *Supernatural issues (1920–32)* vol. II, *Relief of the people (1926–37)* Saigon, Cao Hien Xuat Ban Nam Dai Dao.

Do Thinh (1975), 'The Hanoi City Party Committee Built Its foothold in the Suburbs', *NCLS*, 163.

Duy Minh (1963), 'Some Ideas on the Problem of Feudalism in Vietnamese History', *NCLS*, 55.

Duy Minh (1965), 'The Role of Peasant Uprisings in the Process of development of the Nation', *NCLS*, 81.

Events in Party History, vol. I, 1920–45, and vol. II, 1945–54, Hanoi, Nha Xuat Ban Su That, 1976, 1979.

Fifty Years of Activity of the Communist Party of Viet Nam, Hanoi, Nha Xuat Ban Su That, 1979.

Five Years of Economic and Cultural Construction, Hanoi, Central Statistical Board, 1960.

'Go further to the heart of the general line of the Party in the rural areas', *HT*, 2, 1957.

Ha Ke Tan (1964), 'Irrigation is the leading technical method for developing agricultural production in the North', *HT*, 2.

History of the Communist Party of Viet Nam: Excerpts from Party Documents, Hanoi, Nha Xuat Ban Sach Giao Khoa Mac-Le-Nin, vol. I, 1979.

History of the Struggle of the Vietnamese Workers and Trade Unions (1860–1945), Hanoi, Nha Xuat Ban Lao Dong, 1977.

History of Viet Nam, vol. I, Hanoi, Nha Xuat Ban Khoa Hoc Xa Hoi, 1971.

History of the Vietnamese People's Army, Hanoi, Nha Xuat Ban Quan Doi Nhan Dan, vol. I, 1977.

Hoai Giang (1965), 'Why Did the Other Peasant Risings in the XVIIIth Century Before That of Tay-son Fail?', *NCLS*, 75.

Hoang Van Dao (1965), *The Viet Nam Nationalist Party. A History of Modern Struggle 1927–1954*, Saigon, Nguyen Hoa Hiep.

Hong Chuong (1965), 'The Nam Ky Uprising and Its Lessons', *HT* , 11.

Hong Quang (1962), 'Some Ideas Concerning the Problems of Studying the Historical Meaning and Impact of the Nghe-Tinh Soviets', *NCLS* , 35.

Institute of Minority Studies, Committee for Vietnamese Social Sciences, *The Minority Peoples in Viet Nam*, Hanoi, Nha Xuat Ban Khoa Hoc Xa Hoi 1978.

Le Hoang (1964), 'Concerning the Law of Value and Price Policy in the Economy of the North of our Country', *HT*, 6.

Le Tan Tien (1965), *Looking Back at the Historical Road of the Party*, Hanoi, Nha Xuat Ban Su That.

Le Van Lo (1964), 'The First Step in Studying the Social Systems in the Tay, Nung and Thai Areas During French Rule', *NCLS* , 68.

Le Van Luong (1956), 'Our Present Party-Building Task', *HT*, 3.

Mai Van Nguyen (1947), *The Struggle of the Vanguard Youth*, Saigon, Tu Dan Luu Hanh Xuat Ban Cuc.

'M.N.' (1967), 'Some major features of the workers' movement in Saigon from 1945 to the present', *NCLS* , 95.

The New Reforms of the Government , Hanoi, Office of Information, 1950.

Ngo Tien Chat (1969), 'Some Outlines of the Heroic Struggle of the Viet Bac Minority Peoples in the Resistance Against the French (1945–1954)', *NCLS*, 122.

Ngo Van Hoa and Duong Kinh Quoc (1978), *The Vietnamese Working Class in the Years Before the Founding of the Party*, Hanoi, Nha Xuat Ban Khoa Hoc Xa Hoi.

Nguyen Cong Binh (1961), 'Tentative Comments on the Vietnamese Comprador Bourgeois Class', *NCLS*, 23 and 24.

Nguyen Cong Binh (1975), 'The Vietnamese working class realised its historical task of clearly following the line of the vanguard party', *NCLS* , 160.

Nguyen Dong Chi (1964), 'The Role of Hierarchy and Classes in the Peasant Uprisings and Peasant Wars in the First Half of the XVIth Century and the Middle of the XVIIIth Century', *NCLS*, 60.

Nguyen Luong Bich (1963a), 'Is the Process of Development of the Human Community from Tribe to Nationality, from Nationality to Nation, or Directly from Nationality to Nation?', *NCLS*, 49.

Nguyen Luong Bich (1963b), 'What is the Asiatic Mode of Production?', *NCLS*, 53.

Nguyen Luong Bich (1968), 'The Asiatic Mode of Production in the Highland Areas of Viet Nam During Previous Eras', *NCLS*, 117.

Nguyen Luong Bick (1969) 'What class was the ruling class in Viet Nam from the XVth to the XVIIIth century?' *NCLS*, 128.

Nguyen Ngoc Minh (chief editor) (1966), *The Vietnamese Economy from the August Revolution to the Victory of the Resistance (1945–1954)*, Hanoi, Nha Xuat Ban Khoa Hoc.

Nguyen Phan Quang (1962), 'Some ideas on the Tay Son peasant movement', *NCLS*, 35

Nguyen The Anh (1970), *The Economy and Society of Viet Nam Under the Nguyen Dynasty*, Saigon, Lua Thieng.

Nguyen Thuong Hoa (1962), 'The Law of Value and the Price Situation in our Country', *NCKT*, 8, April.

Nguyen Van Hau (1969), *The Realisation of Hoa Hao Buddhism* , Saigon, Huong Sen Xuat Ban.

Party Members' Training and Investigation Plan, Ha Dong, ICP Executive Committee, 1950.

Phan Huy Le (1963), 'Some Contributions on Problems Concerning the Tay-son Peasant Movement', *NCLS*, 49 and 50.

Pham Ngoc Lien (1963), 'Contribution of a Number of Ideas Concerning the Problem of a Content for Vietnamese History in Accordance with a Fully National Viewpoint', *NCLS*, 48.

Phan Ngoc Lien (1973), 'The Work of Chairman Ho in Mass Campaigns and Education During His Period at Pac Bo', *NCLS*, 149.

The Problem of Agrarian Reform , vol. II, Hanoi, Office of Information, 1950.

The Sacred Resistance of the Vietnamese People , vols. 3 and 4, Hanoi, Nha Xuat Ban Su That, 1960.

Situation and Tasks, printed but np, nd, ICP Central Committee, *c.* 1949.

Thanh Dam (1975), 'Studying the Question of the Middle Strata During the Period of the August Revolution', *NCLS*, 163.

Thirty Years of Economic and Cultural Development of the Democratic Republic of Viet Nam, Hanoi, Nha Xuat Ban Su That, 1978.

The Three Stages of the Long Resistance, Saigon–Cholon, Office of Information, 1949.

Tran Huy Lieu *et al* . (1956–58), *Reference Materials on the History of the Contemporary Vietnamese Revolution*, Hanoi, Su Dia.

Tran Huy Lieu (1969), 'The necessity of finding a theoretical basis for the study of our nation's heroism', *NCLS*, 120.

Tran Phuong (ed.) (1968), *The Agrarian Revolution in Viet Nam*, Hanoi, Nha Xuat Ban Khoa Hoc Xa Hoi.

Tran Truong Kim (1964), *Outline History of Viet Nam* (7th edn.), Saigon, Tan Viet.

Tran Van Giau (1957, 1962, 1963), *The Vietnamese Working Class*, 3 vols., Hanoi, Nha Xuat Ban Su That.

Tran Van Giau (1969), 'Patriotism, the greatest sentiment and idea of the Vietnamese people', *NCLS* , 129.

Tran Van Giau (1972), 'Professor Georges Chesneaux and some problems of Vietnamese History', *NCLS* , 142.

Tran Van Giau (1975), *The Development of Ideology in Viet Nam from the Nineteenth Century to the August Revolution*, vol. I, *The Feudal Ideological System and the Failure of its Historical Mission*, Hanoi, Nha Xuat Ban Su That.

331

Trung Chinh (1961), 'Some Ideas concerning the True Character of the Nghe-Tinh Soviets', *NCLS*, 30.

Truong Chinh (1943), 'The question of the dissolution of the Communist International', in *Liberation Banners*, Hanoi, Nha Xuat Ban Su That, Part I, 1976.

Truong Chinh (1949), *The Three Stages of the Long Resistance*, Saigon–Cholon, Office of Information.

Truong Chinh (1956), *Discourse on the Vietnamese Revolution*, vol. I, Hanoi, Ban Chap Hanh Trung Uong Xuat Ban.

Truong Chinh (1956), 'Rectify Errors and Advance', *HT*, 11.

Truong Chinh (1958), *Unite More Closely to Build a Peaceful, United, Independent, Democratic, Prosperous and Strong Viet Nam*, Hanoi, Nha Xuat Ban Su That.

'Urgently recognise the distinct role and tasks of trade unions', *HT*, 3, 1956.

Van Tan (1967), 'The Reactionary System of the Nguyen Dynasty', *NCLS* 95 and 97.

Van Tan (1968), 'The Centralised Monarchical Regime in Vietnamese History', *NCLS*, 110.

Van Tao (1965), 'Some features of the process of building and developing the Vietnamese revolutionary state in the last 20 years', *NCLS*, 77.

Van Tao (1969), 'The evidently heroic traditions of our nation in the period of struggle at the end of the XIXth century', *NCLS*, 128.

Van Tao and Dinh Thu Cuc (1974), *The Working Class in North Viet Nam 1955–60*, Hanoi, Nha Xuat Ban Khoa Hoc Xa Hoi.

Vo Nguyen Giap (1950), *The Coming Military Task in Moving to A General Counter-Offensive*, Ha Dong, Resistance Administrative Committee.

Vu Huy Phuc (1968), 'The Question of Land in the Nghe-Tinh Soviet Movement', *NCLS*, 108.

Theses and Other Unpublished Works

Brocheux, Pierre (1969), 'L'Economie et la société dans l'Ouest de la Cochinchine pendant la période coloniale (1890–1940)', University of Paris, thèse de 3me cycle, English translation, Cornell University Library.

'Captured Documents and Interrogation Reports', Washington, DC, Department of State Office of Media Services, mimeo., nd.

Catala, J. (nd), 'La Formation de la Nation vietnamienne et les idées et mouvements politiques au Vietnam', mimeo.

Colton, Kenneth Elmer (1969), 'The Failure of the Independent Political Movement in Vietnam 1945–1946', doctoral thesis, American University.

Donnell, John C. (1964), 'Politics in South Vietnam: Doctrines of Authority in Conflict', doctoral thesis, University of California.

Elliott, David W.P. (1976), 'Revolutionary Re-integration: A Comparison of the foundation of post-liberation political systems in North Vietnam and China', doctoral thesis, Cornell University.

Géraud, C. (1971), 'Les Grèves dans les plantations d'hévéas de Cochinchine dans les années 1930', master's thesis, University of Paris.

Ginter, Lawrence E. (1972), 'The Pacification of South Vietnam', doctoral thesis, University of North Carolina.

Gran, Guy (1975), 'Vietnam and the capitalist route to modernity: village Cochinchina, 1880–1940', doctoral thesis, University of Wisconsin.

Hendry, James B. (1960), 'The workforce in Saigon', Saigon, Michigan State University Vietnam Advisory Group, mimeo.

Hinnens, David G. (1961), 'Developments in the Political and Social Systems of Tribal Thai Groups in Northern Indochina Since World War II', unpublished paper, Cornell University.

Huynh Kim Khanh (1972), 'Vietnamese Communism: the prepower phase (1925–1945)', doctoral thesis, University of California.

LaBrie, Norman C. (1971), 'FULRO: the history of political tension in the South Vietnamese highlands', master's thesis, University of Massachusetts.

Library of Congress (1971), 'Communist Vietnamese Publications', microfilm, no. Orien, So. Asia 4.

Mau, Michael P. (1977), 'The Political Evolution of the Village-Commune in North Vietnam 1902–1970', doctoral thesis, University of Pennsylvania.

Moise, Edwin E. (1977), 'Land Reform in China and North Vietnam: Revolution at the Village Level', doctoral thesis, University of Michigan.

Oliver, Victor L. (1972), 'Caodaism: a Vietnamese example of sectarian development', doctoral thesis, Syracuse University.

Phan Huy Le (1986), 'L'Evolution des Formations Socio-Economiques dans l'Histoire du Vietnam', np.

Phan Thanh Son (1968), 'Le Mouvement ouvrier vietnamien des origines à 1945', thèse de 3e cycle, Sorbonne.

Porter, Daniel Gareth (1976), 'Imperialism and Social Structure in Twentieth Century Vietnam', doctoral thesis, Cornell University.

Sampson, Cedric Allen (1975), 'Nationalism and Communism in Viet Nam, (1925–1931)', doctoral thesis, University of California.

'Situation in SVN since the Restoration of Peace to Date', Race Collection, microfilm, Chicago Center for Research Libraries, nd.

'A Study on the Evolution of VM Forces in Nam Bo from 1945 to 1953', Saigon, Translation Section J2–MACV, mimeo., 1964.

Taylor, Keith W. (1976), 'The Birth of Vietnam: Sino-Vietnamese relations to the Tenth Century and the Origins of Vietnamese Nationhood', doctoral thesis, University of Michigan.

Thayer, Carlyle A. (1977), 'The Origins of the National Front for the Liberation of South Viet-Nam', doctoral thesis, Australian National University.

Thompson, Virginia (1945), 'Notes of Labor Problems in Indo-China', typescript, New York, Institute of Pacific Relations.

Tran Nhu Trang (1972), 'The Transformation of the Peasantry in North Vietnam', doctoral thesis, University of Pennsylvania.

Vu Duoc Bang (1971), 'The Viet Nam Independent Education Movement', doctoral thesis, University of California.

Werner, Jayne S. (1976), 'The Cao Dai: The Politics of a Vietnamese Syncretic Religious Movement', doctoral thesis, Cornell University.

White, Christine (1981), 'Agrarian Reform and National Liberation in the Vietnamese Revolution: 1920–1957', doctoral thesis, Cornell University.

Other Sources

Film, 'De Franse oorlog in Indochina', Nederlandse Omroep Stichting and Technisonor co-production, 1978.

Index

337

Comintern, 52, 306
  August Revolution and, 120–22, 124, 126, 140
  Doctrine, 54–8, 301–2, 307, 308
  Far Eastern Bureau, 66
  ICP and, 13, 63–4, 65, 67–8, 70, 73–4
  Lenin and, 8, 9, 11
  polictical economy and, 154, 158–9, 161
Commercial Credit of Viet Nam, 242
Commercial Import Program, 245–6
Committee for Defence of Peace, 251
Committee for Economic Struggle, 181
communal land, 32, 61–2, 74, 88, 91–3, 95–6, 99–100, 187–8
communism, 5, 6–7
  anti- (Campaign of Denunciation), 231–3, 235–7, 241, 246, 252, 254–5
  containment of, *see* containment policies
  revolutionary terrain and, 11–14
  war of position and, 51–75
  see also Cominform; Comintern
Communist Information Bureau, *see* Cominform
Communist Party
  China, 9, 51–2, 56–7, 66, 120–24, 158–60, 181,191, 202, 209–11, 303, 306
  France, 3, 9, 67, 69–70, 122
  Indochina, *see* Indochinese Communist Party
  Italy, 14, 43
  Soviet Union, 9, 11, 84
  Viet Nam, 4, 16, 19–20, 42, 43, 51–4, 55, 80–81, 299
  wartime and, 71–5
  see also Viet Nam Workers' Party

compartmentalization, 213
Confederation of Christian Workers, 232, 251
Confederation of Labour, 153, 182–3, 196–7, 271
Confederation of Vietnamese Workers Unions, 251
Conference on Asian Relations, 209
Confucianism, 21, 37, 39, 40, 42, 44, 82, 86, 91, 93, 96, 101, 118, 239
Constituent Assembly, 236, 237
Constitutionalist party, 58, 68
consumer goods, 33, 90, 104, 151
containment policies, 141, 161, 201, 305
  allies (policies/strategies) and, 202, 208–12
  consolidation in South and, 231–55
  diplomatic struggle, 207, 212–20
  South Viet Nam and, 207, 221–6, 309
cost of living, 197–8, 241
counter–revolutionary regime
  economics of, 240–47
  see also Ngo Dinh Diem
Cuong De, Prince, 119, 123
currency, 27, 102–3, 114–15, 157, 180, 241, 242, 285

Dang Tran Con, 96–7
Dang Xuan Khu, *see* Truong Chinh
D'Argenlieu, Thierry, 139, 166
Decoux, Jean, 114, 119, 120, 199
De Gaulle, Charles, 123, 126
de Lattre de Tassigny, General, 167, 180
'De Lattre Line', 178
democratic dictatorship, 170–71, 180, 182, 183–4
Democratic Party of Viet Nam, 123